Europe and Asia Beyond East and West

This is a timely volume that explores Europe in its relation to Asia in a way that moves beyond simplistic notions of West and East. Rejecting the idea of a clash of civilizations, the contributions highlight the interlinked nature of Europe and Asia and attempt to identify cosmopolitan moments of openness.

From both a historical and a contemporary perspective, it is shown that both Europe and Asia are not based on fixed cultural or geographical foundations. The East is also in the West. Rather than look at Europe and Asia in terms of separate worlds, they can be seen in terms of cultural struggles common to both. A general theme is that the idea of the West as an ideological, cultural and geopolitical construct is becoming increasingly questionable when applied to the current situation, which is one in which West and East are mutually linked. The articulation of a new European identity that includes a recognition of the non-European is now one of the major chances for Europe to define its identity in the world.

Chapters are thematically organized under four headings:

- A post-Western world
- Asia in Europe: Encounters in History
- Between Europe and Asia
- Otherness in Europe and Asia

This major new title will be of great value to students and researchers in the fields of Sociology, European Politics and History, and Cultural Theory.

Gerard Delanty is Professor of Sociology, University of Liverpool. His recent books include (with Chris Rumford) *Rethinking Europe: Social Theory and the Implications of Europeanization* (Routledge, 2005); *Community* (Routledge, 2004). He has edited *Handbook of Contemporary European Social Theory* (Routledge, 2005) and (with Krishan Kumar) *The Handbook of Nations and Nationalism* (Sage, 2006).

Routledge/European Sociological Association studies in European societies

Series editors: Thomas P. Boje, Max Haller, Martin Kohli and Alison Woodward

Europe and Asia Beyond East and West

Edited by Gerard Delanty

Routledge
Taylor & Francis Group

LONDON AND NEW YORK

First published 2006
by Routledge
2 Park Square, Milton Park, Abingdon, Oxon OX14 4RN

Simultaneously published in the USA and Canada
by Routledge
270 Madison Ave, New York, NY 10016

Routledge is an imprint of the Taylor & Francis Group, an informa business

© 2006 Selection and editorial matter, Gerard Delanty; individual
chapters, the contributors

Typeset in Sabon by Wearset Ltd, Boldon, Tyne and Wear
Printed and bound in Great Britain by TJI Digital, Padstow,
Cornwall

British Library Cataloguing in Publication Data
A catalogue record for this book is available from the British Library

Library of Congress Cataloging in Publication Data
A catalog record for this book has been requested

ISBN10: 0-415-37947-4
ISBN13: 978-0-415-37947-2

Contents

Notes on contributors

Johann P. Arnason is Emeritus Professor of Sociology at La Trobe University, Melbourne, and was until recently editor of the journal *Thesis Eleven*. He has published widely on social theory and historical sociology. Recent publications include: *The Peripheral Centre: Essays on Japanese History and Civilization* (TransPacific Books 2002); *Civilizations in Dispute: Historical Questions and Theoretical Traditions* (Brill 2003); (co-edited with Bjorn Wittrock) *Eurasian Transformations, Tenth to Thirteenth Centuries: Crystallizations, Divergences, Renaissances* (Brill 2004); and (co-edited with S. N. Eisenstadt and Bjorn Wittrock) *Axial Civilizations and World History* (Brill 2005).

Ulrich Beck is Professor for Sociology at the University of Munich, and the British Journal of Sociology Professor at the London School of Economics and Sciences. From 1995 to 1998 he was Distinguished Research Professor at the University of Cardiff. From 1995 to 1997 he was member of the Future Commission of the German Government. His interests focus on 'risk society', 'individualization' and 'reflexive modernization'. His most recent research activities include a long-term empirical study of the sociological and political implications of 'reflexive modernization', which explores the complexities and uncertainties of the process of transformation from first to second modernity. Specifically he is working on a sociological framework to analyse the ambivalences and dynamics of 'cosmopolitan societies'. Some of his major publications include: *The Cosmopolitan Vision* (Polity 2006); *Power in the Global Age* (Blackwell 2005); (with E. Beck-Gernsheim) *Individualization* (Sage 2000); *Brave New World of Work* (Polity 2000); *World Risk Society* (Polity 1999); and *What is Globalization?* (Polity 1999).

Alastair Bonnett is Professor of Social Geography at the University of Newcastle. He is the author of *Radicalism, Anti-racism and Representation* (Routledge 1993); *Anti-racism* (Routledge 2000); *White Identities: International and Historical Perspectives* (Pearson 2000); *How to Argue* (Pearson 2001); and *The Idea of the West: History, politics and culture* (Palgrave 2004).

Rémi Brague is Professor of Philosophy at the Univerité Paris 1-Sorbonne and at the University of Munich. He has also taught at Boston University. His books include *The Wisdom of the World: The Human Experience of the Universe in Western Thought* (Chicago University Press 2003) and *Eccentric Culture: A Theory of Western Civilization* (St. Augustine's Press, Indiana 2002).

Fred Dallmayr is Packey J. Dee Professor in the departments of Political Science and Philosophy at the University of Notre Dame (USA). He holds a doctorate from Munich University and a PhD from Duke University (USA). Among his recent publications are: *Beyond Orientalism* (State University of New York Press 1996); *Alternative Visions* (Rowman & Littlefield 1998); *Achieving our World: Toward a Global and Plural Democracy* (Rowman & Littlefield 2001); *Dialogue Among Civilizations* (Palgrave/Macmillan 2002); *Peace Talks: Who Will Listen?* (University of Notre Dame Press 2004); and *Small Wonder: Global Power and its Discontents* (Rowman & Littlefield 2005).

Gerard Delanty is Professor of Sociology, University of Liverpool, UK and has written on various issues in social theory and general sociology. He is editor of the *European Journal of Social Theory*. His publications include *Inventing Europe* (Macmillan 1995); *Social Science* (1997; new edition 2005); *Social Theory in a Changing World* (Polity Press 1998); *Modernity and Postmodernity* (Sage 2000); *Citizenship in a Global Age* (Open University Press 2000); *Challenging Knowledge: The University in the Knowledge Society* (Open University Press 2001); (with Patrick O'Mahony) *Nationalism and Social Theory* (Sage 2002); *Community* (Routledge 2003); (edited) *Adorno: Modern Masters* 4 vols (Sage 2004); (edited with Piet Strydom) *Philosophies of Social Science* (Open University Press 2003); (with Chris Rumford) *Rethinking Europe: Social Theory and the Implications of Europeanization* (Routledge 2005); and has edited the *Handbook of Contemporary European Social Theory* (Routledge 2005) and (with Krishan Kumar) *The Handbook of Nations and Nationalism* (Sage 2006).

Heidrun Friese is currently working on a research project on 'Modernity and Contingency' at the Centre de Recherches Interdisciplinaires sur l'Allemagne, Ecole des Hautes Etudes en Sciences Sociales, Paris and is teaching at the Johann Wolfgang Goethe-University, Frankfurt am Main. Recent publications include: (co-edited with Giuseppe Bronzini, Antonio Negri and Peter Wagner) *Europa, Costituzione e Movimenti Sociali* (Manifestolibri 2003); (as editor) *Identities: Time, Boundaries and Difference* (Berghahn 2002); (co-edited with Antonio Negri and Peter Wagner) *Europa Politica: Ragioni di una Necessità* (Manifestolibri 2002); and (as editor) *The Moment: Time and Rupture in Modern Thought* (Liverpool University Press 2001).

Thomas W. Gallant holds the Hellenic Heritage Foundation Chair of Modern Greek History at York University, Toronto. Professor Gallant received his PhD from Cambridge University in 1982. Previous to receiving the HHF Chair at York in 2002, for seventeen years he was professor of Greek history and anthropology at the University of Florida. He has published six books and over forty scholarly articles. His most recently published books are: *The 1918 Anti-Greek Riot in Toronto* (CHHS 2005); *Modern Greece* (Arnold 2001); and *Experiencing Dominion: Culture, Identity and Power in the British Mediterranean* (University of Notre Dame Press 2002). *Experiencing Dominion* won the 2003 Modern Greek Studies Association's Best Book Prize. He is currently completing two books, *Murder on Black Mountain: Love and Death on a Nineteenth Century Greek Island* and *Violence, Honour and Masculinity in Nineteenth Century Greece*.

Jack (John) Rankine Goody was born in 1919 and educated at St. John's College, Cambridge. He has conducted fieldwork in Ghana, India and China; and he has written extensively on literacy, the family, the Bagre myth of the LoDagaa, and on cuisine and the culture of flowers. His most recent work is: *The East in the West* (Cambridge University Press 1996); *Islam in Europe* (Polity Press 2003); *Capitalism and Modernity: the Great Debate* (Polity Press 2004); and *The Theft of History* (Cambridge University Press, forthcoming).

John M. Hobson is Professor of Politics and International Relations at the University of Sheffield. He has published five books, the two most recent of which are *The Eastern Origins of Western Civilisation* (Cambridge University Press 2004) and (co-edited with Steve Hobden) *Historical Sociology of International Relations* (Cambridge University Press 2002). He works at the intersection of IR/IPE theory and Global History/Historical Sociology, with a primary interest in the issue of inter-civilizational relations, past and present. To this end he is currently finishing a co-edited book called *Everyday IPE: How Everyday Actors Transform the World Economy* (with Len Seabrooke).

David Inglis is Senior Lecturer in Sociology at the University of Aberdeen. He writes in the areas of social theory and the sociology of culture. He has particular interests in the history of modes of consciousness, with reference both to modernity and ancient civilizations. Among his publications are: *Confronting Culture: Sociological Vistas* (Polity 2003); *The Uses of Sport* (Routledge 2004); *Culture and Everyday Life* (Routledge 2005); and, with Roland Robertson, *Globalization and Social Theory: Redefining the Social Sciences* (Open University Press 2006).

Masoud Kamali is Professor of Sociology and Social Policy at Uppsala University (Centre for Multiethnic Research) and MidSweden University (Department of Social Policy). He has published many books and papers in English, Persian and Swedish. Several of his books and articles deal with the questions of modern social movements in Islamic countries. Among his publications are: *Multiple Modernities, Civil Society and Islam: The Case of Iran and Turkey*; and *Revolutionary Iran: Civil Society and Islam in the Modernization Process*. His current research continues to investigate civil societies, movements and multiple modernities in Muslim countries, in particular he is carrying out a comparative analysis of Iranian and Turkish paths to modernization. In addition, he is leading a major European project, The European Dilemma: Institutional Patterns and Politics of 'Racial' Discrimination, in which eight European countries are engaged.

E. Fuat Keyman is Professor of International Relations at Koç University, İstanbul. He is also the director of the Koç University Center for Research on Globalization and Democratic Governance (GLODEM). He works on democratization, globalization, international relations, Turkish politics and Turkish foreign policy. He has produced many books and articles, both in English and in Turkish, in these areas. He is the author of *Globalization, State, Identity/Difference: Towards a Critical Social Theory of International Relations* (Humanities Press 1997); *Turkey and Radical Democracy* (Alfa 2001); *Remaking Turkey: Globalization, Modernity and Democratization* (Lexington, forthcoming); and a co-editor of *Citizenship in a Global World: European Questions and Turkish Experiences* (Routledge 2005).

Jan Nederveen Pieterse is Professor of Sociology, University of Illinois at Urbana-Champaign, and specializes in transnational sociology, his research interests incorporating globalization, development studies and cultural studies. He is the author of: *Culture and Globalization* (Rowman & Littlefield 2004); *Development Theory: Deconstructions/ Reconstructions* (Sage and TCS 2001); *Racism and Stereotyping for Beginners* (Dutch 1994); *White on Black: Images of Africa and Blacks in Western Popular Culture* (Yale UP 1992); and *Empire and Emancipation: Power and Liberation on a World Scale* (Praeger 1989, Pluto 1990); and the editor of *Global Futures: Shaping Globalization* (Zed 2000); *World Orders in the Making: Humanitarian Intervention and Beyond* (Macmillan and St Martin's 1998); *Emancipations: Modern and Postmodern* (Sage 1992); and *Christianity and Hegemony* (Berg 1992).

William Outhwaite is Professor of Sociology at the University of Sussex. He is the author of various books including: *Habermas: A Critical Introduction* (Polity Press 1994); *The Future of Society* (Blackwell 2006); and (with Larry Ray) *Social Theory and Postcommunism* (Blackwell 2005). He is the editor of the following: *The Habermas Reader* (Polity Press 1996); (with Tom Bottomore) *The Blackwell Dictionary of*

Twentieth-Century Social Thought (Blackwell 1993); *The Blackwell Dictionary of Modern Social Thought* (Blackwell 1993); (with Luke Martell) *The Sociology of Politics* (Edward Elgar 1998); and (with Margaret Archer) *Defending Objectivity* (Routledge 2004). He is currently working on a book on society and culture in Europe.

Roland Robertson is Professor of Sociology and Global Society at the University of Aberdeen, Scotland. He is also Director of the Centre for the Study of Globalization at the same university, as well as being Distinguished Professor of Sociology Emeritus at the University of Pittsburgh, USA. He is the author of a number of books, the most well known being *Globalization: Social Theory and Global Culture* (Sage 1992), which is currently being revised for its second edition. He recently co-edited (with Kathleen E. White) the 6-volume set *Globalization: Critical Concepts in Sociology* (Routledge 2003), and is co-author (with David Inglis) of *Globalization and Social Theory: Redefining Social Science* (Open University Press 2006). He has held visiting teaching positions in various countries, his works have been translated into over a dozen languages, and he also serves on the editorial boards of numerous journals.

Chris Rumford is Senior Lecturer in Political Sociology in the Department of Politics and International Relations, Royal Holloway, University of London. His most recent publications include (with Gerard Delanty) *Rethinking Europe: Social Theory and the Implications of Europeanization* (Routledge 2005) and *The European Union: A Political Sociology* (Blackwell 2002). He has recently edited special issues of *European Journal of Social Theory* on 'Theorizing borders', and *Comparative European Politics* on 'Rethinking European Spaces'. He is currently editing two books, *Handbook of European Studies* (Sage) and *Cosmopolitanism and Europe* (Liverpool University Press), and is completing a book for Routledge entitled *Cosmopolitan Spaces: Europe, Globalization, Theory*.

Richard Sakwa is Professor of Russian and European Politics at the University of Kent. He has published widely on Soviet, Russian and post-communist affairs. Recent books include: *Soviet Politics in Perspective* (Routledge 1998); *Postcommunism* (Open University Press 1999); *The Rise and Fall of the Soviet Union, 1917–1991* (Routledge 1999); (co-edited, with Bruno Coppieters of the Vrije Universiteit Brussel) *Contextualising Secession: Normative Aspects of Secession Struggles* (Oxford University Press 2003); and *Putin: Russia's Choice* (Routledge 2004). His current research interests focus on problems of democratic development and the state in Russia, the nature of post-communism, and the global challenges facing the former communist countries.

Natan Sznaider is Associate Professor of Sociology at the Academic College of Tel-Aviv-Yaffo in Israel. His recent publications include: (co-authored with Daniel Levy) *The Holocaust and Memory in the Global Age* (Temple University Press 2005); 'Money and Honor: About the impossibility of honorable restitution' in D. Diner (ed.) *Restitution as New World Politics* (Berghahn 2005); (co-authored with Daniel Levy) 'Forgive and not Forget: Reconciliation between forgiveness and resentment', in E. Barkan and A. Karn (eds) *Taking Wrongs Seriously: Apologies and Reconciliation* (Stanford University Press 2005); (co-edited with Ulrich Beck and Rainer Winter) *Global America: The Cultural Consequences of Globalization* (Liverpool University Press 2003); and (co-authored with Daniel Levy) 'The Institutionalization of Cosmopolitan Morality: The holocaust and human rights', in *Journal of Human Rights* (2004), 3(2): 143–57.

Göran Therborn is Director of the Swedish Collegium for Advanced Study in the Social Sciences, Uppsala, Sweden. His recent books include: *Beyond European Modernity: The Trajectory of European Societies, 1945–1995* (Sage 1995); *Between Sex and Power: The Family in the World, 1900–2000* (Routledge 2004); and two edited volumes, *Asia and European Globalization* (Brill 2005) and *Inequalities of the World* (Verso 2006).

Tong Shijun is Professor of Philosophy of East China Normal University in Shanghai and Deputy President of Shanghai Academy of Social Sciences. He was at the University of Marburg in 1998 and was a Fulbright Scholar at Columbia University in 2001–2002. Among his publications are *Epistemology and Methodology in the Post-Hegelian European Philosophy of 19th Century* (Bergen 1993) and *Dialectics of Modernization: Habermas and the Chinese Discourse of Modernization* (Sidney 2000). He has translated into Chinese Hilary Putnam's *Reason, Truth and History* and Jürgen Habermas's *Between Facts and Norms*.

Bryan S. Turner was Professor of Sociology at the University of Cambridge (1998–2005), and is currently Professor of Sociology in the Asia Research Institute, National University of Singapore. He is the research leader of the cluster on globalization and religion, and is currently writing a three-volume study of the sociology of religion and editing the *Dictionary of Sociology* for Cambridge University Press. A book on human rights and vulnerability is to be published in 2006 by Penn State University Press. Recent publications include *Classical Sociology* (Sage 1999) and *The New Medical Sociology* (W. W. Norton 2004). With Chris Rojek, he published *Society & Culture: Principles of Scarcity and Solidarity* (Sage 2001), and, with June Edmunds, *Generations, Culture and Society* (Open University Press 2002). With Engin Isin, he edited the *Handbook of Citizenship Studies* (Sage 2002).

Preface and acknowledgements

This volume is based on a conference held at Schloss Elmau, Bavaria 4–7 April 2004. I would like to thank Mr Dietmar Müller-Elmau for his generous sponsorship of the conference.

The chapters published in this volume have been extensively revised and are all previously unpublished. Some of the original papers have not been included and others have been added in order to create a thematically integrated volume.

I would also like to thank Gerhard Boomgaarden of Routledge for his interest and support in preparing this volume. I am also grateful to two referees for their helpful comments on an earlier draft of the book.

Gerard Delanty

Introduction

The idea of a post-Western Europe

Gerard Delanty

This volume explores new expressions of European self-understanding in a way that challenges previous conceptions, which have been dominated by the dichotomous ideas of West and East and the more recent post-Cold War ideological notions of the 'clash of civilizations', the 'end of history', the 'new world order' and the 'axis of evil'. The idea of the West as an ideological, cultural and geopolitical construct is becoming increasingly irrelevant to the current political situation as far as Europe and Asia are concerned. The West is no longer the main site of cultural and political defence or of community. With the spread of Western civilization through-out the world, that civilization has ceased to be Western, but has become globalized.[1] It has also ceased to be specifically European. One of the con-sequences of the globalization of Western civilization is that there is nothing essentially distinctive about the West in a cultural sense. Christian-ity, itself divided between the Latin and Orthodox traditions, is no longer the cultural marker of the secular societies in Europe today.[2] As a geopolit-ical entity the West is no longer as homogeneous as it was for much of the second half of the previous century (see Bonnett 2004). Capitalism and democracy are also now global forces and exist in a huge variety of forms throughout the world. Europe, American and the West have become disen-tangled.

The fall of the Berlin Wall symbolically marked the end of an internal East–West divide within Europe. With the end of this internal separation, in which the terms East and West were most vividly defined, there is the beginning of a wider collapse of the distinction. Nonetheless, while notions of the decline or the end of West are as old as the very notion of the West, and may indeed be part of the definition of the West, as the *Abendland*, to speak of the end of the West makes little sense. Even though the East–West distinction within Europe has become less important, to an extent a polit-ical West survives the globalization of the cultural West. The 'West versus the Rest' defines much of global political struggles of the present day. Occidentalism – opposition to the West – is a significant movement in many parts of the world and a force that keeps alive the notion of the West, which is generally associated with the United States but also includes

Europe (see Buruma and Margalit 2004). Such anti-Westernism is of course to be found as much within the West as outside it. China cannot be included within the West, which may come to be defined more closely with respect to China not least because that is the way China views the rest of the world. The West may not exist in Europe, but it exists for much of the non-Western world which has conjured up an image of the West. In this respect what is more significant than the West versus East divide is the North versus the South conflict over global justice.

The resulting situation for Europe is twofold. On the one side, Europe has become a more clearly defined geopolitical area that is part of, but distinct from, the West, while on the other side current developments and a longer view of history suggest a conception of Europe as a multifaceted reality that has been steadily moving eastwards and now covers much of the former communist East (Zielonka 2002). Since the eastern enlargement and the growing importance of relations with neighbouring countries, the European project lacks closure. European integration has given Europe a clearer cultural and political identity, but it has not led to a more homogeneous Europe or a common political project. Europeanization has led to greater contestation over the meaning of Europe (Delanty 1995). Whether due to civilizational encounters in earlier periods, the process known as the 'westernization of the world', imperialism and its consequences, or the globalization of markets, communication and culture, the shape of Europe cannot be accounted for by purely internal factors or by reference to the unity of the West. The EU itself also lacks a clear project and there is no European-wide consensus on what values Europe is based on. The resulting uncertainty of the identity of Europe may be seen less as a sign of crisis than an expression of a questioning attitude and a more critical kind of self-understanding that may be more responsive to the challenges facing Europe. For example, it is not possible to claim that there is widespread public or elite consensus on the identity of Europe as something that excludes Islam. Current debates are more symptomatic of uncertainty than the comfort that comes from a clearly defined set of values. There is an unavoidable recognition that neither self nor other are easily defined. An issue of major significance now is the relation of Europe to the non-European, a relation which must be seen in terms of a model of mutuality and interlinking worlds of shared universes of discourse. This discursive dimension of East–West relations has been much neglected.

This book is addressed to non-dichotomous relations of Europe and Asia from both the historical and contemporary perspective. The contributors address the possibility of a European–Asian cosmopolitanism that is not constrained by the dangers of Eurocentric 'Orientalism' or anti-European 'Occidentalism'. Invoked in this is a cosmopolitan conception of civilizational encounters rather than a clash of civilizations. Encounters can take a variety of forms, including violent clashes and conflicts, but there are also dialogic encounters and ones entailing mutual borrowings as well as forms of co-development.[3] As several contributors point out, such encounters should be seen as an expression of modernity, which as a globalized condition takes a variety of forms, many of which are civilizational (see Eisenstadt 2003; Ben-Rafael and Sternberg 2005; Gaonkar 2001). The notion of cosmopolitanism is relevant here in the sense of a concern with the mutual implications of different social and cultural worlds. As much of cosmopolitan theory suggests, it is no longer possible to exclude the perspective of the other from the self. For example, the struggles going on in the Islamic world are not separate from struggles going on in Europe. The East is also in the West. Rather than look at Europe and Asia in terms of separate worlds, they can be seen in terms of cultural struggles common to both. The notion of a civilizational constellation captures one aspect of this European and Asian cosmopolitanism, namely a continental unity in diversity.

The contributors – sociologists, anthropologists, philosophers and historians – show, from a variety of perspectives, that the conventional equation of Europe both with the West and with modernity must be questioned. Both in terms of new conceptions of modernity and current developments in European integration as well as the wider context of globality, the very meaning of Europe must be re-imagined in a more cosmopolitan direction (see Beck and Grande 2006; Delanty and Rumford 2005; Rumford 2006). The most significant, and until now most unexplored, aspect of this is the possibility of European–Asian cosmopolitanism. Several contributors draw attention to earlier expressions of East–West links in history and to current developments in Asia that call into question assumptions of a great divergence. The history of Europe and Asia can be seen in terms of mutual borrowings, a point made with considerable force by John Hobson in his chapter in this volume (see also Hobson 2004; Ravi *et al.* 2004; Mozaffari 2002). Even in the more qualified terms of Johann Arnason's analysis, the interactive dimension of the relation cannot be neglected. In the context of current debates about Islam and Europe such questions are particularly important. This book offers a view of Islam as integral to Europe, which should be seen in terms of a civilizational constellation rather than a single civilizational model (Bulliet 2004; Goody 2004). This notion of Europe as a constellation of diverse cultures as opposed to a shared common community of fate can be related to the idea of a post-national constellation as advocated by Jürgen Habermas, whose social theory of political community in Europe also stresses the cosmopolitan dimension of the inclusion of the other (Habermas 1998, 2001).

One of the aims of this volume is to establish the basis for a wider social theory of Europe in which questions of post-national community are linked more closely to notions of cosmopolitan community. Until now most of this debate, such as Habermas's contribution, has been confined to internal European developments. This is also reflected in Rémi Brague's conception of a European 'eccentricity' based on borrowing from other cultures to a point that there is no essentially fixed or immutable identity to Europe other than a culture of 'secondarity', as he terms it in his contribution to this volume (see also Brague 2002). Building on such important insights, an attempt is made in this book to show that such a perspective, which can be termed cosmopolitan, is not confined to Europe, but has a wider application for post-universalistic societies. This is clearly a consciousness that is more advanced in the societies of Europe in the present day and which is one of the major expressions of European self-understanding.

There are many reasons why a book on this topic is timely. One reason is that with the expansion of the European Union eastwards and southwards, economic and political encounters with Asia and especially Eurasian societies will become more important than they have been for much of the twentieth century, which was an epoch dominated by the global conflict of Russia and America.[4] Today this dichotomy has crystallized into a number of different encounters, leading to new Euro-Asian relations sustained by transnational migration, trade, changing foreign policy, multiculturalism and tourism. In this case the example of Turkey is particularly illustrative of the changing geopolitical contours of Europe. Current developments in Turkey – the prospect of EU membership, the election in 2002 of the Islamist Justice and Development party and the impact of global civil society – point to a significant reconfiguration of what had been a Western-oriented nation-state within an Asian cultural world. The anti-Westernism of the Turkish Islamist movement has now moved in the opposite direction. In this case there is an important example of the Europeanization of Turkish Islam. Viewed in the context of a wider transformation of the Eurasian world and growing tensions between Europe and the United States, the significance of such developments points to a questioning of a clear separation of West and East. Europe may becoming less Western at precisely the same time Eurasia is becoming less Eastern and that something like a 'post-Western' Europe is emerging.[5] For the first time it is possible to speak of Europeanization emerging to rival Americanization, as far as the transformation of European societies is concerned, since current societal change in Europe cannot be understood in terms of Americanization.[6] The idea of a post-Western Europe does not mean that Europe is ceasing to be Western, but suggests that Europe cannot be defined entirely in terms of a unitary notion of Western civilization or by reference to a political design called the West. This is precisely the case too with Asia, which like Europe must be seen in plural terms, a point made by Göran Therborn in his contribution to this volume. As he points out, although we are accustomed to emphasizing the diversity of Europe, the much larger expanse of Asia is even more pluralized than is Europe.

In addition to the changing geopolitical context there is major societal transformation occurring in a Europe that is perhaps best conceived of in terms of a constellation of diverse elements – cities, regions, nations, groupings of different kinds, cultural and political flows and translations – rather than as a system of enduring cultures and a civilizational order rooted in Western values. As a result of internal diversification, cross-cultural interpenetration, the impact of globalization and the growing momentum of post-national trends, European societies can no longer be understood in terms of national models but also they cannot be simply defined as exclusively Western. As Jack Goody argues in his chapter in this volume, Islam, often regarded as un-European, if not antithetical to Europe, is now a part of many European societies and it is doubtful that xenophobic currents will succeed in channelling post-liberal anxieties into a vision of Europe defined against Islam. The articulation of a new European identity that includes alterity is now one of the major chances for Europe to define its identity in the world. Essential to this tendential cosmopolitanism must be a new relation to Asia. The following chapters explore this problem.

The chapters in Part I provide a general theoretical context for the volume as a whole. With a focus on issues of modernity, globalization and cosmopolitanism these chapters explore a conception of globalization that takes into account the Asian perspective. Part II is concerned with a rethinking of the legacy of history in order to identify what may be called cosmopolitan moments. This is a pronounced theme in several chapters. Other chapters offer different interpretations of links between Europe and Asia. Part III shifts the emphasis to the zones between Europe and Asia, with chapters on Turkey, Russia and Israel as key examples of Eurasian borderlands. Other chapters concern the broader question of changing borders and European enlargement. Finally, the chapters in Part IV explore some of the philosophical aspects of the notion of otherness that has been central to all chapters in this volume. The key theme in these chapters is a notion, which can be associated with the cosmopolitan imagination, of an otherness within the self. This is reflected in different ways with respect to both the idea of Asia and the idea of Europe, neither of which are based on fixed foundations in culture or geography.

Notes

1 According to Hardt and Negri the West has been replaced by Empire, which is not constrained by territorial limits and is formless and decentred (Hardt and Negri 2000).
2 Christianity may be the site of one of the most important cultural differences between Europe and America, for the United States is one of the most religious societies in the world.
3 For some literature on this see Bulliet (2004), Clarke (1997), Deutsch (1991), *Diogenes* (2003) and Dallmayr (1996).
4 On current developments between Europe and Asia see Lawson (2003) and Preston and Gilson (2001).

5 See Delanty (2003) on the idea of a 'post-Western Europe'. See also Delanty and Rumford (2005).
6 On the Americanization of Europe, see De Grazia (2005).

References

Beck, U. and E. Grande (2006) *Cosmopolitan Europe*, Cambridge: Polity Press.

Ben-Rafael, E. and Y. Sternberg (eds) (2005) *Comparing Modernities: Pluralism versus Homogeneity*, Leiden: Brill.

Bonnett, A. (2004) *The Idea of the West: Culture, Politics and History*, London: Palgrave.

Brague, R. (2002) *Eccentric Culture: A Theory of Western Civilization*, South Bend, Ind.: St. Augustine's Press.

Bulliet, R. W. (2004) *Islamo-Christian Civilization*, New York: Columbia University Press.

Buruma, I. and A. Marglit (2004) *Occidentalism: The West in the Eyes of its Enemies*, London: Penguin Press.

Clarke, J. J. (1997) *Oriental Enlightenment: The Encounter Between Asian and Western Thought*, London: Routledge.

Dallmayr, F. (1996) *Beyond Orientalism: Essays on Cross-cultural Encounter*, New York: State University of New York Press.

De Grazia, V. (2005) *Irresistible Empire: America's Advance Through Twentieth-century Europe*, Cambridge, MA: Harvard University Press.

Delanty, G. (1995) *Inventing Europe: Idea, Identity, Reality*, London: Macmillan.

Delanty, G. (2003) 'The Making of a Post-Western Europe: A Civilizational Analysis', *Thesis Eleven*, 72: 8–24.

Delanty, G. and C. Rumford (2005) *Rethinking Europe: Social Theory and the Implications of Europeanization*, London: Routledge.

Deutsch, E. (ed.) (1991) *Culture and Modernity: East–West Philosophic Perspectives*, Honolulu: University of Hawai'i Press.

Diogenes (2003) 'From East to West – Civilizations in a Looking-Glass', *Diogenes*, Special Issue, 50(4).

Eisenstadt, S. N. (2003) *Comparative Civilizations and Multiple Modernities*, Vol. 1 and 2, Leiden: Brill.

Gaonkar, D. P. (ed.) (2001) *Alternative Modernities*, Durham, NC: Duke University Press.

Goody, J. (2004) *Islam in Europe*, Cambridge: Polity Press.

Habermas, J. (1998) *The Inclusion of the Other*, Cambridge: Polity Press.

Habermas, J. (2001) *The Postnational Constellation*, Cambridge: Polity Press.

Hardt, M. and A. Negri (2000) *Empire*, Cambridge, MA: Harvard University Press.

Hobson, J. (2004) *The Eastern Origins of Western Civilization*, Cambridge: Cambridge University Press.

Lawson, S. (2003) *Europe and Asia-Pacific: Culture, Identity and Representations of a Region*, London: RoutledgeCurzon.

Mozaffari, M. (ed.) (2002) *Globalization and Civilizations*, London: Routledge.

Preston, P. and J. Gilson (eds) (2001) *The European Union and East Asia*, Cheltenham: Edward Elgar.

Ravi, S., M. Rutten and G. Beng-Lan (eds) (2004) *Asia in Europe; Europe in Asia*, Leiden: International Institute for Asian Studies.

Rumford, C. (ed.) (2006) *Europe and Cosmopolitanism*, Liverpool: Liverpool University Press.

Zielonka, J. (ed.) (2005) *Europe Unbound: Enlarging and reshaping the boundaries of the European Union*, London: Routledge.

Part I
A post-Western world

1 Europe from a cosmopolitan perspective

Ulrich Beck and Gerard Delanty

Since its foundation in the post-Second World War period the European Union was a project that was shaped by the circumstances of its origins. It was primarily a product of the clashes within Western Europe and in particular between France and Germany. Given the wider context of the Cold War, it was never envisaged by its founders that it would ever be more than an alliance of the major Western European powers. Initially this was of course to be confined to economic cooperation, but increasingly it became a political and finally a social and cultural project, albeit within the limits of the narrowly defined Western Europe of the Cold War era. Gradually more and more countries were incorporated into the EU and since the Single European Act this project has moved far beyond its original justification.

Although the Single European Act may have been the decisive point at which the break with the earlier inter-governmental project had been made, today the European project has entered an entirely new phase that was never anticipated even after the end of the Cold War: the extension of the EU to include much of central and eastern Europe has now reached the point of possible inclusion of a country that has generally been regarded as Asian.

The debate about Turkey and Europe raises major questions about the identity of Europe and the rationale of European integration. This is not just a debate about the incorporation of yet another country into a trans-national political organization. It is a debate about the *raison-d'être* of a polity and culture. Whether or not Turkey eventually becomes a member of the EU cannot be predicted at the present time, but – and the indications are now highly likely that it will – it is evident that the East–West divide has now ceased to be an inner European one but goes beyond the Cold War East and West divide. It has become a question of defining the relation of Europe to Asia, which must now be posed in terms of political community. In addition to this, there is also the growing importance of wider European–Asian relations that have arisen as a result of the economic rise of Asia. What is interesting in this development is a double logic to Europeanization, which operates on internal as well as on external dimensions. The argument advanced in this chapter is that the external dimension is coming increasingly to the fore today and the future of Europeanization will depend to a large degree on successful external cosmopolitanism. The perspective suggested by this is a view of Europeanization in terms of internal and external cosmopolitanism.

From transnationalism to cosmopolitanism

The earlier enlargements of the European Union – the incorporation of the British Isles, southern, Nordic and central and eastern countries from the 1970s – accompanied a gradual movement towards the transnationalization of the nation-state. While there is nothing to indicate that this transnationalization of the state will cease, the current situation is one that suggests something else is also going on and which cannot be fully understood without taking a different perspective. We may term the current situation one of cosmopolitanism as opposed to transnationalization since what is referred to here is not merely a matter of the transformation of statehood but a transformation in the political subjectivity of Europe. The kind of subjectivity emerging today can be termed cosmopolitan in view of its open-ended nature and the fact that it is not underpinned by a substantive identity such as 'a people' but a multiplicity of identities and projects.[1] There are at least four major developments in Europeanization that are a feature of the present day and which are indicative of cosmopolitanism.

First, as mentioned, the nation-state is not being replaced by a supra-state. The modernist drive to create homogeneous structures such as territorial states with a unitary structure is not being replicated on the European level. While the debate on the nature of statehood will continue, it is evident that the EU is not a larger version of the traditional state. The nation-state itself is undergoing tremendous change and for this reason we do not see a dilemma of nation-state or supra-state. This dualism is simply the wrong way to view the current situation. In terms of statehood, the EU is a mixed polity. The creation of interdependencies in every field of politics is not just a form of cooperation which ultimately leaves the nation-states concerned untouched, as the inter-governmental perspective implies. Instead, Europeanization transforms state power and national sovereignty to their very core. The mixed nature of the EU is likely to grow as a result of relations with neighbouring countries. The result of this is not something that can be easily encapsulated in a constitutional design and underpinned by a straightforward appeal to a European people. The European polity has often been described as a reflexive form of integration (Eriksen 2005; Eriksen *et al.* 2005).

Second, the interpenetration of European societies is now a reality. European societies are becoming more and more mixed as a result of a common currency, migration, tourism, a transversal web of cheap airlines, and the common feeling of inhabiting the world risk society. Several decades of European integration have also enhanced the process, which it must be emphasized is not leading to a single European Society any more than it is leading to a supra-state that transcends national states but to different degrees of interpenetration. Resulting from this is a common European public culture. The term is used in the specific sense to refer not to a common European identity but to common concerns and common modes of communication. Although Europeans do not share a common language or read the same newspapers and watch the same TV programmes – despite the existence in almost every country of *Who Wants to be a Millionaire* – they do share certain debates and share certain critical moments. Culture, which is a system of communication, can also be analysed in terms of modes of communication, such as repertories of justification. Looking at European public culture in terms of arguments – including disputes over the nature of Europe – offers in a certain sense a level of analysis that captures the cosmopolitan dimension of cultural commonality. It is in this sense that Habermas's notion of Europe as a post-national constellation of communicative spheres makes sense (Habermas 1998, 2001, 2003). This point will be returned to below when we discuss democratization. As far as identity is concerned, there is now considerable evidence to show that a European identity is not emerging to replace other kinds of identity but exists along side a wide range of other kinds of identity (Herrman *et al.* 2004).

Third, following from the previous point, Europeanization cannot be separated from globalization. There is a tendency to view Europeanization as a reaction to globalization. But this betrays the illusion that globalization can stop at the frontier of the EU. It is a mistake too to suppose that the EU is not vulnerable to the pressures of globalization. Inside and outside cannot be distinguished in a way that separates Europeanization and globalization. Europeanization should rather be viewed as an instance of globalization. The nature of security, for instance, is no longer one that can rely on an Outside from which the Inside must be protected. The implications of this will be discussed in more detail in the final section of this chapter.

Finally, mention can be made of the geopolitics of Europe, which does not have one centre but several and has changing relations of centres to peripheries. It is possible to see the field of Europe as made up of different 'Europes'. In addition to Old Europe (the major Western nation-states) and New Europe (post-communist countries) there are the older geopolitical spatial configurations, such as Central Europe and East Central Europe. Other examples are mega-regional blocs, such as Nordic Europe, Iberia and TransAlpine region. In addition there is the complex web of post-imperial relations that connect Europe to the post-colonial world. More than half of the world's dependencies – some 30 states – are under the direct rule of EU member states (Böröcz and Sarkar 2005: 164). In terms of geopolitics, the global, the national and the European dimensions interact to produce a complex field of borders and rebordering out of which emerge hard and soft borders, open and closed ones, with different degrees of spatial intensity by which regions, networks and flows operate. Another example of the changing relation of the centre to the periphery in Europe is the emergence of a new kind of governance whereby the EU expands its governance beyond the member states to neighbouring regions. Such regions, while being formally excluded from legal membership, are part of a networked political system in which 'fuzzy borders' come into play (Lavenex 2004: 681). Examples of this are accession association (for potential members), neighbourhood association (Mediterranean and near eastern countries), development co-operation (Africa and wider Asian countries) and various kinds of cooperation (see Lawson 2003; Piening 1997). In this context it makes little sense to speak of borders exclusively in terms of the legal boundaries of a given territory. Stein Rokkan referred to these relations on cores and peripheries as a European system of cleavages (Rokkan 1999, cited in Eder 2006).

The first conclusion, then, is that Europeanization entails a process of societal transformation, which can be termed cosmopolitanism to refer to the lack of closure in it due to its multi-levelled orders of governance and its multi-directional expansion. The cosmopolitanism suggested by this should not be equated simply with pluralism. While diversity is an important component of the mosaic of European societies, there is also a process of interaction going on. The interpenetration of societies, the interlinking of different orders of governance, the impact of globalization and transnational movements of all kinds results not just in more diversity, but in societal transformation. Cosmopolitanism is thus not a matter of co-existence, as in multiculturalism, or cultural dialogue, since the various levels and actors co-evolve and as they do emergent realities are produced. Furthermore, the resulting cosmopolitanism, which is variously internal and external, is not a matter of convergence into a uniform framework since the movement itself produces its own terms. There is not a prior plan – such as a master plan or institutional design – or an underlying identity that explains everything. The debates of the present day about the constitution and borders of the EU are an example of this reflexive logic to Europeanization.

Cosmopolitanism and democratization: European public culture

One aspect of democracy that people most commonly associate with the notion is parliament, which is the representative voice of a sovereign people. Viewed in such simple terms it could be argued that there is no European democracy because the European Parliament is not a sovereign institution. This is too simple a view of democracy, which also consists of public debates and civil society outside the formal arena of the state. As a cosmopolitan project, Europeanization entails more not less democracy. In European public culture new discourses about political community are being articulated. These discourses are not controlled by any one social actor and in them competing conceptions of political community are worked out. Actors constantly have to re-situate themselves as the discourses lack fixed reference points. The debate about the draft European Constitution is a pertinent example. This is a process of contestation, persuasion and power in which multiple actors were involved. What is clear from this is that there are no authoritative definitions of what constitutes the 'we' of the political community and also there is no clear definition of who the 'Other' is.

As previously suggested, Europe is now indefinable for precisely these reasons; both Self and Other are not easily defined in ways that can lead to a clear-cut identity that could be encapsulated in a constitution or in a territorially defined polity. Europeans are divided on whether Europe includes Turkey and they are divided on whether Europe can be defined by Christianity. They are divided on whether Europeanization is good or bad and what its limits should be. Much of this is an expression of democratic self-criticism, but much of it is fuelled by xenophobia and a failure to see the connection between the reality of cosmopolitanism and the expansion of democracy.

All of a sudden, a European discourse of origins is on everyone's lips. Those who want to keep the Turks out discover that the roots of Europe lie in the Christian West. Only those who have always been a part of this 'occidental community of shared destiny' is 'one of us'. This becomes clear when we ask 'Where do you stand on Turkey?', which has become the critical question of European politics. It divides opinion and ignites the conflict between the old national and a new cosmopolitan Europe. The term 'cosmopolitan Europe' can be understood as precisely the negation of this sort of territorial social ontology which seeks to block all paths to the future. The idea of a 'cosmopolitan Europe' has an empirical meaning in drawing attention to the diverse and ever-changing world in which we live, for example, that the Turks some people want to keep out have long since already been inside. Turkey arrived in European space a long time ago, as a member of NATO, as a trading partner, as one pole of transnational forms of life. Moreover, large parts of Turkey are Europeanized.

To allow a Christian-occidental principle of ethnic descent to be resurrected from the mass graves of Europe is to fail to understand Europe's inner cosmopolitanism. It is to deny the reality of the roughly 17 million people living in the EU who cannot recognize this ethnic-cultural heritage of 'Europeanness' as their own, because they are Muslims or people of colour, for example, yet who understand and organize themselves culturally and politically as Europeans. The history of the eastern contribution to Europe and the contribution of migrants to the cultural dynamics and moral self-understanding of a cosmopolitan Europe has yet to be written.

In the world of the twenty-first century there is no longer a closed space called 'the Christian West'. With growing transnational interconnections and obligations, Europe is becoming an open network with fluid boundaries in which the outside is already inside.

There is no doubt that the current state of the European Union deserves criticism. But where can we find suitable standards of criticism? They cannot come from the national self-image or from laments over the loss of national sovereignty. The concept of a cosmopolitan Europe makes possible a critique of EU reality which is neither nostalgic nor national but radically European. The reality of Europeanization is the reality of democratization. It was not too long ago that many of the present EU member states were anything but democratic. Germany ceased to be a totalitarian state after 1945 while Greece, Portugal and Spain made the transition to democracy only in the 1980s. The process by which the central and Eastern European countries made the transition to democracy since 1990 was enhanced by the accession to the EU. In addition to establishing a framework for peace and democracy in post-war Europe, the EU has now the capacity to influence democratization in its neighbouring countries. This is evident in Bulgaria and in Romania. Nowhere is this more evident than in the case of Turkey, where the impact of democratic reforms has been extensive. It is also evident that the EU is able to use effectively further enlargement in the Balkans as an instrument of foreign policy. The prospect of eventual membership for Croatia, and likely membership in the near future for Serbia, has been a huge inducement for democratization. This is also becoming evident in the case of Ukraine, one of Europe's least democratic countries. With this capacity to develop democracy in neighbouring countries the EU has the means to become an important power. The prospect of Europe becoming such a cosmopolitan player will be discussed below.

There is a further democratizing dimension to European public culture that must be highlighted: the culture of resistance that was created after the Second World War. While much of this heritage has been claimed by national identities, there is a dimension that has a strong cosmopolitan side to it. Cosmopolitan Europe was consciously initiated after 1945 as the political antithesis to a nationalistic Europe and its moral and physical devastation. This cosmopolitan Europe is a Europe which struggles morally, politically, economically and historically for reconciliation. The adjective 'cosmopolitan' stands for this openness limited by the critique of ethnonationalism which clamours for recognition of cultural difference and diversity.

The creation of an international court from its origins in the Nuremberg Trials was the first step in the direction of a cosmopolitan Europe (see Fine 2000). It is remarkable that it was a creation of legal categories and a judicial procedure beyond national sovereignty. This made it possible to capture the historical monstrosity of the systematic, state-organized extermination of the Jews in legal concepts and court procedures. It can and must be interpreted as a primary source of the new European cosmopolitanism that has a powerful external dimension. Cosmopolitan Europe expresses a genuinely European self-contradiction in a moral, legal and political sense. If the traditions from which colonialist, nationalist and genocidal horror originate are European, then so are the evaluative standards and legal categories in terms of which these acts are proclaimed as crimes against humanity before a global public. The dilemmas of an institutionalized cosmopolitanism are especially evident in the commemoration of the Holocaust. In this sense, the commemoration of the Holocaust is a monitory memorial against the ever-present modernization of barbarism (Levy and Sznaider 2002). The negativity of modernity and European awareness of it is not merely a pose, an ideology of the tragic. It reflects the historical invention of a modernity distorted by the nation and the state which has inexorably developed the potential for moral, political, economic and technological disaster like a chamber of horrors of a real laboratory without concern for its own destruction. The mass graves of the twentieth century – of the two World Wars, the Holocaust, the atomic bombs dropped on Hiroshima and Nagasaki, the Stalinist death camps and genocides – testify to this. As Daniel Levy and Natan Sznaider have argued, radical, self-critical European commemoration of the Holocaust does not destroy, but rather constitutes, the identity of Europe. Paradoxically formulated, it can enable Europe to find its continuity in its break with the past. In the commemoration of the Holocaust, the break with the past draws its power for the future. What is at stake is the institution of future-oriented forms of memory for a cosmopolitan self-critique of Europe in opposition to national founding and warrior myths. A similar challenge is posed, incidentally, by post-colonialism and also by the nascent revolutionary consequences of developments in human genetics, nanotechnology and electronic communication.

However, it would be a mistake to see all criticism of Europeanization as anti-democratic. The relationship between the intensification of Europeanization and the rise of neo-nationalism and right-wing populism has often been noted. While European nation-states are becoming caught up in processes of mutual absorption, combination and synthesis, the national imagination reigns more than ever in people's heads, as a sentimental ghost, a rhetorical gesture, in which the fearful and bewildered seek a refuge and a future. What is going on here is a diverse cacophony of voices, not all of which are due to the inherent appeal of nationalism. What needs to be appreciated is that the relation between elites and masses has changed.

It is this change that lay at the core of the momentous No votes in May 2005 when the French and Dutch voters overwhelmingly rejected the draft EU constitution. The event – the first popular hard choice for the test of the EU – marked a fundamental turning point in the relation of the masses to the elites. This was the first major revolt in the history of the EU of the masses against the elites. But the revolt was not due to a simple reflex of a primordial and backward national identity – a demos backed up by an ethnos – revolting against the cosmopolitanism of the elites. The masses do not constitute a substantive peoplehood but are, as in these cases, a diverse coalition of social interests mobilized by democratic processes. The relation between elites and masses has changed in the following respects. First, the elites can no longer rely on traditional forms of authority and deference; second, the popular arguments for European integration as enhancing the national interest have been challenged by global threats which did not exist at the time of the Treaty of Rome; third, paradoxically a more advanced level of formal democratization – including widespread availability of information – has allowed the elites to be challenged in ways that were not possible during earlier stages in European integration; and finally, contemporary culture is more diverse than before, making it more difficult for consensus to be achieved.

The case of the constitutional crisis in 2005 is an example of the masses not only rejecting the messages of the elites but of articulating different positions with a wider field of contestation. This field is likely to grow in the future and as it does so a European public culture of democratic contestation is likely to become more important in framing the terms of national politics. Unavoidably the global context will be more present. To this external dimension to the cosmopolitan nexus we now turn.

Europe and the rise of Asia: globalization as cosmopolitanism

The relevance of a cosmopolitan perspective for the present day is not simply due to factors specific to the internal transformation of Europe. Attention must also be paid to external context. Of particular interest and much neglected is the relation of Europe to Asia. The relation with the United States has been much discussed and there is no doubt that the formative phase of European integration has been closely tied to the United States and a Western orientation. The United States has itself been a strong advocate of European integration and clearly American business and political elites see a strong Europe as part of an American-led West.

The relation of Europe to America cannot be easily described since it has many dimensions, ranging from a general acceptance of a Western way of life and belief in the values of freedom and the worth of the individual to more political alliances. It has been widely commented that since 11 September 2001 the relation has grown more tense. Although this has often been exaggerated, since most European countries continue close relations with the United States, there are clear signs of a rift. First, as the memory of the Second World War fades, so too does the symbolic role of America as the saviour of Europe. Especially since the fall of communism,

Europe has slowly evolved its own public culture which cannot be seen as a consequence of Americanization. European culture can be seen in terms of cosmopolitanism, as examples from sport, media, health and transport attest (Roche 2006). Second, the European tradition of social solidarity and social justice is stronger than in the US and is increasingly becoming more and more a basis of a European model of society (Rifkin 2004). It is possible to envisage the social question becoming the driving force in the future. The present crisis concerning the European constitution is one such example of how a debate about the constitution became a debate about capitalism and the free market eroding social and economic securities. Third, there are clear political differences between Europe and America on issues of human rights and global justice. It is likely that these differences will grow in the future due, on the one side, to the growing momentum of the Europeanization and, on the other, the rise of an increasingly unilateralist and militaristic United States. Finally, there is the longer perspective of history. The United States emerged out of very different historical circumstances – a settler and largely agrarian society whose spirit of independence was closely linked to millennial religious movements, a weak state, the absence of feudalism and monarchy – than did European states whose traditions of revolution were very different. Although the EU was not born out of a revolutionary act of liberation as such, the values that underpin it express the European republican, radical and cosmopolitan currents. Viewed in historical perspective it is possible to envisage further differences between Europe and America.

What is becoming clear is that the unitary notion of the West is increasingly irrelevant to the current situation. Europe and America do not constitute the West in any meaningful sense. But rather than speak of the decline of the West, it is more accurate to speak of its fragmentation and global restructuring. It is possible to see in this a re-orientation of Europe as a power between America and Asia. With the United States becoming more and more a supra-power – albeit one that does not have unlimited military power – the opportunities are created for Europe to become a cosmopolitan power. The critical factor in this is the relation to Asia.

Like Europe, Asia is also changing, although at an unprecedented rate and far more than anything like what is happening in Europe (Sharma 2005). It would not be inaccurate to refer to change in Asia as Westernization, since on one level that is clearly what is occurring, but it is too simple. The tremendous transformation of Asian societies, in particular India and China in recent years, cannot be seen simply in terms of the adoption of a Western way of life. The new Asian world is in part a product of diverse histories and vastly different societies. As these societies become more and more economically and technologically advanced the rest of the developed world will have to reconsider their relations to Asia. Given the wider context of the globalization of markets, Asia will be a major power in the world. Countries such as India and China will overtake Japan in economic influence. China is already third largest producer of manufactured goods. In demographic terms these countries will overtake Europe as a new global social dynamic comes into play. By 2020 the population of China is expected to be 1.4 billion and the population of India is expected to reach 1.3 billion. The implications go beyond trade and manufacture. As Asian countries become more prosperous the implications for energy are huge and pollution will increase due to inefficient use of energy and weak environmental protection. The political implications are also likely to be far-reaching as parts of Asia become marginalized from the rising centres. Inevitably new political alignments will emerge with the scales of global power shifting from the West to Asia.

The diversity of Asia – which is greater than in Europe – will prevent anything like a common political community emerging comparable with the EU (see Oommen 2004; Therborn in this volume). However, regional trade organizations such as Asia–Europe Meeting (ASEM) are comparable in terms of its economic influence (see Preston and Gilson 2001). Trade within Asia is growing at nearly three times the global rate and already there is pressure from Asian countries for more free trade agreements. Since the first ASEM in 1996, the EU has been developing relations with Asian countries and Asian transnational organizations (see Lawson 2003). It may be suggested that as the relation with Asia becomes increasingly more important, opportunities will arise for Europe to become more self-consciously cosmopolitan. Trade is clearly central to this but there are also wider social, cultural and political questions at stake. Just as Europe–American relations defined the identity of Europe, so too will Europe–Asian relations define the identity of Europe. This is the opportunity for Europe to give a new meaning to its cosmopolitanism, one in which the external dimension will complement the internal one in important ways.

The danger however exists for a protectionist reaction against trade liberalization. There is no easy solution to this as Europeans can legitimately expect protection from cheap imports from Asia. The position of the UK government encourages trade liberalization and the movement of Western firms to Asia has already made a huge impact on European industry. But cosmopolitanism is not simply a matter of open markets. The combined labour population of India and China is almost 2.4 billion allowing these countries to produce a huge volume of manufactured goods and increasingly too services at a fraction of the cost in Europe. With low levels of social and environmental protection, Europe is put on the defensive by an unfettered capitalism in Asia and a corporate culture in Europe wishing to escape the restraints that exist within the EU. What is the solution?

It would appear from the current debate that Europe either embraces the liberal global market in open terms with the result that a nationalist reaction will be triggered or Europe maintains protectionist barriers which guarantee social and economic securities but at the price of erecting a

Fortress Europe. So Europe can retreat into its social democracy to protect itself from an Asian capitalism that is not restrained by democracy. If it does, the creation of a Fortress Europe will in turn only serve to provoke anti-European sentiments in Asia. Rather than choose between these two positions, there is a third option for Europe to pursue and which is congruent with its cosmopolitan currents.

This option would be to devise cooperative links with Asian countries whereby Europe can use its influence to exert Asian governments and firms to promote social protection for workers and to devise safer and more environmentally sustainable modes of production than is presently the case. Only by recognizing the reality of the world risk society which both Europe and Asia inhabit, and the global gains in the promotion of democracy and social justice, can genuine cooperation be achieved. The availability of cheap labour in Asia may be an attractive resource for Western firms, but for Asian firms it does not solve all problems. As Asian countries become more developed with capital-intensive manufacturing they will come to depend increasingly on Western technological expertise until they can create their own knowledge-based economies: cheap labour is only one cost in industrial production in knowledge-based economies. Firms in India and China are already short of qualified workers and are often forced to move operations to Europe. The resulting global interdependence may lead to less exploitative labour relations. It is thus possible to suggest that European countries through the EU and European–Asian summits such as ASEAN and the World Economic Forum should promote ways of controlling capitalism, such as developing and extending a corporate culture of global responsibility.

One of the achievements of European modernity was in creating dynamic relations between the market, the state and civil society. Promoting such positive models of modernity to Asia is an example of cosmopolitanism and not of Eurocentric nationalism. The achievement of European modernity was that the rule of the market was always limited by democracy. In the present day, globalization has released capitalism from such limits in much the same way as colonialism allowed Europeans to plunder the rest of the world. Bringing globalization under the control of cosmopolitan politics is the only way Europe and Asia will survive in the world risk society. This will not be easy, but it is difficult to see an alternative. It is undoubtedly the greatest challenge of the EU, which until now has been successful in opening markets within Europe without undermining social securities. Already the EU is gradually extending the free movement of goods, capital and services to those countries within its neighbouring regions. It is not impossible for the EU to find ways of responding to the challenge of globalization without surrendering the commitment to social justice that is already being challenged within Europe by nationalist reaction.

The point of the present discussion can be summed up as follows. Until now Europe has been mostly defined in terms of its historical relation with the United States. With the expansion of the EU east and southwards, on the one side and on the other the changing identity of the US as a global military power, the Western alliance is likely to become weaker. While Europe of course still remains more tied to the US, the question of its relation to Asia will become more important in the present century. The opportunity exists for Europe to devise new relations with Asia at a time when Asia is itself undergoing major change.

Conclusion: the reality of cosmopolitanism

The national outlook not only misunderstands the reality and future of Europe. It reduces the solution to two options: a federal state (federalism) or a confederation (inter-governmentalism). Both models are empirically false. Understood in normative and political terms, they deny the very thing at stake now and for the future: a cosmopolitan Europe. Our main conclusion then is that cosmopolitan realism implies that Europe will never be possible as a project of national homogeneity. To build the common European house according to the national–international logic is neither realistic nor desirable; on the contrary, it is counterproductive. Only a cosmopolitan Europe which (as its founders intended) both overcomes and acknowledges its national tradition – overcomes it by acknowledging it (and hence excludes a national Greater Europe, but celebrates national diversity as an essential characteristic of Europe) – is both European (in the sense of non-national) as well as national, because it is plural-national, hence European. The internal cosmopolitan project that has been a feature of much of Europeanization until now must be complemented by a strengthening of what can be called an external cosmopolitanism.

We have argued that a cosmopolitan Europe cannot be created only from within Europe; it must also involve an engagement with Asia. As discussed above, already a movement in the direction of a cosmopolitan engagement with the Outside can be discerned in the way in which the enlargement of the EU is serving to democratize foreign policy in the neighbouring regions of Europe. In this blurring of the difference between Inside and Outside there is also a rescaling of the difference between Self and Other. Increasingly Europe is being defined on its borders (Balibar 2004). Instead of being the edge of Europe, the border has become the point at which the political community becomes conscious of itself. The upshot of this is that the cosmopolitan perspective complements the view that the Other cannot be excluded since it is already part of the Self. In other words, Europe can no longer be defined by the exclusion of Asia, which is already part of Europe.

Note

1 On cosmopolitanism and Europe see Beck (2006) Beck and Grande (2006), Delanty (2005), Delanty and Rumford (2005) and Rumford (2006).

References

Balibar, E. (2004) *We the People of Europe: Reflections on Transnational Citizenship*, Princeton: Princeton University Press.

Beck, U. (2006) *The Cosmopolitan Vision*, Cambridge: Polity Press.

Beck, U. and E. Grande (2006) *Cosmopolitan Europe*, Cambridge: Polity Press.

Böröcz, J. and M. Sarkar (2005) 'What is the EU?', *International Sociology*, 20(2): 153–73.

Delanty, G. (2005) 'The Idea of a Cosmopolitan Europe: On the Cultural Significance of Europeanization', *International Review of Sociology*, 15(3): 405–21.

Delanty, G. and C. Rumford (2005) *Rethinking Europe: Social Theory and the Implications of Europeanization*, London: Routledge.

Eder, K. (2006) 'Europe's Borders', *European Journal of Social Theory*, 9(2).

Eriksen, E. O. (ed.) (2005) *Making the Euro-Polity: Reflexive Integration in Europe*, London: Routledge.

Eriksen, E. O., E. Fossum and A. J. Menendez (eds) (2005) *Developing a Constitution for Europe*, London: Routledge.

Fine, R. (2000) 'Crimes Against Humanity: Hannah Arendt and the Nuremberg Debates', *European Journal of Social Theory*, 3(3): 293–311.

Habermas, J. (1998) *The Inclusion of the Other: Studies in Political Theory*, Cambridge, MA: MIT Press.

Habermas, J. (2001) 'Why Europe Needs a Constitution', *New Left Review*, 11, Sept./Oct.

Habermas, J. (2003) 'Toward a Cosmopolitan Europe', *Journal of Democracy*, 14(4): 86–100.

Herrman, R. K., T. Risse and M. B. Brewer (eds) (2004) *Transnational Identities: Becoming European in the EU*, New York: Rowman & Littlefield.

Lavenex, S. (2004) 'EU External Governance in "Wider Europe"', *Journal of European Public Policy*, 11(4): 680–700.

Lawson, S. (2003) *Europe and Asia-Pacific: Culture, Identity and Representations of a Region*, London: RoutledgeCurzon.

Levy, D. and N. Sznaider (2002) 'Memory Unbound: The Holocaust and the Formation of Cosmopolitan Memory', *European Journal of Social Theory*, 5(1): 87–106.

Oommen, T. K. (2004) 'Socio-Politician Transition in the Indian Republic and the European Union', *European Journal of Social Theory*, 7(4): 519–37.

Piening, C. (1997) *Global Europe: The EU in World Affairs*, London: Reiner.

Preston, P. and J. Gilson (eds) (2001) *The European Union and East Asia*, Cheltenham: Edward Elgar.

Rifkin, J. (2004) *The European Dream: How Europe's Vision of the Future is Quietly Eclipsing the American Dream*, New York: Tarcher/Penguin.

Roche, M. (2006) 'Cultural Europeanization and the "Cosmopolitan Condition"', in C. Rumford (ed.) *Cosmopolitanism and Europe*, Liverpool: Liverpool University Press.

Rumford, C. (ed.) (2006) *Cosmopolitanism and Europe*, Liverpool: Liverpool University Press.

Sharma, R. (ed.) (2005) *India and Emerging Asia*, London: Sage.

2 Post-Western Europe and the plural Asias

Göran Therborn

Seriously relating Europe and Asia today seems to require two fundamental intellectual operations. One is to distinguish current Europe from the "West", both as a historical signifier and as a contemporary notion of allegiance, or denunciation, as "Western civilization" or as "West-toxification" or "occidentalism" (see Buruma and Margalit 2005). The other is to take systematic account of the incomparable plurality of Asia. That is, while Europe historically as well as today can be grasped as (approximately) one unit, Asia is irreducibly divided, now as yesterday.

On the basis of these considerations, this chapter will end by looking into tendencies of future positions and relations of Europe and the Asias in the world. Such tendencies have to be seen in the shadow of the imperial cloud of the American superpower, in particular of the recent US manifestations of what had better be called Occidental Despotism. Both the global tendencies affecting Europe and the Asias, and the current thrust of the USA will call for important cultural adjustments of Europe.

The sketch below is framed in terms of structural contours and abstracted shapes of trajectories, its author being well aware of his lack of the linguistic competence and deep cultural erudition characteristic of the great Eurasian scholarly traditions, including that of classical Orientalism, often too easily dismissed by fast readers of Edward Said, another great scholar. While rarely explicitly invoked, there is a frequent practice of *licentia sociologicae* – of sociological licence to write on topics without proper research – of which non-sociologists, and also several sociologists, are justly suspicious. However, it may also be argued that within proper limits, bird's eye topographies and profiles may add something to close-up and profoundly penetrating studies. In the world of today, the methodological nationalism constitutive of modern historiography, political science and sociology is a hindrance to new cognitive discoveries.

Europe and the "West"

The old European, and to some extent also Asian, conception and discussion of "East" and "West" underwent a crucial mutation after 1945. The historical cultural dichotomy became one party's designation of the Cold War divide. Among the dominant political currents of Western Europe and North America, and their allies and clientele in the rest of the world, "the East" became "the Eastern bloc", i.e. the Communist world. Above all, "the West" in this perception now became synonymous with the United States and its allies. Europe, in this world view, became only a part or an appendix of the USA.

In American discourse this notion of the West survived the Cold War. Its tenacity is well illustrated by Samuel Huntington's (1996) important and influential *The Clash of Civilizations*. There is no European civilization, only a "Western" one, which is supposed to divide Europe into, on one hand, an extension of North America, and, on the other, an "Orthodox" civilization, comprising Greece and the legacy of Orthodox Christianity. In Europe, however, first the thaw and then the end of the Cold War, and the advancing integration of Western Europe, led to a re-emergence of "Europe" from under the shadow of the "West". Instead of "Western" values, "Western" culture and "Western" civilization, the mainstream literature, sustained by EU research funding, now begins to focus on "European" values, culture and civilization, and their roots. This did not amount to a denial of the West, or any critique of "*Westbindung*" (bonding with the USA), only to an affirmation of a European identity of its own.

Any dialogue today on the traditional conception of East and West cannot escape the decisive Cold War transformation of it. From a notion roughly synonymous with Europe, the international power constellation and the geopolitics after 1945 made it, for practical purposes, a synonym of the USA. In this way, the question of the West has become a key part of questions about the possibilities of Europe, about its autonomy, and about its position and future in the world.

Recent developments have been contradictory in this respect. The Cold War East–West division became irrelevant with the collapse of European Communism. The enlargement and the deepening in the 1990s of what the Anglo-Saxons liked to call the "Common Market" into a European Union, as the world's most potent trading entity and with an increasing coordination of its foreign policy, meant a re-assertion of "Europe" as distinctive from "the West". Under the Chairmanship of Jacques Delors and of Jacques Santer, the European Commission also affirmed a European social model, derived from the two major reformist traditions of Continental Western Europe, Social Democracy and Christian Democracy.

In the negotiations over a Spanish, Portuguese and Greek entry to the (predecessor of) EU, the principle was established that only effective democracies could become members of this Europe in the making. This was the first time ever that democracy was made a *sine qua* non qualification for membership of an inter-state organization. Democracy, ethnic minority rights, and social rights including trade union rights, became crucial guidelines for post-Communist Eastern Europe aspiring to EU membership.

However, in the last 5–10 years the distinctiveness of the EU is eroding, by internal corrosion as well as by external shelling. The social conception of Europe, once a widely shared part of European political identity, common to Christian as well as to Social Democrats and to the Gaullists, is being ideologically abandoned, even if the institutions are still in place, in Western Europe and even in part of Eastern Europe. Tony Blair and his entourage have been the pivots in swinging Europe to the neoliberal right, obliterating the formal European Social Democratic ascendancy in the late 1990s. German Christian Democracy hoisted the flag of neoliberalism by selecting the Director of the IMF as the new German President. Now, the October 2005 German elections showed, there is no majority for neoliberalism, as there was never a popular majority for Mrs Thatcher. But the Christian Democratic *Soziallehre* is clearly on the wane.

The United States has, on the whole, been supportive of the European project. In the Cold War the latter was both perceived and intended as a contribution to the war of the West. But after the end of the Soviet Union, divergent world views and strategies have developed. While Europe has emphasized negotiations, agreements, law and exchange (or trade), the USA has concentrated on military force, military alliance and ideological confrontation.

NATO, the American Cold War alliance, which was never committed to democracy but included Fascist Portugal and militarist Turkey – and but for some stern European opposition would have included Fascist Spain as well – has not only been kept after the end of the Cold War. It has been expanded enormously, in its range of operations as well as in its membership. It has been changed from a North Atlantic defensive military alliance to a political instrument for legitimating new US wars of attack, in Kosovo and in Afghanistan, and is also in spite of European opposition used for providing auxiliary occupation forces in Iraq to the extended US empire.

The violent, deadly, but largely symbolic attack on the World Trade Center, the Pentagon and some other, never certainly identified, US target in September 2001 ripped "the West" apart, and created-cum-highlighted differences between Europe and the USA, and among European political elites. The dramatic event also brought forth renewed efforts at re-affirming a Western civilization and Western values. In sober thought, this underlines the urgency of clarifying the current relations of Europe and "the West".

The Bushmen and the re-launching of Occidental Despotism

The Bush regime of the US, saw "9/11" as the proper moment to declare a Third World War, labelled the "War on terrorism". While explicitly siding with the USA in combating the few scores of Islamist radicals taking on the superpower of the world, most Europeans have had difficulties in seeing it as a full-scale "war". The current course of the USA has, on the one hand, fundamentally divided the West by cutting off connections to a crucial contemporary European norm, the rule of law.

The Bush government is asserting the USA as the world ruler, above any law, intervening anywhere in ways it sees fit. Its legal advisers even argue that the American President as commander on chief is unbound from any constitutional or human rights constraints. The latest US wars have blatantly flaunted the UN Charter and the Geneva Convention on Prisoners of War. The USA has opposed the International Criminal Court, and has forced its clientele states to recognize the exemption of the United States from any war crimes prosecution. What we are witnessing here is the rise of an *Occidental Despotism*.

The American war has both undermined Europe, and, unintendedly, reinforced it. Europe has been undermined by the British unconditional support of the war and of its repressive implications. The enormous, historical task of unifying Eastern and Western Europe, on the agenda with the 2004 enlargement of the EU, was sidelined for the American strategic aim of West-binding Turkey in the EU. Similarly, the American Kosovo war had precipitated a much larger and accelerated eastern enlargement of the EU than planned. However one should evaluate the intrinsic value of these openings, it is clear that both the popular legitimacy and the institutional capacity of the EU have been over-extended by these cavings-in to American demands and time-schedules.

On the other hand, there is the widening rift between current American policy and the European legal tradition, pre-1914 and post-1945. The European state system generated very early a legal framework transcending the various polities – it would be anachronistic to call it international law. Originally it derived from the coexistence of a number of powerful princes and a common Christian religion. In the seventeenth century it was secularized as *ius gentium*, the law of peoples. It was no protection against state violence, although it did gradually raise some regulation of wars and of their aftermath. International law is the basis of the European Union – with the *effet direct* of European nation upon member states – as well as the Council of Europe (see Therborn 2002).

The new Atlantic gap was highlighted in late October 2005, when the EU started an inquiry into the revelations of the *Washington Post* and other US media of secret American torture chambers in Poland and Romania. The US rejection of the Geneva Convention on humane treatment of prisoners of war, and of the International Criminal Court, has not been publicly endorsed by a single European government. On the contrary, the official position of every government is the opposite of the Washington view.

The liberal democratic US reaction to the dramatic but basically symbolic attack of 11 September 2001 should make the violence of popular revolutions, like the Russian Bolshevik in 1917–1920, more understandable, if not necessarily more pardonable. When an overwhelming superpower, with no serious rival for power in sight, finds it necessary to protect liberalism by worldwide abductions, a global network of torture centres and concentration camps, and two full-scale wars of invasion, what could reasonably be expected of a socialist revolution in a despotic country besieged by an array of foreign armies – British, Czech, French, German, Japanese – as well as by an armed and amply-officered domestic counter-revolution?

The recent American embrace of Occidental Despotism – reverting to the times of the Indian wars and expulsions and to the invasions of Cuba and The Philippines a century ago – is one major part of the recent undoing of the Euro-American "West".

The other is the rise of Christian fundamentalism (and of Jewish militantism) in the USA, while secularism is widening and deepening in Western Europe. In spite of post-Communist promotion of official religion, Europe is, with a few national outliers – Croatia, Ireland, Lithuania, Poland – the most secularized part of the world, whereas the USA is one of the most God-believing and God-invoking (Inglehart *et al.* 2004: 12, F050ff).

In summary, with the rise of USA, Europe was no longer synonymous with the West. Indeed Europe became a "dispensable" part of the West, to which only the United States was the "indispensable nation", as Clinton's Secretary of State Madeleine Albright put it. But with the recent cultural-political divergence, Europe is no longer meaningfully part of a common North Atlantic West. Europe is coming to itself, but it is still struggling with Western ties and allegiances.

Above both Europe and Asia there is an imperial cloud under which any serious East–West discussion today takes place, and which the latter has to relate to. The consequences are direst for West Asia, also the weak centre of the violent resistance to the American empire. In Central Asia, imperial geopolitics is propping up the authoritarian regimes, paying them, arming them, legitimating them. Where the attempts to enlist Japan and South Korea as imperial auxiliaries will lead is difficult to tell, but the encouragement of Japanese armed interventions overseas is likely to increase regional tension and worries. China is likely to concentrate on its own growth for the foreseeable future. There will be more attempts to draw India into the American orbit, which are likely to increase domestic conflict.

One Europe, several Asias

Like the East–West distinction, the Europe–Asia comparison has to be deconstructed. Europe may be seen as one, but Asia cannot. How to show that argument as non-arbitrary? There are at least three different basic criteria, each having its own time-span, which may be used. One refers to conscious historical cultural legacy. What is the classical canon of the culture? Its classical, perhaps sacred, language(s), its classical literature and its philosophy. The classical legacy seem to be less difficult and arbitrary to handle for modern purposes than the concept of civilization, however defined. The second concerns the trajectory into the modern, the timing and, above all, the line-up of forces for and against, and the shape of their struggles. In brief, the roads to modernity. As the current weight and value of the classics and the route to modernity cannot be determined a priori, it will appear wise to deploy also a third criterion, the recent and current pattern of political, economic and cultural relations. On all three criteria we can discern some unity or singularity of Europe. On none of them, is there one Asia – although all parts of the continent may be located within a world system.

In terms of civilization as well as in terms of roads to modernity it is meaningful to talk of Europe in singular, although the continent is not flat like a shopping-mall parking-lot, and its political divisions seem to be currently increasing. There is a sense, in which we may talk about one Europe, and not primarily because of the enlargement of the European Union of May 2004. In terms of world history, Europe is basically one civilization, with a common Antiquity or Classicism – of philosophy, art and architecture – derived from the city states and empires of Greece and Rome 2,500 to 1,500 years ago, and a common Christian religion, although deeply divided for a thousand years.

It is sometimes argued that Eastern Europe falls outside this civilization, for not having had the resurgence of this Antiquity in what in Europe is called the Renaissance of the fifteenth and sixteenth centuries. However, this was the time, after the fall of Constantinople to the Muslim Ottomans in 1453, that the religious and political authorities of Muscovy began to refer to Moscow as the "Third Rome", that Italian builders were recruited to build the main churches of the Kremlin, albeit in a Russian style with only secondary Italianate elements (Kaufmann 1995: 30ff). The border treaty of Nerchinsk between Russia and China in 1689 was negotiated in Latin and Manchu with the help of Jesuit interpreters (Spence 1990: 67) From the eighteenth century Greek-Roman architecture became part of Russian imperial Classicism, while French became the language of the Russian court and nobility. Most of the showpieces of the new capital of St Petersburg were built by Italian architects, for example, the Alexander Nevsky monastery by Trezzini, the Senate and the Synod by Carlo Rossi, the Winter Palace by Rastrelli (Pilipenko 1993). Germanic as well as Slavic Europe were outside the Roman empire, and Sweden did not even exist on the maps of Ancient geographers, but later on an Ancient legacy of Latin and Greek was learnt and claimed all over European high culture.

There is a basically common European road to modernity, beginning with Britain in the seventeenth century, with its scientific breakthroughs and its political civil wars, and winning the centre stage through the eighteenth-century Enlightenment and the French Revolution, but then having to fight its way all through the long nineteenth century, and only becoming victorious with the outcome of the First World War. This is a road of endogenous development, of internal conflict, civil wars and revolutions. Dynasties – with the brief eighteenth-century qualification of "Enlightened Absolutism", stretching from Lisbon to St Petersburg – aristocracies and all established churches (Catholic, Orthodox and Protestant) were against a rupture with traditional sources of authority. Burghers, artisans, secular intellectuals, dissident aristocrats and, increasingly, the big city populace, the new industrial workers and nationalistically aroused peasants were in favour. European modernity was no inherent emanation, and it had to fight its way forward. But the conflicts, violent or peaceful, revolutionary or reformatory, were usually internal to existing polities, and from the French Revolution to the Russian Revolution increasingly involved class conflict, while Europe's modern war paths were largely shaped by the vicissitudes of colonialism overseas. To this day, the democratic party systems of Europe have a class-rooted left–right cleavage pattern.

Europe also has a common, traumatic twentieth-century history, being the main theatre of the two World Wars and of the global Cold War – all three originating and decided in Europe. This traumatic war experience has had two important consequences in particular. One is the drive for overcoming the violent divisions of the past, first of the Franco-German wars, which led to the creation of what is now the European Union, then of the Cold War division of Germany into German Reunification, and third, of the Cold War "Iron Curtain", to be overcome in part (if not fully) by the "Eastern enlargement" of the EU in 2004. Left out after 2004 are Bulgaria and Romania, which have been given clear prospects of later membership, the remaining states of the former Yugoslavia, Albania, Belarus, Russia and the Ukraine, whose European future is still uncertain, and, in the cases of Ukraine, Russia and Belarus, still controversial.

Second, pioneered by post-Second World War Germany, twentieth-century history has taught Europe guilt. European culture has become significantly preoccupied with digging up, commemorating and redeeming its crimes of the past; mainly, but by no means exclusively, the Nazi genocide and the collaboration or collusion with it, and also the dictatorship of Communism, the dirty Cold War by the West and the crimes of colonialism.

Europe's loss of its colonies and of its Big Powers have been remarkably little traumatic, although they do form a very relevant background to the Rome Treaty of 1957, which launched the European Economic Community. Those losses, and in particular the former, were overshadowed by the unprecedented boom of the European economies after the war, which already in the early 1960s made the European continent a magnet of immigration, reversing an almost 500-year-old tradition of out-migration.

European civilization as well as European modernity have a strong universalistic, missionary streak. Christianity is a world religion of salvation, and European explorers, traders and conquerors were usually from the very beginning accompanied by Christian missionaries, who ventured into Sub-Saharan Africa, South America and East Asia by the sixteenth century. The European scientism and the rationalism of the seventeenth and eighteenth centuries were also explicitly universalistic, which did not exclude a high respect and admiration for some non-European cultures, the Chinese in particular, revered by some of the greatest minds of the European Enlightenment, like Leibniz and Voltaire. But universalism is inherently self-righteous. In the twentieth century, European Communism, Social Democracy and Liberalism have all continued this universalistic Europeanness.

This common European legacy of classicism, modernity and twentieth-century traumas has always been full of conflict, opposing interpretations and exclusivist claims. The commonality of Europe is by no means a cultural emanation, but a commonality of conflict, of war, as well as of bargaining, truces and compromise. It has resulted in the current European Union, which is now bridging one of the most ancient cultural divides of Europe, the Trieste–St Petersburg line, separating Eastern and Western European marriage systems. The line can be traced back to the Eastern limits of the Germanic expansion eastwards in the early Middle Ages (see Therborn 2004: 144ff). Also in this way "Europe" has become post-Western.

The plurality of Asia

There is no Asia in the same sense. "There is no common tradition in Asia to define the Great Books of the East", as the American Orientalist de Bary put it in a valiant attempt to construct an Asian canon (de Bary 1990: 42). Not even the wonderful Pan-Asian journal *Inter-Asia Cultural Studies* has a fully Pan-Asia basis, restricting itself to the huge area from India to Japan (inclusive). The range of the grand Singaporean millennium conference "We Asians" (Kwok Kian-Woon *et al.* 2000) is the same, repeating the stretch a century earlier by Okakura Tenshin and a couple of other Japanese artists going to Calcutta and linking up with Bengali culture for a Pan-Asian effort. When Okakura (1903) opened his *Ideals of the East* by saying "Asia is one", he was proclaiming a new Japanese intellectual programme, against the anti-Asianness of the early Meiji modernizers, who with Fukuzawa Yukichi called for a dissociation with Asia, "datsu-A ron". But he was thinking primarily of the Sinic and the Indic civilizations (see Karatani 1993). The Japanese concept of "the East", *toyo*, which was established as a topic of historiography on par with "the West" from the 1890s, did formally include Eurasia east of Europe, while excluding what is now seen as Southeast Asia, and was in fact centred on Sino-Japanese relations (Tanaka 1993).

While recognizing that there has been a continental Asian group at the

UN and that there are continental Asian Games, Koh refrains from trying to define anything commonly Asian, concentrating instead on talking about "East Asia". The great Sino-American Confucian scholar Tu Weiming recently summarized Asia as "East Asia, South Asia, and South-east Asia" (interviewed in Hutanuwatr and Manivannan 2005: I:137), a restriction also adopted (without motivation) by an ambitious German orientalist overview of the continent (Weggel 1989). In Chinese, the concept of Asia is derived from the English name of the continent. Then it so happens that the characters used to render the English word-sound may be read as "Inferior Continent", surrounding the Central Kingdom (China). (I owe the former insight to the German Sinologist Christoph Harbsmeier, oral communication, the latter to Korhonen 2002.)

How many Asias exist that are more or less equivalent to "Europe" is a question hardly raised seriously before, and one that is unlikely to have a non-controversial answer. De Bary and Bloom (1990) opted for four "major traditions", the Islamic, the Indian, the Chinese and the Japanese. Any number higher than three, and any further sub-division, can expect at least some objections. Let us start with the three irreducible Asias.

The West, the East and the South

West Asia is clearly one Asia, the birthplace and the centre of Islam, with a culture historically further shaped by the Arabic script, by a learned knowledge of the Arabic language and Arab-language learning of law, history and science, by Persian poetry and other secular culture of refinement, and by Turkic military prowess and command language. Architectural styles came to differ, mainly between a Western one developed by the Ottomans and one spreading east from Persia, but monumental building had a common base, centred on military fortresses for the rulers and mosques and *madrasas* (schools) according to the same planning principles. It was a society moulded by mounted warriors, pastoralists and merchants, knit together by caravans and their routes across deserts and steppes. In the sixteenth to eighteenth centuries this was a civilization stretching from the Balkans and Morocco to what is today Uzbekistan and Bangladesh. Its main political carriers then were the Ottoman and the Mughal empires with Persia and smaller-scale emirs and khans between them or on the margins.

While the Mughals of India finally succumbed to the British, the main West Asian road to modernity was one of Reactive Modernization, initiated and directed from above under acute external threats, and largely imported from abroad. The Ottomans and after them Atatürk and the nationalists of Turkey led the way, followed by the Persians/Iranian rulers, and by Arab monarchs and nationalists. In the twentieth century, major parts of this Asia have become the world's premier rentier economies, whose enormous oil wealth has made possible peculiar blends of modernity and tradition, political and religious.

Contemporary West Asia is fractured, a fact highlighted by Turkey's bid to join Europe, about a century after Japanese nationalists discussed whether modern Japan should leave Asia. The post-World War establishment of a Jewish state in Palestine furnished a common enemy, but the US-backed and US-financed formidable Israeli army has repeatedly defeated any Arab unity. The oil economies are similar and competing rather than complementary, although they have occasionally formed a functioning cartel. Attempts at Islam-based cooperation have not been very successful either, due to the divisions between the mostly Sunni Arabs, the Shia Iranians and the secularized Turks.

At the other end is East Asia, the realm of the Sinic civilization, from Korea to Vietnam, with the Middle Kingdom at its centre, having a common elite culture of a secular Confucian classical canon and a common script and language of erudition, conveying a common corpus of ethics, aesthetics and poetry. Well into the twentieth century the Chinese characters could function, like medieval European Latin, as a common means of communication between intellectuals of the region. There was also a similar Buddhist tradition. The pre-modern East Asian commonality was nevertheless varied and complex, most easily summed up in the development of Japanese, Korean and Vietnamese scripts below the supreme culture of classical Chinese. In addition, the Shogun's Edo was not built according to the same strict symmetrical principles as imperial Beijing (compare the maps of seventeenth-century Edo in McClain and Merriman 1994: 20ff with any of Beijing).

Whatever arguments may be marshalled in favour of separating modern Japan from this East Asia, Japan clearly shared its classical background with China (and the rest of East Asia). Until the nineteenth century the Japanese elite saw China as their cultural centre, and even intellectual pioneers of Japanese cultural nationalism, like Aizawa – who wrote the intellectual rationale for the external closure edict of 1825 – or Shiratori, initiating oriental history in the first decades of the twentieth century, formulated their theses in classical Chinese terms. Japan had now become the Middle Kingdom and the base of true Confucianism, respectively (Wakabayashi 1986; Tanaka 1993).

Japan was the first and the most successful example of Reactive Modernization, so rapidly successful that it soon became a colonial ruler, the only non-European in modern history. As a colonial power it was also more successful or progressive than anybody else, manifested in the development of schooling and the economy of Korea and Taiwan. Should this unrivalled Japanese success be interpreted as a break up of East Asia? I don't think that would be a very fruitful, and certainly not an analytically parsimonious, approach to Asia. Qing and Republican China did embark on the same route of Reactive Modernization, very much under Japanese inspiration, and was never really colonized. The Japanese aggression and Soviet example and support did introduce a large-scale European-type class struggle into China. But after the end of Maoism China has embarked on a new wave of modernization from above with the help of Chinese émigré (and Japanese) capital.

The roads to modernity did diverge in East Asia, with colonialism by the French and Japanese, with Communism and massive class conflict. However, since the 1980s they are converging again, without ending in one single lane.

The region was kept together by its involvement in the big global wars of the twentieth century, hot and cold, although on opposite sides in the Second World War and in the Cold War. This de facto integration through conflict is a basis for the extensive economic ties of the countries of the region, ties which have been deepened and strengthened in recent decades because of the booming markets of South Korea, Taiwan and, then and above all, China, in part also Vietnam. The weakness of the region is the absence of any post-nationalist politico-cultural reconciliation between Japan and Korea, and between Japan and China.

Between those two wings of Asia, there is the Indic civilization, the core of current South Asia, with its own classical language, Sanskrit, its own classical canon of huge epics, holy Vedic scriptures, and legal code, the Law of Manu, and with an ancient tradition of polytheistic religion, of mathematics and of science. There is also something else common to South Asia, perhaps even more important: a tradition of multiculturalism, of coexistence of different religions – Hinduism, Islam, Jainism, Sikhism, Zoroastrism, Christianity, earlier Buddhism – of many different languages and several scripts, and of a complex, heterogeneous culture different from political power. A great deal of the latter originated in the Muslim warrior cultures of Central Asia, for instance the Sultanate of Delhi and its successor the Mughal empire, founded by a fugitive from Samarkand, Babur. More indigenous Indian polities were also multilingual. The Vijayanaga state, important between 1340 and 1565, was ruled by speakers of Tulu and Kannadu, but its court literature was mainly written in Telugu, Tamil and Sanskrit (Pollock 2001: 400–1). On the eve of Indian colonial subjugation Sanskrit became a dying language, like eighteenth-century Latin. The administrative language in Bengal and other parts of the decaying Mughal empire was Persian, the first literary language of the great early nineteenth-century Bengali intellectual Rammohan Ray (Robertson 1995: 24ff). The Mughals developed their own variant of Islamic architectural splendour, in imperial mausolea and fortresses (the Taj Mahal and the Red Fort, for example), as well as in mosques, alongside the gaudy-coloured, sculptured Hindu temples.

South Asia had to travel the typical Colonial Road to Modernity: conquest, occupation, identification with the aggressor (the conquering culture) and rebellion against the role model by turning his own model against him. The South Asian variant had remarkably little anti-colonial violence – but more ethno-religious communal violence at the times of

Partition, between India and Pakistan, and later between Bangladesh and Pakistan – and a remarkable cultural complexity and sophistication. The alliance of the thoroughly British-educated modernizer Nehru and the critical Indianist anti-modernist Gandhi foregrounds a picture, to which their opponent the Anglicized Muslim lawyer Ali Jinnah, the founder of Pakistan, makes up a fitting addition. Half a century after independence, English remains the main public language, although South Asian polyglotism also remains impressive. Cricket has been adopted as the national sport.

In spite of a body of regional cooperation, which regularly assembles government ministers and leaders for talks, there is hardly any regional economic integration. However, the countries remain geopolitically locked into each other. India and Pakistan have their constantly running, albeit up and down, conflict over Kashmir, once a wonderful summer resort to Mughals and British alike. India helped Bangladesh to independence against Pakistan, but has opposite water interests to its smaller and poorer neighbour.

Between these three major regions of Asia there have, of course, been contacts and exchange, but no commonalities corresponding to Greco-Roman Antiquity, Christianity, Latin and later French languages, and inter-marrying dynasties and aristocracies in pre-modern Europe, or to the European modernity of scholars, scientists and *philosophes* from the seventeenth century and on to the Enlightenment and beyond, of the French revolutions (of 1848 and 1830 as well as of 1789), nineteenth-century nationalism and historicism, or the big wars of the twentieth century, hot and cold.

Many of the most important inter-Asian encounters occurred very early, and then declined in significance, or were discontinued. Between India and China the most fruitful exchanges took place in the seventh century CE, plus and minus a couple of centuries. Culturally, the Chinese import of Buddhism and translations of sacred and scientific texts from Sanskrit was the high point (see Sen 2005: ch. 8). After the Chinese Tang dynasty contacts tended to dry up. Under British rule India became a major supplier of opium to nineteenth-century China.

Muslim missionaries from West Asia arrived in Beijing, and Arab and Chinese military commanders battled each other in today's Uzbekistan (near the ancient city of Talas or Taraz, north-west of Samarkand) in 751. The Arabs won a decisive victory, and the Chinese were confined to current Sinkiang (Soucek 2000: 67ff). Islam and the Arabic script became enduring features of Central Asia.

The Silk Road of caravans connected West and East Asia across the deserts, steppes and mountains of Inner Asia. It provided the basis of the wealth and the cultural florescence of oasis cities like Bokhara. Its strenuous plodding could connect, but not unite, the two wings of Asia, and after the seventeenth-century it fell into decline.

What we now call Central Asia would have been the pivot, if there had been one Asia. Bold attempts were made, and not without success, but never for very long. Most successful were the Mongols of Genghiz Khan and his grandsons, who were by the end of the thirteenth century ruling Inner Asia from the Yellow Sea to the Black Sea. They were succeeded by another formidable commander of mounted warriors, the Turkic Tamerlane (as Amir Temur the patron saint of current Uzbekistan). But Temur died, in 1405, at the very beginning of his China campaign, and the Timurids held, for a good century, a basically West-cum-Central Asian empire, from today's Afghanistan to the Black Sea (see Soucek 2000: chs 7–8).

The centre and the southeast

If one should extend the division of Asia beyond the number of three, two more might very well be added, Central and Southeast Asia.

In spite of its sparse population Central Asia may be singled out as a fourth Asia. Its continental significance has derived primarily from its pre-modern Mongol and Turkic warriors. Bokhara and Samarkand were also major cultural centres of West Asian civilization, from the ninth century of al-Bukhari, the most renowned and revered editor of *hadith*, i.e. of sayings of the Prophet Muhammad, to the fifteenth-century statesman and astronomer Ülugbek (or Ulug Beg), whose astronomical calculations were translated into Latin by English seventeenth-century scholars, on proud display today in the little museum at his former observatory in Samarkand. The authors of today's literary classics of Central Asia wrote in Arabic, and were part of a West Asian culture, to whose centres, Baghdad, Damas-cus, Cairo, Shiraz, they also travelled. A case in point is the tenth-century philosopher al-Farabi, now beginning the display at the Kazakhstani Book Museum in Almaty – which ends with literature on the 60th anniversary of the victory in the Great Patriotic War, 1945 – and adorning the *tenge* ban-knotes of Kazakhstan. The plundered wealth of Temur and his successors was used to turn Samarkand into a wonder of Islamic architecture, drawing on expertise and resources from Azerbaijan to India.

The "classicism" characteristic of Central Asia cannot be formulated in literary terms. It was the far-ranging military exploits fostered by its harsh nomadic culture that produced Genghiz Khan and the Genghisids, Tamer-lane and the Timurids, and Babur, the descendant of them both, who founded the Mughal empire. But the Mongol rulers left little culture behind them, the rule of the Timurids was rather short. Immediately after Temur's death the imperial capital was moved from Samarkand to Herat, and the Mughal empire became more Persian than Central Asian. In other words, if it had been only for its short-lived and often destructive powerful empires, Central Asia might have been left as a (virtually) empty hole in the middle of Asia.

However, it had a distinctive path to modernity, combining elements of

(Russian) colonialism and European class conflict. Modernity came to Central Asia with the Russian Revolution, igniting Russian railwaymen and soldiers of Tashkent and other centres of what had in the late nineteenth century become Russian Turkestan, and young Central Asian nationalists rebelling against the emirs and the khans protected by crumbling Czarism. The legacy of the Russian Revolution is now viewed critically, but it is not denied and denounced. Victory in the Second World War is regarded as a national victory in the post-Soviet states of Central Asia. When Lenin was taken down in the (then) capital of Kazakhstan, Almaty, he was replaced by two female war heroes of the Second World War. The last pre-perestroika Communist leaders of Kazakhstan and Uzbekistan, Kunaiev and Rashidov, respectively, are naming major boulevards in Almaty and Tashkent. The party boss who Gorbachev fired for corruption has posthumously become a consensual national statesman. The Kazakhstan opposition recently placed a basket of flowers at the official post-independence monument of Kunaiev (*The Kazakhstan Monitor* 28 October 2005: 2).

Enormous gas and oil findings in above all Kazakhstan and Turkmenistan, with some much smaller ones in Uzbekistan, are approximating the region to its ancient cultural configuration, West Asia. Like the latter, Central Asia today is no region with a common voice. While inter-state wars have not arisen – unlike the Caucasus and former Yugoslavia – previous contacts have thinned. There are no longer any direct train or bus connections between the two largest cities, Tashkent and Almaty, and visas are required to Tajikistan and Turkmenistan, the latter country turning itself into the isolationist North Korea of the area. The Central Asian University has significantly become the law faculty of the State University of Tashkent. The unity that occurs is mainly part of big power games. The Russians are proposing a Eurasian Gas Alliance, and the Chinese and the Russians are pushing their regional security interests in the Shanghai Group (assembling two Eurasian big powers and Central Asia except for Turkmenistan). The Americans have a military base in Kyrgyzstan, at an airport named after the country's national poet, Manas. The smartest players try to turn the big power courting to their own advantage. Kazakhstan and its President Nasarbaiev definitely belong to that class. A recent example of it is the internationally released film of the modern Kazakh national epos Nomads. It has three directors, a Russian, an American and a Kazakh.

The case for Southeast Asia as a fifth Asia would also have to be complex. Though richly endowed with ancient high culture, it has no common classicism. Its classics include Javanese high Malay culture (of music, literature, etiquette), the norms of *adat*, influences of Hinduism in the Indonesian archipelago – still visible in the temple ruins of Borobodur in Java, and in the predominant culture of Bali and Lombok – later on followed by Islam, also coming by Indian merchants. They also include enduring Buddhism in today's Sri Lanka (a major centre historically), Myanmar and Thailand – with its ancient sacred language of Pali, its scriptures and characteristic architecture – a Catholic Christian input into The Philippines, and a Chinese culture with pre-modern ancestry in the region. Its road to modernity was mainly colonial, with different colonial rulers – Dutch, British, French, Spanish, Portuguese, even American – but the region also includes Siam, today's Land of the Thais, which took the slow lane of Reactive Modernization.

Why single out Southeast Asia then? For two reasons mainly. First, a global study of the family in the twentieth century (Therborn 2004) revealed an interstitial region between the Indic and the Sinic civilizations, and at the crossroads of Buddhism, Islam, Christianity, Confucianism and Hinduism, upon a receptive and mellowing Malay culture. The stern patriarchies of the main Asian civilizations, and even of Hispanic Catholicism, had softened in this area, from Sri Lanka to The Philippines, due mainly to Malay customs and to Buddhist insouciance with respect to family matters.

Second, in ASEAN, Southeast Asia has currently the only really functioning institution of regional cooperation, economic and political, on the continent. It was established in 1967, out of earlier Malaysian and Filipino initiatives, largely as a conservative, Cold War outfit, not unlike the EEC, with an edge against China, as Chinese as well as Communist. A very large part of modern economic development has been pushed and carried by more or less assimilated Chinese capitalists, producing ethnic tensions much less lethal but culturally rather similar to those of Germans and Jews, and Turks and Armenians (see Chua 2003).

Part of Southeast Asia is also a cross-roads where the different Asias actually meet. The Singapore invocation of Asian values may have something hollow about it, coming from a city-state that has embraced its colonial (British) background more thoroughly than any other Asian state, including naming the business class of Singapore Airlines, Raffles Class, after the British colonial founder of the city. But it may also be seen as coming out of a regional watch-tower. Neighbouring Malaysia is in fact the meeting ground of all the major cultures of Asia. Alongside its Southeast Asian Malay majority, it has very sizeable Chinese and Indian (Tamil) minorities. Through its increasingly emphasized (majority) Muslim character, it is also connected to West Asia, and to the latter's holy places and educational centres of Islam. In the wake of West Asian withdrawal from an increasingly unreliable and hostile America and Europe, Malaysia is also wooing West Asian capital. Islam bridges cultures. The first democratic President of Indonesia after the bloody dictatorship of general Suharto, Abderrahman Wahid (aka Gus Dur), was educated in Cairo and in Baghdad.

Declining Europe, rising Asias

Recent "globalization" discourse to the contrary, contiguous space, trans-national regions has become more important, at least in some respects. Trade flows, for instance, have become more inter-regional, in Europe, in East Asia, in North and South America. South and West Asia have little intra-regional trade, but also there, like in Africa, East and Southeast Asia, and in the Americas, are tendencies towards more regional political coop-eration. Europe has here been an important source of inspiration (see Therborn 2006). Trans-national popular culture has strong regional pro-files, with an East and Southeast Asian circuit of pop music, film and tele-vision. In South Asia there is an Indian radiation across national political barriers, there is an African music scene, a common Arab culture – whose gravity is shifting from Egypt to the Gulf – and a Latin American frame-work with Mexican and Brazilian centres. Europe has several regional cul-tural features and institutions, ranging from the European Song Festival to the Franco-German Arte Channel.

In this context of trans-national regionalization, the prospects of regions acquire their significance. A demographic-cum-economic perspect-ive here predicts a long process of European decline of relative wealth and power in the world, a rise of China and of East Asia generally, except for Japan, and a rise of India and South Asia. For the foreseeable future, the United States can be expected to maintain itself much better than Europe.

There are three crucial factors here: the size of the population, the age composition of it and the effects of age on economic growth. Western Europe and Japan have for decades had a fertility rate well below replace-ment, and this is now beginning to affect population developments seri-ously. The post-Communist trauma of Eastern Europe has also led to a precipitous decline of the birth rate there. Russian and Ukrainian popula-tions are already declining, while immigration is still offsetting the natural decrease of Germany and Italy. The USA is the only significant part of the developed world that is roughly on replacement level – mainly due to the fertility of Hispanic and other recent immigrant women (see UNFPA 2005: 111ff; Therborn 2004: 288ff). A UN prognostic gives a hint of the future numbers involved (Table 2.1).

Europe, Japan and Russia are bent on becoming the big demographic losers of the new century, with declining populations, and, in particular and particularly serious, declining working-age populations (Bloom *et al.* 2002: table 3.1). From contemporary projections of population and of economic growth China may come to dwarf its Russian and Japanese neighbours. In 1900 Europe housed a quarter of the world's population, in 2000 one-eighth, and in 2050 it is predicted to harbour only one-fifteenth of the human beings of the earth. South Asia, and perhaps also Sub-Saharan Africa, are heading for overtaking East Asia as the most populous region of the world. The natural riches of Africa and the demonstrated

Table 2.1 Regional population prospects of the world 2000–2050 (in millions)

	Prognosticated population in 2050	Change 2000–2050
Sub-Saharan Africa	1,680	+1,045
Latin America & Caribbean	806	+280
Northern America	438	+120
USA	397	+111
Eastern Asia	1,665	+173
China	1,462	+177
Japan	109	−19
South Asia[a]	2,345	+933
India	1,572	+547
Pakistan	344	+199
Southeast Asia	800	+170
Indonesia	311	+97
West Asia and North Africa[a]	920	+457
Europe[b]	603	−123
Russia	104	−44
World	9,322	3,186

Source: UNFPA (2001).

Notes
a Afghanistan and Iran here transferred to West Asia.
b Enlarged EU and the Balkans.

productive capacity of India make it not inconceivable that their population weight may in the end get an economic base to stand on. The West Asian–North African heartlands of Islam are likely to become demographically heavy-weight, although the educational changes just started may bring down the current estimates. Their economic future is even more uncertain.

The balance of power in the world will be affected, not only by the distribution of missiles and other weapons of mass destruction, but also by population movements.

So far, ageing has attracted much more attention than population decline and shifts of demographic weight. Even under assumptions of continued immigration and of some recuperation of the fertility rate, the future of Europe and Japan looks rather grey. By 2000, there were already more people aged 65 and older than there were children under 15 in Japan, and in Germany, Greece, Italy and Spain. In 2015 this appears likely to be the case over the whole of Europe (UNDP 2002: table 5). The UN Population Division (UNFPA 2000: table A11) for 2050 predicts that one Japanese in three will be 65 or more, as well as almost one in three (29%) of the inhabitants of the current European Union. The median age of Japanese and Europeans will be 49 and 48, respectively. The US prognostic is one in five being 65 or older.

Ageing populations have natural difficulties in being innovative and dynamic. There are recent tendencies in theories of economic development to emphasize the importance of the age composition of a population for the growth of its economy. Other things being equal, a large and growing proportion of prime-age people, say 20 to 40, is conducive to economic growth, whereas large proportions of old people or of children tend to slow it down (see Bloom *et al.* 2002).

Now, demography, like all the social sciences, is subject to the inexhaustible whims of human creativity, so these long-term predictions have wide margins of uncertainty. However, the tendencies pointed to above do provide a reasonable starting point for reflections about the future of Europe and Asia. A relative decline and a relative rise, respectively, then seem to be what should be expected. But within such a framework, what are the main regional options? And, what will be the cultural implications of the shifts of positions in the world?

The necessity and the options

Europe is bound for a relative decline of power. But its world significance will also depend on its own choices. A focus on continental integration and a development of the European social pattern and of the European tradition of international law will make it an influential world player, a kind of Scandinavia writ large. The important Asian and North African immigration could be given a chance to stimulate a multicultural Renaissance. On the other hand, a neglect of continental integration, an abandonment of the specific social form of capitalism, and an abdication from defending principles of law and human rights, in favour of an alignment with the USA, as a *Hilfspolizei* in the American crusades around the world, and of attempting to emulate American domestic markets, may contribute to a defence of a "Western civilization" in the American sense. But that option, not unrealistic, is likely to accelerate the decline of Europe, economically, socially, culturally and politically.

Currently, Europe is drifting, without any responsible leadership in sight. No part of Asia is yet ready to do anything more in the world than to raise itself, which is of course both legitimate and important.

In the longer run important cultural adjustments will be called for. Both European and Asian civilizations had better become learning civilizations. The European or "Western" canon will not be able to maintain universalistic claims. Asian forms of cognitive thought, of aesthetics and of values will no longer be ignorable or marginalizeable. From the experimental psychology of Richard Nisbet (2003) we are beginning to catch a glimpse by hard evidence of interesting, fundamental differences of cognition. East Asians, for instance, tend to perceive the world more in contextual, relational, contradictory and spatial terms than Euro-Americans, who focus more on actors' dispositions, on objects and their categorization, on abstract rules and on an excluding logic of either/or. These and other similar findings likely to emerge into view will require some cultural re-orientation.

East and South Asian values and worldviews will become more import-ant and more widespread, although their concrete content cannot be extrapolated from their ancient civilizations. Questions like Tu Weiming's (in Hutanuwatr and Manivannan 2005: I:154) are likely to be raised with mounting insistence:

> Why should we have more emphasis on liberty than on justice? Why is there too much emphasis on rationality at the expense of compassion and sympathy? Why is there such a strong emphasis on legality rather than on civility? Why is there too much emphasis on individual rights rather than on individual responsibility? Why is there too much emphasis on individualism rather than a stronger emphasis on the communal, or on the idea of a person as a centre of relationships rather than as an island of individualism?

But Asian values will also have to confront the coming wealth and power of the region, a task which the thought-rich collection of interviews on *The Asian Future* (Hutanuwatr and Manivannan 2005) avoids because of its perspective of "Alternatives to Consumerism". Asia is actually more likely to have to manage a rising and spreading consumerism, than to follow the alternative of a "simple lifestyle" advocated by some of its greatest minds.

India and, in particular, China have little of the cultural universalism and sense of mission propelling European and American empires. *Ceteris paribus* this will mean a more peaceful world, with less violent interven-tions. But it will also make the development of international law and global governance more difficult.

The Islamic world shares the sense of mission with Euro-American Christianity. The crusaders and the jihadis are of the same kin. But the long-term global influence of Islam will largely depend on the outcome of the current violent resistance and of the American aim at crushing it. For Islamic influence to spread, terrorism has to stop, without West Asia being pulverized by the USA.

Sooner or later, the big powers of Asia, China and India will have to confront, in one form or other, the American mission to rule the world. The rational interest of Europe will be to stay out of that conflict, to step out of the "Western" shadow and out of the imperial cloud.

References

Bary, W. T. de (1990) "Asian Classics as 'The Great Books of the East'", in W. T. de Bary and I. Bloom (eds) *op. cit*: 25–60.

Bary, W. T. de and I. Bloom (eds) (1990) *Approaches to the Asian Classics*, New York: Columbia University Press.

Bloom, D., D. Canning and J. Sevilla (2002) *The Demographic Divided: A New Perspective on the Economic Consequences of Population Change*, New York: RAND.

Buruma, I. and A. Margalit (2005) *Occidentalism*, London: Penguin.

Chua, A. (2003) *World on Fire*, London: William Heineman.

Huntington, S. (1996) *The Clash of Civilizations and the Remaking of World Order*, New York: Simon & Schuster.

Hutanuwatr, P. and R. Manivannan (eds) (2005) *The Asian Future*, 2 vols, London: Zed Books.

Inglehart, R. *et al.* (eds) (2004) *Human Beliefs and Values*, México: Siglo XXI.

Karatani, K. (1993) "The Discursive Space of Modern Japan", in M. Miyoshi and H. D. Harootunian (eds) *op. cit*: 288–315.

Kaufmann, T. D. C. (1995) *Court, Cloister and City: Art and Culture of Central Europe, 1450–1800*, London: George Weidenfeld & Nicolson.

Koh, T. (2000) "Opening Address", in Kwok Kian-Woon *et al.* (eds) *We Asians*, Singapore: Singapore Heritage Society, pp. 9–14.

Korhonen, P. (2002) "Asia's Chinese name", *Inter-Asia Cultural Studies*, 3(2): 253–70.

Kwok Kian-Woon *et al.* (eds) (2000) *We Asians*, Singapore: Singapore Heritage Society.

McClain, J. and J. Merriman (1994) "Edo and Paris: Cities and Power", in J. McClain, J. Merriman and K. Ugawa (eds) *op. cit*: 3–40.

McClain, J., J. Merriman and K. Ugawa (eds) (1994) *Edo and Paris*, Ithaca: Cornell University Press.

Miyoshi, M. and H. D. Harootunian (eds) (1993) *Japan in the World*, Durham: Duke University Press.

Nisbet, R. (2003) *The Geography of Thought*, London: Nicholas Brealey.

Okakura, K. (1903) *The Ideals of the East*, London: John Murray.

Pilipenko, V. (1993) *St Petersburg*, Saint Petersburg: Zvezda Library.

Pollock, S. (2001) "The Death of Sanskrit", *Comparative Study of History and Society*, 43(2): 392–419.

Robertson, B. C. (1995) *Raja Rammohan Ray*, New Delhi: Oxford University Press.

Sen, A. (2005) *The Argumentive Indian*, London: Allen Lane.

Soucek, S. (2000) *Inner Asia*, Cambridge, Cambridge University Press.

Spence, J. (1990) *The Search for Modern China*, New York: W. W. Norton.

Tanaka, S. (1993) *Japan's Orient*, Berkeley: University of California Press.

Therborn, G. (2002) "The World's Trader, the World's Lawyer", *European Journal of Social Theory*, 5(4): 403–18.

Therborn, G. (2004) *Between Sex and Power: Family in the World, 1900–2000*, London: Routledge.

Therborn, G. (2006, in press) "Europe and Asias: In the global political economy and in the world as a cultural system", in G. Therborn and H. Khondker (eds) *Asia and Europe in Globalization*, Leiden: Brill.

UNDP (2002) *Human Development Report 2002*, New York.
UNFPA (2000) *Replacement Migration*, New York.
UNFPA (2001) *The State of the World Population in 2001*, New York.
UNFPA (2005) *The State of the World Population in 2005*, New York.
Wakabayashi, B. T. (1986) *Anti-Foreignism and Western Learning in Early-Modern Japan*, Cambridge MA: Harvard University Press.
Weggel, O. (1989) *Die Asiaten*, München: C. H. Beck.

3   Civilizational constellations and European modernity reconsidered

Gerard Delanty

The idea of civilization has made a return to the contemporary scene. What is noteworthy about the idea of civilization today is the emphasis on the plural: it is a matter of civilizations. The universalistic notion of civilization went into gradual decline over the last twenty years or so as a result of four major discourses, which can be summed up as discourses of civilizational mastery, civilizational hybridity, clashes of civilizations and civilizational cross-contamination.

The first can be associated with Edward Said's orientalist thesis, which, as is well known, claimed that Western civilization required for its self-description a notion of another civilization that was less developed or superseded by the Western civilization (Said 1979). In this view, which laid the foundation for postcolonialism, the very notion of civilization required a binary relation of self and other whereby it was the self, the West, that created the terms of the relation and thus established its mastery over the other, the Orient. This thesis has been much discussed and it will suffice to state that the significance of the orientalist thesis is that it introduced a notion of civilization that highlighted the relational dimension of West and East and, moreover, suggested a view of civilization as a term of discourse.

Where Said drew attention to the discourse of mastery in the constitution of civilizations, the next generation of postcolonial thought stressed the hybrid nature of civilizations and the capacity of the dominated to resist. Building on Said's notion of an orientalist discourse of mastery, postcolonial scholarship influenced by the confluence of postmodernism and globalization theory noted the mixed character of civilizations. Notions of hybridity, creolization, cross-fertilization, globalization and entangled modernities suggested a view of East and West as mutually implicated in each other and, moreover, stressed the political role of the subaltern in resisting the West (Chakrabarty 2002; Nederveen Pieterse 2004). The emphasis shifted to resistance.

From an entirely different background, Samuel Huntington introduced the popular theory of civilizations locked in a primordial clash as a result of incommensurable religious worldviews (Huntington 1996). With the decline of oppositional political ideologies, such as capitalism/democracy versus communism, civilizations become the new scene for geopolitics with clashes between the Christian West and a resurgent Islamic and Confucian East shaping world politics. Although some aspects of this have been discredited – such as the assumed link between Islam and Confucianism – the argument has some resonance in the current political situation and has been very influential (see Burke 1997). In any case, the notion of a clash of civilizations has itself drawn attention to tensions between cultural models and collective identities that have a basis in civilizational routes to modernity.

Finally, a more recent conception of civilizational relations has emerged around the notion of Occidentalism. Where Huntington stressed the defensive stance of the West and the need to adjust to the post-Cold War context, the Occidentalist charge, as stated most forcibly by Ian Buruma and Avishai Margalit, highlights the rise of a non-Western counter-civilization arising in the East and which paradoxically had its intellectual origins in the West (Buruma and Margalit 2004). This is a thesis of civilizational cross-contamination: the bad ideas of the West found their expression in non-Western civilizations and have given rise to a powerful and authoritarian counter-civilization, which is principally represented by radical Islamism. A different version of this is represented by Asianism, with the Russian Eurasianist movement being the chief example of this anti-Western current based on a notion of the uniqueness of Russian civilization as distinctly un-Western (Billington 2004).

In their very different ways what is suggested here is a picture of civilizations in tension, whether through violent conflict, resistance or mastery. Undoubtedly far too big claims are made for civilizations as actors akin to states and as having unified and coherent identities. Civilizations are much more diffuse and some of the most violent conflicts have been within them, not between them. Civilizations are not cultures and nor are they, as Buruma and Margalit imply, systems of ideas, but what has been called 'families of societies'. The very term the West is now questionable and it is doubtful that Europe and the United States form a common culture (Bonnett 2004). The postcolonial thesis avoids to some extent some of the more extreme claims, albeit at the cost of overstating colonial hybridity or generalizing national cases to a wider notion of civilization and, moreover, does not adequately account for civilizational encounters not shaped by colonial relations, as in East Asia, or precolonial relations with the East. It is not the aim of this chapter to dismiss these positions. Rather the purpose is to identify a cosmopolitan conception of civilizational interactions. The aim of this exercise is to draw attention to the hermeneutical dimension of civilizations in dialogue. To do this the notion of a civilizational constellation will be proposed and applied to what will be called European–Asian inter-civilizational cosmopolitanism. In proposing such a notion, the intention is not to deny the fact that the interactions of civilizations have often been violent and nor is it intended to over-play a harmonious conception of civilizational interactions. Civilizations and wider civilizational constellations have indeed, as Johann Arnason (2003) has argued, destructive dimensions and constitute fields in which radical interpretations of the world are articulated.

The intellectual background to this is threefold: comparative sociological civilizational analysis, focusing on the work of S. N. Eisenstadt and Johann Arnason; critical hermeneutical philosophy; and theories of cultural translation. This will be briefly clarified before the notion of a civilizational constellation is introduced with some remarks concerning the European context of application. The implications of this for an inter-civilization cosmopolitanism will be considered by way of conclusion.

Multiple modernities and civilizational analysis

In contrast to the contemporary discourses of civilizations in tension, a hermeneutical conception of civilization can be associated with the comparative sociological analysis of Benjamin Nelson, who introduced the notion of civilizational encounters into what had been a universalistic understanding of Western civilization and various cyclical notions of civilization (notably Spengler and Toynbee). Drawing from, but going beyond, Weber's comparative studies on the religious origins of the major world civilizations, Nelson was interested in the relations between civilizations in terms of cultural encounters (Nelson 1976, 1981). Weber's own concerns did not lie in hermeneutics, given his preoccupation with tracing the development of processes of rationalization, which he believed to be universal and dominated by formal and instrumental rationality as embodied in capitalism and law. Nelson's framework emphasized the plurality of civilizations as embodied in different forms of consciousness. This theory of civilizational encounters was not at the expense of a notion of universalism or an overriding concept of modernity. Although incomplete and tending to ignore the economic and political structures of civilizations, his approach had the merit of highlighting cultural encounters and also drew attention to the suggestive notion of a civilizational complex.

Nelson's pioneering work in comparative historical sociology was reflected in the theory of world history, as developed by William McNeil. He argued that a global perspective on world history had been established on the basis of earlier works but the full implications of this had not been realized (McNeil 1980). Accordingly his aim was a strong argument for civilizations in the plural and driven by communicative cultural links between multiple centres of power. We have also in this the suggestion of a communicative concept of culture. Civilizations develop through borrowings and learning. Although McNeil did not explicitly advocate a hermeneutical concept of civilizational interrelations, it was implicit in his approach. In addition, his world history approach provided a sound basis for a pluralistic theory of civilizations as well as a theory of globalization as having its roots in civilizations (see Mozaffari 2002; Robertson 1992).

Along with Nelson and McNeil, Fernand Braudel can also be mentioned as a pioneer in civilizational analysis. In his studies of the Mediterranean, Braudel portrayed the interaction of a plurality of civilizations within the unity of the Mediterranean: Christian, Jewish, Islamic and Orthodox civilizations interacted and the cross-fertilization of their cultures produced the world of the Mediterranean which he associates with the multi-ethnic Roman Empire (Braudel 1972/73, 2002). Braudel never developed his concept of civilization, which remained a vague, suggestive notion entailing both unity and pluralism within it and at the same time included an inter-civilization dynamic that was creative and transformative. Cultural trade, diasporas, translations, cultural diffusions and cross-fertilizations produced the world of the Mediterranean and its civilizations. Finally, for the purpose of this brief sketch, the work of Eisenstadt has been significant in preparing the ground for a new theory of civilizational analysis that is now best represented by the work of Johann Arnason.

The study of the Axial Age civilizations, a term borrowed from Karl Jaspers, provided a context for an analysis of the relations between cultural, civilizational visions and institutional frameworks (Eisenstadt 1986; see also 1983, 1987). Eisenstadt argued that the Axial Age civilizations were characterized by a sharp distinction between the social division of labour and the charismatic dimensions of the social order. In these civilizations cultural visions are never fully encapsulated in social structures because they are borne by social groups – autonomous cultural elites such as intellectuals – who emerge as distinct social actors. This point is connected with the argument that there is a close connection between autonomous cultural elites and new types of social movements, such as sects and heterodoxies, which articulated alternative visions of social order in their collective identities. What in fact crystallizes with the Axial Age is a fundamental tension between the transcendental and the mundane orders and, more importantly, different conceptions on how to institutionalize such heterodox visions. The quest for major social reorganization driven by the transcendental visions – as expressed in ideologies and collective identities – as interpreted by particular social groups has made the entire world potentially subject to continuous social, political and cultural reconstruction. What emerged, then, with the Axial Age was a cultural predisposition towards social transformation as a result of an entirely new conception of social agency. Where this has been the case there has been a strong tendency towards revolution.

Not all civilizations have been shaped by an Axial Age transformation. Eisenstadt has been struck by the fact that the uniqueness of Japanese civilization did not have an Axial Age discord between the transcendental and the mundane. This has been the subject of a major study of Japanese civilization (Eisenstadt 1996).

On the basis of the civilizational theory of the Axial Age, in the course of the last five years or so Eisenstadt has developed an entirely new conception of modernity as multiple (Eisenstadt 2003). Modernity emerged out of the cultural and political programme of one Axial Age civilization, the Christian-European civilization; it manifested itself first in various heterodoxies which all sought to bring the Kingdom of God to earth. These revolutions gave rise to the belief in the possibility of bridging the gap between the transcendental and mundane orders; they were based on the belief in the capacity of conscious human agency to realize in the mundane orders some of the transcendental and utopian visions. In the Great Revolutions from the wars of religion in the seventeenth century to the Enlightenment these heterodoxies and the modern secular equivalents moved the new transcendental vision closer to the centre where they became institutionalized in, what can be called, a 'second Axial Age' and thus ceased to be marginal sectarian projects. According to Eisenstadt, this all began in Europe, but spread to the rest of the world. Beginning with America, the fundamental legacy of the Axial Age has been taken up by different groups and institutionalized in numerous different ways. This legacy, which constitutes a new civilization, is 'modernity'. But modernity is not able to overcome the basic antinomies or contradictions of the Axial Age and entails the continuous reinterpretation and reconstruction of its themes, especially those produced in the tension between the totalizing and pluralistic conceptions of human experience and social life. It is not just for this reason that modernity did not give rise to a homogeneous civilization. The civilization of modernity, which developed first in Europe, spread to the entire world but crystallized in numerous forms. The resulting condition of multiple modernities challenges the classical theories of modernization and signals a particular view of the contemporary world in terms of a multiplicity of cultural and political projects.

Whereas Eisenstadt tends to see modernity as a distinct civilization, Johann Arnason in a major work on civilizational theory argues for a pluralistic theory of civilization and a related argument concerning multiple modernities (Arnason 2003). Briefly, Arnason's position is one that brings a strong hermeneutical dimension to civilizational analysis. Although this is implicit in the work of Eisenstadt, it was not developed. Arnason's starting point is Castoriadis's theory of the imaginary component in cultural models of interpretation, which are a central feature of the self-constitution of every society (Castoriadis 1987). For Arnason, Castoriadis broke new ground in philosophy and had an important message for the analysis of civilization in that his notion of a radical social imaginary can be seen as the mechanism that lies at the core of civilizational encounters. In this approach civilizations are contested grounds in which different visions of the world emerge and undergo transformation, central to which are dynamics of encounters and syntheses.

The multi-dimension, pluralist dimension of civilizations is much more evident in Arnason's approach, which is based on the key insight that civilization unity is compatible with a plurality of political centres and cultural models. Civilizations are 'families of societies', not holistic units and, unlike Eisenstadt, he stresses not 'cultural programmes' but 'cultural problematics'. Although Arnason does not make the claim, it could be argued on the basis of his ideas that a civilization is marked not by a worldview as such but by a particular logic of imaginary signification. Thus a civilization is not defined by an unchanging set of cultural values or systems of belief but formations of the *long durée* open to significant change and adaptation to new conditions (Arnason 2003: 304). The hermeneutical trust of this is clear: civilizations are internally plural and exist within a plurality of civilizations and all are based on frameworks of interpretation which can be appropriated in different ways by many social actors within and beyond the contours of the given civilization. Such frameworks constitute fields of interpretation for more or less radical interpretations of the world. For this reason Arnason is doubtful about the application of civilizational analysis to cosmopolitanism (see his chapter in this volume).

However, the connection with modernity is a central aspect of his argument. Modernity is the major example of internal conflict and contested identity, he claims, and as such it bears the imprint of the fundamental tension of the imaginary significations of civilizations. The divergent patterns of modernity should thus be seen as combinations of civilizational complexes. The argument can be summed up in his own words as the endeavour 'to link the civilizational perspective to an important but underdeveloped theme in the theory of modernity: the dynamics of tensions and conflicts, between basic orientations (such as the cumulative pursuit of power and the more ambiguous moves towards autonomy) as well as between divergent institutional spheres – economic, political and cultural – with corresponding interpretative frameworks' (Arnason 2003: 49–50). This emphasis on the self-transformative capacity of societies is thus grounded in a pluralistic vision of civilizations and of modernity.

Critical hermeneutics and cosmopolitan possibilities

The previous analysis attempted to show that there is considerable support within comparative historical sociology for a conception of civilization that highlights the plural and hermeneutical aspects of civilizations. The work of Eisenstadt and Arnason, in addition, makes a connection with civilizational analysis and notions of multiple modernities. One of the implications of this is a view of civilization as critical of both postcolonial and occidentalist notions of Eurocentrism, that is the assumption or accusation that Western civilization is inherently based on universalistic premises and that therefore the very notion of civilization is inseparable from a logic of mastery. The aim of this chapter is to develop this by demonstrating, both theoretically and empirically, a view of civilizational encounters pointing in the direction of a new cosmopolitanism. A hermeneutical conception of civilizational encounters suggests a cosmopolitan political standpoint. Two dimensions of this will be taken in order to clarify the theoretical foundations of such a cosmopolitanism: first, the critical hermeneutics as formulated by Jürgen Habermas and Paul Ricouer and, second, Rémi Brague's critique of Eurocentrism. What we have here are two very different critiques of the Eurocentrist fallacy with demonstrations of a certain cosmopolitanism inherent in the European civilization.

The notion of critical hermeneutics is best associated with the work of Habermas and Ricouer, who in their different ways have outlined the foundations of a hermeneutical philosophy that is characterized by a strong critical thrust. Critical hermeneutics as developed by Habermas draws attention to the transformative dimension of human communication, for the act of interpretation entails evaluation, reflection and critique (Habermas 1987, 1996, 1998). In this view, culture is constantly being scrutinized by an emancipated rationality, the bearers of which are enlightened and open up communicative spaces for society as a whole. In Habermas's communication theory it is the very nature of language, which is the ground of culture, that cultural frameworks of meaning can be critically interrogated. Under the conditions of modernity this becomes an enhanced capacity and is the hallmark of modernity itself, which Habermas more or less equated with critical reflection and learning. In his social theory, modern European civilization was the first to give expression to a hermeneutical culture of critique and reflection. In constitutional law, radical social movements, democracy and modernity unfolded in the form of a struggle of communicative reason versus the instrumental reason of capitalism and authoritarianism.

In Habermas's work a critical hermeneutical conception of culture gives a privileged place to Europe as the site of its emergence, but the implication is a limited universalism which can be seen as the basis of cosmopolitanism. According to Habermas, because this culture emerged in Europe it does not mean it is specifically European, for all societies have the learning capacity for critical reflection. This is a universalistic position to the extent to which it is based on the thesis that the capacity for critical self-reflection is present in the very nature of human communication and that, moreover, every society and civilization has a capacity for self-critique. It is a limited universalism in that it makes no claims as to which cultural values should be considered important. In short, it is a universalism of communicative reason as embodied in democracy. Although Habermas's approach is not necessarily free of Eurocentrism, there is the basis of a cosmopolitan vision of cross-civilizational hermeneutics in it that has not been properly developed by Habermas (Delanty 1997). The tendency in his thought more recently is towards a position that simply posits that people can transcend cultural contexts of particularity to engage in discursive dialogue that is free from culturally specific limits. From the perspective of democratic theory this is no doubt interesting and important, but from the point of view of a social theory of civilizational encounters and the search for a wider cosmopolitanism it leaves unresolved the question as to the cultural foundations of inter-civilizational encounters. Nevertheless, the basis of critical hermeneutics has been established and there is considerable value in building up this to develop the notion of multiple modernities. As argued in the previous section, the analysis of the roots of a hermeneutical conception modernity in civilizations and civilizational encounters is the key to a genuine cosmopolitan theory of modernity.

Where Habermas asserts the inherent cosmopolitanism of communication as tendentially trans-civilizational and the essence of any inter-civilization encounter, Brague has offered a quite different position, which can be briefly discussed. As noted above, Habermas's idea of critical hermeneutics is located on the level of discourse rather than on the level of cultural imaginaries or the distinctive cultural models of civilizations. In contrast, Brague sees within European civilization a distinctive culture characterized by a logic of distantiation from its own origins, the result of which is that this European culture can only see itself through the eyes of the other. Thus what distinguishes Europe is its mode of relating to itself, which is one of distance, Brague claims. Europe constantly has to confront a consciousness of having borrowed everything from sources that can never be regained. Brague associates with Rome an eccentric culture that is based on nothing more than the re-working of the culture of others. The Romans were the bearers of innovation and brought innovation itself to the centre of culture. His thesis is that Europe distinguishes itself from other cultural worlds by its particular mode of relation to its own: 'the appropriation of what is foreign' (Brague 2002: 90). The fundamental trait of modernity therefore is contained in Europe's relation to its past. This is a relation that is essentially hermeneutical: the past cannot be known, but it can be interpreted. European culture thus is a culture of, what he calls, 'secondarity'. In this view, European culture is by its nature inherently cosmopolitan, since to travel along its route is to go back to non-European sources: 'For Europe, the source is what is external' (Brague 2002: 137). The relation to a European Self must therefore be a relation to an Other. What Brague has done is to draw attention to the form of European culture in order to demonstrate that culture is more than what is carried as content. The distinctive feature of the form of European culture in his provocative characterization is the mode of transmission.

Brague may be going too far in claiming that this hermeneutical mode of cultural transmission is distinctively Roman. We cannot enter into an assessment of that claim here. It can be suggested, however, that what he has pointed to is a feature of modernity that is present to varying degrees in all cultures, namely the tension between the present and the past along with the consciousness of globality, which brings with it different visions of the world. This theme has been at the centre of philosophical work on hermeneutics and the confluence of European and Indian thought (Dallmayr 1996), studies on the Enlightenment and the East (Clarke 1997; Osterhammel 1998) and recent historical sociology that draws attention to the Eastern origins of Western civilization (Hobson 2004). The main point to be made in the present context concerns the implications of a hermeneutical understanding of civilizational interactions for cosmopolitanism. This will now be briefly commented on.

Cosmopolitan thought has now moved beyond the limits of earlier conceptions of cosmopolitan to recognize that there is a plurality of cosmopolitan projects and that therefore we should conceive of cosmopolitanism in the plural (Breckenridge *et al.* 2002; Cheah and Robbins 1996; Vertovec and Cohen 2002). Both the Ancient and Enlightenment conceptions of cosmopolitanism were Eurocentric in the assumption that the context of cosmopolitanism was Europe and that cosmopolitanism was a civilizing force in the world. Enlightenment cosmopolitanism reflected the superiority of the French language and has often been associated with a particular kind of individualism, suggesting the capacity of every individual to transcend their immediate social context. Current theorizing on cosmopolitanism has moved beyond this limited horizon to what might be called a post-universal cosmopolitanism that is critical and dialogic with diversity as the goal rather than the creation of a universal order, such as a cosmopolis. This is a view that enables us to see how people were cosmopolitan in the past as well as now and how different cosmopolitanisms existed before and despite Westernization. The message in all cosmopolitan philosophy is the challenge of living in a world of diversity and a belief in the fundamental virtue of embracing the values of the other.

Cultural translations and multiple modernities

We have now reached the main contention of this chapter. One of the central dynamics that characterizes the cosmopolitan and hermeneutical logic of civilizational encounters is cultural translations. The notion of a cultural translation includes a hermeneutical dimension as well as a cosmopolitan orientation.

It has been widely recognized that translation is not a simple act of replication. As Hans-Georg Gadamer has argued, 'every translation is at the same time an interpretation' (Gadamer 1975: 346). The very idea of translation refers to something that transcends both self and other. In Gadamer's words: 'The horizon of understanding cannot be limited either by what the writer had originally in mind, or by the horizon of the person to whom the text was originally addressed' (Gadamer 1975: 356). Translation can never overcome the fundamental gulf between two languages he argued in this seminal work on the nature of truth, tradition and interpretation. Translation arises, he argues, because of a need to bridge this gap, but it cannot overcome it. While Gadamer makes the point that translation is never the norm in 'ordinary communication' (which is based on mutual understanding of a shared language), or even when one speaker is speaking a foreign language, it is increasingly becoming the space in which many forms of communication are played out. Migration, globalization, and new information and communication technologies have changed the nature of communication to a point that cultural translation has become a central category.

The capacity for translation – of languages, memories, narratives, experiences, knowledges, identities, religion – is the basis of communication, tradition and cultural possibility and entails a continuous process of social construction. The nature of translation is that it entails a relation to an otherness. This can be to another culture, the past, to a universal culture or whatever is experienced in terms of a cultural logic of distance or loss. Translation arises in the first instance because of the fact of cultural difference and plurality, but never overcomes the fact of difference. As Gadamer has argued, translation can never overcome the fundamental gulf between languages (Gadamer 1975). Translation occurs because of the fact of difference. Cultural translations cannot be discussed without considering some of the negative aspects that may arise from cultural difference; that is, the dislocations of culture, mutations and even pathologies than can result when cultures meet each other. Whether we are talking about secularization, vernacularization, the 'invention of tradition', or multiculturalism, cultural translations can have a destructive or unsettling moment built into them, producing reifications, racisms, misunderstandings, symbolic violence or misrecognition. It is the nature of cultural translations that they destroy stable reference points and constitute new locations; producing costs as well as benefits for those who live in their margins. This is to address the question of 'failures' of translation; whether failures will result in self-conscious critical awareness, in acts of resistance or empowerment (Clifford 1997: 182–3).

If cosmopolitanism entails the capacity to view oneself from the eyes of the other, then cultural translation might be the medium in which one views one's own culture as foreign (Ricoeur 1995, 1996). This is a medium which is in particular a feature of modernity. While the capacity for translation has always existed, at least since the advent of writing; it is only with modernity that translation, or translatability, has itself become the dominant cultural form. Prior to modernity, translation served the function of communication and was not the basis of a given culture. The tendency to multiplicity within modernity was always present, but is only becoming fully apparent today when the logic of translation has extended beyond the simple belief that everything can be translated into a universal global culture to the recognition that every culture can translate itself and others. Modernity should thus be defined neither in the singular nor in the plural as such; it is a condition that arises as a result of universal translatability and expresses itself in the belief that every culture can translate itself and others. Modernity is specifically defined by a mode of cultural translation in which culture is itself a mode of translation. Modernity might be seen as a condition in which the form of culture is one of translation. The encounter of self and other, local with the global, past and present takes multiple forms, determined largely by the forms of cultural translation influenced by civilizational patterns and historical interactions and conflicts. Globalization – as a process that intensifies connections, enhances possibilities for cultural translations and deepens the consciousness of globality – is the principal motor of modernity.

The idea of a civilizational constellation and the multiple modernities of Europe

The term constellation, as used by Walter Benjamin and Theodor Adorno, refers to a juxtaposed rather than a fixed or integrated cluster of changing elements, which do not have a common foundation or underlying meaning. It is relevant to the notion of civilizational encounters discussed in this chapter and will be considered in what follows with respect to Europe. A civilizational perspective on Europe draws attention to two important matters. First, Europe consists of several civilizations and not one and should be understood as a constellation of interacting civilizations. Second, the multiple dimensions and routes to modernity within Europe can be related to the diversity of its civilizations.

Viewed as a civilizational constellation Europe consists of three civilizations: the Western Judaeo-Christian, Russian-Slavic and Islamic Turkish civilizations. Within each of these of course are a wide diversity of societies and state traditions. Confining the designation civilization to the first of these under the general heading 'European Civilization' reduces the term civilization too much to purely cultural expressions, quite aside from what in the view of many are ideological characteristics associated with the term. Associating the term with the West presents as many difficulties, for Europe refers to something broader than the geopolitical notion of the West. Moreover, viewing Europe as a civilizational constellation shifts the focus away from states as the major reference points in European history. Although states have been the major actors in shaping history, a perspective on civilizations highlights the cultural, geographical and political factors that together have been constitutive of modernity. Modernity cannot be explained exclusively by reference to state formation but requires reference to other matters such as consciousness of globality. One of the major shortcomings in the recent literature on multiple modernities is precisely this tendency to relate modernity to the nation-state with the result that the multiple condition of modernity is ultimately a multiplicity of national routes to modernity (Eisenstadt 2000, 2003; Gaonkar 2001). A civilizational approach avoids a purely numerical view of modernity while at the same time recognizing the multiple nature of modernity.

There is an additional reason why a civilizational approach to Europe is timely. There are changing perceptions of European civilization in the direction of its Eastern origins and global connections (Jardine and Brotton 2000; Brotton 2002). In an assessment of the 'rise of the West' thesis, John Hobson has argued that the origins of European civilization were in the appropriation of Eastern civilizations (Hobson 2004). Jack Goody has argued that Islam must be viewed historically as part of Europe (Goody 2004). The case for a multiple conception of European civilization made in this chapter draws from these arguments and, more specifically, the claim that a large part of the European civilization has itself been formed in relation to two Eurasian civilizations, the Russian and Islamic civilizations. Underpinning all three was the Judaic tradition, which cannot be exclusively related to the Western Christian tradition. European civilization has been formed by precisely the interaction, cross-fertilization, cultural borrowing and diffusions of its civilizations. For this reason it is plausible to claim that Europe must be seen as a constellation consisting of links rather than stable entities or enduring traditions or an overarching civilizational idea. The following remarks are for reasons of space necessarily brief.

The main components of the European civilizational constellation can be said to be the Western Judaeo-Christian, Russian-Slavic and Islamic Turkish civilizations simply because of their pivotal role in world history and European history in particular. By civilization is meant a family of societies, or a constellation of societies, formations of the *long durée* which are open to significant internal changes and adaptable to new circumstances (Arnason 2003: 304). A civilization has a foundation in material life and while not reducible to a specific spatial location, it can be related to a geopolitical field. This definition reduces the number of possible entities to a few. The Renaissance was not a civilization in itself but part of a wider civilization, indeed one that in the view of Jardine and Brotton was an inter-European civilization. Judaism in itself is not a civilization, but a culture and diaspora. Civilizations are loosely defined categories that nevertheless have a tangible form, in geopolitics, culture and material life. Often their form becomes coherent only in the longer perspective of history.

In a departure from conventional wisdom the contention of this chapter is that Europe is as much Eastern as it is Western. Russia is part of the European civilizational constellation, which includes an Asian dimension. The Slavic dimension of course was part of a wider cultural world that was divided between East and West, with the Poles being amongst the most Western of the Slavs. Southern Russia has been part of Europe far longer than many regions which we consider to be core European countries. Through the Byzantine heritage and Orthodox religion Russia preserves a distinct European inheritance (Arnason 2000; Buss 2004). Yet, Russia also represents a civilization in its own right – Slavic, Eurasian – in the sense that it is distinct from Western civilization. This mix of European and Asian components was the defining feature of Russian civilization and the basis of its route to modernity through the synthesis of the Western (the national state tradition), Eurasian (Slavic) and classical (Byzantine) traditions.

Islam is also part of the European civilizational constellation. Islam like Christianity is not in itself a civilization, owing to the great diversity of its forms. Only in combination with other forces did Islam and Christianity constitute civilizations. Throughout the Middle Ages, both Spain and Russia were under Islamic rule, but these expressions of Islam did not give rise to a civilization and eventually disappeared, while leaving important traces. However, Islam did give rise to a civilization that had a major European component. The Ottoman Empire was a multi-ethnic and multi-national trans-continental empire that brought Islamic civilization into the heart of Byzantine Europe. It is a key part of the European civilizational constellation and is today principally represented by Turkey. Islam has the same roots as the Judaeo-Christian civilization and has played a key role in European history, not as an enemy but as a cultural mediator.

Whether Islam is part of Europe is a question that is being asked more and more today in light of the growing number of Muslims within Western Europe, EU intervention in the Kosovo War on behalf of Albanian Muslims, and the likely entry of Turkey into the European Union. Jack Goody has argued Europe has never been entirely isolated and purely Christian (Goody 2004: 14). The Mediterranean face of Europe, which Braudel argued formed the basis of European civilization, is becoming more and more important in the wider trans-continental redefinition of Europe.

The upshot of a civilizational approach is that the cultural diversity of Europe can be seen as an expression of the interaction of the civilizations that make up Europe. Rather than reducing such diversities to nation-states, a civilizational analysis suggests a deeper and also a wider level of analysis. Civilizations are developmental, cumulative and multi-linear. Furthermore, modernity can itself be conceived as a multiple condition, with the divergent patterns of modernity to some extent grounded in civilizational frameworks. Modernity in Europe must be regarded as both multiple and hybrid. There is no single European modernity, but several; even though one of these, the Western European one, played a decisive role in shaping the wider European civilizational constellation. However, the argument must go beyond multiplicity and hybridity to a clearer statement of the interactive and transformative impetus that is the key dynamic of modernity.

Relating the diverse forms of modernity to civilizational frameworks, a more deeply rooted historical sense of modernity as a transformative project becomes more plausible. One important aspect of this is the role of civilizational encounters since, as previously argued, the European civilizations have not been separated from each other, but are part of what has

been called a civilizational constellation. For this reason, too, the modernities that developed in Europe have borne the imprint of their civilizational
context and encounters.

This argument goes beyond the claim that the civilizations of Europe
are connected as a result of cross-fertilization, borrowings and encounters
of various kinds. The stronger claim, which is not to be equated with
hybridity, is that modernity itself was shaped by the hermeneutical interaction of the civilizations of Europe. In this view, the essential point is less
the multiple expressions of modernity than the civilizational dynamic that
gave to modernity its pluralism and self-transformative impetus.

Conclusion

This chapter has tried to defend the idea of civilizations as fluid and constituted in interactions with other civilizations. Europe itself is a fertile
ground for such an analysis, which calls into question both the idea of civilizations locked in combat and the notion of a single universal Western
civilization. The civilizations of Europe are plural and characterized by
cultures and political centres that extend beyond Europe. Contrary to the
notion of the clash of civilizations, the borders of European civilization are
vague (Morin 2002; Zielonka 2002). The civilizations of Europe have
developed in interaction with each other, not in isolation. This hermeneutical notion of civilizations' encounters is not intended to replace the militaristic and colonial narrative with a dialogic one. Rather the aim is to
identify common roots and shared histories of an inclusive Europe of
cosmopolitan possibilities.

The implication of such an approach points towards a European–Asian
inter-civilizational cosmopolitanism. With the borders of the EU moving
closer to Russia and with the eventual entry of Turkey, extending into
Asia, the identity of Europe is becoming more and more 'post-Western'
(Delanty 2003). This is not an anti- or a non-Westernism, but a condition
defined increasingly by the legacy of an earlier modernity which will have
to be negotiated with other modernities. There is no evidence of a clash of
civilizations. The differences between the 15 new member countries and
the older 15 member states fall within the extremes that already exist
within the latter group (Laitin 2002). It is less a clash of civilizations than
a reconfiguration and reconstruction of modernities. If the West is under
threat it is more likely to be because of growing differences within it. The
United States and Europe no longer constitute a common Western Civilization. With Europeanization moving eastwards and a more inclusive
European Union taking shape, the differences between Europe and an
increasingly militaristic United States are growing.

Finally, then, what is Europe? Europe is a term that is best used to refer
to the relation amongst things that are different and all that constitutes its
reality is precisely the mode of relating to otherness, a relation that

includes a relation to its own history. The European civilizational constellation is a structure that is apparent only in multiple links. As a result of centuries of cultural translations, the civilizations of Europe are overlapping and interpenetrating.

References

Arnason, J. (2000) 'Approaching Byzantium: Identity, Predicament and Afterlife', *Thesis Eleven*, 62: 39–69.

Arnason, J. (2003) *Civilizations in Dispute: Historical Questions and Theoretical Traditions*, Leiden: Brill.

Billington, J. (2004) *Russia in Search of Itself*, Baltimore: Johns Hopkins University Press.

Bonnett, A. (2004) *The Idea of the West: Culture, Politics and History*, London: Palgrave.

Brague, R. (2002) *Eccentric Culture: A Theory of Western Civilization*, South Bend, Ind.: St. Augustine's Press.

Braudel, F. (1972/3) *The Mediterranean and the Mediterranean World in the Age of Philip II*, London: Fontana.

Braudel, F. (2002) *Memory and the Mediterranean*, New York: Vintage Books.

Breckenridge, C. A. *et al.* (eds) (2002) *Cosmopolitanism*, Durham, NJ: Duke University Press.

Brotton, J. (2002) *The Renaissance Bazaar: From the Silk Road to Michelangelo*, Oxford: Oxford University Press.

Burke, V. L. (1997) *The Clash of Civilizations: War Making and State Formation in Europe*, Cambridge: Polity.

Buruma, I. and A. Margalit (2004) *Occidentalism: The West in the Eyes of its Enemies*, London: Penguin Press.

Buss, A. (2004) *The Russian Orthodox Tradition and Modernity*, Leiden: Brill.

Castoriadis, C. (1987) *The Imaginary Institution of Society*, Cambridge: Polity Press.

Chakrabarty, D. (2000) *Provencializing Europe: Postcolonial Thought and Historical Difference*, Princeton: Princeton University Press.

Cheah, P. and B. Robbins (eds) (1996) *Cosmopolitics: Thinking and Feeling Beyond the Nation*, Minneapolis: Minnesota University Press.

Clarke, J. J. (1997) *Oriental Enlightenment: The Encounter Between Asian and Western Thought*, London: Routledge.

Clifford, J. (1997) *Routes: Travel and Translation in the Late Twentieth Century*, Cambridge, Mass.: Harvard University Press.

Dallmayr, F. (1996) *Beyond Orientalism: Essays on Cross-cultural Encounter*, New York: State University of New York Press.

Delanty, G. (1997) 'Habermas and Occidental Rationalism: The Politics of Identity, Social Learning and the Cultural Limits of Moral Universalism', *Sociological Theory*, 15(3): 30–59.

Delanty, G. (2003) 'The Making of a Post-Western Europe: A Civilizational Analysis', *Thesis Eleven*, 72: 8–24.

Eisenstadt, S. N. (1983) *Tradition, Change and Modernity*, New York: Wiley.

Eisenstadt, S. N. (ed.) (1986) *The Origins and Diversity of the Axial Age Civilizations*, New York: SUNY Press.

Eisenstadt, S. N. (ed.) (1987) *Patterns of Modernity*, Vol. 1: *The West*, London: Pinter.

Eisenstadt, S. N. (1996) *Japanese Civilization in a Comparative Perspective*, Chicago: Chicago University Press.

Eisenstadt, S. N. (ed.) (2000) *Daedalus*, Special Issue on Multiple Modernities, 129(1).

Eisenstadt, S. N. (2003) *Comparative Civilizations and Multiple Modernities*, Vol. 1 and 2, Leiden: Brill.

Gadamer, H.-G. (1975) *Truth and Method*, London: Sheed & Ward.

Gaonkar, D. P. (ed.) (2001) *Alternative Modernities*, Durham, NC: Duke University Press.

Goody, J. (2004) *Islam in Europe*, Cambridge: Polity Press.

Habermas, J. (1987) *The Theory of Communicative Action*, Vol. 2, Cambridge: Polity Press.

Habermas, J. (1996) *Between Facts and Norms: Contributions to a Discourse Theory of Law and Democracy*, Cambridge: Polity Press.

Habermas, J. (1998) *The Inclusion of the Other: Studies in Political Theory*, Cambridge, Mass.: MIT Press.

Hobson, J. (2004) *The Eastern Origins of Western Civilization*, Cambridge: Cambridge University Press.

Huntington, S. (1996) *The Clash of Civilizations and the Remaking of the World Order*, New York: Simon & Schuster.

Jardine, L. and J. Brotton (eds) (2000) *Global Interests: Renaissance Art between East and West*, London: Reaktion Books.

Laitin, D. (2002) 'Culture and National Identity: "The East" and European Integration', *West European Politics*, 25(2): 55–80.

McNeil, W. (1980) *Poly-ethnicity and National Unity in World History*, Toronto: University of Toronto Press.

Morin, E. (2002) 'European Civilization: Properties and Challenges', in M. Mozaffari (ed.) *Globalization and Civilizations*, London: Routledge.

Mozaffari, M. (ed.) (2002) *Globalization and Civilizations*, London: Routledge.

Nederveen Pieterse, J. (2004) *Globalization and Culture*, New York: Rowman & Littlefield.

Nelson, B. (1976) 'Orient and Occident in Max Weber', *Social Research*, 43(1): 114–29.

Nelson, B. (1981) *On the Roads to Modernity*, New York: Rowman & Littlefield.

Osterhammel, J. (1998) *Die Entzauberung Asiens*, Munich: Beck.

Ricoeur, P. (1995) 'Reflections on a New Ethos for Europe', *Philosophy and Social Criticism*, 21(5/6): 3–13.

Ricoeur, P. (1996) *Oneself as Another*, Chicago: University of Chicago Press.

Roberston, R. (1992) *Globalization: Social Theory and Global Culture*, London: Sage.

Said, E. (1979) *Orientalism*, New York: Vintage.

Vertovec, S. and R. Cohen (eds) (2002) *Conceiving Cosmopolitanism*, Oxford: Oxford University Press.

Zielonka, J. (ed.) (2002) *Europe Unbound: Enlarging and Reshaping the Boundaries of the EU*, London: Routledge.

4 Oriental globalization

Past and present

Jan Nederveen Pieterse

The critique of Eurocentrism has gone through several rounds. The first round was primarily a critique of Orientalism. Edward Said and Martin Bernal, among others, focused on cultural bias and racism in Eurocentric history. Others addressed Eurocentric biases in development thinking (Samir Amin, Paul Bairoch, Stavrianos) and historiography (Eric Wolf, James Blaut, Jack Goody).

In the second round, history from the viewpoint of the global South such as Subaltern Studies in India and revisionist history of Africa contributed different perspectives. In addition, global history generated critical historical studies that document the significance of in particular Asia and the Middle East in the making of the global economy and world society. Janet Abu-Lughod focused on the Middle East, Marshall Hodgson on the world of Islam, K. N. Chauduri on South Asia, Andre Gunder Frank on East and South Asia, Kenneth Pomeranz, Robert Temple and Bin Wong on China, Eric Jones on Japan, and Anthony Reid on Southeast Asia along with many other studies. This body of work not merely critiques but overturns conventional Eurocentric perspectives and implies a profound rethinking of world history that holds major implications for social science and development studies.

These studies break the mould of Eurocentric globalization that dominates the globalization literature. Eurocentric globalization is geographically centred on the West and preoccupied with recent history: post-war (in most economics, political science, international relations and cultural studies), post-1800 (most sociology), or post-1500 (in Marxist political economy and world system theory).[1] In history curricula the latter periods figure as the 'modern' and 'early modern eras'. In this view, the radius of globalization is typically if not invariably from the West outward. The oriental globalization literature adopts a longer time frame and reverses this relationship: the radius is principally from the East outward. In this discussion I review the arguments of oriental globalization in the past and draw out some of their implications. In the second section I turn to contemporary oriental globalization and 'the rise of Asia' and discuss the continuities between oriental globalization past and present.

Oriental globalization past[2]

Arguably, the recent global history literature converges on a single major thesis: the Orient came first and the Occident was a latecomer. Andre Gunder Frank's *ReOrient* settles on 1400–1800 as the time of 'Asian hegemony': 'The two major regions that were most "central" to the world economy were India and China' (1998: 166). This centrality was based on 'greater absolute and relative productivity in industry, agriculture, (water) transport, and trade' and was reflected in their favourable balance of trade, particularly of China (127). Pomeranz's *The Great Divergence* offers meticulous comparisons of developments in China and Britain that confirm this thesis and argues that the great divergence of Europe from the rest of the world is a myth. Geoffrey Gunn (2003) draws attention to exchanges between Southeast Asia and Europe from the sixteenth century onward as part of 'first globalization', while A. G. Hopkins (2002) and John Hobson (2004) synthesize this literature.

In general outline the Orient first thesis runs as follows. Global connections may go back to 3500 BCE or earlier still, but 500 CE may rank as the start of oriental globalization and 600 as the beginning of the big expansion of global trade. This timing is based on the revival of camel transport between 300 and 500. At the time the global economy was centred on the Middle East with Mecca as a global trade hub. For instance, in 875 Baghdad ranked as a 'water-front to the world' linked to China (Hobson 2004: 40). Other sources concur: 'Around 900 CE ibn Khordādbeh, postmaster of the Arab province of al-Jibāl in Persia, compiled his eight-volume *Book of the Roads and Countries* as a guide for the postal system. He described roads and sea routes as far as Korea, giving detailed directions, distances, weather conditions, and road security' (Hoerder 2002: 31). The Middle East remained the 'Bridge of the World' through the second millennium, but by 1100 (or later, by some accounts)[3] the leading edge of accumulation shifted to China, where it remained until well into the nineteenth century.

According to Hobson, in China's 'first industrial miracle', 'many of the characteristics that we associate with the eighteenth-century British industrial revolution had emerged by 1100' (2004: 50), with major advances in iron and steel production, agriculture, shipping and military capabilities. From Japan to the Middle East, the East was the early developer – far ahead of Europe in agriculture, industry, urbanization, trade networks, credit institutions and state institutions. Many historians concur that 'none of the major players in the world economy at any point before 1800 was European' (Hobson 2004: 74).[4]

Europe was not only a late developer, but Eastern ideas and technologies enabled European feudalism, the financial revolution in medieval Italy and the Renaissance: 'oriental globalization was the midwife, if not the mother, of the medieval and modern West' (Hobson 2004: 36). This much had been established in studies of science and technology, as in the work of Needham (1956) and Goonatilake (1999). The profound influence of the Islamic world on the European Renaissance is on record as well. Many studies such as Donald Lach on the role of Asia in the making of Europe document the Asian influences on Europe and the Enlightenment (e.g. Marshall and Williams 1982; Nederveen Pieterse 1994). What the recent studies add to this picture is an emphasis on political economy and economic institutions.

In Marshall Hodgson's words, the Occident was 'the unconscious heir of the industrial revolution of Sung China' (in Hobson 2004: 192). Hobson dates China's central role earlier, to about 1100, and extends it later than Andre Gunder Frank does. In shares of world manufacturing output, according to Hobson, China outstripped Britain until 1860 and 'the Indian share was higher than the whole of Europe's in 1750 and was 85 percent higher than Britain's as late as 1830' (77, 76). In terms of GNP the West only caught up with the East by 1870; in terms of per capita income, a less representative measure, the West caught up by 1800. I will discuss three specific critiques of Eurocentrism that the recent studies contribute and then give an assessment of this literature.

One of the cornerstones of Eurocentrism is the idea that in the fifteenth century after the return of Zheng He's naval expeditions China turned away from maritime trade and that this caused its gradual decline and opened the way for the expansion of European trade in Asia. The revisionist literature argues that the closure of China (and also Japan) is a myth and the diagnosis of decline is likewise mistaken. It is true that China did not choose for the path of maritime expansion or empire, but Western historians have mistaken the official Chinese imperial legitimation policy of upholding the Confucian ideal and condemning foreign trade with the actual trade relations, which continued and flourished. That China remained the world's leading trading power shows in the 'global silver recycling process', in which 'most of the world's silver was sucked into China' (Hobson 2004: 66; Frank 1998: 117).

Another cornerstone of Eurocentrism is Oriental despotism (and variations such as Weber's patrimonialism). In contrast, the revisionist literature argues that states such as China and Japan had at an early stage achieved 'rational' institutions including a 'rational-legal' centralized bureaucracy, minimalist or laissez-faire policies in relation to the economy and democratic propensities, while the European states during the 1500–1900 'breakthrough period' were far less rational, more interventionist and protectionist, and less democratic: 'eighteenth century China (and perhaps Japan as well) actually came closer to resembling the neoclassical ideal of a market economy than did Europe' (Pomeranz 2000: 70). Light taxation and laissez-faire attitudes to enterprise were common in the East long before the West, and throughout the period of comparison trade tariffs were consistently far higher in the West than in the East, which shows that the Oriental despotism thesis is faulty.

A centrepiece of Eurocentrism is the judgement that other cultures lacked the European commitment to enterprise and accumulation. Weber highlighted the Protestant ethic and described Islam and Confucianism as obstacles to modern development. But many observers since then have noted the origins of Islam amid a trading culture and the penchant for commerce in the Islamic world (e.g. Turner 1994; Kazim 2000; Wolf 2001).

Viewing Confucianism as an obstacle to development involves historical ironies too: what ranked as an obstacle in the early twentieth century was recast in the late twentieth century as the Confucian ethic hypothesis to account for the rise of the Asian Tigers. An additional irony is the influence of Confucianism on European thinking. That behind Adam Smith stood Francois Quesnay and the Physiocrats is a familiar point; but the Physiocrats' critique of mercantilism was inspired by Chinese policies and the philosophy of *wu-wei* or non-intervention, which goes back to well before the common era (Hobson 2004: 196; Marshall and Williams 1982). Thus, Confucius (or rather, a European version of Confucius) ranks as a patron saint of the Enlightenment.

What is the significance and status of the oriental globalization literature at this stage? There are echoes of dependency theory in this body of work for if it wasn't European genius or other endogenous factors that turned the tide, the role played by colonialism and imperialism in changing the global equation must be larger than is acknowledged in Eurocentric perspectives. One thinks of Eric Williams's work on slavery, Walter Rodney on Africa and other studies. But recent global history generally interprets the nineteenth-century advance of the West in terms of wider combinations of geography and history. Dependency theory was structuralist, while the recent revisionist history rejects a global structural approach (such as world system theory) and reckons with contingency and devotes attention to agency and identity formation: 'material power in general and great power in particular, are channeled in different directions depending on the specific identity of the agent' (Hobson 2004: 309). Dependency thinking came out of the era of decolonization, while the allegiance of revisionist history is to global history rather than to history viewed through the lens of a particular region and time period. It looks past Fernand Braudel's 'Mediterranean world' and past world-system theory and its preoccupation with the Low Countries and the Baltic, to wider horizons in the tradition of William McNeill's global history. This literature is part of a wider literature that situates globalization in the *long durée* (Nederveen Pieterse 1989, 2004a; Robertson 2003).

At times there is a rhetorical surcharge to this literature, which reflects its character as a polemical position. This comes across in a recurrent problem: though the *portée* of its findings is that the East–West divergence is a fiction and is really a continuum, at times the oriental globalization literature reverses the current of Eurocentrism by centring the East and marginalizing the West, thus replaying East–West binaries in reverse. Addressing this problem and taking global history beyond East–West binaries is the thrust of other studies (Lieberman 1999, 2003; Pomeranz 2002; Whitfield 2003; Bayly 2004). At times, as one would expect, this involves the theme of Eurasia (Moore 2003).

The oriental globalization literature is uneven in that it represents a kind of retroactive Sinocentrism and Indocentrism. For various reasons China, India and the Middle East have been more extensively studied and are more salient than other areas. There is frequent mention of the 'Afro-Asian global economy', but the African part remains sketchier than the Asian side. Also Southeast Asia, Central Asia and the Mongol Empire often fall between the cracks of the world's major zones. The oriental globalization thesis needs to integrate finer grained regional histories. Janet Abu-Lughod also suggests triangulation with local histories, but notes, 'We can never stand at some Archimedean point *outside* our cultures and outside our locations in space and time. No matter how *outré* we attempt to be, our vision is also distorted' (2000: 113).

It is interesting to note how the paradigms of the present are the lenses through which history is read and reread (see Zurndorfer 1997). Eighteenth-century Europeans admired China for its 'enlightened despotism', while in twenty-first-century accounts what matters is 'rational institutions' and laissez-faire economic policies, thus echoing the current status of rational choice and neoclassical economics.

While the oriental globalization literature has grown rapidly and is increasingly substantial, it is by no means dominant. Mainstream thinking continues to view the West as the early developer and the East and the global South as laggards or upstarts. At the turn of the millennium – following the Soviet demise, the Asian crisis and neoconservative belligerence in Washington – American triumphalism, though increasingly hollow, sets the tone as part of an entrenched 'intellectual apartheid regime'. The Washington consensus is as steeped in Orientalist stereotypes and historical myopia as the neoconservative mission to bring freedom and democracy to the world. Eurocentric economic history à la David Landes (*The Wealth and Poverty of Nations*) and Roberts (*Triumph of the West*) rhymes with Samuel Huntington's clash of civilizations, Bernard Lewis's account of Islam (*What Went Wrong?*), Fukuyama's ideological history (*The End of History*) and Mandelbaum (*The Ideas that Conquered the World*). A general mindset of Western triumphalism informs IMF and World Bank policies (economics without history, without anthropology) as well as American aspirations in the Middle East (politics without memory), as if development and democracy are virtues that the West chanced upon first and only.

Besides the usual ignorance and arrogance, there is something deceptive about Eurocentrism-as-policy, a trait that Ha-Joon Chang (2002) summed up as *Kicking Away the Ladder*. In the nineteenth century, free trade was used as a means to deindustrialize colonial economies and now WTO statutes and free trade agreements that uphold the intellectual property rights of multinational corporations seek to short-circuit industrialization in the global South. In this regime of truth, institutionalized amnesia and intellectual apartheid serve as instruments of power.

As the oriental globalization literature overtakes the indulgent West-centric view of globalization, perhaps the global realignments that are now gradually taking shape will also catch up with the material side and the political economy of American supremacism. This diagnosis of the 'global confluence' arrives on the scene at the time that China, India and East Asia are re-emerging as major forces in the global economy; historiography catches up with the present just when the present is coming full circle with past trends in the world economy. But a synthesis that is yet to take shape is that of the historical oriental globalization thesis with the cutting edge of contemporary globalization in the making. On this point I will make some tentative notes.

Oriental globalization present

> We've had a couple of hundred bad years, but now we're back.
> (Economist in Shanghai, cited in Prestowitz 2005: 225)

Globalization isn't what it used to be. Paul Kennedy noted, 'we can no more stop the rise of Asia than we can stop the winter snows and the summer heat' (2001: 78). According to cautious IMF estimates, China's GDP is likely to pass that of Japan around 2016 and approach the size of the US by 2040, or earlier in terms of its domestic purchasing power (Prestowitz 2005: 74). The Indian economy is also moving ahead swiftly. In a structural fashion economic advantages are moving east and to newly industrializing societies. Asian demographics include young populations – unlike in Europe, the US and Japan – with great social densities and fast rising levels of education, growing technological capabilities and rising levels of development. Other variables in the rise of Asia are geographic proximities and what Abdel-Malek calls 'the depth of the historical field'. At times there is mention of the possibility of hegemonic rivalry and American military intervention; but let's note that these are generally not variables that are amenable to geopolitical intervention.

A different global equation is in the making and Asia plays a central role in this along with the emerging BRIC countries, including Brazil and Russia, countries such as South Africa and the wider radius of oriental globalization. The question I want to ask is what is the relationship between oriental globalization past and present. To what extent and in which ways does oriental globalization in the past form the basis of, shape and inform oriental globalization in the present? To what extent and in what sense is the rise of Asia not just a rise but a come-back? This is a question of limited status for obviously the discontinuities are as interesting as the continuities. New patterns, combinations and hybridities arising from the interactions with Western societies and the adoption of new technologies are as interesting as continuities with the past. Yet they are also enabled by continuities with the past, so there is merit to raising this question.

With respect to culture and civilization, continuities between oriental globalization past and present are commonly recognized. Confucianism in the circle of Sinic influence and the idea of a neo-Confucian ethic are part of this (Tu Weiming 2000). The Teen Murti school in New Delhi has been concerned with Indic civilization rather than just India (Kumar and Chandhoke 2000). Continuities with regard to nationhood and states are also widely recognized. China ranks among the 'continuous nations' with a national identity and state existence stretching back to well before the Common Era (Abdel-Malek 1981; Cohen 2000). Besides these fairly common points of reference, we can consider the role of trade routes and migrations and diasporas. These are brief notes, pending the patient revisiting of regional histories, focusing on Asia rather than on the wider radius of oriental globalization.

This kind of inquiry is not uncommon. In the Annales school and Braudel's work the *long durée* refers to long-term structural and institutional changes. Evolutionary economics and institutional economics address institutional legacies as part of economic dynamics; a strong instance of this is path dependence. Robert Putnam (1993) argues that the success of administrative decentralization in northern Italy and its failure in southern Italy since the 1970s was in large measure attributable to the history from medieval times onward of city states in the North in contrast to kingdoms in the south and other forms of governance that involved less civic allegiance. Thus, configurations going back to medieval and Renaissance times account for contemporary dynamics even though other political and economic configurations have intervened.

State capability and 'bureaucratically coordinated capitalism' is widely recognized as a crucial component in the rise of East Asia (Weiss 1996). Dedicated public service and skilful civil servants cannot be fully understood without the long legacy of political Confucianism.

In language, culture and arts, the civilizational interconnections persist.[5] The Indo-European languages are a case in point (Mallory 1991). History is part of the cultural and institutional capital of nations. The theme of continuity is well on the map in Asia and overseas. References to the depth of civilization and the interspersion of the traditional and the modern, and the idea that the rise of Asia is a Renaissance (Ibrahim 1996) are common.

These continuities are symbolically acknowledged or intimated in the recurrent use of the Silk Routes metaphor, which is often more than a metaphor and also a memory and a future project (Abdel-Malek 1994; Wood 2003). When opening the new Ceyhan oil pipe line from the Black

Sea to the Mediterranean in July 2005 the President of Turkey referred to it as 'the new Silk Road'. The Asia–Europe intergovernmental meetings have also been viewed as 'new Silk Routes' (Brennan *et al.* 1997). The 'new Silk Roads' images that reinvoke historic continuities and geographic contiguities remind us that the links of past times ramified widely and that the ripples of past waves of globalization still linger.

Traces of old accumulation treasure and savvy persist in collective memory, circumstances and artefacts. In many places the remnants of old trade infrastructures and institutions still exist and at times the new trades reactivate ancient trade routes and old nodal points. From Kaifeng in China to Damascus and Istanbul, remnants of the Silk Roads still exist: the actual roads and ports (Broëze 1989), the caravanserais, the ruins or remains of forts, palaces and temples (Whitfield 2004). Through most of Asia and the Middle East, as in much of Europe, the physical traces of thousands of years past are just around the corner. The current industrial and commercial buzz in Asia has been foreshadowed in the great Asian bazaar of old times. The industriousness and savvy of Asian markets, abuzz with merchants and workshops, trade emporia and far flung trade networks, is part of a deep infrastructure of social densities that predates capitalism.

Migration and diaspora routes serve as two-way carriers of knowledge and technology, language, skills, goods and investments. They also play a major role in Asia's resurgence. In China's rapid rise as an industrial exporter, investments by the Chinese diaspora from the Pacific Rim back into the mainland play a significant part, notably from Taiwan (Chen 2005; Liu 1998; Seagrave 1996). In India, the role of the NRIs or non-resident Indians as investors and intellectual and social capital is also rapidly growing and actively courted. These relations reactivate old migration links that wire Asian countries with worldwide links. Scholars and entrepreneurs in India are rediscovering their many civilizational and economic links with the Arab world and with Persia and Central Asia (Shanker 2005). The trails of the Mughals and the Parsi traders were two-way routes then and may be so again (Nederveen Pieterse 2003). India now seeks to re-establish its links with Central Asia as an avenue of commerce and energy supplies.

In mapping the Southwest Silk Road, Bin Yang (2004) discusses the ancient confluence of China, India and Persia in trading and civilizational networks. The ancient trading links between Yunnan, Burma and India go back to 200 BCE. Routes of trade and migration between China and Southeast Asia also have great historical depth (Thapar 1992; Sugiyama 1992; Dobbin 1996) and carry over into present times (e.g. Yamashita and Eades 2003). Xiangming Chen (2005) focuses on the role of cross-border and regional social capital in Asian economies and maps processes of de-bordering and re-bordering over time. He traces trade and migration routes back to the seventeenth century and finds that some areas of high activity in the past such as the Pearl River delta are active also now. These inquiries show that cultural and economic efflorescence, past and present, has been typically a cross-border or regional phenomenon. Yet most history, particularly since the nineteenth century, is the history of nation-states and statistics record data primarily in nation-state units.

Arif Dirlik (2000) criticizes Samuel Huntington's 'clash of civilizations' thesis and contends that the tensions refer instead to capitalist competition between different cultural centres. Dirlik's view is certainly more pertinent than that of Huntington; but it invites two qualifications. One is obvious; of course the relations are not just those of rivalry but also of collaboration. The second is that capitalism and capitalist rivalry themselves are categories with limited or contingent explanatory validity. Andre Gunder Frank's historical work eventually led him to look beyond capitalism as a central explanatory category:

> Far from arguing that capitalism is five thousand years old, I suggest that we should dare to abandon our belief in capitalism as a distinct mode of production and separate system. Why? Because too many big patterns in world history appear to transcend or persist despite all apparent alterations in the mode of production. It therefore cannot be the mode of production that determines overall development patterns.... World history since 1500 may be less adequately defined by capitalism than by shifts in trade routes, centers of accumulation, and the existence/nonexistence and location of hegemonic power.
>
> (Frank 1996: 44)

Earlier I noted that

> This implies a profound challenge to critical political economy; it suggests that many explanations that are held to be fundamental are in fact conjunctural and reflect not just limitations of geography but also limitations of the time frame. Global political economy may overcome the limitations of geography, but the limitations of time are of a different order; it makes a profound difference whether the time frame of explanation is from 1800 or from 1000 BCE or 500 CE.
>
> (Nederveen Pieterse 2005: 386)

The study of oriental globalization past and present shows that in economics and technology just as in culture and civilization, the taken-for-granted units of analysis – such as nation-states, capitalism – are but provisional approximations, conceptual conventions that in seeking to map the ebb and flow in time and space may lead us astray as much as guide us. It is not surprising that history of the *long durée* should unsettle our analytical categories, such as the nation-state and capitalism, for concepts are embedded in time. Decolonization involves epistemic decolonization ('emancipate yourself from mental slavery') and the decolonization of imagination. It is interesting that the road to epistemic emancipation runs as often via history as via theory.

The idea of regional technological independence (e.g. Chamarik and Goonatilake 1993), past or present, is probably a fiction. Silk production was exported from China to the Ottoman Empire and Europe, porcelain making travelled from China to Europe in the seventeenth and eighteenth centuries (witness Delft, Wedgwood, Sèvres), Chinese agricultural technologies revolutionized English agriculture, and Indian textile crafts imbued British textile production (as in Paisley, Scotland). In the late nineteenth and twentieth centuries, industrial skills and technologies journeyed from West to East. In the late-twentieth and twenty-first centuries, Asian technologies travel West again (such as Japanese Toyotism and Indian software). This back and forth motion of technologies and the overlaps between old and new routes of trade and migration in the *long durée* suggest underlying affinities.

Between oriental globalization in the past and the present, oriental globalization has circled the globe. Eurasia was part of the terrain that was traversed (Moore 2003 traces the role of Eurasia from the eleventh century) and Eurasia makes a come-back in the present, in discussions of capitalisms and Asian–European dialogue (Nederveen Pieterse 2004b). Seen from the viewpoint of oriental globalization past and present, European development, Eurocentrism and occidental globalization appear as episodes and phases in a much wider multicentric global process.

Notes

1 On social science disciplines in relation to globalization studies and the periodization of globalization, see Nederveen Pieterse 2004a, chapters 1 and 4.
2 An earlier version of this section appears in *Theory Culture and Society*, 2005.
3 According to Kazim (2000) the Arab world remained dominant in world trade until 1500.
4 The East was also expansive; Hobson argues that the 'Afro-Asian age of discovery' preceded Columbus and Vasco da Gama by about a millennium (2004: 139).
5 Yo-Yo Ma has turned from interpretations of Bach and Brahms, to a long-term Silk Road project with the cooperation of musicians from Turkey to China in the Silk Road Ensemble.

References

Abdel-Malek, A. (1981) *Civilizations and Social Theory*, 2 Vols, London: Macmillan.

Abdel-Malek, A. (1994) 'Historical Initiative: The New "Silk Road"', *Review*, 17(4): 451–99.

Abu-Lughod, J. L. (2000) 'Book Review of A. G. Frank', *ReOrient: Journal of World History*, Spring: 111–14.

Bayly, C. A. (2004) *The Birth of the Modern World, 1780–1914*, Oxford: Blackwell.

Brennan, B., E. Heijmans and P. Vervest (eds) (1997) *ASEM Trading New Silk Routes: Beyond Geopolitics and Geo-economics: Towards a New Relationship Between Asia and Europe*, Amsterdam, Transnational Institute and Bangkok, Focus on the Global South.

Broeze, F. (ed.) (1989) *Brides of the Sea: Port Cities of Asia from the 16th–20th Centuries*, Honolulu: University of Hawaii Press.

Chamarik, S. and S. Goonatilake (eds) (1993) *Technological Independence: The Asian Experience*, Tokyo: UN University Press.

Chang, H.-J. (2002) *Kicking Away the Ladder*, London: Anthem.

Chauduri, K. N. (1990) *Asia before Europe: Economy and Civilization of the Indian Ocean from the Rise of Islam to 1750*, Cambridge: Cambridge University Press.

Chen, X. (2005) *As Borders Bend: Transnational Spaces on the Pacific Rim*, Boulder, CO: Rowman & Littlefield.

Cohen, W. I. (2000) *East Asia at the Center: Four Thousand Years of Engagement with the World*, New York: Columbia University Press.

Dirlik, A. (2000) 'Reversals, Ironies, Hegemonies: Notes on the Contemporary Historiography of Modern China', in A. Dirlik, V. Bahl and P. Gran (eds) (2000) *History After the Three Worlds: Post-eurocentric Historiographies*, Boulder, CO: Rowman & Littlefield, pp. 125–56.

Dobbin, C. (1996) *Asian Entrepreneurial Minorities: Conjoint Communities in the Making of the World-economy, 1570–1940*, Richmond, Surrey: Curzon Press.

Frank, A. G. (1996) 'The Underdevelopment of Development', in S. Chew and R. Denemark (eds) *The Underdevelopment of Development*, London: Sage, pp. 17–55.

Frank, A. G. (1998) *ReOrient: Global Economy in the Asian Age*, Berkeley: University of California Press.

Goonatilake, S. (1999) *Toward a Global Science*, Bloomington: Indiana University Press.

Gunn, G. C. (2003) *First Globalization: The Eurasian Exchange, 1500–1800*, Lanham, MD: Rowman & Littlefield.

Hobson, J. M. (2004) *The Eastern Origins of Western Civilization*, Cambridge: Cambridge University Press.

Hoerder, D. (2002) *Cultures in Contact: World Migrations in the Second Millennium*, Durham, NC: Duke University Press.

Hopkins, A. G. (ed.) (2002) *Globalization in World History*, New York: Norton.

Ibrahim, A. (1996) *The Asian Renaissance*, Singapore: Times Books.

Kazim, A. (2000) *The United Arab Emirates AD 600 to the Present: A Socio-discursive Transformation in the Arabian Gulf*, Dubai: Gulf Book Centre.

Kennedy, P. (2001) 'Maintaining American Power: From Injury to Recovery', in S. Talbott and N. Chanda (eds) *The Age of Terror: America and the World after September 11*, New York, Basic Books, pp. 53–80.

Kumar, R. and N. Chandhoke (eds) (2000) *Mapping Histories: Essays Presented to Ravinder Kumar*, New Delhi: Tulika.

Lieberman, Victor (ed.) (1999) *Beyond Binary Histories: Re-imagining Eurasia to c.1830*, Ann Arbor: University of Michigan Press.

Lieberman, Victor (2003) *Strange Parallels: Vol. 1: Integration of the Mainland:*

Southeast Asia in Global Context, c. 800–1830, Cambridge: Cambridge University Press.

Liu, H. (1998) 'Old Linkages, New Networks: The Globalization of Overseas Chinese Voluntary Associations and its Implications', *The China Quarterly*, 155: 582–609.

Mallory, J. P. (1991) *In Search of the Indo-Europeans: Language, Archaeology and Myth*, London: Thames & Hudson.

Marshall, P. J. and G. Williams (1982) *The Great Map of Mankind: British Perceptions of the World in the Age of Enlightenment*, London: Dent.

Moore, R. I. (2003) 'The Eleventh Century in Eurasian History: A Comparative Approach to the Convergence and Divergence of Medieval Civilizations', *Journal of Medieval and Early Modern Studies*, 33(1): 1–21.

Nederveen Pieterse, J. (1989) *Empire and Emancipation: Power and Liberation on a World Scale*, New York: Praeger.

Nederveen Pieterse, J. (1994) 'Unpacking the West: How European is Europe?', in A. Rattansi and S. Westwood (eds) *Racism, Modernity, Identity: On the Western Front*, Cambridge: Polity, pp. 129–49.

Nederveen Pieterse, J. (2003) 'Social Capital and Migration: Beyond Ethnic Economies', *Ethnicities*, 3(1): 5–34.

Nederveen Pieterse, J. (2004a) *Globalization and Culture: Global Mélange*, Boulder, CO: Rowman & Littlefield.

Nederveen Pieterse, J. (2004b) *Globalization or Empire?*, New York: Routledge.

Nederveen Pieterse, J. (2005) 'Paradigm Making While Paradigm Breaking: Andre Gunder Frank', *Review of International Political Economy*, 12(3): 383–6.

Needham, J. (1956) *Science and Civilization in China*, 2 Vols, Cambridge: Cambridge University Press.

Pomeranz, K. (2000) *The Great Divergence: China, Europe and the Making of the Modern World Economy*, Princeton, NJ: Princeton University Press.

Pomeranz, K. (2002) Beyond the East–West Binary: Resituating Development Paths in the Eighteenth Century World, *Journal of Asian Studies*, 61(2): 539–90.

Prestowitz, C. (2005) *Three Billion New Capitalists: The Great Shift of Wealth and Power to the East*, New York: Basic Books.

Putnam, R. D. (1993) *Making Democracy Work: Civic Traditions in Modern Italy*, Princeton, NJ: Princeton University Press.

Robertson, R. (2003) *The Three Waves of Globalization: A History of a Developing Global Consciousness*, London: Zed.

Seagrave, S. (1996) *Lords of the Rim*, London: Corgi Books.

Shanker, S. (2005) 'From the Silk Route to the IT Highway', *International Herald Tribune*, May 25: 9.

Sugiyama, J. (1992) 'From Chang an to Rome: Transformation of Buddhist Culture', in *The Significance of the Silk Roads in the History of Human Civilizations*, Osaka: National Museum of Ethnology, pp. 55–60.

Thapar, B. K. (1992) 'India's Place on Ancient Trade Routes', in *The Significance of the Silk Roads in the History of Human Civilizations*, Osaka: National Museum of Ethnology, pp. 117–26.

Tu Weiming (2000) 'Implications of the Rise of "Confucian" East Asia', *Daedalus*, 129(1): 195–218.

Turner, B. S. (1994) *Orientalism, Postmodernism and Globalism*, London: Routledge.

Weiss, L. (1996) 'Sources of the East Asian Advantage: An Institutional Analysis', in R. Robinson (ed.) *Pathways to Asia: The Politics of Engagement*, St Leonard's: Allen and Unwin, pp. 171–201.

Whitfield, S. (2003) 'The Perils of Dichotomous Thinking: Ebb and Flow rather than East and West', in *Marco Polo and the Encounter of East And West*, Toronto: University of Toronto Press.

Whitfield, S. (ed.) (2004) *The Silk Road: Trade, Travel, War and Faith*, Chicago: Serindia Publications.

Wolf, E. R. (2001) *Pathways of Power*, Berkeley: University of California Press.

Wood, F. (2003) *The Silk Road: Two Thousand Years in the Heart of Asia*, Berkeley: University of California Press.

Yamashita, S. and J. S. Eades (eds) (2003) *Globalization in Southeast Asia: Local, National, and Transnational Perspectives*, New York: Berghahn.

Yang, B. (2004) 'Horses, Silver and Cowries: Yunnan in Global Perspective', *Journal of World History*, 15(3): 281–322.

Zurndorfer, H. T. (1997) 'China and "Modernity": The Uses of the Study of Chinese History in the Past and the Present', *Journal of the Economic and Social History of the Orient*, 40(4): 461–85.

Part II

Asia in Europe

Encounters in history

5   Contested divergence

Rethinking the "rise of the West"

Johann P. Arnason

Interpretations of the distinction between East and West are more or less explicitly linked to historical accounts of changing constellations and inter-relations. Even when the dichotomy is grounded in meta-historical meanings or principles, there is room for a narrative of self-discovery, oblivion and articulation. But the most influential and intellectually productive approach to this problematic allows for a more formative historical factor. The "rise of the West" is – despite widely divergent views on details – commonly seen as a world-historical process which changed the relationship between the ascendant region and the rest of the world, while at the same time transforming both sides. As I have argued elsewhere (Arnason 2003), a suitably redefined concept of the West is separable from the much less tenable notion of a uniform or undivided East, and the same must apply to the historical model to be discussed here. One of the questions to be raised when comparing its different versions is to what extent they still reflect a residual influence of the dichotomy.[1]

The "rise of the West" has been one of the key themes in twentieth-century scholarship on world history; William McNeill's classic work (1963) is perhaps the best-known example (and by the same token, McNeill's reconsiderations and second thoughts – set out in later essays – are particularly relevant to further debate). The following discussion will treat this model as a *Denkfigur* which sums up historical experience from a specific perspective, but must for that very reason be subject to revision from what McNeill calls the "moving platform of the present"; as I shall try to show, some inherited assumptions need rethinking both on the basis of growing historical knowledge and in light of current trends; but reflections in that vein will also have to deal with the problems and limits of an underlying conceptual framework.

To put the issues in perspective, it should be noted that scenarios for a counter-offensive have also figured prominently in twentieth-century discourses on contemporary history. The "rise of the rest" (Amsden 2001) has sometimes been proclaimed in sweeping and totalizing "tricontinental" terms, but the more serious arguments tended to focus on Asian responses to Western ascendancy. Visions of an Asian resurgence – imminent or in progress – were not uncommon during the shorter twentieth century; Bolshevik hopes for revolutionary mobilization throughout Asia, after the failure in Europe, were perhaps the first variation on this theme. In the last quarter of the century, the success of East Asian developmental states inspired a very different line of analysis and speculation, with a more specific regional focus (but not incompatible with the search for alternatives to Western models). On the other hand, the *fin de siècle* also saw a revival of simplistic and polarizing ideas on both sides. The notion of the "anglosphere" as a distinctive and superior civilization, destined to reshape the world, is an intellectually impoverished and ideologically inflated version of the rising West. At the other end of the spectrum, some parts of the postcolonial nebula seem to identify with the pursuit of ideological power on metropolitan ground, and with the mythical transfiguration of this strategy into a part of the supposedly global struggle against imperialism. But for the purposes of constructive debate, it seems best to bypass the battle between anglospherics and postcolonials. I will therefore try to disregard the ideological conjuncture and focus on questions that should – although certainly not irrelevant to issues in world politics – not be subordinated to any kind of political apriorism.

The first section will recapitulate the most salient conclusions that can now be drawn from comparative historical research. On this basis, the idea of a "rise of the West" seems defensible as a macro-historical construct, but it must be reformulated with a view to avoiding short-circuits and misconceptions that have often gone together with it. The notion of a self-contained process is no less misleading than the now more fashionable reduction of Western success to a mere reflection of failure in other quarters. There is no tenable monocausal explanation of the "great divergence", no valid reason for crediting the West with any kind of inherent radical exceptionalism, and no precisely datable turning-point that would mark the beginning of irresistible ascent. A whole series of historical constellations set an emerging West apart from other Eurasian regions and gave it some decisive advantages over rivals and victims; the overall dynamics of the process can only be understood in a global context of intercivilizational encounters with mutually formative effects. Such perspectives are now often subsumed under the label of cosmopolitanism (but the present writer should confess in passing that he belongs to those who remain unenthusiastic about this particular use of the term: it seems more suited to ideological demarcation than to scholarly work). The second section then moves on to discuss more controversial points. If comparative history helps to make a balanced case for the "rise of the West", it is also true that critical reflection on the driving forces and social-historical dimensions of the process in question will open up horizons of contested meaning beyond the narrative basics. Culture matters, but so do the structures of social power and the changing ways of wealth creation; the ongoing conflict of interpretations within each of these thematic fields will inevitably translate into rival readings of history, not least of macro-historical processes on the scale to be considered here.

Situating the West: internal and external contexts

The "rise of the West" should be understood as an abridged label for three sets of historical developments: the emergence of Western Europe (or Western Christendom, to use a more adequate term for the formative phase) as a distinctive civilization; the achievement of global supremacy – technological, economic, political and ideological – by this civilization and its trans-Atlantic offshoots; and the diffusion of Western models, often reinterpreted in significantly variant ways, throughout the previously non-Western world. All three processes are discussed in the literature on the subject (even if their relative weight varies widely), and there are good reasons to retain the triple focus. A strong emphasis on the second theme – the breakthrough to global primacy – is evident in recent scholarship, but it should not obscure the importance of the other two. If it is now increasingly accepted that the expanding West gained a decisive edge over other civilizations at a later date than the received view would have it, this does not mean that earlier innovations and transformations on a more limited scale were insignificant. The marginality of Western Christendom in the overall Eurasian context did not prevent it from developing specific capacities and institutions that could later serve to sustain new initiatives in a changed global environment. An exclusive concern with the climactic phase would therefore screen out a whole range of relevant questions. Similarly, no account of the "rise of the West" would be complete without an analysis of the dynamic that gave a global but at the same time contested meaning to historical forces set in motion by the West (not on its own, but more effectively than by other actors in the field). As will be seen, this problematic has to do with the relationship between Westernization and modernization, and with the place of Western patterns within the framework of "multiple modernities" (both early and advanced).

This provisional definition should suffice to mark out a field of inquiry. The next step is to note the most basic criteria to be met by an up-to-date interpretation; they may be seen as minimal conclusions emerging from advances in comparative history and historical sociology.

First, the "rise of the West" must be analysed as a multi-dimensional process. This point has a twofold meaning. On the one hand, it concerns the sources and the driving forces of the process. In that regard, it reaffirms an insight clearly formulated by Max Weber, but often ignored by his critics and not always fully understood by his disciples. In the introduction to his collected essays on the sociology of religion (arguably the most seminal statement on "the rise of the West", even if it does not use that expression), Weber refers to the "concatenation of circumstances" (*Verkettung von Umständen* – Weber 1963: 1) that has shaped the distinctive developmental path of Western civilization. In every phase and at every juncture, decisive turns have been due to interactive combinations of mutually irreducible factors, rather than to any single underlying principle or orientation. A brief recapitulation could begin with Western Christendom's roots in the radically different cultural tradition symbolized by Athens and Jerusalem, brought together in the setting of a mutating Roman Empire and reactivated in other contexts at later stages. The decomposition of imperial structures in the West led to the rise of kingdoms with more or less marked ethnic identities, alongside the gradual consolidation of a religious power centre on a civilizational scale; this constellation became the background to the medieval maturing of Western Christendom as a distinctive civilization. During the High Middle Ages, new strategies and patterns of state formation interacted with the sociocultural dynamic of urban communities in quest of autonomy, as well as with a progressive articulation and institutionalization of potentialities inherent in the Christian universe of meaning. Finally, the phase that brought about a global breakthrough was – as Weber saw – characterized by the interplay of the three modernizing mega-machines: industrial capitalism, the post-absolutist bureaucratic state and organized science.

The same applies to the epoch-making results and global ramifications of the process: they are best understood in terms of multiple trends without systemic coordination. The world-transforming inventions of the West include not only the union of capitalism and science that led to the institutionalization of permanent technological progress, but also new techniques of control and mobilization, perfected in the course of state formation and taken to extremes in totalitarian projects, and the cultural polarization of Enlightenment and Romanticism (to which there seem to be only limited analogies elsewhere), together with the ideological formations that grew out of it. On the international level, new patterns of economic interdependence were pioneered by the West, and models of political organization were diffused across cultural boundaries; but on the other hand, the "rise of the West" (in the broad sense defined above) involved the appropriation of Western countercultures and protest ideologies by non-Western forces striving to combine emulation and resistance. These points may seem elementary, but they must be reiterated against the pervasive economism of contemporary thought.

Second, the "rise of the West" was – as McNeill stressed in one of his retrospective essays – a long-term process (McNeill 1986). His perspective is implicit in a definition that links the technological and geopolitical take-off to the *long durée* of medieval and early modern Western Europe. The most obvious way to clarify it is to single out successive turning-points which have set lasting preconditions for later developments. It is now widely agreed among historians that the eleventh and twelfth centuries CE saw the definitive crystallization of Western Christendom as a distinctive civilization; although it has proved more difficult to identify the specific factors at work and explain the dynamic of their interaction, the "papal revolution", i.e. the consolidation of the Catholic Church as an integrative institution on a civilizational scale, can safely be singled out as a crucial part of the process. No similar case of centralized ideological power – alongside political fragmentation – can be found in any other civilizational context. Within this institutional framework, religious conflicts could have a correspondingly far-reaching impact. The realization of their schismatic potential depended on a variety of other factors; but the unparalleled civilizational bifurcation that resulted from the sixteenth-century split of Western Christendom could only happen in the historical setting that had taken shape during the first half of the millennium. The most acute phase of religious conflict coincided with another turning-point: early modern European expansion. It is true that traditional views on the European conquest of the Americas have come in for de-mythologizing criticism, but one basic fact remains indisputable: this was the first case of trans-oceanic empire-building, and it paved the way for further distinctive developments. The slave plantation economy of the New World should, as C. A. Bayly (2004: 41) argues, be included in the category of "industrious revolutions" that preceded the industrial one: they represented "a flexible, financially sophisticated, consumer-oriented, technologically innovative form of human beastliness" (it is perhaps worth recalling that both the prehistory and the proper history of the rising West were marked by episodes of particularly pronounced dependence on slavery: this applies to crucial phases of classical antiquity, but also to the role of the slave trade in the early medieval European economy [McCormick 2001], and to the controversial but clearly not insignificant contribution of trans-Atlantic slavery to the "great divergence" that put the West ahead of the rest). But there was more to the trans-Atlantic opening than a new chance to rationalize exploitation. Comparative historical approaches (Eisenstadt 2003b; Veliz 1994) have increasingly highlighted the New World transformations of European civilizational premises, as well as the contrasts between Anglo- and Ibero-American versions of this pattern. Seen as a case of civilizational divergence, the Atlantic divide within the West invites comparison with other examples, but next to no work has so far been done on such questions. One crucial aspect of a broader picture may be noted: intra-imperial differentiation created preconditions for imperial schisms of a new kind, which could in turn draw on European ideological traditions and re-interpret them in new contexts. This would seem the most adequate view of the New World breakthroughs to independence.

The imperial schisms resulted from multiple developments, but they took place in a specific socio-political and geopolitical setting that should be included among the most salient junctures of the long-term process in question. The historical experience of European absolutism – not least the tension between a far-reaching rationalization of state strategies and an attempt to reinvigorate the idea of sacred kingship – and the democratic response to it interacted with the rivalry of states in pursuit of imperial power; this complex dynamic culminated in a conjuncture of revolutions and wars at the end of the eighteenth century and the beginning of the nineteenth. These events preceded the decisive impact of the industrial revolution (to the extent that a commercial middle class was involved, we can speak of a connection with the "industrious revolutions"), but they added up to a formative moment on a world historical scale. As C. A. Bayly's recent analysis (2004) shows, the progress of governmental activism – accompanied by the rise of "critical publics" in various guises – was not unique to Europe; but the same author traces a process which transformed difference in degree into more radical regional innovations with global consequences. French historians have described this aspect of the "rise of the West" as "occidentalisation de l'ordre politique" and as a "greffe de l'Etat" (Bayart 1996), worldwide transfer of a Western invention. Such terms must be qualified to stress the importance of interaction – asymmetric, but less so in some cases than others, and far from insignificant on the global scale.

This observation brings us to the last general point: the "rise of the West" is best understood as an interactive process. To put it another way, the dichotomy of internalist or externalist accounts is misguided. It is true that both these supposed alternatives are represented in recent work (Jones 2003 is often quoted as a prime example of the internalist view, whereas Frank 1998 takes the externalist one to caricatural extremes). But the only viable approach is one that allows for changing combinations of factors internal and external to the West as a civilizational complex.

To clarify this claim, let us briefly revisit McNeill's evolving interpretation of world history. He had from the outset taken an emphatically interactionist view: both the trajectory of civilization in the singular and the vicissitudes of the variants which can be singled out as civilizations in their own right were to be analysed in terms of the hypothesis that learning new skills from strangers was the main driving force of historical change. The "rise of the West" appeared as the last of several successive shifts from one civilizational centre to another, and it had begun with intensive learning from other civilizations, before going on to develop new skills and resources that ensured a decisive advantage. In a much later essay (McNeill 1990), he found the original approach insufficient and proposed to take the interactionist perspective one step further: as he now saw it, interaction between separate civilizations gave rise to trans-civilizational constellations or "ecumenical world-systems". The first formation of that kind was the ancient Middle Eastern ecumene, and the "global cosmopolitanism" that had prevailed since the mid-nineteenth century could be seen as the final stage. For present purposes, it may be useful to recast both parts of the argument. The learning of skills is one aspect of the broader problematic of intercivilizational encounters, which can also involve other kinds of one-sided or mutually formative contact; as for the second step, it is perhaps best to drop the notion of a world system (a "conceptual misalliance", as an early and acute critic [Zolberg 1981] suggested), and allow for a variety of intercivilizational constellations. The interactionist perspective would then take into account not only the direct impact of civilizations on each other, but also the effects of changes to the overall constellations which they share.

The emphasis on interaction is not meant to pre-empt answers to specific questions about historical transitions and turning-points. It is, for example, a matter of debate among economic historians whether it makes sense to see the industrial revolution in Britain as a response to more competitive artisan techniques of textile production elsewhere, and to what extent it was financed by wealth generated through trade and exploitation outside Europe. No general considerations will settle such controversies. But in the overall perspective, the interactionist view is a necessary corollary of the two preceding points. A long-term perspective must take into account the changing relations between Eurasian civilizations, and the impact of intercivilizational dynamics on European development; only a multi-dimensional frame of reference, allowing for cultural as well as political and economic factors, can do justice to the varying levels and mechanisms of these macro-regional connections. A more detailed narrative would have to start with the transformation of the Roman world (this formulation, which has now to all intents and purposes replaced the traditional picture of a "decline and fall of the Roman Empire", sums up a paradigm shift of major dimensions, and its long-term implications have yet to be fully clarified). Western Christendom emerged as one of three successor civilizations, alongside Byzantium and Islam, and its distinctive characteristics were not unrelated to this broader background (one point worth noting is that the superior dynamism of the two less directly affiliated successor civilizations, Islam and Western Christendom, clearly had something to do with more innovative mixtures of traditions). And although the details of the record are debatable, further interaction with the Byzantine and Islamic worlds was of some importance to the medieval transformations of the West. Evidence of that can be found at very different levels of socio-cultural life: from the early medieval slave trade with the Islamic world (see the above reference to McCormick) to the reappropriation of classical sources (crucial to the twelfth-century renaissance) through Byzantine and Arabic intermediaries. A new constellation took shape with the Mongol conquest of most of Eurasia. Western Christendom was one of the marginal regions left outside the short-lived Eurasian empire; it was less seriously threatened than the others, and it briefly developed a more diplomatic and inquiring relationship with the ascendant power. But it can also be argued that in the longer run – after an initial destructive impact – the Mongol input gave a new lease of life to Islamic empire-building (Hodgson's "gunpowder empires"), most obviously in the case of the Ottomans, who were to initiate a new phase of the conflict between Islam and the West.

Early modern European expansion, beginning with the long sixteenth century, gave a new twist to the whole process. But as debates during the last quarter of a century have shown, the notion of a Europe-centred and unilaterally imposed world system is very misleading: European powers acquired new possessions and established networks of new footholds around the globe; they gained access to pre-existing channels of exchange; and when they opened up new channels (as they did through conquest of the Western hemisphere), the consequences were largely beyond their control. Economic historians now seem to agree that the impact of American silver on the East Asian economic zone and its unfolding "second commercial revolution" may have been more important than any intra-European effects.

Finally, the interactionist perspective has a direct bearing on the most recent phase. The "rise of the West", in the most comprehensive sense, involves not only attempts to reproduce Western models in order to counter Western expansion or escape Western control, but also borrowings from Western counter-cultural traditions by non-Western societies in search of strategic prescriptions for change and revival; in the most significant cases, combinations of Western and indigenous inputs give rise to alternative projects that challenge the ascendant West. This derivative rise of the "West against the West", exemplified by the Communist regimes of the twentieth century, was a world-historical episode of major dimensions. It took different turns and came to different ends in Russia and China; their respective exits from Communism can now serve as starting-points for a retrospective comparison of the roles played by Western influences and Westernizing aspirations in the history of these two revolutionized and reconstructed empires.

Reinterpretations

So far, I have only summarized basic lessons of comparative historical inquiry, with particular reference to the "rise of the West" and the current requirements for a tenable account of it. My line of argument was loosely aligned with McNeill's narrative. More specifically, the above considerations do not go beyond the view that subsumes the "rise of the West" under a more general historical pattern. The trajectory that began on the Western Eurasian frontier and continued across the Atlantic had a more global impact than any earlier rise to primacy, but did not amount to a radical departure from precedent. Nor is there any compelling reason why it should be the last of its kind. McNeill's version of the story culminated in a global ecumene, but his original model does not seem incompatible with the prospect – suggested by various writers on more or less plausible grounds – of East Asia overtaking the West and becoming (at least in some respects) the vanguard of development.

A closer look at conceptual frameworks and their theoretical implications will shift the focus to a more contested field. As I shall try to show, this leads to stronger emphasis on unique aspects of the "rise of the West", but also – paradoxically – to conclusions that undermine the very idea of regional hegemony and indicate other ways to make sense of the process in question. The West appears less as a dominant part of the world than as a vehicle of forces or principles that follow a global logic and find their most adequate expression on a global scale. Here I can only indicate some key themes of an open debate. They are most easily identified in relation to the three points made above: the multi-dimensional, long-term and interactive character of the process in question. Each of these three aspects can be – and has been – qualified or problematized in ways that raise far-reaching questions.

Notwithstanding the historical evidence of a multi-dimensional dynamic, it can be argued that one factor has been decisive and tended to absorb all the others. The "rise of the West" is, above all else, a matter of power and its multiple sources. The Western pursuit of power has, on this view, been uniquely successful on three levels. From the maritime skills evident in early European expansion to the pioneering of industrial trans-formations, the superior resources of European powers gave them a deci-sive advantage over other civilizations, including the previously more advanced ones. This shift in the global balance of power forced the non-Western contestants to import or imitate models first invented by the winning side. In other words, the Western pursuit of power triggered pre-ventive or defensive Westernization in widely varying settings, with corre-spondingly different outcomes. Finally, the borrowing of power techniques proved conducive to less controllable changes, affecting the cultural identi-ties and presuppositions of the societies in question. In that sense, the ulti-mate triumph of Western power was the general de-stabilization of non-Western cultural worlds.

This power-centred approach tends to portray Western domination as a vehicle of developments that obey a more general logic and can result in more evenly balanced global changes. A shift in this direction may be noted in McNeill's *Pursuit of Power*, where the history of warfare in general and of Western military power in particular is first outlined in terms of "macroparasitism", an evolving pattern of specialists in violence gaining direct or indirect control over their social environment and impos-ing their priorities, but then reconstructed in a more detailed fashion without using that language, and allowing for more "symbiotic" relation-ships between societies and their armed forces (McNeill 1982: VII). The conceptual ambiguity evident at the beginning resurfaces in a double-edged diagnosis of contemporary trends. The accelerated progress of military technology would have been impossible without the more general inter- and intra-civilizational dynamics that made the West central to world history, but industrialized warfare – the pursuit of power at its most extreme – has moved so far out of step with other aspects of social life that the very possibility of survival is in doubt. McNeill concluded – a quarter of a century ago, well before the end of the Cold War – that "a global sovereign power", an "empire of the earth" (McNeil 1982: 383), radically different from all known forms of hegemony, would solve the problem. The "rise of the West" would thus culminate in a self-abolishing leap to higher levels of social organization. But the idea of an inherently globalizing competitive pursuit of power can lead to other conclusions. Those who now envisage a transition from American hegemony or imperial rule (by implication the last form of Western ascendancy) to a multi-polar world are relying on basic assumptions of that kind.

From another point of view, the shift that really matters is not so much from Western domination to multi-polarity as from an external to an internalized form of Western hegemony. This perspective prevails in some versions of postcolonial theorizing: the main target of criticism is a model, or more precisely a meta-model (not always identified in the same terms), imposed on non-Western cultures by Western conquerors but adaptable to a wide range of backgrounds and circumstances. Theodore von Laue's analysis of the "world revolution of Westernization" (von Laue 1987) proposes a more nuanced variation on the same theme. As he sees it, a Western breakthrough to higher levels of power forced states and societies in other parts of the world to compete within a framework established by the strongest players; and the most influential strategies developed for that purpose mix direct imitation with imagined alternatives (for von Laue, even the Communist challenge to the West fits into this category). After a long history of – in the last instance – unsuccessful counter-projects, the only hope for a more constructive global regime lies in self-critical reflection on both sides: the West should accept the blame for its destructive impact on the rest, while non-Westerners in search of alternatives might reconsider the one-sided perceptions – of both problems and possibilities – on which dominant developmental models have hitherto been based.

To round off this first part of our survey, Samuel Huntington's well-known work on the "clash of civilizations" may serve to illustrate yet another view. His most provocative claims have to do with macro-historical cultural identities and the conflicts between them, but this line of argument is backed up by a less explicit account of power and its changing role in intercivilizational relations. Huntington insists that the West was Western long before it went modern; when it embarked on the path of modernizing transformations (industrialization, urbanization etc.), the first effect was to empower it against other civilizations, and this global supremacy was reinforced by the Westernizing projects that grew out of the borrowing of modern techniques (in the broadest sense). But for Huntington, this is not the end of the story: the conflation of modernization and Westernization gives way to what he calls "second-generation indigenization", and the ultimate effect of modernizing processes is to re-entrench the traditional plurality of civilizations. In that sense, modernization has self-cancelling consequences: it returns history to the traditional pattern of mutually incompatible and uncomprehending (or at best partially comprehending) cultural worlds. From Huntington's point of view, the "rise of the West" is thus a confusing notion: it lumps together two very different things, the original constitution of the West as a distinctive civilization and the temporary advantages which the West derived from its pioneering role in a process that ultimately re-empowers its adversaries.

Multi-dimensionality reappears when we go on to trace connections between the accumulation of power and the diverse sources on which it draws. In the long run, economic and technological capacities were crucial: the power–wealth nexus must therefore be central to the story. The growth of power and wealth was in turn sustained by cognitive progress in general and institutionalized science in particular. The connection between power and knowledge thus calls for further reflection. Inasmuch as the world-historical dynamic of the West has depended on the initiatives of individual and collective actors, an evolving synergy of power and freedom was of major importance. Last but not least, we should note a connection between power and meaning: despite the unending controversies about the role and relative weight of specific traditions, it is widely agreed that distinctive interpretations of the world and the human condition contributed to the "rise of the West". They focused on visions of human autonomy and self-empowerment, implemented through rational domination of the world as well as through sovereign reconstruction of social order, and articulated in rival ideologies of progress.

No extensive coverage of this problematic can be attempted here. The following remarks will centre on particular themes – more specifically wealth and meaning – and underline the need to locate them in a broader context; they will thus single out some focal points of a debate that remains open to new approaches. Some of the most challenging recent contributions have come from those who stress the fundamental importance of wealth and the impact of changing ways of wealth creation. Various writers have put forward ideas in this vein during the last decade, but the case has been stated most forcefully and comprehensively by Jack Goldstone (2000, 2002 and forthcoming). On this view, the decisive "great divergence" (Pomeranz 2000) between the West and the rest was a later development than historians had tended to assume: it resulted from the industrial revolution, and closer analysis of this epoch-making event has shown that the real turning-point – in terms of economic and social impact – came later than traditional accounts would have it, in the early nineteenth rather than the late eighteenth century. The foundational achievement of the industrial revolution was a breakthrough in energy use, but its long-term significance lay in what Goldstone calls the marriage of science-based engineering and visionary entrepreneurship. It gave rise to an economy based on accelerated innovation and risk-taking (one salutary side-effect of Goldstone's argument is that it helps to puncture the much-inflated notion of "risk society": we have been living in a risk society for two centuries). Goldstone describes this historical shift as a transition from traditional to modern wealth creation: the latter centres on permanent innovation.

The conventional idea of a "rising West" reflects the historical experience of the industrial revolution but in a misleading way: the breakthrough occurred in Britain, rather than on a broader regional basis. It presupposed a contingent, localized and exceptional interplay of many factors: economic, political, religious and cultural. The new mode of production (the Marxian term seems appropriate) expanded beyond its birthplace, at first most effectively in the European and North American context, but some parts of the rest responded more actively than some parts of the West. More generally speaking, the diffusion of the industrial revolution is best understood in terms of networks of developmental centres, rather than whole countries or regions (let alone civilizations). We are, in other words, dealing with a radically new form of economic life, born of a mutation which could only happen in a very particular place, and whose subsequent global reach could only be sustained by privileged foci of dynamism. This revised account diverges very sharply from established conceptions of the "rise of the West".

Goldstone's arguments add up to a powerful challenge to traditional views on the "rise of the West". Here I can only indicate what I think is the most plausible way of countering it. We can accept the late dating, the local (rather than regional) character, and the contingency of the industrial breakthrough, and still insist on preconditions (necessary but not sufficient) and connections that enable us to speak of a "rise of the West" on a broader basis and in a more long-term perspective. The cultural currents and social forces (including the transformative potential of Protestantism as well as what Joel Mokyr [2002] calls the "industrial enlightenment") that crystallized in an unprecedented conjuncture in eighteenth-century Britain can only be understood in the context of a long-term and large-scale transformation of European civilization. As for the relationship between innovation and accumulation (Goldstone's line of argument involves a critique of all accumulation-centred theories of development, including practical recommendations to developing countries), it is no doubt true that the cultural and institutional opening to innovation needs to be put more firmly at the centre of the picture; but it was only in conjunction with a socio-economic regime geared to the accumulation of capital as well as knowledge that the newly institutionalized innovative capacities changed the world. Finally, the effort to rationalize innovation into a regular component of wealth creation is also a part of the capitalist historical universe, and the aspiration to do better in that regard became the starting-point for the most important counter-project of the twentieth century: the Communist model of an alternative modernity.

The cultural factors that enter into genealogies of the industrial revolution can also be credited with a transformative dynamic of their own; when taken to the most radical conclusions, this line of argument posits a cultural mutation that set the West – more specifically the modern West – farther apart from other civilizations than any previous developments had done. In historical terms, such interpretations have foregrounded the sixteenth-century fragmentation of Western Christendom, the seventeenth-century take-off of the scientific revolution, or the eighteenth-century Enlightenment. Irrespective of chronological variations, the common ground is a conceptual switch with critical implications for the historical picture summarized above. The idea of a cultural mutation seems, at first sight, to single out one dimension of the social–historical world, but critics of purely culturalist approaches can argue that innovations on the level of formative meaning draw on multiple sources and take practical shape through multiple channels. Similarly, while the emphasis on discontinuity in regard to the most basic cultural orientations must at the very least modify our understanding of long-term processes, a case can be made for genealogical perspectives that link the moments of breakthrough to cumulative background trends on one hand and gradually unfolding articulations on the other. Finally, the notion of a radical and unparalleled transformation within a regional and civilizational framework amounts to a major qualification of the interactionist thesis, even if it does not exclude a global view of preconditions as well as of the ramifications that lend world-historical meaning to the locally initiated changes. At the same time, the idea of an epoch-making change to cultural orientations undermines all constructs of an enduring Western identity: the episodes often taken to represent the most decisive triumphs of the West now appear as harbingers of a new historical formation, no more reducible to older sources than confinable within its original limits.

The argument so far outlined on a very abstract level has found more concrete expression in contemporary social theory. The most promising starting-point for further discussion is S. N. Eisenstadt's interpretation of modernity as a new civilization that took shape through mutations at the very core of the European (or more precisely West European) world but rose to dominance in the global arena and crystallized into diverse forms in different contexts (for the most condensed programmatic statement, see Eisenstadt 2003a). Cultural premises are as central to this civilization as to traditional ones; the most distinctive innovations in that regard have to do with visions of human autonomy, intertwined but not identical with the ability to master the natural world and transform the social one. These new perspectives on the human condition and its inherent possibilities were articulated – in unequally developed ways – across a broad spectrum of social practices, but most ambitiously in the philosophical projects that accompanied the transition to modernity. Conflicting interpretations translate the common theme – the new horizons of human autonomy – into divergent images of society, ideological models and operative definitions of social power.

This civilizational view of modernity is related to other theoretical innovations in the same field. To cut a long and unfinished story short, early modernities are perhaps best understood as partial transformations, occurring separately in various regional and civilizational contexts, but only coalescing into a civilizational pattern in the specific setting of the expanding and mutating West; "multiple modernities" would then represent variants of that pattern unfolding on a global scale. This is not to imply that the Western crystallization of modernity as a civilization was a self-contained process. The regional concentration presupposes a global conjuncture, and vice versa. The most ambitious and erudite global history of "the birth of the modern world" now available admits European specificity in no uncertain terms: it refers to the "particular buoyancy of the European idea of knowledge and its material rewards" (Bayly 2004: 80). As the same author notes, destructive consequences of this distinction were no less important than the productive ones; but that does not alter the fact that his analysis converges with the civilizational approach. There is, on the other hand, no denying that the latter needs further clarification. Eisenstadt's formulations leave some room for doubt as to whether modernity should be seen as a new civilization, fundamentally comparable with older ones, or a civilizational formation of a new type, departing from traditional patterns in unprecedented ways. Other unresolved issues will emerge when his views are compared with those of classical and contemporary authors who have developed more implicit but often insightful arguments in the same vein. Even so, the civilizational frame of reference seems particularly relevant to the problems that arise when the historical trajectory of the West is subjected to theoretical questioning.

Note

1 Thanks are due to Jack Goldstone, for making unpublished manuscripts available; and to participants in the discussion at Schloss Elmau in April 2004. The title of the paper is, of course, inspired by Kenneth Pomeranz's book, *The Great Divergence*.

References

Amsden, A. (2001) *The Rise of the Rest: Challenges to the West from Late Industrializing Economies*, Oxford: Oxford University Press.

Arnason, J. P. (2003) "East and West: From Invidious Dichotomy to Incomplete Deconstruction", in G. Delanty and E. Isin (eds) *Handbook of Historical Sociology*, London: Sage, pp. 220–34.

Bayart, J. F. (1996) *La greffe de l'Etat*, Paris: Karthala.

Bayly, C. A. (2004) *The Birth of the Modern World, 1780–1914*, Oxford: Blackwell.

Eisenstadt, S. N. (2003a) "The Civilizational Dimension of Modernity: Modernity as a Distinct Civilization", in id., *Comparative Civilizations and Multiple Modernities*, vol. 2, Leiden: Brill, pp. 493–518.

Eisenstadt, S. N. (2003b) "The First Multiple Modernities: The Civilization of the Americas", in id., *Comparative Civilizations and Multiple Modernities*, vol. 2, Leiden: Brill, pp. 701–22.

Frank, A. G. (1998) *Re-Orient: Global Economy in the Asian Age*, Berkeley: University of California Press.

Goldstone, J. (2000) "The Rise of the West – or Not? A Revision to Socioeconomic History", *Sociological Theory*, 18(2): 175–94.

Goldstone, J. (2002) "Efflorescences and Economic Growth in World History: Rethinking the 'Rise of the West' and the Industrial Revolution", *Journal of World History*, 13(1): 323–90.

Goldstone, J. (forthcoming) *The Happy Chance: The Rise of the West in Global Context, 1500–1850*, Berkeley: University of California Press.

Huntington, S. P. (1997) *The Clash of Civilizations and the Remaking of World Order*, New York: Simon & Schuster.

Jones, E. L. (2003) *The European Miracle. Environment, Economies and Geopolitics in the History of Europe*, Cambridge: Cambridge University Press.

McCormick, M. (2001) *Origins of the European Economy: Communications and Commerce AD 300–900*, New York: Cambridge University Press.

McNeill, W. (1963) *The Rise of the West: A History of the Human Community*, Chicago: Chicago University Press.

McNeill, W. (1982) *The Pursuit of Power: Technology, Armed Force, and Society since AD 1000*, Chicago: Chicago University Press.

McNeill, W. (1986) "The Rise of the West as a Long-term Process", in id., *Mythistory and Other Essays*, Chicago: Chicago University Press, pp. 43–67.

McNeill, W. (1990) "The *Rise of the West* after Twenty-five Years", *Journal of World History*, 1(1): XV–XXX.

Mokyr, J. (2002) *Gifts of Athena: Historical Origins of the Knowledge Economy*, Princeton: Princeton University Press.

Pomeranz, K. (2000) *The Great Divergence: China, Europe, and the Making of the World Economy*, Princeton: Princeton University Press.

Veliz, C. (1994) *The New World of the Gothic Fox: Culture and Economy in English and Spanish America*, Berkeley: University of California Press.

Von Laue, Th. (1987) *The World Revolution of Westernization: The Twentieth Century in Global Perspective*, New York: Oxford University Press.

Weber, M. (1963) *Gesammelte Aufsätze zur Religionssoziologie, Bd. 1*, Tübingen: J. C. B. Mohr.

Zolberg, A. (1981) "Origins of the Modern World System: A Missing Link", *World Politics*, 23(1): 253–81.

6 Discovering the world

Cosmopolitanism and globality in the 'Eurasian' renaissance

David Inglis and Roland Robertson

> The nature of all other creatures is defined and restricted within laws which We have laid down; you, by contrast, impeded by no such restrictions, may, by your own free will ... trace for yourself the lineaments of your own nature. I have placed you at the very centre of the world, so that from that vantage point you may with greater ease glance round about you on all that the world contains ... in order that you may, as the free and proud shaper of your own being, fashion yourself in the form you may prefer.
>
> (Mirandola 1998: 12)

Such are the words of God in the much-quoted lines of the 'Oration on the Dignity of Man', written by the Italian humanist scholar Pico della Mirandola in the year 1486 (1998). Pico's Oration has often been understood as the key philosophical manifesto of that set of phenomena that we in the present day are accustomed to call the European Renaissance, a philosophical and literary movement that is conventionally located primarily as beginning in the Italian peninsula and starting in the fifteenth century. In the extract above, we see both the kernel of Pico's thought, and also, it is frequently claimed, the essence of the overall Renaissance mindset. The revival of the secular and inquiring spirit of ancient Greek and Roman learning throughout the fifteenth century created a condition in which, it is said, the shackles of Catholic religion and the dead-weight of suffocating medieval tradition were increasingly sloughed off, in favour of a dawning realisation that the human being is the only creature on earth which can shape its own nature, and thus its own destiny. Just as each individual human has that capacity to choose the nature and style of his or her own endeavours, so too does the species as a whole, the essence of the human character being the capacity to transcend the barriers set in each epoch upon achievement and aspiration. When we think today of the Renaissance, we tend to think of mankind's Promothean capacities, its abilities to shape itself in a never-ending series of self-induced transformations, and, in so doing, enactments of successively more impressive achievements (Greenblatt 1980).

In what has come to be the standard view of the European Renaissance, the individual human's internal discovery of his or her Promethean potentials is thought to be a purely 'European' phenomenon. What allegedly differentiates 'Europe' from other parts of the world is based on what is seen as the unique mental capacity of the 'European', which encompasses both the ability to fashion one's own self, free of the ascribed identities imposed by group membership, and also the aptitude to utilise the latter skill in the building of future social and cultural conditions that are unfettered by the constraints of tradition and convention. While 'Asia' and 'Africa' are seen to remain forever caught within the confines of 'traditional' thought, practice, selfhood and social arrangements, the European has the unique ability to look forward into a limitless horizon of the future, a panorama of unlimited possibilities vis-à-vis how the person sees him- or herself and how she lives in association with others (Goody 1996). This powerful and seductive vision of the apparently exceptional potential of the European person lies at the heart of the idea of 'Europe' dominant in modernity, an imagining of the latter as the only place in the world where the freedom of the self to make itself leads in turn to virtuous cultural conditions (the rejection of irrational tradition, an empirical and questioning mindset, the championing of liberal values) and social arrangements (freedom of individual expression, political liberty and the absence of despotism). These values and conditions have come to be expressive of the dominant mode of self-understanding of Europeans for the last two centuries and more. While they are often associated with the Enlightenment of the eighteenth century, nonetheless mainstream commentaries regard the roots of the tendencies of the latter as being firmly locatable within, and having grown out of, Renaissance thought and practice (Pater 1980).

Such a view, which since the mid-nineteenth century has become the dominant interpretation of the influence of Renaissance mores on subsequent European socio-cultural development, leads to a curious paradox as regards issues to do with 'cosmopolitan' outlooks and practices. On the one hand, Renaissance practices and attitudes of self-fashioning suggest an openness to endless possibilities, including learning from those living in other parts of the world, respecting their cultural otherness, and including certain aspects of their thinking and lifestyles within one's own sense of self and social existence. We can see this in the above quotation, where Pico makes God pronounce to the human that s/he has been made in such a way that s/he 'may with greater ease glance round about you on all that the world contains'. Despite the human's capacity to gaze upon all the varieties of life the world has to offer, it remained the case in this conceptualisation that only certain aspects of others' thinking and lifestyles could be included in one's own, namely those aspects that did not threaten one's capacity constantly to mould the self anew, by suffocating that capacity under the weight of traditional and irrational dogmas. Nonetheless,

Renaissance self-fashioning strongly implies an openness to cultural alterity and a willingness to learn from it.

On the other hand, openness to others and other cultures seems to be a purely 'European' capacity: only the European, with his or her culture of self-fashioning, is in a position to be a cultural cosmopolitan, because non-Europeans are seen to remain embedded within 'traditional' mindsets and social structures. Thus while the European may admire (to some degree) and learn (a little) from, for example, the apparent stoicism in the face of the vagaries of life and the universe embodied by the Hindu and the Buddhist, the latter are felt by the European unable to engage in the same practices of admiration and learning, for they remain too stuck within their respective mindsets ever to engage in the form of reflexive self-questioning and self-fashioning that is seen to be the sole preserve of the European. Paradoxically, then, only Europeans apparently can have cosmopolitan attitudes towards the wider world, because all non-European others are unable to engage in the practices of the self that allow cosmopolitan attitudes in the first place. A further paradox follows: the Europeans' cosmopolitan sensibilities are themselves expressive of, and rooted in, a strong form of cultural chauvinism: *we* are cosmopolitans but *you* are not (Goody 1996).

This outcome inexorably follows from the starting-point of this sort of argument, namely that the Renaissance is solely and simply a European phenomenon, and that the apparently virtuous mental capacities it unleashed, including cosmopolitan dispositions towards other cultures, are conveyed only on Europeans or on those who fully embrace a 'European' mindset, the very mindset that was allegedly formed in and by the Renaissance. In this chapter, our aim is to take apart the commonplace notion that the set of phenomena contemporary observers have come to call the 'Renaissance' is simply an unabashedly 'European' institution. By examining empirically the genesis and operation of those phenomena usually referred to under the blanket term 'Renaissance', we will unpack the complex of inter- and trans-national processes that lie behind them. In particular, we will see that far from being simply 'Europe's other', the Islamic world of the Ottoman empire was a very important player in the international processes of mutual trade and cultural influence that can be discerned as the generating mechanisms behind, and the characteristic expression of, what can be called – in inverted commas – the 'Renaissance world'. In this way, we will see that the 'Renaissance' is better understood as a 'hybrid' and indeed 'Eurasian' set of processes rather than simply as a solely 'European' innovation.

In terms of issues to do with cosmopolitanism, we will show that it was in fact 'cosmopolitan' conditions of inter- and trans-national cultural influence, cultural emulation and trade (in art forms and luxury goods especially) which were both the conditions of possibility, and the characteristic means of expression, of 'Renaissance culture'. We will delineate how this state of affairs meant that a strong and increasingly sophisticated sense of 'globality' – the idea that the world is a single place, and that all parts of it are connected in various ways with all other parts (Robertson 2001) – was characteristic of the thinking of the Renaissance period. In that sense, we will see that the 'cosmopolitan' aspects of Renaissance thought were predicated upon 'cosmopolitan' conditions of socio-cultural connectivity, especially as these pertained between the 'Christian West' and the 'Islamic East'. We will also briefly examine the role of Renaissance cartography, itself bound up in practices of international trade, in the forging of what can be called Renaissance globality. By demonstrating the interplay between 'Renaissance', cosmopolitanism and globality, we will suggest that a much less chauvinistic reading of the former term is possible, a reading that has implications for what we in the present day think 'Europe' and 'European culture' are and how they may be thought of in the future.

Reconfiguring the Renaissance

The conventional view of the European Renaissance – that which sees it as a purely 'European', and more especially Italian, phenomenon, and as a revolution in mentalities and mores with profound effects on later Western history – is itself a product of the nineteenth century. The French historian Jules Michelet, the Swiss historian Jacob Burckhardt, and the English *litterateur* Walter Pater are perhaps the most influential exponents of what became the hegemonic view, described above, of what 'the Renaissance' was, what it involved, and what ramifications it had. Unsurprisingly, revisionist historians of a variety of hues working in the present day have sought to overthrow what they see as an idealisation of the cultural tendencies of the period under scrutiny, an idealisation which they see as expressive more of the nineteenth-century liberal's eulogisation of the individual and their rational capacities than of the concrete socio-cultural conditions of the fifteenth and early sixteenth centuries. Indeed, in many present-day historiographical circles, the very word 'Renaissance' itself has become tabooed, to be replaced by what is felt to be the more analytically neutral term 'early modern'.

Nonetheless, certain contemporary historians have argued for the need to retain the term 'Renaissance', for it captures certain dynamics that are irreducible to a focus on 'early modernity'. Foremost among these are the UK-based scholars Lisa Jardine and Jerry Brotton, whose work, written both individually (Jardine 1997; Brotton 1997; Brotton 2002) and collaboratively (Jardine and Brotton 2000), we will draw significantly upon in this chapter. If it is the case that each epoch reinvents the past in light of its own characteristic interests and obsessions, then this general rule certainly applies in the work of Jardine and Brotton, in that what they offer is a deepening and problematisation of the 'Renaissance', both as a period and as a set of mental and practical endeavours, regarded in light of present day analytic concerns with globalisation, globality and cosmopolitanism. As Jardine (1997: 436) argues, 'the world we inhabit today, with its ruthless competitiveness, fierce consumerism, restless desire for ever wider horizons, for travel, discovery and innovation, a world hemmed in by the small-mindedness of petty nationalism and religious bigotry but refusing to bow to it, is a world which was made in the Renaissance'.

Lest this sound like an uncritically Eurocentric account of world history, based on the claim that the European Renaissance is the source of all subsequent happenings in the world, it is important to note that both Jardine and Brotton reject wholeheartedly the nineteenth-century construct of the Renaissance as solely 'European' in origin and nature; they also dismiss and attempt to transcend the contention that the practices associated with Renaissance culture appeared unexpectedly and *sui generis* in the Italian peninsula, rather than, as they see it, out of the fertile ground of the material–cultural interplay, and corresponding sense of globality, characteristic of the whole of the 'European' and Mediterranean worlds of the time.

This position obviously involves noting that the 'Renaissance' should be seen as a pan-European set of processes, rather than as wholly an Italian 'invention', with different national contexts all playing a part, in their own culturally distinctive manners, in the fostering of new modes of sensibility and activity. Even nineteenth-century historiography, with its particular focus on the Italian roots of Renaissance, acknowledged that by the mid-fifteenth century there was an international 'republic of letters' in and through which scholars such as Erasmus and Thomas More corresponded, argued and developed their ideas, a situation that can be represented as something akin to a free-flowing, Latin language-based ideal speech situation, relatively unhindered by the national barriers to dialogue and communication that would characterise European life in a later age of fully-formed, linguistically autarkic nation-states.

Modern scholarship, however, goes further in stressing the inter- and trans-national characteristics of Renaissance intellectual and artistic production. For a historian such as Kirkpatrick (2002), 'Renaissance' refers to processes and developments that are as much 'Northern' European as 'Southern'. For example, the remarkable outburst of creativity and innovation in polyphonic music composition taking place in Flanders in the 1490s, and the new sensibilities and stylistics embodied in the paintings of Pieter Breughel indicate that if the period is to be seen as characterised by cultural effervescence, then the latter should be seen as happening in some ways as much in more northerly climes than in sunny groves of the south. One might also point to the 'international' aspects of the careers of 'star' artists of the time. The German-born Hans Holbein (1497–1543), for example, who was heavily influenced by the newer Italian styles of composition, worked first in Switzerland and then settled in London and flourished there. As Brotton (2002: 19) argues, he absorbed cultural, political, and intellectual influences that were remarkably global. This made his painting strikingly hybrid, and very different from many of his Italian contemporaries'. From this perspective, it is precisely Holbein's hybrid stylistics and international career that make him a quintessential cultural producer of the – wider, pan-European – Renaissance.

Enter the Ottomans

Although the redefinition of Renaissance as pan-European rather than simply Italian in nature is very important, it does not fully problematise what is meant by 'European', nor does it consider how 'non-European' factors may have played a role in the genesis and operation both of 'Renaissance' and of the very idea of 'Europe' that was developing at that period. One of the most valuable aspects of the researches of Jardine and Brotton is that they are able to mount convincing arguments to the effect that it was the highly symbiotic relationship between 'west' and 'east', that is to say between the Christian states north and west of Turkey and the Ottoman empire, which was productive of the conditions that nineteenth-century historiography conjured away as a purely 'western', indeed narrowly 'Italian', set of phenomena.[1] As Brotton (2002: 53) succinctly puts the point:

> There were no clear geographical or political barriers between east and west in the 15th century. It is a much later, 19th century belief in the absolute cultural and political separation of the Islamic east and Christian west that has obscured the easy exchange of trade, art, and ideas between these two cultures. Europe was very aware that the culture, customs and religion of Islam were very different from its own, and the two sides were often in direct military conflict with each other. However, the point is that the material and commercial exchanges between them were largely unaffected by political hostility: instead, the competitiveness of business transactions and cultural exchanges produced a fertile environment for development on both sides.

From this perspective, what happened in the pan-European Renaissance is empirically, and thus also analytically, inseparable from the wider cultural dynamics characteristic of 'European' and Ottoman relations of the period. Neither political fractiousness nor religious differences between the two entities – and the 'European' bloc was itself highly diverse, both politically, culturally, and after Luther, religiously – prevented dense dynamics of cultural interconnection, self-conscious rivalry and mutual emulation. The importance and influence of the Ottomans in 'European' life and letters of the period was indeed unavoidable, ever since they had captured the capital of the Byzantine empire, Constantinople, in 1453, and thus had come to occupy a pivotal position, both geographically, politically, militarily and economically, in the Eastern part of the Mediterranean world. We can illustrate this situation in various ways.

In the first place, just as it would be wrong to posit a homogeneous 'Europe' in a united manner facing the Ottoman foe, so too would it be a grave mistake to regard the latter as simply an 'Islamic' entity, implacably ranged against the 'West'. On the 'European' side, different 'European' political units moved in and out of treaties with the Ottoman Sultan throughout the later fifteenth and sixteenth centuries. While political entities such as Hungary, which had territories perilously close to the Ottoman-controlled Balkans, were in an almost constant state of war with the Sultan, other 'European' political actors, whose territories were less in the path of apparent Ottoman conquest, were more than happy to operate in terms of peaceful coexistence with the Sultan. This was especially the case with the great trading entities Venice and Genoa, whose mercantile interests were well served by their trading links with the Turks; tellingly, both cities sent envoys to Constantinople to establish friendly trading relations, just months after the fall of the Byzantine capital, the greatest disaster to face Christendom according to clerics but a great opportunity for furthering trade as far as the Venetians and Genoese were concerned.

After the initial shock experienced by 'Christendom' as to the conquest of Constantinople had been absorbed, a succession of Popes found it almost impossible to mount any serious concerted action against the Ottomans to retrieve lost 'Western' territories; this was because at any one time, some European states would be in bellicose relations with the Turks, while others would be pursuing lucrative trading relations with the latter, especially in terms of the trade in spices from the east, a very important part of the whole European economy of the time. While political and religious rhetoric of the period stressed the antagonistic relations between Islam and Christianity, the actual practices at the ground level between these two apparently homogeneous entities are such as seriously to call into question any characterisation of there being a single 'West' facing a monolithic 'East'.[2]

Such empirically existing conditions of widespread European trade with the Ottomans were the ground upon which sprang much of the literary and artistic processes of the period. This can be seen in the fact that just as the 'West' was not a monadic entity, neither was the Ottoman empire culturally homogeneous and hermetically sealed off from the wider world. In the years after the conquest of Constantinople, the Sultan Mehmed II was concerned to erect a capital of his empire worthy of the greatest rulers the earth had seen. What is particularly interesting about the case of Mehmed is that a person whom Christian propaganda of the age characterised as the 'Grand Turk', the most feared and wicked man of the time, was himself a lover of the classical literature of ancient Greece and Rome. While engaged in the siege of Constantinople, he employed various

Italian humanist scholars – *the* quintessential figures of what we can now regard as the clichéd view of the Renaissance formulated in the nineteenth century – to read to him 'from ancient historians such as Laertius, Herodotus, Livy and Quintus Curtius and from chronicles of the popes and the Lombard kings' (Babinger 1978: 112). Mehmed styled himself not on Islamic predecessors but on the Roman emperors he had read about and, above all, on that great stylist of the self and Renaissance idol, Alexander the Great.

In addition, just like other powerful men of the period, such as the Medicis in Italy and, at a later date, the Fugger banking family in Germany, Mehmed coveted copies of classical texts that 'Renaissance' humanist scholars both eulogised for their wisdom and made a point of recovering from dusty monastery libraries. In the great library that Mehmed built up in his new capital were classical works in Greek, Latin, Hebrew and Arabic. Quite apart from the personal interest he had in the contents of such texts, Mehmed like the Medicis, the Fuggers and other power-brokers of the period, regarded a library stuffed full of rare classical texts, carrying within their pages gems of ancient learning, as a powerful symbolic embodiment and notice to the wider world of the refinement and wisdom both of themselves and of their domains. As Jardine (1997) stresses, possession of the right sort of cultural capital – in this case, classical texts so highly regarded in this period – was a crucial part of a prince's armoury of symbolic power and prestige, allowing him to gain 'world-wide' fame as a learned man and patron of scholarship and the arts. This was as much the case in the latter half of the fifteenth century for the Ottoman Sultan as it was for the monarchs of the West, indicating that there was a shared sensibility, ranging from Britain in the north-west to Syria in the south-east, that the comprehension of classical learning was a *sine qua non* of the repertoire of a modern, 'civilised' ruler. In this sense, 'Renaissance' was not just pan-European but in fact a markedly 'Eurasian' phenomenon.[3]

Mehmed's capital was deliberately intended by him as both a cultural powerhouse, whose fame for refinement and learning would be known to the far reaches of *both* Islam and Christendom, and as a central node of international trade networks. Through Istanbul passed a vast array of different wares, moving both from east to west, and vice versa. The more obvious sorts of goods involved included carpets, pottery and silks, and it is noteworthy that in the decorative arts, it was Ottoman – and more broadly, Islamic – styles that were fervently copied by the artisans of the Renaissance West, such styles feeding in various ways into the artistic productions of the period. One of the most striking examples of the powerful Islamic influence on Western visual practices of the time is the city of Venice itself: engaged in dense trading relations with both the Ottomans, and their Islamic rivals, the Egyptian Mamluks, the architects and builders of *La Serenissima* enthusiastically took up both designs and building methods first developed in Egypt and Palestine (Howard 2000; Mack 2002).

Beyond this interplay in visual representations between the Ottomans and their western neighbours, there was also an exchange of armaments (money-making activities overcoming whatever scruples there may have been on either 'side' as to the arming of the apparent religious enemy), tulips (the Ottoman supply of which would come at a later period to be the source of the speculative buying frenzy in Holland) and horses. The trade in equine thoroughbreds was an important network that connected the Ottoman and Western ruling classes, both in that they exchanged horses with each other, and in that the possession of fine specimens by a prince or aristocrat was a potent marker of power, a semiotic situation understood equally throughout east and west (Jardine and Brotton 2000).

Just as both horses and books were the common currency of symbolic display amongst the powerful of both west and east at the time, so too was the hiring of the services of well-known artists. As is very well attested (e.g. Wolff 1981), it is in the later fifteenth century in Italy that the notion of the 'artist' as a unique figure of wholly individualised genius begins first to develop. Conventional historiography stresses the rejection by figures such as Leonardo da Vinci and Michelangelo of the humble role of artisan in favour of a self-representation of self-willed creator, taking this development as one of the cornerstones of the Renaissance revolution in mentalities. What has been subjected to much less comment is that the Ottoman rulers just as much as their counterparts to the west understood the cachet of luring a famous artist to work in their service. In the space encompassing all the lands within the figure formed by drawing lines between London, Moscow, Jerusalem and Cairo, 'cultural exchanges between prominent patrons, facilitated by artistically and intellectually gifted individuals, were the arteries along which Renaissance art and specialist knowledge flowed' (Jardine 1997: 243).

Leonardo, for example, entered into correspondence with Qaitbay, the highly cultivated Mamluk Sultan of Cairo. One of the key artistic and architectural practitioners of what is conventionally taken as the Italian Renaissance, Leon Battista Alberti, was highly popular among Italian rulers for his brand of grandiose imperial architecture, so much so that it rapidly became an 'internationally' recognised style. Eyeing with some envy the designs Alberti had constructed for the palaces of his Italian peers, Mehmed II hired a number of Alberti's pupils, such as de Pasti, Michelozzo and Filarete to work on the new Topkapi palace, a situation that resulted in its mixed Islamic, Italian, Greek and Roman influences. Filarete's international career is attested by his next project, the new Kremlin palace built for the Tsar of Russia. It was not only the Sultan who copied the Italians; the Italians also copied the Sultan. For example, Federico, ruler of the principality of Urbino, tasked his architects to ape the style of the Topkapi palace; and Justus of Ghent, another international artistic 'name' of the time, was hired by Federico to paint representations of such Renaissance heroes as Plato and Aristotle. The style he used to carry out his commission was remarkably 'Ottoman' in nature (Brotton 2002: 148–52). In these various ways, we can see that far from being uniquely 'Italian' or even broadly 'European', cultural production and innovation in the period were marked strongly by east–west, trans-European and cross-Mediterranean currents and flows.

Global sensibilities

Thus far we have reviewed some very good reasons for seeing what conventional historiography has called the 'Renaissance' as in actual fact a set of 'cosmopolitan' practices and outlooks, centred around both pan-European dynamics and a dense network of east–west and Islamic–Christian encounters. Equally well it may be argued that we should see the Renaissance as an epoch in which a strong sense of 'globality' comes to the fore in the affairs of those human beings, both in west and east, who were engaged in the cross-cultural, inter- and trans-national exchanges that we have so far described. What we mean here is that what is conventionally taken as 'Renaissance culture' – the revival of classical learning, and the creation of new modes of subjectivity – should be enlarged to encompass senses, felt by people of the time, that the whole world in which they lived was becoming more and more 'one place', in the sense that all parts of it were connected in increasingly complex ways to all other parts, and that events in one part of the earth could have multiple ramifications in many other parts.

A common misapprehension of much of the contemporary scholarship on 'globalisation' is that such a sensibility is a purely modern phenomenon. In his review of the history of thoughts as to globality, Scholte (2000: 62, 65) argues that while 'global consciousness began to tease secular minds half a millennium ago ... [it] touched few minds [before the nineteenth century] ... Even for that small minority, globality was usually a passing rather than a central thought'. We have shown in various other contexts (e.g. Inglis and Robertson 2005; Robertson and Inglis 2004) how this claim is invalid, in that a strong sense of global connectivity was present first in Hellenistic Greece from the third century BCE onwards, and then in both Republican and Imperial Rome. For example, the Greek orator Aelius Aristides (1953: 896) wrote of Rome about the year 200 CE that it was truly a 'world city' in that 'whatever is grown and made among each people cannot fail to be here at all times and in abundance ... the city appears a kind of giant emporium of the world'.

Our contention is that it was not only 'classical learning' that was 'reawakened' during the Renaissance. What was also brought back more strongly into consciousness than had been the case in the high medieval period was the Hellenistic and Roman sensibility that the world was becoming ever 'smaller' because all of its various parts were becoming more and more regularly connected with each other, a situation brought about not least through trade, often over long distances. Consider, for example, the words of the Venetian cleric Pietro Casola, writing in the 1490s. Notice how his description of trade in and through Venice clearly recalls the words of Aristides written some 1200 years earlier:

> It seems as if all the world flocks here, and that human beings have concentrated there all their force for trading ... who could count the many shops so well furnished they seem almost like warehouses ... so many cloths of every make, carpets of every sort ... silks of every kind ... warehouses full of spices, groceries and drugs...!
>
> (cited in Brotton 2002: 38)

A cliché of conventional views of the Renaissance, in addition to those we have already mentioned, is that it was a period in which the 'discovery' (or rediscovery) of mankind's inner capacities occurs at the same time as more 'outer' discoveries, namely the voyages of Europeans around the globe for the first time and the apprehension, and subsequent conquest, of the Americas. Even the Italo-centric account of Renaissance given by Burckhardt (1995: viii) explicitly formulates the twin 'inner' and 'outer' senses of new horizons encountered at this period as 'the discovery of the world and of man [sic]', presenting each process not just as happening simultaneously but as in some sense – though not clearly adumbrated by Burckhardt – symbiotically connected.

Clearly Burckhardt and all the many others who have followed him in this judgement do have a point. For example, it is not difficult to see the European discovery of hitherto unknown (especially 'American') 'others' as having a profound impact on what it means to have a self. Thus in Michel de Montaigne's famous meditation 'On the Cannibals', one of the major works of Renaissance philosophical anthropology, Montaigne's (1991: 231) reading about the habits of the newly 'discovered' natives of Brazil compels him to conclude that there are no such things as 'barbarians' because 'every man [sic] calls barbarous anything he is not accustomed to'. By coming up against the relativity of customs and mores, through reflection on the forms of life to be encountered in the Americas, Montaigne comes to a conclusion already familiar from Pico: while the self can be a prisoner of tradition and prejudice, it is the imperative of the educated person to fashion a self less parochial and more 'cosmopolitan', one able to appreciate the ways of others, to learn from them and, in so doing, to fashion one's own self anew.

However, there is more to Renaissance globality than just this dimension, as important as it is. One of the great services both Jardine and Brotton have provided to contemporary scholarship is their conjoining of two, hitherto largely separated, modes of historiographical endeavour, namely Renaissance studies and the history of cartography. By emphasising the mercantile dynamics of the period, and locating Renaissance aesthetics and thought-processes within them, they have opened up the possibility of examining two closely interrelated phenomena. First, how maps and globes – which were literally depictions of the 'world as a whole' – were caught up in relations of trade and inter-state economic rivalries. Cartographic implements were seen by Europeans of the time to be the keys to the control and colonisation of newly accessible areas, both to the east (especially in terms of controlling the far eastern spice trade) and the west (especially in terms of controlling the slave trade in the Americas). New maps and globes were commissioned by rulers, and kept in the most secret conditions, lest they be stolen by spies from enemy powers seeking economically vital information. Particularly in the rivalry between Spain and Portugal to control the spice trade, maps and globes were crucial tools of power, which could be used to justify which state had control over which parts of the world.

Second, and following on from this, Jardine and Brotton also allow us to see how cartographic implements both expressed, and were instrumental in creating, forms of global consciousness. These sensibilities were truly 'global' in nature, in that maps and globes depicted the 'whole world'. But they also helped shape the modern sense of 'Europe', in that what was identified as a particular tranche of land with the name 'Europe' was located in a particular part of the globe, and given a precise earthly location. This not only helped solidify European senses of self-consciousness, modes of self-awareness that ran alongside and fed into the 'discovery' of self described by Pico. It also gave Europeans *and* Ottomans (for the latter were also engaged in similar map-making enterprises) of all vocations – not just rulers, but also merchants, sailors, shop-keepers and others especially involved in trade – a strong feeling of the wholeness and connectedness of the entire planet, and of the place of the individual self within it. This was both a rediscovery of antique forms of globality first felt by the Hellenistic Greeks and Romans, and also a new departure, as for the first time, the whole globe, rather than just the Eurasian part of it alone, was now truly graspable in the imaginations of many people, and not just elites.

Conclusion

In this chapter, we have pulled apart some of the common historiographical misconceptions that have, from the nineteenth century onwards, been attendant upon the understanding of the 'European Renaissance'. We did this for the purposes of dealing with the problem that, if a cosmopolitan selfhood directed towards the appreciation of cultural otherness is to a significant degree a function of Renaissance innovations vis-à-vis self-development, and if the latter is itself exclusively a 'European' phenomenon, then it follows that cosmopolitan dispositions will paradoxically be strongly culturally chauvinist, in that it is thought that only European self-hood has the self-fashioning capacities that allow cosmopolitan dispositions.

In order to deal with this problem we turned to empirical historiography, especially that of a revisionist bent, to consider how the senses of self developed during what is conventionally called the Renaissance are not simply 'European' in nature at all. We saw in the first instance how 'Renaissance' is certainly not simply an 'Italian' phenomenon but must be conceived of, at the least, as a pan-European movement. We then turned to see how, following the important arguments of Brotton and Jardine, one may discern the markedly 'Eurasian' aspects of Renaissance, in that the latter involved cultural interplay and connection between the Christian 'west' and the Ottoman 'east'. This mode of analysis in itself suggests that what have been taken to be quintessentially 'European' phenomena are actually the products of 'east'/'west' encounters and interactions. At the very least, we believe that one is compelled to admit that 'Renaissance self-fashioning' is not *sui generis* and indigenous to an entity called 'Europe'. Rather, it arose out of the 'European' engagement with the Ottoman and Islamic 'east', and to that extent is not a simple indigenous and endogenous outgrowth of an undifferentiated entity called 'Western culture'. Indeed, the latter became part of 'Westerners' self-consciousness to a large degree through the 'western' encounter with the 'east'. More radically, one might go so far as to claim that the Renaissance of the fifteenth and early sixteenth centuries, especially the self-fashioning that apparently is a primary constituent part of it, is a simultaneously 'western' and 'eastern', 'Christian' and 'Islamic', 'European' and 'Ottoman' phenomenon, born of both 'sides' in the encounter, but irreducible to either. If that is the case, the so-called 'European Renaissance' is in fact best described as part of an entity we may call 'Eurasian culture': it is a product of the permeable cultural boundaries that exist in ages and areas of engagement, encroachment and rapprochement between units that see themselves as different, yet which, often unintentionally, create commonalities between themselves as they both emulate and differentiate themselves from each other. We may also add, given our examination of the nature of senses of globality and self in the period under consideration, that a sense of one's place in a much wider and truly earth-spanning arena was part of the warp and woof of life for many people in the period we conventionally call the European Renaissance. It is not, we think, too much to claim that one of the most profound 'inventions' of the period is not just a self that can interrogate its own evolving tendencies, but also a self whose tendencies were integrally connected to global consciousness and cosmopolitan forms of thought and practice. Self-fashioning, in other words, is very closely connected to awareness of a much wider world around one, and the diversity of different cultural modes that co-exist within it. If we recall both that fact and the potentially 'Eurasian' provenance of Renaissance self-fashioning, we may see that cosmopolitical dispositions cannot simply be regarded as the sole birthright of present-day Westerners.

Notes

1 There are strong parallels here with Bernal's (1987) 'Black Athena' thesis, in which the author alleges that in their eulogisations of the apparently purely 'Western' nature of the beginnings of 'Western civilisation', classical scholars of the nineteenth century systematically purged ancient Greece of its empirically existing 'Afroasiatic' cultural characteristics.
2 For an analogous argument, this time in the context of the British Empire in India, see Jasanoff (2005).
3 We are using the appellation 'Eurasian' to describe interactions between the 'European'/Christian and Ottoman/Islamic worlds as much for rhetorical and polemical reasons as for analytic ones. The dynamics we are talking about did not directly involve the 'eastern' part of the Eurasian landmass, that is all those parts to the east and north-east of the Ottoman empire (Robertson 1990). 'Eurasian' therefore in the present context does not refer to the entirety of the geographical expanse of Eurasia, nor does it refer to what Kroeber (1945) calls 'Eurasian culture', the set of practices and values that can be argued to be common to most, or all, of the cultural units existing in the expanse between Ireland to the west and Japan to the east. Rather, 'Eurasian' here refers to a particular set of cultural interchanges, between 'Europe' and Ottoman Islam in the period under consideration, which occurred in a particular geographical context (particularly, the Eastern Mediterranean and the Levant) that can be seen as, in some senses, at the very centre of the geo-cultural formation that is Kroeber's 'Eurasian culture'. What we call the 'Eurasian Renaissance' of the fifteenth and sixteenth centuries CE can in fact be seen as but one element within the chronologically and geographically wider processes of cultural movement and diffusion that Kroeber sees as characteristic of cultural dynamics within Eurasia 'as a whole' over a very long sweep of human history.

References

Aristides, A. (1953) 'Roman Oration', in James H. Oliver 'The Ruling Power: A Study of the Roman Empire in the Second Century after Christ through the Roman Oration of Aelius Aristides', *Transactions of the American Philosophical Society*, New Series, Vol. 43, Part I: 873–999.
Babinger, F. (1978) *Mehmed the Conqueror and His Times*, Princeton: Princeton University Press.
Bernal, M. (1987) *Black Athena: The Afroasiatic Roots of Classical Civilization*, London: Free Association Books.
Brotton, J. (1997) *Trading Territories: Mapping the Early Modern World*, London: Reaktion Books.
Brotton, J. (2002) *The Renaissance Bazaar*, Oxford: Oxford University Press.
Burckhardt, J. (1995) *The Civilization of the Renaissance in Italy*, London: Phaidon.
de Montaigne, M. (1991) 'On the Cannibals', in *The Complete Essays*, M. A. Screech (ed. and trans.), Harmondsworth: Penguin, pp. 228–41.
Goody, J. (1996) *The East in the West*, Cambridge: Cambridge University Press.

Greenblatt, S. (1980) *Renaissance Self-Fashioning*, Chicago: Chicago University Press.

Howard, D. (2000) *Venice and the East*, New Haven: Yale University Press.

Inglis, D. and R. Robertson (2005) 'The Ecumenical Analytic: "Globalization", Reflexivity and the Revolution in Greek Historiography', *European Journal of Social Theory*, 8(2): 99–122.

Jardine, L. (1997) *Worldly Goods: A New History of the Renaissance*, Basingstoke: Macmillan/Papermac.

Jardine, L. and J. Brotton (2000) *Global Interests: Renaissance Art Between East and West*, London: Reaktion Books.

Jasanoff, M. (2005) *Edge of Empire: Conquest and Collecting on the Eastern Frontiers of the British Empire*, London: Fourth Estate.

Kirkpatrick, R. (2002) *The European Renaissance, 1400–1600*, Harlow: Longman.

Kroeber, A. (1945) 'The Ancient Oikoumene as an Historic Culture Aggregate', *The Journal of the Royal Anthropological Institute of Great Britain and Ireland*, 75(1/2): 9–20.

Mack, R. E. (2002) *Bazaar to Piazza: Islamic Trade and Italian Art, 1300–1600*, Berkeley: University of California Press.

della Mirandola, P. (1998) *On the Dignity of Man*, New York: Hackett.

Pater, W. (1980 [1893]) *The Renaissance: Studies in Art and Poetry*, Berkeley: University of California Press.

Robertson, R. (1990) 'Japan and the USA: The Interpretation of National Identities and the Debate about Orientalism', in N. Abercrombie, S. Hill and B. S. Turner (eds) *Dominant Ideologies*, London: Unwin Hyman, pp. 182–98.

Robertson, R. (2001) 'Globality', in N. J. Smelser and P. B. Baltes (eds) *International Encyclopaedia of the Social and Behavioural Sciences*, 9, Oxford: Elsevier/Pergamon Press, pp. 6254–8.

Robertson, R. and D. Inglis (2004) 'The Global Animus: In the Tracks of World-consciousness', *Globalizations*, 1(1): 38–49.

Scholte, J. A. (2000) *Globalization: A Critical Introduction*, Basingstoke: Palgrave.

Wolff, J. (1981) *The Social Production of Art*, Basingstoke: Macmillan.

7 Revealing the cosmopolitan side of Oriental Europe

The eastern origins of European civilisation

John M. Hobson

> Rather than the manufactured clash of civilisations we need to concentrate on the slow working together of cultures that overlap, borrow from each other, and live together.... But for [this] kind of wider perception we need time and patient and sceptical enquiry supported by faith in communities of interpretation that are difficult to sustain in a world demanding instant action and reaction.
>
> (Said 2003 [1978]: xxii)

It was with these cosmopolitan words that Edward Said closed the 2003 preface to the reprint of *Orientalism*. And it is these poignant words that provide my point of departure. Nevertheless an obvious paradox or seeming contradiction immediately confronts us here. For as Said's argument has been received, the possibility of cosmopolitan interaction between the West and East becomes seemingly impossible given that the former's identity has been defined negatively against the latter through the construction of orientalism. Moreover, it is clear that most of us naturally think that European history has long been defined by recurring confrontations or clashes with the East. In our popular imagination these began with the Crusades between 1095 and 1291, progressed forwards through the Voyages of Discovery after 1492/1498 before culminating in the age of European colonialism down to the 1970s. But focusing mainly, let alone solely, on this side of Europe's identity or history obscures the cosmopolitan side that has played an extremely important role in the development of Europe after the eighth century.

To pursue this further it helps to disaggregate two core aspects of Europe's cosmopolitanism. First, while medieval European perceptions of the Eastern peoples were often characterised by bizarre images (e.g. the Sciopods, Blemmyae and Anthropophagi), nevertheless the Europeans were cognisant of, and sometimes awestruck by, the richness if not the economic and cultural superiority of many Eastern societies between about 800 and 1780. This was certainly true of Egypt and China, both of which Europeans long held as 'positive examples of higher and finer civilisations.

Both were seen to have had massive material achievements, profound philosophies and superior writing systems' (Bernal 1991: 172). And paradoxically, even during the Age of Crusades the Europeans found much to admire and envy in the civilisation of Islamic West Asia.

The second aspect of cosmopolitanism flows on from the first: that respect for other civilisations was crucial in leading the Europeans to emulate and borrow the superior aspects of their economies and cultures in order to promote Europe's own development. And here we return to one of the paradoxes that emerges from viewing European identity only within racially or religiously antagonistic terms. For as we shall see below, at the very time when the Europeans were engaged in military confrontation with Islam, they not only continued trading with the Muslims but were avidly borrowing a wealth of Islamic ideas, technologies and institutions that propelled Europe forward. Notable too is that at the very time when Dante was consigning Muhammad to the eighth circle of Hell in his book *Inferno*, he was simultaneously borrowing many of his ideas from Islamic philosophers (which was why he consigned them to Purgatory rather than Hell in his book). In other words, focusing only on the European clash with Islam serves to obscure the many peaceful and beneficial interactions that have occurred between the two.

Thus while I do not seek to dismiss the existence of Europe's clashes with various civilisations, nevertheless to a certain extent I call for a deconstruction of the manufactured idea of the 'clash of civilisations'. For this enables us to reveal the many forms of beneficial, if not harmonious, cosmopolitan inter-civilisational interactions that Europe has for so long participated in but which have been obscured by the headline idea of the 'clash of civilisations'. And paradoxically it is this alternative emphasis on cosmopolitanism that, I think, Said has in mind when he penned those words in his 2003 preface.

The chapter's argument is also situated within an anti-Eurocentric problematique. The major theories of the rise of Europe suffer from a Eurocentric bias (Blaut 1993; Frank 1998: ch. 1; Hobson 2004: ch. 1), which has served to obscure Europe's cosmopolitan inter-civilisational relations. Eurocentrism or Orientalism emerged fully in the nineteenth century. As Said originally pointed out, it was this discourse that suddenly pronounced the superiority of Europe over the inferior East (Said 2003 [1978]). This entailed two critical assumptions: first, that what had previously been thought of as interlinked, if not symbiotic, regions were suddenly relocated along either side of a constructed 'civilisational line of apartheid'. And second, Europe was pronounced as qualitatively superior to the East because it allegedly had uniquely progressive and exceptional characteristics, while the East supposedly had only regressive properties.

The key point is that this Orientalist discourse was at its height precisely at the time when the major theories of the rise of Europe were constructed – most notably those of Marx and Weber. Thus having endogenised Eurocentrism, these theorists – as do their successors – explain Europe's rise by looking only to causal variables that exist squarely within Europe. This was thought to be appropriate given that they accepted uncritically the twin Eurocentric notions of Europe's separation from the East on the one hand and Europe's uniqueness/exceptionalism on the other. And for these theorists, it was this that ensured the inevitability of Europe's breakthrough to modern capitalism and its impossibility in the East. In sum, Eurocentric scholars assume that the rise of capitalist modernity was pioneered solely by the Europeans without any help from the Easterners.

But the problem with the prevailing Eurocentric meta-narrative is that it obscures the considerable role that Eastern influences have played in the rise of Europe. Deconstructing the 'civilisational line of apartheid' that was constructed by Eurocentric thinkers so as to separate out the superior West from the inferior East, necessarily reveals the many ways in which the two have been promiscuously entwined. In short, deconstructing Eurocentrism as well as the idea of the clash of civilisations enables us to reveal the European West as a *hybrid* entity that has been shaped by the East; hence my preference for the label of the 'Oriental West' or 'Oriental Europe'. For it is this notion of hybridity that connotes Europe's cosmopolitan origins.

The chapter proceeds in four stages. The first part provides the groundwork by reconsidering the definition of Europe in order to reveal its fluid and malleable nature, while the second part provides the link to the third and final parts. It provides a sketch of oriental globalisation and the Eastern-led global economy that emerged after the sixth century. I then reveal the Eastern ideational influences (part three) and Eastern technologies (part four) that diffused across the Eastern-led global economy to enable the subsequent rise of Europe.

Redefining Europe as an inclusive and malleable moral idea

It is necessary to begin by noting that Europe has never been defined by rigid geographical boundaries that definitively demarcate it from the 'non-European' world. Rather it has always been a moral idea and its geographical boundaries have waxed and waned in response to the shifting idea of what constitutes Europe at a particular point in time (Hay 1957; Delanty 1995). Yet more importantly, the dominant idea of what constitutes a 'pure Europe' obscures the many 'non-European' influences that have resided within it and which have, no less, given much impetus to defining Europe. In the interests of space I shall deal briefly with two major issues to illustrate the point at stake.

The first issue concerns the Greek heritage of Europe. Today we take it as axiomatic that Greece was the birthplace of Europe. For it was there where science and rational thinking were allegedly first established, only to be reclaimed after the Dark Age interlude during the so-called Italian

Renaissance. But this notion of Greece is a fabrication – an idea that was constructed by European thinkers only as late as the end of the eighteenth century (Bernal 1991). Prior to then, the dominant view of a pure European Greece did not exist – and it was certainly one that the Ancient Greeks did not share. They viewed Greece as fixed firmly within the 'Hellenic Occident'. Indeed 'Greece was linked spiritually and culturally to the East; and ... the attempt to turn away from, or to deny, this eastern heritage has always implied for Greece a cheapening and coarsening of spiritual and cultural values' (Campbell and Sherrard 1965: 71). That Europe has always been an idea as opposed to a geographical reality is reflected by the fact that 'Europa' herself was in Greek mythology the daughter of Agenor, King of Tyre, situated on the coast of Lebanon. And note too that Troy was in fact *east* of the Dardanelles. Moreover, that Ancient Greece owes so much to Ancient Egypt (as the Greeks readily acknowledged), wreaks havoc with the notion of a pure Aryan lineage of Europe that is cherished by Eurocentric thinkers (Bernal 1991). In short, tracing the European heritage back to Ancient Greek should be to acknowledge the significant Eastern roots of Europe.

Second, if a 'pure European Greece' was not the birthplace of a 'pure Europe', so the notion of Europe-as-Christendom was equally a fabrication that obscures its West Asian foundations. Of course, Christianity was an oriental religion, and one that shared many things in common with Islam. But more importantly, the definition of Europe-as-Christendom obscures the many Islamic impulses that came to provide such a profound and positive influence on the subsequent shape and course of European development and thinking. By 711 CE Islam had entered Spain and was consolidated in 756 when Abd al-Rahman set up the Ummayad polity. Islam also took root in Portugal and later in Sicily in 902 and, yet later on, in Eastern Europe via the Ottoman Empire. These formed the final ramparts of the Islamic *Bridge of the World*, across which flowed not just Eastern trade but, above all, many Eastern 'resource portfolios' (ideas, institutions and technologies) that were assimilated by the Europeans. And to return to the paradox mentioned above, it was precisely during the time of the Crusades that Europe's assimilation of Islamic ideas escalated. Moreover, behind the headlines of the 'Crusading clash with Islam' lay a less dramatic picture wherein Christians and Muslims as well as Jews peacefully co-existed for many centuries in cosmopolitan Islamic Spain (Menocal 2002) and elsewhere in Europe. And it was principally from these sites whence many Jewish and especially Islamic ideas seeped out to redefine the very idea of Europe (see also Goody 2004).

To sum up then, it is apparent from these two examples alone that the Eurocentric idea of an exclusive or pristine Europe is a fabrication that obscures the many Eastern impulses and influences that in large part helped shape and redefine the very identity of Europe over time. And even if Europe was not linked into a wider Afro-Asian world lying outside of

Europe, the claim that it has been a hybrid entity would still hold. But the fact that Europe was fundamentally embedded within a wider Afro-Asian-led global economy, through which many Eastern resource portfolios diffused across, consolidates or clinches the notion of a hybrid 'Oriental Europe'.

Oriental globalisation: Europe's dependence upon the Eastern-led global economy, *c.*500–1800

My aim here is to provide a very quick sketch of the Afro-Asian-led global economy between 500 and 1800 for three principal reasons. First it reveals the considerable inter-connectedness of Europe with Afro-Asia; second it reveals some of the channels or diffusion paths along which the more advanced Eastern resource portfolios traversed to fuel the rise of Europe; and third it reveals Europe's dependence upon the more advanced Eastern global agents, which reinforces the claim of the next two sections – that the rise of Europe owes a massive debt to the Easterners.

But to contextualise the immediate discussion it bears noting at the outset that Eurocentric analyses of globalisation deny its existence prior to 1500 (if not before 1850), thereby undermining the basis for my own alternative analysis. This date is highly significant because it connotes in traditional historiography the point at which Europe emerged in capitalist form at the top of the world's economic hierarchy. This in turn justifies the claim that the period between 1492 and 1800 constituted one of Western-led proto-globalisation, as the superior Europeans expanded outwards into the world. For in the process they supposedly 'battered down the walls' that had hitherto isolated the regressive East from the progressive West, thereby creating for the first time the outlines of an emergent world-economy. This was supposedly initiated through the so-called Voyages of Discovery. But as will become apparent shortly, these might better be labelled the Voyages of Rediscovery, given that the Europeans were *directly* entering an established inter-linked Afro-Eurasian economy that had been forged by Eastern capitalists since the sixth century.

Particularly important to the emergence of the global economy after the sixth century was the formation of a series of inter-linked regions or empires. These comprised T'ang China (618–907), the Islamic Ummayad/Abbasid empire in West Asia (661–1258), the Ummayad polity in Spain (756–1031) and the Fatimids in North Africa (909–1171). Moreover the kingdom of Śrīvijaya in Sumatra was important in that it constituted the vital entrepôt that connected China to the Indian Ocean between the seventh and thirteenth centuries. These inter-linked regions were vital in promoting an extensively pacified space that fostered considerable trade and enabled the transmission of Eastern resource portfolios.

While a number of capitalist agents were important here – including Africans, Jews, Indians, Chinese and Javanese – the prime role in setting up the global economy was performed by the West Asian Muslims. The global economy comprised three prime routes, though the two most important ones were the Middle and Southern routes (Abu-Lughod 1989). The Middle route had a land component which linked the Eastern Mediterranean with China and India, and a sea route that passed through the Persian Gulf. The Southern route linked the Alexandria–Cairo–Red Sea complex with the Arabian Sea and then, as with the Middle sea route, the Indian Ocean and beyond to Southeast Asia, China and Japan. These routes ensured that Europe was fundamentally connected to the Afro-Asian-led global economy after about the eighth century. And *contra* Eurocentrism, this situation continued throughout the period between 1000 and 1800 when the various leading European powers were at their height.

With the 'Fall of Acre' in 1291, the Venetians came to rely on the dominant Southern route which was presided over by the Egyptians. As Abu-Lughod claims, 'Whoever controlled the sea-route to Asia could set the terms of trade for a Europe now in retreat. From the thirteenth century and up to the sixteenth that power was Egypt' (Abu-Lughod 1989: 149). Moreover, Venetian trade did not dry up after 1291 but continued on, especially given that the Venetians managed to circumvent the Papal ban and secured new treaties with the Sultan in 1355 and 1361. And right down to 1517, Venice survived because Egypt played such an important role within the global economy. Moreover, after 1517 Venice continued its trading connection through the Ottomans.

Nevertheless, Eurocentrism claims that after 1492/1498 the Portuguese and Spanish initiated the process of proto-globalisation, before the global batten of power was passed on to the Dutch and then the English. But in fact European trading connections intensified thanks largely to the role played by the Muslims and Indians but, above all, the Chinese who sat at or near the centre of the global economy between *c*.1450 and 1800. And for a whole variety of reasons, the paradox here was that the official 1434 Chinese ban on foreign trade came just before Chinese trade escalated (see Hobson 2004: ch. 3). The conversion of the Chinese economy onto a silver standard in the mid-fifteenth century was the seminal moment. For as a result of the huge demand that the Chinese economy had for foreign silver owing to its large trade surplus, global trade rapidly intensified (Flynn and Giraldez 1994; Frank 1998).

Simultaneously it led to the opening up of a new trade route that went from South America across to The Philippines and thence into China via the Spanish Manila galleon. Above all, it was this Chinese input that ultimately sucked Europe *directly* into the trading and financial global system (rather than vice versa as Eurocentrism preaches), given that the Europeans had been only indirectly linked in previously. For it was the plundered Spanish bullion that not only enabled the Europeans to finance their trade deficit with Asia in general and China in particular, but also to finance their activities within the Indian Ocean in the first place.

To sum up, then, the arrival of the Europeans in the Indian Ocean in 1498 did not mark a key turning point in world history. For all they were really doing was *directly* joining the global economy that had been created during the previous 1,000 years and which remained dominated by the Afro-Asians right down into the nineteenth century (Hobson 2004: chs. 2–4, 7; Frank 1998). It is clear, then, that from the eighth century onward Europe was embedded within a gradually intensifying Eastern-led global economy. Moreover, while oriental globalisation began during Europe's 'Dark Age', its ultimate significance lay in the fact that it was the midwife, if not the mother, of modern Europe. For it was along the sinews of the Eastern-led global economy that Eastern resource portfolios diffused across to enable European development, as we shall now see.

Oriental globalisation and the transmission and assimilation of the Eastern idea in the rise of Europe

The Oriental Renaissance and Scientific Revolution

Italy is famous for the Renaissance, which in turn set Europe off into the post-feudal era. This intellectual revolution is traditionally thought to have been in effect a recalling of the scientific and rational ideas that had been pioneered by the Ancient Greeks (hence the importance of fabricating Greece as purely European). The immediate problem here – as was noted earlier – is that many of the ideas that were 'invented' in Greece were actually derived from Ancient Egypt (Bernal 1991). But perhaps more important is the point that the Renaissance owes a huge debt to the contemporary Muslims, as did the Scientific Revolution (Hobson 2004: ch. 8; Goody 2004).

This claim, of course, immediately stands at odds with the traditional interpretation, not least because the Renaissance thinkers themselves were in part anxious to forge a new European identity that was independent of the Islamic world. Indeed 'the return to the classical [Greek] world was seen as the answer to the [perceived] threat from Islam to European culture' (Goody 2004: 48). And so we come to the paradox of the Renaissance: that it was in part created to differentiate Europe from Islam and yet it was from Islam that the Renaissance scholars drew so many of their new ideas. How then did Islamic thinkers help shape the Renaissance and the subsequent Scientific Revolution?

Islamic breakthroughs in mathematics including algebra and trigonometry were vital. The former term was taken from the title of one of al-Khwārizmī's mathematical texts (as a result of the translation made by the Englishman, Robert of Ketton, in 1145). And by the beginning of the tenth century all six of the classical trigonometric functions had been defined and tabulated by Muslim mathematicians. Developments in public health, hygiene and medicine were also notable. Al-Rāzī's medical works were translated and reprinted in Europe some forty times between 1498 and 1866. And Ibn Sīnā's *Canon of Medicine* became the founding text for European medical schools between the twelfth and fifteenth centuries (having been translated in the twelfth century). The Muslims developed numerous medicines and anaesthetics and pioneered the study of anatomy. Notable here is that the Egyptian physician, Ibn al-Nafis (d. 1288), whose work on the human body which contradicted the traditional position of the Greek physician, Galen, fully pre-empted the much heralded work of William Harvey by 350 years. The Muslims were also keen astrologers and astronomers and their ideas were avidly borrowed by the Europeans. Ibn al-Shātir's mathematical models bore an uncanny resemblance to those used by Copernicus 150 years later. And as early as the ninth century, al-Khwārizmī calculated the circumference of the Earth to within 41 metres. Last but by no means least, the Baconian idea that science should be based on the experimental method had already been pioneered by the Muslims (not the Greeks).

Nevertheless, the standard Eurocentric reply here asserts that all these ideas were in fact derived from Ancient Greece (given that the Muslims had held and translated much of their work). It is certainly true that the Muslims had learnt much from the Ancient Greeks. But they were not mere 'librarians' who held the original Greek texts in custody before passing them back once the Europeans were ready to receive them. For the fact is that they not only built on the original 'Greek ideas' and took them much further, but at times they were highly critical of them and provided novel departures (the insistence on the experimental method being a case in point). Moreover, to answer the possible Eurocentric retort that this could all have been mere coincidence, it is necessary to reveal the transmission paths of these ideas.

Increasingly, after about 900, Europeans began translating Islamic texts into Latin (as mentioned above). Islamic scholarship developed not only in West Asia but also in Spain, where it was proactively encouraged by the second Ummayad Caliph (al-Hakkam II, 961–976). The fall of Spanish Toledo was especially important for it was from its vast library where the Europeans managed to get hold of many of the relevant books to translate. Learning from Islam was actively continued by the Spanish King, Alfonso X (1252–1284), though largely through Jewish intermediaries. Much the same was true of the situation in Portugal. Moreover, Ancient Egyptian Hermetic texts also featured in the Italian Renaissance, given that they were translated after 1460 by Marsilio Ficino at the Court of Cosimo de Medici. Islamic ideas also entered Europe via the Ottoman Empire which was heavily embroiled in Eastern Europe, especially in the Balkans. Finally, Islamic ideas entered Venice through the trade route from West Asia and North Africa as well as from Islamic Sicily after 902. Notable here was the profound Arabic influence on the School of Salerno after 1050.

The Oriental Enlightenment

As most agree, the Enlightenment was a crucial defining moment in the remaking of Europe after about 1700. But to see this once more as a purely European creation is to obscure the considerable debt that was owed to the Chinese. Indeed it was more than mere coincidence that the year 1700 also constituted the 'year of transition in which the affections of the learned [European] world were turned towards China' (Reichwein 1967: 78). Indeed between 1700 and *c.*1780, much of Europe formed a virtual love affair with the world of rococo and sought to emulate many aspects of Chinese civilisation. This was considerably helped by the wealth of translated Chinese pamphlets and books that flooded Europe after about 1650, some of which were transmitted by the Jesuits.

The link between the European Enlightenment and Chinese thought was ultimately bridged by the shared faith in reason as the centre of all things. Reason enabled the discovery of the autonomous 'laws of motion' that were allegedly inscribed within all areas of social, political and 'natural' life. In 1687, a book on Confucius was translated (*Confucius Sinarum Philosophus*) and in the Preface the author asserts that:

> One might say that the moral system of this philosopher is infinitely sublime, but that it is at the same time simple, sensible and drawn from the purest sources of natural reason. . . . Never has Reason, deprived of divine Revelation, appeared so well developed nor with so much power.
>
> (cited in Rowbotham 1945: 227)

Indeed this book in particular had a major impact in Europe and was received by Europeans with astonishment. While many Enlightenment thinkers positively associated with China and its ideas, Voltaire was undoubtedly the major Sinophile. He drew on Chinese conceptions of politics, religion and philosophy – all of which were based on rational principles – in order to attack the European preference for hereditary aristocracy. Indeed, many of the major Enlightenment thinkers derived their preference for the 'rational method' from China. Chinese ideas also played a very important part in influencing British culture. Indeed Britons developed a strong taste for Chinoiserie, ranging from tea drinking to wallpaper to Anglo-Chinese gardens, as well as to ideas about political economy.

In the Anglo-Saxon canon *the* central European political economist was the Scotsman, Adam Smith. But while Anglo-Saxons parochially think of Smith as the first political economist, the fact is that behind Smith lay François Quesnay, the French 'Physiocrat'. And crucially, behind Quesnay lay China (Maverick 1946). Indeed:

Quesnay's revolutionary ideas amounted to a liberation from the economic orthodoxy of ... mercantilism ... and his influence on the free-
market theories of Adam Smith was profound. What is often omitted
in accounts of Quesnay's place in modern thought is his debt to China
– unlike in his own day when he was widely known as 'the European
Confucius.

(Clarke 1997: 49)

Quesnay, not Smith, was the first European to critique the ideas of mercantilism. The term 'physiocracy' means the 'rule of nature'. The significance of his ideas, derived from China, was at least twofold: first, he saw in
agriculture a crucial source of wealth (which became an important idea
that lay behind the British Agricultural Revolution). Second, and more
importantly, he believed that agriculture could only be fully exploited
when producers were freed from the arbitrary interventions of the state.
Only then could the 'natural laws' of the market prevail (as the Chinese
had long realised). Quesnay's debt to Chinese conceptions of political
economy was found in many ideas, the most important being that of *wu-
wei* – which is translated into French as *laissez-faire*. Indeed around 300 CE
Kuo Hsiang described *wu-wei* as that which lets 'everything be allowed to
do what it naturally does, so that its nature will be satisfied'. And once this
had entered the mind of Adam Smith, as they say, 'the rest was history'.
None of this is to say that the European Enlightenment was the *pure*
product of Chinese ideas, for clearly there were some Enlightenment
thinkers who rejected China as a model for Europe – most notably Montesquieu and Fénelon; but it would be entirely remiss to ignore the Chinese
input.

Oriental globalisation and the transmission and assimilation of Eastern technologies in the rise of Europe

In the interests of space I shall omit discussion of the many Eastern technologies that diffused into Europe after about 800, all of which were
crucial in enabling an energy revolution as well as the rise of agricultural
production, commerce, proto-manufacturing and finance (Hobson 2004:
chs 5–6). Instead I shall concentrate on those technologies that diffused
across to enable some of the most vital turning points: the Voyages of
Rediscovery, the military revolution and the British industrial revolution. I
shall take each in turn.

Before the Voyages of Rediscovery could begin, numerous challenges to
extant European shipping design and navigational techniques that oceanic
sailing entailed had to be solved. But it was to the Easterners – especially
the Muslims (often via the Jews) as well as the Chinese – that the Iberians
turned (Seed 1995: 107–28; Hobson 2004: chs 6–7). The first challenge
was the need to tack into the strong head-winds that blew up south of

Cape Bojador. This was solved in the 1440s by the construction of *caravels* that had a stern-post rudder attached to a square hull, and were rigged with three masts, one of which bore a lateen sail. But the origins of the caravel date back to the Islamic *qārib*. The square hull and stern-post rudder were invented by the Chinese around 400 CE with the design subsequently diffusing westward to enter Europe around 1180. The new triple mast system was almost certainly borrowed from the Chinese who had long had multiple-mast systems. And the lateen sail was almost certainly an Islamic invention that was also passed on to the Europeans.

The critical navigational techniques were borrowed mainly from the Muslims. Because the lateen sail led to a zigzagging (or triangular) sailing path, this necessarily made it much harder to calculate the linear distance travelled. This was solved by the use of geometry and trigonometry, which had been developed by, and was borrowed from, the Muslim mathematicians (as noted above). Moreover the strong tides south of Cape Bojador that could beach a ship or simply destroy it required knowledge of the lunar cycles (since the moon governs the tides). This had been supplied at the end of the fourteenth century by the Jewish cartographer resident in Portugal – Jacob ben Abraham Cresques. Oceanic sailing also required a wealth of more accurate navigational charts and techniques. Here Islamic astronomy enabled the Europeans to calculate the size of the earth and thereby calculate the distance travelled by using degrees. Moreover, longitude and latitude tables as well as solar calendars were also supplied by the Muslims (as well as the Jews). Finally the importation of the astrolabe was especially important. And though sporadic mentions are made of this technology in a few Ancient Greek texts, it was certainly the Muslim astronomers who perfected it before it was transmitted into Europe via Islamic Spain in the mid-tenth century.

The only problem with the concept of the European military revolution (1550–1660) is its adjective. For all the major technologies that formed the core of this revolution were in fact invented during the world's first modern military revolution (850–1290) that occurred in China. These comprised the Chinese invention of gunpowder (850), the metal barrelled gun firing a metal bullet (1275) and the cannon (1288).

Conventionally it is thought that the first cannon was invented in England (1327), as revealed in picture form in the famous manuscript by Walter de Millemete. But this picture is an exact replica of the earlier Chinese cannon (Pacey 1991: 47). It might be replied that this could have been an entirely coincidental event. But the giveaway here is that claims for an independent European invention are rendered problematic by the fact that no military expert has ever been able to produce any evidence for the necessary military developments that must have preceded the 1327 English cannon. For such an invention presupposes a long line of prior developments. But such a lineage is readily available in the Chinese context stemming back to *c*.850. Moreover, strong circumstantial evidence exists to suggest that the cannon, as well as the gun and the recipe for gunpowder, diffused across to Europe where they were subsequently assimilated (Needham *et al.* 1986).

Finally, the familiar claim that the first industrial revolution occurred in eighteenth-century Britain obscures the much earlier industrial miracle of eleventh-century Sung China. Moreover, the claim that the British industrial revolution was allegedly the pinnacle of British ingenuity obscures the fact that it was the earlier pioneering Chinese inventions that were avidly borrowed by the British to promote their 'own' revolution (see Hobson 2004: ch. 9). Thus while Eurocentrism celebrates James Watt for his pioneering skills in inventing the steam engine, the fact is that he owed much to the Chinese. The essentials of the steam engine go back to Wang Chên's *Treatise on Agriculture* (1313), which in turn go back to the Chinese invention of the water-powered bellows (31 CE). Moreover, Chinese breakthroughs in cannon/gun manufacturing were also important in enabling the later invention of the steam engine (given that the cannon or gun is in effect a one-cylinder combustion engine and all of our modern motors are descended from it). And although it was the British who finally developed the steam engine, this should not obscure the many ideas and prior inventions made by the Chinese in the absence of which the world might never have heard of James Watt.

While the British are conventionally thought to have been the first to use coal in producing iron ore, this in fact began in eleventh-century Sung China. The Chinese also led the way in steel production, beginning in the fifth century CE. Not surprisingly, therefore, British iron and steel producers (e.g. Benjamin Huntsman of Sheffield) undertook detailed studies of Chinese production methods in the eighteenth century in order to develop their manufacturing techniques. The other great pillar of the British industrial revolution was cotton-manufacturing. John Lombe's machines, that he used in the silk industry were subsequently used in the Derbyshire cotton mills. But while it has been acknowledged that he copied the Italian silk machines, it is not generally recognised that the Italian machines replicated the earlier Chinese invention right down to the last detail (having diffused to Italy in the thirteenth century).

Conclusion

None of this is to say that the Europeans did not succeed in eventually taking the transmitted Eastern resource portfolios further. But it is to say that without them, there would have been little or nothing to have taken further. And without them we might be debating today why Europe remains on the periphery of the Afro-Asian-led global economy. Nevertheless, it is clear that deconstructing the civilisational-apartheid perspective of Eurocentrism as well as the manufactured idea of the clash of civilisations reveals the Europeans as having consistently engaged in cosmopolitan inter-civilisational relations since the eighth century. By no means is this to deny the point that Europe has clashed with 'non-European' civilisations, most notably through imperialism (Hobson 2004: 162–73, 219–42, 257–77). But it is to say that this idea has obscured Europe's cosmopolitan inter-civilisational relations with the East that have not only significantly shaped and fuelled the course and direction that European history has taken, but have even entered into defining and redefining the very idea of Europe. And most importantly of all, in rediscovering our global collective past we make possible a better future for all.

References

Abu-Lughod, J. (1989) *Before European Hegemony*, Oxford: Oxford University Press.

Bernal, M. (1991) *Black Athena*, I, New York: Vintage.

Blaut, J. M. (1993) *The Colonizer's Model of the World*, London: Guilford.

Campbell, J. and P. Sherrard (1965) 'The Greeks and the West', in R. Iyer (ed.) *The Glass Curtain between Asia and Europe*, London: Oxford University Press, pp. 69–86.

Clarke, J. J. (1997) *Oriental Enlightenment*, London: Routledge.

Delanty, G. (1995) *Inventing Europe*, London: Macmillan.

Flynn, D. O. and A. Giraldez (1994) 'China and the Manila Galleons', in A. J. H. Latham and H. Kawakatsu (eds) *Japanese Industrialization and the Asian Economy*, London: Routledge, pp. 71–90.

Frank, A. G. (1998) *ReOrient*, Berkeley: University of California Press.

Goody, J. (2004) *Islam in Europe*, Cambridge: Polity.

Hay, D. (1957) *Europe: The Emergence of an Idea*, Edinburgh: Edinburgh University Press.

Hobson, J. M. (2004) *The Eastern Origins of Western Civilisation*, Cambridge: Cambridge University Press.

Maverick, L. A. (1946) *China A Model for Europe*, I, San Antonio, Texas: Paul Anderson.

Menocal, M. R. (2002) *The Ornament of the World*, Boston: Little, Brown.

Needham, J., Ho-Ping-Yü, Lu Gwei Djen and Wang Ling (1986) *Science and Civilisation in China*, V (7), Cambridge: Cambridge University Press.

Pacey, A. (1991) *Technology in World Civilization*, Cambridge, Mass.: MIT Press.

Reichwein, A. (1967) *China and Europe*, Taipei: Ch'eng-Wen Publishing Co.

Rowbotham, A. H. (1945) 'The Impact of Confucianism on Seventeenth Century Europe', *The Far Eastern Quarterly*, 4(3): 224–42.

Said, E. W. (2003 [1978]) *Orientalism*, London: Penguin.

Seed, P. (1995) *Ceremonies of Possession in Europe's Conquest of the New World*, 1492–1640, Cambridge: Cambridge University Press.

8 Europe and the Mediterranean

A reassessment

Thomas W. Gallant

The sea changes related to the end of the Cold War, the advance of globalization and all that it entails, and the expansion of supra-national regional political and economic entities, such as the European Union, have inaugurated discussion and debate about reconceptualizing the world by deploying frames of analysis other than the nation-state. In the context of this intellectual ferment, scholars, such as those represented in this volume, are interrogating some of the central ideological props of the modern era, like the division of the world into regions on the basis of abstractions like East and West and Oriental and Occidental. A crucial element of this re-imagining of the world is a reassessment of the relationship between Europe and the Mediterranean and how the Euro-Mediterranean fits into the wider world of the twenty-first century.

What is it to be 'European'? What is it to be 'Mediterranean'? What is Europe? What is the Mediterranean? Indeed, what do these terms express? Are they merely expressions of geography? Or do they connote something else – identity, for example? What has been the relationship between the two over the *longue durée*? None of these questions are susceptible to easy or straightforward answers, though they have been frequently posed and debated, especially in the case of the Mediterranean. They are becoming even more important as the European Union expands to include more countries from the Mediterranean and as policies such as the Euro-Mediterranean Partnership define and structure the nature of the relationship between Europe and the Mediterranean. These developments are perforce having an impact on how this 'Greater Europe' will be situated into the emerging reconfiguration of regionalizations on a global scale.

In this chapter, I argue that an examination of the relationship between Europe and the Mediterranean over the long sweep of history from antiquity to present suggests that the emergence of a Euro-Mediterranean region in the late twentieth century is in fact nothing but a new phase in what has been a long and enduring relationship. Of course, the precise nature of that relationship changed frequently in the past and was often in a state of flux; also, throughout history, the directionality of dominance and power within and between the two regions was invariably unequal and subject to change.

This thesis challenges the dominant view that emphasizes heterogeneity and division as the defining characteristics of the historical relationship within and between the two regions, and that the recent movement toward greater articulation between them must overcome this legacy. Geography and identity are often adduced to support this view. After all it would seem self-evident that Europe and the Mediterranean occupy two separate geographical spaces and have never in the past occupied the same symbolic space. To the extent that there developed in the recent past a European self-identity it did not include the peoples of the Mediterranean and there has never existed in the latter's social imaginary a self-evident Mediterranean identity. I find neither of these persuasive.

I focus first on the geo-physical issue. As much recent work has shown, in the case of the Mediterranean in spite of great environmental diversity the degree of interconnectedness, the fluidity of communications, and the dense web of interdependencies creates a form of unity.[1] Much the same could be said for Europe. Ideas grounded in notions of fluidity, movement and networking have replaced older models that emphasized fixity, immobility and separation. Nor can the view that the boundaries between North and South are rooted or fixed by physical geography be substantiated. The areas that were imagined to be Europe, the Mediterranean, and the border between them have been shown to vary over time and have traditionally been very malleable conceptualizations (Ben-Artzi 2004; Leontidou 2004; Liotta 2005; Purcell 2003). All spatial configurations are expressions of mental maps, a form of symbolic geography. What area constituted Europe? The Mediterranean? To what degree were the two ever imagined to be one and the same? The answers to any of these questions are different depending on which historical era one is talking about. Borders and boundaries, then, were the product of politics and power plays, not geography.

This was true in the past and it is even now. Take, for example, the case of the North Atlantic Treaty Organization, which has for close to half a century included Greece and Turkey, even though they are obviously not located along the North Atlantic. They had a place in the symbolic, not physical, space of NATO. The European Union is likewise an expression of symbolic rather than physical geography, and this will increasingly be the case as new countries are added to it. Regarding its boundaries in the twenty-first century, then, I agree with Liotta that 'in the broadest sense, the "new" map of Greater Europe includes Turkey, Ukraine, the Russian Federation, and perhaps even Christian Armenia and Georgia and Muslim Azerbaijan' (Liotta 2005: 69). It being taken for granted that the Mediterranean region is obviously part of the new Greater Europe. In the reconfiguration of globalized regions, the Mediterranean will function, as it has for centuries, as the hinge connecting Greater Europe with Asia and

Africa. In sum, my argument is that while the idea of a symbolic Euro-Mediterranean space may only be emerging now, the reality of a Euro-Mediterranean regionalization based on social, demographic, political and economic ties has existed for millennia.

Much of the literature on the relationship between Europe and the Mediterranean emphasizes the historical separation of the two, especially in the Modern era. Indeed, some have gone so far as to propose that the idea of 'Europe' was formed in opposition to the Mediterranean, a zone which, they argue, represented Europe's 'Other'. Consequently, historians have proposed numerous moments in the past when they believe that the Mediterranean became the East and Europe the West. For some, the fateful moment was when the military forces of the Hellenic League turned back the invading forces of Persian King Xerxes in 479 BCE. The defeat of the Persian Empire's mighty military supposedly brought down a barrier that separated Asia from Europe and created a civilization fault-line that would separate East from West forever. Others situate the locus of separation later in time. For Henri Prienne and his followers it was the Arab invasions of the seventh century CE that were most critical by imposing religion as the barrier between 'Us' and 'Them'. Still others look to the capture of Constantinople and the demise of the Eastern Roman Empire as the key event. Some opt for 1571 or 1683 when the course of Ottoman expansion north and westward was halted at the battles of Lepanto or Vienna, respectively. Some look to longer term developments rather than solitary events as being most important. In the view of these scholars, it was the Enlightenment and the shift of economic and political power northward and westward that set the Mediterranean on a developmental trajectory different from Europe. Reinforcing the impact of these structural revolutions was the rise of the nation-state. Either carved out of the remnants of the old empires or formed through the coalescence of previously independent polities, the newly formed states accentuated differences between peoples and cultures. Each new state would develop along its own, perhaps even unique, path. Also as national identities formed they did so by creating dichotomies between nations; the alterity of the 'Other' enabled groups to delineate an image of themselves. In short, the forces that divided the peoples of the Mediterranean from one another and that separated them off from the cultures of Europe were even more powerful and efficacious in the Modern era than in previous epochs.

While not denying the importance of these events and developments, I argue that their significance has been greatly overrated. I demonstrate, first, that dichotomous categories like East and West and Oriental and Occidental have never accurately described the social, political and economic realities that structured lives of peoples in the Mediterranean region. Put more bluntly, the economic, demographic, cultural and political interactions between the cultures of the Mediterranean have over time been so intense, so long-standing and so multifaceted as to create a degree of interconnectedness that makes it impossible to understand its history except on a regional basis. This process of Mediterraneanization continues to the present and is a vital element in the reconceptualization of the Mediterranean in a global context (Morris 2003). Second and related to this first point, the level and magnitude of interaction and interconnectedness between the cultures and states of the Mediterranean and Europe over the millennia have been such that the history of one region cannot be understood without reference to the other.

The idea of 'Europe' was born in the Eastern Mediterranean. There is the Greek myth of how Zeus metamorphosed into a bull and seduced the Phoenician princess, Europa, into riding on him so that he could abscond with her to the island of Crete where he raped her. She then became one of his lovers and bore him three sons, one of whom, Minos, became the mythical founder of the 'Minoan' civilization (Delanty, this volume; Leontidou 2004). The myth stands as a metaphor for the close, indeed, intimate relationship between Europe and the Mediterranean, which in antiquity were one and the same. While not gainsaying the importance of this and other imaginative constructs of Europe and Asia in antiquity, I want to focus on another ancient phenomenon that created an actual, physical relationship among cultures in the Mediterranean and between them and the cultures that occupied what would later become the geographical expression of Europe, namely colonization. Beginning in eleventh or tenth century BCE, Greeks and Phoenicians began to found settlements all around the Mediterranean basin and along the shores of the Black Sea. Some of the most famous cities of the ancient world (many of which are still prominent cities today) began life as Greek or Phoenician colonies. This dense network of colonies enabled a process of 'Mediterraneanization' to develop and this facilitated trade, cultural interaction and political relations across the region (Morris 2003; Horden and Purcell 2000). In addition, these colonies became nodes from which tendrils of trade and exchange extended northward, connecting the various cultures of Western and Central Europe to the more advanced civilizations of the Mediterranean. It would be upon this fragile and tenuous network of links that subsequent interaction between Europe and the Mediterranean would be built (Winks and Mattern 2004). Colonization, then, recommenced a new manifestation of the process of Mediterraneanization, but for many historians its life-span was quite short-lived as the unity it created was destroyed by the clash between Greek (Western) and Persian (Eastern) civilizations.[2]

At first glance, the argument that the great conflict between the Persian Empire and the alliance of Greek states was the historic moment when East and West became made manifest entities would seem to have much going for it. After all, the defeat of the Persian military in 479 BCE ensured that 'Oriental despotism' would remain an Eastern phenomenon and that Greek society could continue to develop the ideals and institutions that would provide the foundation on which Western civilization would be based. A closer examination, however, demonstrates how simplistic and misleading this view is. The Persian Wars were neither a clash between East and West nor were they a conflict just between Greeks and Persians. Arrayed in the forces of the empire were peoples drawn from all across the Middle East, the Levant, Asia Minor and the Balkans. Indeed, more Greeks fought with the Persian army than fought against it. Nor did Persian defeat create a barrier between East and West. Commerce and trade that spanned the Mediterranean and the Black Sea continued to connect the domains of the empire with Greeks states, and indeed may even have become more intensive after than they had been before the wars. Moreover these economic ties connected not just those numerous Greek states that remained in the empire with the independent Greek states but also other non-Greek cultures within the imperial domains, like Egypt and the cities of Phoenicia. Along with the flow of the goods the movement of people continued long after the war had ended. Even politically, the Persian Wars did not separate East from West. It was, after all, Persian gold and resources that tipped the balance in favour of Sparta over Athens in the Mediterranean-wide Peloponnesian War of the late fifth century BCE, and right down until Alexander the Great seized the Persian throne Greek warriors took their place in the ranks of the Persian army.

The connections between Mesopotamia, North Africa, the Near East, Asia Minor and the Mediterranean that survived the wars of the fifth century underwent a phase of renewal and expansion with the conquests of Alexander the Great. One need not subscribe to the old view that Alexander sought to create a unity of mankind to accept that his conquests brought together into a single polity the major civilizations of the eastern Mediterranean and the Middle East. Though his own reign was short-lived and the empire he forged soon split, the kingdoms ruled over by his successors perpetuated the social, political and economic connections established earlier. These ties were extended further when all of the Hellenistic kingdoms fell to the great power from the Western Mediterranean: Rome.

The Roman Empire spanned Europe and the Mediterranean. It was created out of conquests by a people originally from central Italy and their domain eventually extended over all three of the coastlands of the Mediterranean – Asian, African and European – and deep into the hinterlands behind them: in the east they incorporated the kingdoms of Alexander's successors which extended eastward as far as Armenia and Mesopotamia; Roman *imperium* extended southward as far as the cataracts of the Nile and the Sahara; and northwards it projected outward into Gaul and Britain and the delta of the Rhine, and north-eastward along the Danube. Though marked by great diversity, nonetheless the incorporation of these regions into a single polity strengthened even more the web of interconnections that had been developing for the previous 800 to 1,000 years.

A line of thought stretching from Edward Gibbon to Henri Prienne and beyond proposes that the division between Europe and the Mediterranean and the fragmentation of the Mediterranean were brought about by the two major invasions of the first millennium of the current era. Arab and Slavic invasions, according to this argument, ushered on to the scene peoples who possessed cultures and, in the case of the Arabs, a religion that were so radically different from the old Mediterranean civilizations as to create a civilizational fault-line so wide and deep that it split the world that the Romans had made.

The Eastern Roman Empire, of course, survived both of these invasions and indeed, managed by 1000 BCE to regain some of the territory it had lost to one of the invaders and largely incorporated the other into its cultural orbit. Moreover in spite of the schism between the Catholic and Eastern orthodox churches and even the sacking of Constantinople by Latin knights in 1204, the Mediterranean was still interconnected in fundamental and important ways (Abulafia 2000). For these and other reasons, some prefer to see the split between East and West as commencing in 1453 with the fall of Constantinople and the incorporation of what remained of the Byzantine Empire into the domain of the new suzerain of the region: the Ottomans. As this Islamic empire spread northward toward Vienna and south and West along the coast of Africa, it divided the Mediterranean more sharply than ever before and exacerbated the rift between East and West. Moreover, it was not a coincidence that 'the Western twentieth-century concept of Europe was based on the ideas of sixteenth century historians and it should be noted that it excludes the original idea that was Europe: the modern Bulgaria, Albania, Serbia and Greece' – all by then part of the Islamic empire of the Ottomans (Pocock 1997: 12). The sixteenth was the century when the Ottoman Empire attained its zenith and threatened the continental kingdoms of Europe the most. The rise of an Oriental, Islamic empire brought into sharper relief the common cultural heritage that Europeans shared and it foregrounded the differences that distinguished them from the East. This, then, would seem to be the moment when East and West sprang from the European imagination. Once again, however, material realities tell a different story and it is one that emphasizes interconnectedness, both within the Mediterranean and between the Mediterranean and Europe (Greene 2000).

In some ways, the rise of the Ottoman Empire brought into sharper relief perceived differences between East and West in some ways, while in others, it showed how interrelated Europe and the Mediterranean were. By the seventeenth century, the Ottoman Empire had become the centre of a vast and strongly interconnected commercial and economic system that spanned much of the globe and that articulated European economies to those of East Asia and the Indian subcontinent. Christian and Muslim merchants from Ottoman cities such as Istanbul, İzmir, Alexandria, Aleppo and Baghdad were deeply integrated into a commercial network that spanned from Calcutta, Bandar Abbas, Surat and Cambay to the south and east and to Vienna, Kiev, Moscow, Danzig, Amsterdam, Venice and London to the north and West. Economically, then, for much of the Early Modern period, the Ottoman Empire was the hinge that connected the rapidly growing economies of Europe with those of the East. Not only goods but people moved along the lines of communication that closely connected the various regions (Bayly and Fawaz 2002; Goffman 2002). By 1700, according to one estimate, close to one million Christian merchants from the Ottoman Empire resided in northern and central Europe. Perhaps as many as another quarter of a million lived in port cities and towns in the Western Mediterranean. At the same time substantial numbers of merchants from Europe and the Western Mediterranean relocated to the major port cities of the Ottoman Empire (Braudel 1972: 415–18; Aymard 1974). It was not just goods but people, ideas and culture that flowed along this vast and intricate web of connections. These people breathed life into the network that connected the various regions of the Mediterranean and that articulated it to Europe during the Early Modern period.

It is no coincidence that the two works most closely associated with the argument in favour of seeing the Mediterranean as a viable, perhaps even necessary, frame of analysis, those of Braudel, and Horden and Purcell, empirically concentrate mainly on the pre-modern eras. During the eighteenth and especially the nineteenth centuries, as the mania of nationalism spread to the region and nation-states emerged from the dismantling of the old multi-national empires or from the coalescence of the tiny polities that dotted some regions in the Early Modern period, the new states superseded all other entities as the central reality in peoples' lives. As has been often noted, one of the most powerful aspects of nationalism was its ability to elevate a national identity above all others; even though, as was almost always the case, that identity was largely the product of imagination and acculturation. In any case, as the old polities of the Early Modern period fell on to history's trash heap and new political configurations arose, no indigenous imaginary identity of being 'Mediterranean' developed in the cultures around the great sea.

Concomitant and related to this development, European historians increasingly promoted the nation-state as the paramount geographical frame for scholarly research. Telling of the story of each nation's rise and accounting for its particular *volksgeist* came to be seen as the historian's primary task. Nineteenth-century historiography, then, dovetailed nicely with the broader public discourse and, particularly through the dissemination of school textbooks, helped to elevate a unitary national identity that superseded all others, including both sub-national and super-national ones. At the same time, other academic discourses either formed or persisted in European universities and learned societies that focused on the Mediterranean. These are well known and therefore do not require much elaboration here. Two of them, Romanticism and classicism, elevated Greco-Roman antiquity to the status of Europe's progenitor. These intellectual movements reified the 'West' as a European phenomenon, while, of course, simultaneously denying contemporary Mediterranean cultures a place in this imaginary space. To the extent that Greeks, Italians and others shared in this glorious heritage it was at best tangential and debased. Greatly contributing to this process of distancing the Mediterranean from Europe was the discourse of 'Orientalism'. As Edward Said showed, during the Nineteenth century, French philologists led the way in constructing an exoticized identity for the peoples of the Mediterranean as Europe's 'Other'. Arguably, then, it was during the nineteenth century that the divide between East and West, Occident and Orient, became truly and fully substantiated.

Two additional elements would seem to bolster this conclusion and to support the complementary argument that even within the Mediterranean barriers, division and cultural distinctiveness held sway. The first of these is that the nationalistic orientation of academic history and public discourse, noted above, predominated in the major universities in the region. Greek, Serbian and Italian historiographies, for example, developed very much as extensions of the national discourse and as foundational props for nation-building. This discourse tended to exaggerate national differences and deny the importance of transnational phenomena. The greater Mediterranean region, to the extent that it was discussed at all, was seen as merely a geographical expression and nothing more; and even this view was borrowed from outside (Ben-Artzi 2004). Second, indigenous academics and local societies by and large accepted and internalized the dichotomous categories of East and West. What caused disagreements among them was not whether or not they were Occidental or Oriental, but rather over whether or not they should strive to be Westernized (Tsoukalas 2002). It would seem, then, that the argument made earlier that the level and degree of interconnectedness among the cultures of the Mediterranean and between them and Central and Western Europe do not apply in the Modern era. In other words, that the consensus view that the emergence of the nation-state changed everything is correct.

An examination, however, of the history of the nineteenth century and the first half of the twentieth century that focuses less on what scholars and nation-builders said and more on the developments and events that structured the realities of everyday life shows once again that there was a high and marked degree of interrelatedness and networks of economic, social and political connections both within the Mediterranean and between it and Europe – just as in earlier periods (Rein 1999). But, the precise nature of those connections was yet again different from those of earlier epochs.

Before examining them, however, it needs to be pointed out that even at the level of ideology and social imagination, the Occidental versus Oriental dichotomy fails to capture fully the complex interplay within and without the region over identity. To take one specific example, that of the encounter between Britons and Greeks on the Ionian Islands, the British did not construct an oriental identity for their Greek subjects but instead saw them as the Irish of the Mediterranean (Gallant 2002). While still creating social space and alterity between Britons and Greeks, it also underscored a view of the Greeks as fellow Europeans: but, like the Irish (in British eyes), it constructed them as Europe's less fortunate and only marginally civilized distant relative. The same conclusion is evident if we expand the discussion to include how the British and Germans, for example, saw Italians, Spaniards, Serbs or Maltese. In sum, the canonical Orientalist paradigm so powerfully expressed by Said and others fails to capture accurately the complexity and malleability embedded in the discourse over Mediterranean identities in the Modern era.[3]

The orthodox view becomes even less tenable when we analyse economic and commercial developments, demography and population movements, and politics and international relations. From the time that Napoleon dreamed his dream of a French empire that spanned continents until the end of the Second World War, the Mediterranean was the space where the European powers came to fight. In addition to actual military conflicts, the Mediterranean was also the space where the Great Powers played out their ambitions for imperial expansion. Because the region did not fall neatly into the sphere of influence of any one of the Great Powers, it became the field more than any other where the 'Great Game' of empire was played. The list of episodes where one or more of the major powers interfered in the states along the shores of the Mediterranean is long and well-known to the extent that one can almost speak of the provincialization of the Mediterranean.

The long-standing commercial and economic relations between the Mediterranean and Europe continued and indeed became even closer in the nineteenth century and into the twentieth century. The mercantilism that characterized economic relations between the two regions during the eighteenth century persisted, but was now augmented by two new developments, both of which were related to industrialization and the global advance of capitalism. The first of these was related to the uneven pace of industrialization. As mass manufacturing took off in Northern and Western Europe, older forms of production persisted in the Mediterranean creating a situation whereby indigenous products became increasingly expensive compared with imports. At the same time, the Mediterranean increasingly became a net exporter of raw materials and foodstuffs. In the parlance of world-systems theory, the Mediterranean became semi-peripheralized and a dependent appendage to the industrializing north. The flow of goods from the Mediterranean did not even come close to offsetting the value of goods imported into the region, creating chronic trade deficits that would impair the economic development of all of the Mediterranean countries (Aerts and Valério 1990).

The other novel development in the nineteenth century was the advent of a massive flow of capital from the north to the south. The governments of the newly formed nation-states and the older polities needed huge amounts of capital funding to underwrite the costs of projects like building a military and creating an infrastructure that would encourage economic growth in manufacturing to occur, and for social spending to deal with the host of problems associated with modernization. By the end of the century, every country around the Mediterranean was deeply indebted to European creditors. The nineteenth-century economic encounter between Europe's industrializing states and their neighbours to the south led to the further provincialization of the Mediterranean, which, if anything, strengthened the bonds of dependency between Europe and the region.

The nineteenth and the first half of the twentieth centuries witnessed yet again a massive movement of people both within the Mediterranean and from the region outwards. Population shifts during this period took on three general forms. The first of these was associated with nation-building and entailed the exchange or unidirectional movement of people from one country to another, usually one with whom the migrants shared some ethnic or religious bond. The most prominent of this type of population movement was the exchange of peoples between Greece and Turkey in 1923 after the Greco-Turkish War of 1920–1922 (Hirschon 2003). But this was just one, albeit a very prominent one, of a number of such transnational population shifts between countries. All told, millions of people relocated within the Mediterranean and this helped to reinforce social and cultural connections across the region (Aymard 1974).

The second form of population movement that helped to break down ties of localism and to facilitate the formation of even more extensive transnational connections was internal migration. All across the Mediterranean a combination of population growth and economic depression compelled millions of people to leave their rural villages and relocate to the burgeoning urban centres (see for example Douglass 1983; Leontidou 1990; Reher 1990). Residence in the city exposed people more directly to the cultural and educational institutions responsible for national-building. At the same time that people internalized a canonical national identity at the expense of a localized one, they were also exposed to the more cosmopolitan ways of life and multiculturalist ethos found in the city. This was especially the case in port cities, which, as Henk Driessen has shown, acted as nodes to connect people from the city and its hinterland to the wider world (Driessen 2005).

The third major migration stream during this period was the flow of people from the Mediterranean outwards, primarily to North and South America but also to Central and Western Europe. The experience of living abroad in a foreign culture helped to consolidate the predominance of a national identity over localized ones and, because so many of the migrants were lumped together in the social imaginary of the host country, it helped to foster a sense of solidarity that planted the seeds of an identity of importance other than a national one; in this case as being 'Mediterranean' or 'Southern European'. In the modern era, as before, migration created dense and extensive strands of connections that created networks connecting the peoples of the Mediterranean in Europe and beyond.

It can be argued, then, that even in the heyday of nationalism and the formation of ethno-nationalistic states, the many-stranded linkages that connected cultures and countries persisted and may have even strengthened, when we should have expected to see an ever more marked degree of fragmentation and separation, as so many contemporary writers believed.

The trends and patterns of interconnectedness and interpenetration among the cultures of the Mediterranean and between them and Europe that I have argued had been developing for centuries became even denser and more developed during the second half of the twentieth century: precisely when Cold War rhetorical and political realties were reifying the dichotomy between East and West. Once again, however, the nature and form of the linkages within and between the region and Europe experienced profound change and though connected, of course, to what came before were quite different.

As we have seen, in academic discourse the idea of the Mediterranean as a coherent frame of analysis originated among nineteenth-century German geographers. Historians, however, largely remained rooted to the national paradigm as is shown by their response to the publication of the first edition in French of Braudel's *magnum opus* in 1949. As Marino has pointed out, the response to the book during the 1950s and 1960s was tepid at best and mostly antagonistic – even in the fields of economic, diplomatic and Renaissance history that were closest to Braudel's work (Marino 2002, 2004). The book only began to have a major impact after the publication of the second English edition in 1972, due to the confluence of numerous factors, an important one of these being the emergence of the Mediterranean as a field site for anthropological research, primarily among English and American anthropologists.

Beginning in the 1950s anthropologists began to seek out sites in the Mediterranean to conduct ethnographic field research. A number of practical and intellectual factors contributed to this development. Among the latter was the growing sense that because of common ecological circumstances, which Braudel so minutely and authoritatively described in his work, and a shared history, the Mediterranean was an ideal location 'for fruitful comparative research' (Albera and Blok 2001: 20). The 1960s saw a continuation of this trend and by the mid-1970s a sufficient number of case studies had been published to allow for an attempt at a synthesis – John Davis's *People of the Mediterranean* (1977). Subsequently, the strong case for viewing the Mediterranean as a cultural area in the anthropological sense was put forward by David Gilmore (1982; see also Boissevain 1979). There ensued a heated debate about this proposition with Michael Herzfeld emerging as the leader of those who contested it (Herzfeld 1984,

1987). By the end of the decade, the debate has lost much of its currency and fire (Pina-Cabral 1989; Driessen 2001).

In the early 1990s, the discipline of history, and especially European history, underwent a crisis. A number of widely divergent developments, the end of the Cold War, the emergence of a more united Europe, the promulgation of new philosophical and epistemological schools of thought (such as postcolonialism and postmodernism), and the so-called 'culture wars', created an intellectual climate conducive to challenging many of the old verities of the historical profession. And none of these tried and trusted bastions of the old order was more directly challenged than that of the centrality of Europe in the meta-narrative of the Modern era. As John Gillis put it, 'Europe has lost its spatial and temporal centrality' in the story of the modern world (1996: 5).

Gillis's was only one voice among many proclaiming that the end of modern European history as we knew it was at hand. By far the largest chorus focused on the question of Eurocentrism, i.e. the propensity of historians to view global developments primarily from a European perspective, and the need to toss this Eurocentric view of the world on to the scrap heap of history. These developments called into question some of the historiographical elements that constituted the very foundation of modern European history. The decentring or provincialization of Europe within the master narrative of the modern age had wide ranging repercussions (Chakrabarty 2000). As Peter Gran noted, 'the dominant paradigm [of European history] seems likely to be eclipsed sooner or later for intellectual reasons or for purely practical ones' (1996: 7). The increasingly hostile reaction to 'Eurocentrism' has not been the only threat to European history. Other developments also pulled at the fabric of the core-constituting element of traditional modern European history: the nation-state.

Another aspect of the 'crisis of European history' centred on the primacy of the nation-state as modern history's primary analytical unit. If the nation-state was one of the central elements of modernity, and if we have moved beyond the modern age to something else, then this raises the question of the role of the nation-state. The development of transnational political organizations, the move toward greater integration of nations into them, the collapse of the central props of Cold War identities and their replacement with different, often smaller, and contested ones have all contributed to a push to conceptualize the political, social and cultural geography of Europe in novel ways. As Gillis observed, 'the very concept of the nation is much more problematic than it once was and no longer provides a self-evident frame for historical investigation' (1996: web page 5). Another historian put it much more succinctly: historiographically, 'the nation is dead' (Hans Mommsen quoted in Applegate 1999: 1157 and note 5). In the wake of its demise, there was a move to shift the emphasis of interest to super-national or sub-national regionalizations.

There are a number of reasons why the Mediterranean emerged in the

1990s as an important frame of historical research. First, there was Braudel's work, which had long before achieved the status as a modern classic of historical research. Though empirically based in the Early Modern period it nonetheless stood as a model for those interested in pursuing regional-based research in the Modern era (Horden 2005). Next, the early 1990s witnessed the so-called 'historic turn in the human sciences' which strengthened the ties between historians and anthropologists (McDonald 1996). The Mediterranean region, of course, came to figure prominently. Even though the 'Mediterranean debate' was running out of steam among anthropologists at this time, there was still the substantial body of work they had produced, and the debate itself resonated with historians who tended to side more with those who favoured the idea of unity. This corpus of anthropological scholarship of exceptional depth, breadth and quality provided a foundation on which historians could build. Also, in the 1980s and early 1990s, for reasons to be discussed below, the Mediterranean emerged as a recognized category of analysis in a number of cognate disciplines, such as political science, international relations, economics, geography, environmental studies and sociology. One need only cite the very large number of journals and serials produced in those fields that include Mediterranean in their titles to make this point (Gallant and Esenwein 1996; Alcock 2005). The last development that solidified the status of the Mediterranean as an important focus of historical research was the publication of Horden and Purcell's *The Corrupting Sea* (2000) and the rich body of works that engaged it.[4]

Other, more practical, developments that have their roots earlier in the twentieth century complemented the purely academic ones discussed so far and together they have contributed to the emergence of a Mediterranean identity and the strengthening and deepening of the bonds between Europe and the Mediterranean that had been developing for centuries. I focus first on population movements. The second half of the twentieth century witnessed once again a massive movement of people between the two areas, and as was the case in the past the flow of migrants took on different forms. The first major migration was from the Mediterranean northward. Seeking better paying jobs in the more industrialized north, millions of workers relocated to countries like France, Germany, The Netherlands, Belgium and elsewhere. These guest-workers at first migrated with the idea of returning to the homeland after a short stay abroad, and many of them did eventually return. Very substantial numbers chose to stay, adding yet another layer of peoples from the Mediterranean to the communities that had formed in earlier times.

Mass tourism created another large and important migratory flow. Starting from a trickle during the 1950s the seasonal movement of people from the north to the south became a flood by the 1980s and 1990s. This had a number of important consequences. First, it facilitated a cultural dialogue between visitors and hosts, an important dimension of which related to identity. This dialogue augmented and complemented a process that had, as we have seen, been ongoing for centuries. Second, it helped to consolidate a specific image of the Mediterranean and its cultures. It was during this period that the archetypal image of the Mediterranean as a land of sea and sand, bronzed babes in bikinis and *la dolce vita*, 'anything goes' lifestyles came into being (Liakos 2003). In an ironic twist, this Mediterranean beach culture, which is now so closely associated with the region in popular imagination, was a foreign construction that has been internalized over the last twenty years by indigenous cultures. In any event, tourism contributed to the ongoing intercultural dialogue (Apostolopoulos *et al.* 2001).

Finally, the third, and most recent, migration stream connecting the Mediterranean and Europe was created by the movement of peoples from outside either region, primarily, Africa, the Middle East and East Asia, especially The Philippines, which has some well-known problems but which has also helped to solidify a common Euro-Mediterranean identity in the face of new 'Others' (King 2001; Riba Mateos 2005 – to cite only two major works among the large and ever-growing body of literature). Transnational migration in the age of globalization, then, as it had done in the past, has helped to break down barriers, facilitate intercultural dialogue and further enhance cosmopolitanism. Yet again what we see in the region is a form of unity at one level in spite of great diversity at another.

Obviously the most important factor shaping the economic and political life of the Mediterranean since the middle of the twentieth century has been the establishment of the European Union. The establishment of the Euro-Mediterranean Partnership (EMP) at the Barcelona conference in November 1995 elevated to new heights the economic bonds that linked the two regions which had been developing over thirty years. It also strengthened political and cultural ties within the EU Mediterranean countries and between them and the other EU countries. EU expansion to include more countries from the Mediterranean will advance this process further. While, of course, not without its problems the EMP has had an impact on nearly every facet of society, economy and politics in the Mediterranean, including identity.[5]

The Euro-Mediterranean moment has arrived. I have argued that the current state of play is the end result of a process that has been ongoing for centuries and has experienced many different developmental phases. I end by focusing on one aspect of the current that is unique – the development of a Euro-Mediterranean identity. Like all identities, it is an imaginary construct and just as has happened in the nineteenth century with national identities, it will take root only through a process of acculturation underpinned by strategic initiatives by various political and cultural entities. Contributing to this process will be the practical and cultural consequences of EU policies for the establishment of the Mediterranean as an academic discourse. A Mediterranean self-identity that is simultaneously a European identity is becoming manifest. While it has not replaced a national identity as the dominant one in the popular social imaginary yet and may never do so completely (Tsoukalas 2002; Herzfeld 2005; Moulakis 2005; Pace 2005), nonetheless it is certainly becoming more prominent in shaping how people see themselves and their place in the world. Moreover, at least part of the reason that an identity as being Mediterranean is gaining currency is precisely because of the belief that to be Mediterranean is to be European (Malkin 2005; Nocke 2005). The emergence of a Euro-Mediterranean identity represents, as I have demonstrated above, the final chapter in a historical relationship that has spanned millennia. As Greater Europe reassesses its place in the changing global schema of regionalizations, the Mediterranean will serve, as it has so often in the past, as its hinge or gateway to the wider world.

Notes

1 My views on this subject have been shaped especially by the work of Horden and Purcell (2000). All future research on this subject will begin with their superb study. In the debate over the idea of Mediterranean unity, lip service has all too often been paid to 'history'. Besides Horden and Purcell and the excellent collection of essays edited by Abulafia (2003), few have actually engaged the historical record.
2 I use the verb 'recommence' here because much recent archaeological research indicates that there were networks of trade and settlements developed during the prehistoric Bronze Age that spanned the Mediterranean.
3 Indeed, it has been argued that by focusing primarily on philologists, Said underestimates the far more varied and nuanced ways that French scholars and scientists exploring the Mediterranean understood it; see Bourguet (1998).
4 An excellent review of the Mediterranean debate after the historic turn in the human sciences can be found in Sant Cassia and Schäfer (2005).
5 The literature on the European Union and the Mediterranean and the EMP is vast. My thinking about it has been most influenced by Luciani (1984), Gillespie (1997), Pierros *et al.* (1999), Featherstone and Kazimias (2001), Xenakis and Chryssochoou (2001) and Pace (2005).

References

Abulafia, D. (2000) *Mediterranean Encounters, Economic, Religious, Political, 1100–1550*, Aldershot: Ashgate.
Abulafia, D. (ed.) (2003) *The Mediterranean in History*, London: Thames & Hudson.
Aerts, E. and N. Valério (eds) (1990) *Growth and Stagnation in the Mediterranean World in the 19th and 20th Centuries*, Leuven, Belgium: Leuven University Press.
Albera, D. and A. Blok (2001) 'The Mediterranean as a Field of Ethnological Study: A Retrospective', in D. Albera, A. Blok and C. Bromberger (eds) *Anthropology of the Mediterranean*, Paris: Maisonneuve et Larose: Maison méditerranéenne des sciences de l'homme, pp. 15–42.
Alcock, S. E. (2005) 'Alphabet Soup in the Mediterranean Basin: The Emergence of the Mediterranean Serial', in W. V. Harris (ed.) *Rethinking the Mediterranean*, Oxford: Oxford University Press, pp. 314–36.
Apostolopoulos, Y., P. J. Loukissas and L. Leontidou (eds) (2001) *Mediterranean*

Tourism: Facets of Socioeconomic Development and Cultural Change, London: Routledge.

Applegate, C. (1999) 'A Europe of Regions: Reflections on the History of Sub-national Places in Modern Times', *American Historical Review*, 104: 1157–82.

Aymard, M. (ed.) (1974) *Les Migrations dans les pays méditerranéens au XVIIIéme et au début du XIXéme*, Nice: Université de Nice, Centre de la Méditerranée moderne et contemporaine.

Bayly, C. A. and L. Fawaz (2002) 'The Connected World of Empires', in C. A. Bayly and L. Fawaz (eds) *Modernity and Culture: From the Mediterranean to the Indian Ocean*, New York: Columbia University Press, pp. 1–27.

Ben-Artzi, Y. (2004) 'The Idea of a Mediterranean Region in Nineteenth- to Mid-Twentieth-Century German Geography', *Mediterranean Historical Review*, 19(2): 2–15.

Boissevain, J. (1979) 'Toward an Anthropology of the Mediterranean', *Current Anthropology*, 20: 81–93.

Bourguet, M.-N. (1998) *L'invention scientifique de la Méditerranée: Egypte, Morée, Algérie*, Paris: Ecole des hautes etudes en sciences sociales.

Braudel, F. (1972) *The Mediterranean and the Mediterranean World in the Age of Philip II*, London: Collins.

Chakrabarty, D. (2000) *Provincializing Europe: Postcolonial Thought and Historical Difference*, Princeton: Princeton University Press.

Davis, J. (1977) *People of the Mediterranean. An Essay in Comparative Social Anthropology*, London: Routledge and Kegan Paul.

Douglass, W. A. (1983) 'Migration in Italy', in M. K. Kenny and D. I. Kertzer (eds) *Urban Life in Mediterranean Europe: Anthropological Perspectives*, Urbana: University of Illinois Press, pp. 162–202.

Driessen, H. (2001) 'Divisions in Mediterranean Ethnography: A View from Both Shores', in D. Albera, A. Blok and C. Bromberger (eds) *Anthropology of the Mediterranean*, Paris: Maisonneuve et Larose: Maison méditerranéenne des sciences de l'homme, pp. 625–44.

Driessen, H. (2005) 'Mediterranean Port Cities: Cosmopolitanism Reconsidered', *History and Anthropology*, 16(1): 129–41.

Featherstone, K. and G. A. Kazimias (eds) (2001) *Europeanization and the Southern Periphery*, London: F. Cass.

Gallant, T. W. (2002) *Experiencing Dominion: Culture, Identity and Power in the British Mediterranean*, Notre Dame: University of Notre Dame Press.

Gallant, T. W. and G. Esenwein (1996) 'The Future of European History: One Alternative', *Perspectives*, December: 25–6.

Gillespie, R. (ed.) (1997) *The Euro-Mediterranean Partnership: Political and Economic Perspectives*, London: F. Cass.

Gillis, J. R. (1996) 'The Future of European History', *Perspectives*, April: 1–5.

Gilmore, D. D. (1982) 'Anthropology of the Mediterranean Area', *Annual Review of Anthropology*, 11: 175–205.

Goffman, D. (2002) *The Ottoman Empire and Early Modern Europe*, Cambridge: Cambridge University Press.

Gran, P. (1996) *Beyond Eurocentrism: A New View of Modern World History*, Syracuse, NY: Syracuse University Press.

Greene, M. (2000) *A Shared World: Christians and Muslims in the Early Modern Mediterranean*, Princeton, NJ: Princeton University Press.

Herzfeld, M. (1984) 'The Horns of a Mediterraneanist Dilemma', *American Ethnologist*, 115: 439–54.

Herzfeld, M. (1987) *Anthropology Through the Looking Glass: Critical Ethnography in the Margins of Europe*, Cambridge: Cambridge University Press.

Herzfeld, M. (2005) 'Practical Mediterraneanism: Excuse for Everything, Epistemology to Eating', in W. V. Harris (ed.) *Rethinking the Mediterranean*, Oxford: Oxford University Press, pp. 45–63.

Hirschon, R. (ed.) (2003) *Crossing the Aegean: An Appraisal of the 1923 Compulsory Population Exchange between Greece and Turkey*, New York: Berghahn Books.

Horden, P. (2005) 'Mediterranean Excuses: Historical Writing on the Mediterranean since Braudel', *History and Anthropology*, 16(1): 25–30.

Horden, P. and N. Purcell (2000) *The Corrupting Sea: A Study of Mediterranean History*, Oxford: Blackwell.

King, R. (ed.) (2001) *The Mediterranean Passage Migration and New Cultural Encounters in Southern Europe*, Liverpool: Liverpool University Press.

Leontidou, L. (1990) *The Mediterranean City in Transition: Social Change and Urban Development*, Cambridge: Cambridge University Press.

Leontidou, L. (2004) 'The Boundaries of Europe: Deconstructing Three Regional Narratives', *Identities: Global Studies in Culture and Power*, 11(4): 593–617.

Liakos, A. (2003) 'I Mesoyeios kai To Soma', *To Vima*, 13929 (3 August), section B: 29.

Liotta, P. H. (2005) 'Imagining Europe: Symbolic Geography and the Future', *Mediterranean Quarterly*, 16: 67–85.

Luciani, G. (ed.) (1984) *The Mediterranean Region: Economic Interdependence and the Future of Society*, London: Croom Helm.

Malkin, I. (2005) 'The Mediterranean Option', paper presented at the conference on *Constructions of Mediterranean Nostalgia*, T. Gallant and A. Liakos (organizers), Athens.

Marino, J. A. (ed.) (2002) *Early Modern History and the Social Sciences: Testing the Limits of Braudel's Mediterranean*, Kirksville, MO: Truman State University Press.

Marino, J. A. (2004) 'The Exile and His Kingdom: The Reception of Braudel's Mediterranean', *Journal of Modern History*, 76: 622–52.

McDonald, T. J. (1996) 'Introduction', in T. J. McDonald (ed.) *The Historic Turn in the Human Sciences*, Ann Arbor: University of Michigan, pp. 1–16.

Morris, I. (2003) 'Mediterraneanization', *Mediterranean Historical Review*, 18(2): 30–55.

Moulakis, A. (2005) 'The Mediterranean Region: Reality, Delusion, or Euro-Mediterranean project?', *Mediterranean Quarterly*, 16: 11–38.

Nocke, A. (2005) 'Mediterraneanism in Israel: Narratives of the Past and the Construction of Modern Israeli Identity', paper presented at the conference on *Constructions of Mediterranean Nostalgia*, T. Gallant and A. Liakos (organizers), Athens.

Pace, M. (2005) *The Politics of Regional Identity: Meddling with the Mediterranean*, Abingdon, Oxfordshire: Routledge.

Pierros, F., J. Meunier and S. Abrams (eds) (1999) *Bridges and Barriers: The European Union's Mediterranean Policy, 1961–1998*, Aldershot: Ashgate.

Pina-Cabral, J. d. (1989) 'The Mediterranean as a Category of Regional Comparison: A Critical View', *Current Anthropology*, 30: 399–407.

Pocock, J. G. A. (1997) 'What Do We Mean by Europe? (Europa: The Past and Future of an Idea)', *The Wilson Quarterly*, 21: 12–40.

Purcell, N. (2003) 'The Boundless Sea of Unlikeness?: On Defining the Mediterranean', *Mediterranean Historical Review*, 18(2): 9–29.

Reher, D. S. (1990) 'Urbanization and Demographic Behaviour in Spain', in A. van der Woude, A. Hayami and J. de Vries (eds) *Urbanization in History*, Oxford: Clarendon Press, pp. 282–99.

Rein, R. (1999) *Spain and the Mediterranean since 1898*, London: F. Cass.

Ribas Mateos, N. (ed.) (2005) *The Mediterranean in the Age of Globalization: Migration, Welfare, and Borders*, New Brunswick, NJ: Transaction Publishers.

Sant Cassia, P. and I. Schäfer (2005) ' "Mediterranean Conundrums": Pluridisciplinary Perspectives for Research in the Social Sciences', *History and Anthropology*, 16: 1–23.

Tsoukalas, C. (2002) 'Between "East" and "West", the Meaning of the Mediterranean in Modern Greece and Possibly Elsewhere as Well', *Mediterranean Historical Review*, 17(2): 32–46.

Winks, R. W. and S. P. Mattern (2004) *The Ancient Mediterranean World: From the Stone Age to A.D. 600*, New York: Oxford University Press.

Xenakis, D. and D. N. Chryssochoou (eds) (2001) *The Emerging Euro-Mediterranean System*, Manchester: Manchester University Press.

9 Europe and Islam

Jack Goody

The current tendency in much European thought is to consider Europe in opposition to Islam, the former being characterized by many politicians as Judaeo-Christian civilization in contrast to the Muslims. It has a long history. But there is another view altogether. We need to start by going back to the societies that emerged after what the prehistorian Gordon Childe (1964 [1942]) referred to as the Urban Revolution of the Bronze Age. That radical change involved the development of a more advanced agriculture including the plough and irrigation, together with animal traction and the wheel, as well as the associated division of labour, artisanal specialisms and the invention of writing itself that made life in the towns both so much richer and so much more complex.

Civilization in the sense of urban culture evolved in parts of Asia, and to a minor extent Europe, from the third millennium BCE Subsequently European writers, beginning with the Greeks, have opposed European and Asian societies, especially with regard to their political traditions, democracy as opposed to despotism. The states of Antiquity, a notion that applied only to Europe, that is, to Greece and Rome, were seen in opposition to the oriental empires. Antiquity led on to feudalism, feudalism to capitalism, while the East was left to pursue its own different line ('Asiatic exceptionalism') originating in their earlier irrigation societies, seen as highly centralized. Considerable intellectual damage has been caused by trying to separate that classical, European world, not only in terms of historical knowledge but by politicians down the ages, by over-emphasizing and indeed creating supposed differences. The distinction then becomes polarized, Europe (us) being positively valued, Asia (them) negatively. Europe is the land of democracy, Asia of despots. Europe made it, Asia did not.

Just as Asia had its own political system, epitomized in recent times by 'despotic' Turkey, so too the Near East had its own religion, Islam, which was inextricably associated with its more 'backward' economy. But the notion of opposing civilizations or continents seems less than appropriate. All these three major religions, Judaism, Christianity and Islam, arose in the Near East, technically in Asia rather than Europe, and they spread widely throughout the world. In any case the Eastern Mediterranean, on whose borders these religions arose, is badly served by a geographical distinction between Europe and Asia since it was an area of constant interaction, economic, political, cultural, and over a long period, with influences coming from Africa (Egyptian), some from Asia (Semitic) and some from Europe itself, especially from the classical world.

That perception has dominated much European thinking about the present and the past, together with the idea that Europe achieved modernization on its own, that it 'invented invention', democracy, individualism, freedom, even love. In fact these features, in so far as they can be satisfactorily defined, were found in Western Asia as well as in Western Europe, especially following the expansion of Islam in the seventh century. In this chapter I want to touch upon three aspects of this relationship: first, the similarities in character, values and intellectual orientation between Islam and its sister religions; second, the importance of contacts with the Near East for 'modernization' in Europe; and third, the actual physical penetration of Islam into Europe.

The development of writing gave birth to written religions, religions of the Book, including the Near Eastern trilogy. These written religions take a different shape from earlier 'oral' ones, partly because the use of writing produces a text that acquires a permanent, timeless status as the 'holy scriptures' (as distinct from the relatively flexible and changing religions of earlier society).[1] That relative permanency of the sacred text, which contrasts not only with the changing nature of most oral communication but with the cumulative nature of other kinds of written production, such as science, has certain consequences that are highly significant in the contemporary world. While processes of adjustment and adaptation do take place within such religions, and even tendencies towards secularization and agnosticism occasionally appear, there is always the potential possibility of what have been called fundamentalists returning to the original religious text. Equally there are those who go back to earlier pronouncements in order to 'reform' the religion. Thus Reformation (and in the arts Renaissance) was on a par with fundamentalism. That was the case with the Taliban of Central Asia who rejected the construction of figurative icons as blasphemous and therefore destroyed the Buddhist masterpieces of Bamiyan. Similar destruction was found in many Protestant movements that tended to reject Catholic iconicity in favour of unadorned churches where sculpture and painting were thrown out or damaged because they were considered to be forbidden to early Christians. In a different form fundamentalism appears in Orthodox as distinct from Reformed Jewish groups, notably in the long-haired, bearded, traditionally-dressed inhabitant of Me'ah She'arim in Jerusalem, as well as among many of the members of settlements of the West Bank in Palestine, committed as they are to following the pronouncements of a text that was composed 2,000 years ago. In all these contexts the social and political consequences are enormous.

In the Far East followers go back to the words of Confucius or to the early texts of Buddhism, inscribed in stone. But it is particularly true of the three Near Eastern religions that refer to versions of the same Holy Scriptures, as well as having additions of their own. They share most of the same myths and importantly many of the same values, despite widespread views to the contrary. It is true that the three religions have often been opposed to one another on the ground and have persecuted their neighbours in intolerable ways. Nevertheless (although this is perhaps less true of Judaism) similar universalistic ideas are found within each community which enjoin its members to love not only brothers and clansfolk but all those who convert to the same faith. That conversion is often more significant than affiliation to race or class. One could 'legitimately' enslave only the non-believer, not a fellow member; the same was in principle true of marriage, since endogamy was greatly preferred, and even enforced. Marriage entailed conversion to the faith, in Catholic Christianity, in Islam, in Judaism. In Islam in particular, once converted an adherent could rise through the ranks to become Vizier or admiral; the other two religions also provided ladders to power, reputation or wealth, but more restrictedly. That opportunity permitted a measure of mobility, and freedom, for some individuals.

One of the values that Islam shared with Judaism and with early Christianity (as well as with some later branches of Protestantism) was the aversion to figurative representation, originally embodied in the Commandment, Thou shalt make no graven images. The destruction of the statues of the Buddha at Bamiyan, the defacing of statues of the Virgin in Ely Cathedral, the absence of figurative ornament in Jewish synagogues, these all reflect the same religious traditions and indicate the strong and enduring links between the religions of the Book. In this respect the destructive actions of one group are no more barbarian than those of another. Certain features associated with an ancient text are found in all written religions. The tendency to apply norms universally is one of these. Written religions are boundary-maintaining and hence involve conversion rather than just compromise or incorporation. Sometimes this is achieved by voluntary means, sometimes by conquest, which leads to the inclusion of members of different socio-cultural groups.

It is clear that toleration was not confined to Christians, nor was charity, despite popular views that *caritas* was primarily a Christian virtue. All post-Bronze Age societies display a substantial measure of economic stratification, of class differentiation. All these religions make provision for helping those members of the community (and sometimes others too) who are worse off, by gift, by bequests, by investments, sometimes direct but usually through the church, mosque or synagogue, as well as to others requiring the blessing of God. It was under Christianity that most charitable gifts were probably needed because, of the three religions, this was the only one that had an establishment consisting of monasteries as well as of bishops and clergy. However Islam came a close second with its use of endowments (*waqf*) to support the mosques and their attached markets, caravanserai, hospitals and schools as well as those made to help poor members of the family. Jews too have institutions for helping members of the faith of this kind, but given their dispersal did not have the same need to support major institutions.

So too other values and emotions often regarded as uniquely Christian or as acquired from the Greeks are found in slightly different forms in the other religions. Freedom, claimed by Finley (1985) as an invention of the Greeks, is as much regarded in the other creeds. In the eighteenth century the British admiral Slade praises this quality in Turkish life, even though in popular mythology all citizens were seen as 'slaves' of the Sultan. He admires the way that ordinary soldiers could rise to the highest rank, of people's freedom from tolls and taxes. Restraint is a virtue sometimes thought to be completely lacking in Islam because of the practice of polygyny and the promise of sexual pleasure in the next world. But polygyny on any scale is only for the few, who have their fill of pleasures in most stratified regimes. In fact Islam restrains the behaviour of its members in many ways, insisting on generosity (the weekly saddaq or gift), the five daily prayers, the requirement of the pilgrimage and above all the annual month-long day-time fast.

Individualism is another of those virtues that Westerners attribute to themselves. It is part of the Robinson Crusoe and parallel myths that seem to contribute to entrepreneurship and capitalism. In fact humanity in general has seen something we can call 'individualism' increase in certain spheres over time. But to regard the modern economy with its tight organizations in factory, in office, in theatre or in school as more individualistic than earlier forms of work organization is another myth of the West, which always sees itself as more 'individualistic' than the 'collective', 'primitive', of the East. There is no evidence to support the contention that individualism is absent from Islamic societies, whose members over a long period were the major traders in the Indian Ocean as well as along the silk route and who participated actively in early capitalist activities. It was Muslims who led the famous fifteenth-century Chinese expedition to Africa and it was a Muslim who piloted Vasco da Gama to India. There was no shortage of individual entrepreneurs.

One of the aspects of the inner life that Christians have tried to appropriate at the expense not only of Islam is love itself, at least romantic love, which has been seen as the 'innovation' of the troubadours of twelfth-century France. That notion has been firmly promoted by historians, such as Duby (1996), by sociologists such as Giddens (1991), by psychologists such as Person (1991) and by cultural theorists such as de Rougemont (1956). In Europe it is seen by demographers and family historians as linked to the constellation of the European nuclear family, which again is thought to have a unique connection with the development of capitalism.

However, love poetry of a romantic kind is found in early China, in Sanskritic India and very widely in Arab and Persian societies. Indeed it seems highly likely that the courts of Southern France where the troubadours performed were strongly influenced by Muslim Spain where love poetry was a popular genre. Once again there is little to distinguish the emotional disposition of the Christian and Muslim worlds, and if anything it was the latter that influenced the former.

This and other similarities in 'value orientation' have been obscured by the conflict situation often, but not always, existing between them. Not always, because Islam gave a limited recognition to other religions of the Book. They had to pay a special tax but then had many of the privileges of citizenship. Communities of Jews and Christians lived reasonably successful lives in Cairo in the early Middle Ages, as we see from Goitein's (1967) vivid picture drawn from the Geniza manuscripts. That was particularly the case with Jews in North Africa; unlike Christians, they represented no political threat, spoke Arabic and continued to make important contributions to medicine, science and philosophy in these regions. Many returned to North Africa with the Muslims when these were finally expelled from Spain, preferring exile to coming under Christian rule.

Part of the supposed contrast with Europe has taken the form of seeing Islam as having not only values that were very different but also institutional systems that prevented it from 'modernizing' and therefore from becoming 'capitalist'. Politically Turkey for example was considered 'despotic' in an Asiatic fashion as distinct from European democracy. But that democracy of the contemporary kind only effectively manifested itself after the French and American revolutions. While Turkey may not have had exactly the same form of feudalism, which many Western writers have seen as an essential stage in the run-up to capitalism, they certainly had a system of land tenure that was of the same genre, involving what Maine called a 'hierarchy of rights' and a degree of long-term security. And they developed capitalist institutions well before the West, at least at the level of mercantile capitalism. For they were not only warriors, but heavily involved in the long-distance trade with the East as well as with the West, largely through Venice and the Italian city states. They were also engaged in the manufacture of commodities that were exchanged in that trade.

Islam stood at the centre of the known world, known that is to Europeans and Asians, each of which was known to the other at least from the classical period, if not from the Bronze Age. Before 1592 the Muslim religion stretched continuously from the south of Spain to the borders of China, acting as a conduit for information, inventions and commodities. It was along this route that the manufacture of paper developed, invented in China around the beginning of the Christian era, and which had such a dramatic effect on Europe and the Near East. Paper was manufactured on a mass scale using the water mill, as happened in early textile factories. The making of silk thread, another import from China, used mechanized and indeed industrial techniques which were probably transmitted to Italy. Certainly the Islamic world saw a huge growth in the production of silk thread and silk cloth, some of which was exported to Europe and became critical to the trade of Venice and other Italian cities when commerce revived. Indeed it has been said of the old Ottoman capital of Bursa that the economy was built on the trade in silk (and its production and manufacture), both locally but especially to Europe, with which the materials, thread and cloth were exchanged for woollen cloth as well as for bullion. The export of woollen cloth was particularly associated with the town of Florence, whereas other North Italian towns, especially Lucca, but also Genoa, Bologna and Venice, took up the manufacture of silk, first using imported thread but eventually planting mulberry trees, cultivating silk worms and producing their own materials which they made with the aid of water-driven threading machines that seem to have been based on a Chinese model (Elvin 1973).

It was these machines that helped turn Bologna into what Poni describes as 'an industrial city'. The secrets of these processes were eventually pirated by one Lombe, a member of an English weaving family, and taken back to help construct the Great Mill at Derby in 1718, before the industrialization of cotton production that is usually seen as marking the beginning of the Industrial Revolution. In other words these early processes of industrialization and mechanization were transmitted to Europe by way of Islam, to be developed later on in the eighteenth century for the factory production of cotton and other items. There was therefore a measure of continuity between the economies of Europe and Asia not only in the long-distance trade on which part of the prosperity of both continents depended, but in the transmission of techniques, processes and inventions between them. The crude dichotomy between a potentially or actually capitalist Europe and a backward, 'traditional' Asia quite misrepresents the past relationships between them and is a poor guide to the future, even if it had some limited justification in the nineteenth century.

So it was not only that 'values' and intellectual orientations in the Eastern Mediterranean were more similar to those in the West than was then imagined, but so were the economic activities. It is true that Islam has apparently been more faithful to Biblical injunctions against usury than either Christianity or Judaism, nevertheless that has not been a serious handicap to trade. Mahomet himself was a trader and Mecca a centre of market activity. Muslims travelled widely in their trading ventures, to the eastern coast of India, to Singapore and Malaysia, to Indonesia and to China.

Reciprocal trade and the associated manufactures lay at the heart of the revival of Europe at the end of the Middle Ages. Mercantile capitalism led to increased production and to industrial capitalism. That input from the East went back much further in time. The collapse that followed the fall of the Roman Empire did not affect eastern towns and eastern culture in the same drastic way. In the West there was an extreme reaction; in Britain towns collapsed, literacy disappeared and even Christianity may have vanished. Trade, manufacture and commerce received a severe setback. In the East, which was to become Islamic from the seventeenth century, the urban cultures of port cities like Alexandria and inland towns like Cairo continued to prosper partly because they were still trading with countries yet further East, in Persia, Arabia, India and China. Those towns became of great importance to Europe when trade began to pick up. As early as the ninth century, Venice entered into relations with Christian Constantinople as well as with Muslim Alexandria, from which port it acquired not only commercial goods but the very relics of its patron saint, Mark.

It was this revival of trade in the Mediterranean that developed Europe's trade with the East, with India and China. That revival had two results. It led to the rising mercantile capitalism of Italian towns and to the development of their manufactures, especially substitutes for eastern imports, silk from Muslim lands, porcelain originally from China and later cotton cloth from India, the basis of the Industrial Revolution in England. All these activities came through Muslim lands, as did paper-making and many intellectual advances. They came not only through exchange but also because of Islam's penetration into Europe by way of conquest and conversion, Arabs (and Berbers) to southern Spain between 711 and 1492 as well as to Sicily, Southern Italy and Cyprus. In Greece and the Balkans it was the Turks who extended their empire, creating permanent Muslim enclaves in Albania and Bosnia. Further north it was the Mongols who arrived, later converting to Islam, and leaving behind them Muslim communities in the Crimea and the Caucasus. Many of these invaders were forced to withdraw, but not before they had contributed significantly to the revival of Europe through the exchange of goods and knowledge. Indeed it has recently been argued that capitalism and the modern world generally had an Eastern origin (Hobson 2004). While that argument may put the case too strongly, the influence of the 'advanced' East was certainly significant in helping a 'backward' Europe to catch up and overtake its Eastern counterparts.

Such influences were particularly important from Andalusia and Sicily as these Muslim regions were obviously close and could be visited by Europeans. In the twelfth century, Andalusia had great libraries such as the royal collection in Cordoba (open to others), as well as great scholars, Jews such as Maimonides, Muslim students of Greek philosophy and medicine, such as Ibn Rashd (Averroes), an expert on Aristotle who proposed a doctrine of Universal Reason. But quite apart from local scholars and local resources, both Andalusia and Palermo were in touch with the rest of the Islamic world that stretched through Persia, north India, Central Asia to the borders of China; all these lands contributed to its store of knowledge, widely transmitted both by travelling scholars and by books. Islamic cultures had not only taken over part of the classical learning that Europe had lost or set aside during the upheavals following the fall of the Roman Empire and the rise of Christianity, but acquired other discoveries from India, such as the so-called Arabic numerals that transformed mathematical calculation, as well as the many inventions brought in from China, including the Baconian trilogy that he saw as creating the modern world, the compass, gunpowder and printing. Very important for Europe was the medical knowledge that had been developed in Hellenistic times in the works of Hippocrates and others, and in the Roman period in the writing of Galen and his colleagues. It had been in Alexandria during Hellenistic times that Herophilus had developed the practice of surgery, based upon the dissection of the human body. That is not an activity encouraged by many cultures, even in early literate societies. It was equally taboo to Christians and other followers of the Abrahamic religions for which the body was God's creation. Consequently anatomy fell into desuetude during the Middle Ages, and many other aspects of medicine too since they were enshrined in pagan texts. In any case disease was often seen as the result of sin, which could only be cured by confession, prayer and repentance. The Muslims and Jews had fewer qualms about such literature and continued to translate the texts and to practise medicine. Much medieval knowledge and practice came to Europe through these scholars and practitioners.

If the Islamic world contributed so much in the past, what gave rise to the present situation in which the Western world clearly has a competitive advantage in the economy as well as in other spheres such as education and possibly in political representation? The knowledge revolution beginning in the West in the sixteenth century was partly related to the commercial and economic successes in Europe, whose economy had broken through to new levels. But of great importance were changes in the means of communication. The early adoption of paper had given Islam a great competitive advantage, enabling it to build up much larger libraries than was possible in Europe where writers had to use parchment made from animal skins or papyrus imported from Egypt. But for religious reasons to do with the reproduction of the name and word of God and his prophet, or even of their language, the printing press, which like paper was invented in China, was not adopted in the Muslim world until very late. That rejection left them out of the great advances in printing with an alphabetic script that Eisenstein (1979) among others regarded as so significant for scientific, informational and literary developments in the Renaissance and that Ong (1974) sees as so important for the growth of education. In all these spheres changes in the speed and extent of communication corresponded to an increase in diversity; the range of written material available for an individual to consult increased enormously. That proliferation was associated with a period of 'disenchantment of the world', at least for some, of freeing certain areas of thought from their religious constraints. We find similar periods in Islam that have been described as 'humanism' but there was nothing so radical as occurred in Europe where even though some religious beliefs became more 'fundamentalist' in the Protestant return to the text, other areas of enquiry definitely became more free, especially under the Reform. Islam got left behind, not only in the economy but in secular learning and education. In many areas, Muslim schools remained committed to learning the Qu'ran before all else, at a time when religion played a lesser part in Western education either at schools or universities. Islam has remained more firmly committed to its faith and its text for longer than either Christianity or, later, Judaism.

So Christianity and Islam, Europe and the Muslim world, were linked in many ways right from the beginning of the latter religion which centred itself upon the Mediterranean and its cultures. In religious terms there was of course an earlier opposition not so much in terms of intellectual achievement and economic action but in matters of festivals, of holy days, of ritual, of prophets, of recruitment rather than of a monotheistic faith and values. The boundaries between Europe and Asia are largely inconsequential; the opposition between Christianity and Islam largely a question of politics, war and regimes. In other ways there was a great deal of movement between the two spheres, mainly from East to West since the East was more advanced economically and in knowledge systems, at least until the Renaissance.

Note

1 This and related differences are elaborated in Goody 1986.

References

Childe, V. G. (1964 [1942]) *What Happened in History*, Harmondsworth: Penguin.
Duby, G. (1996) *Féodalité*, Paris: Gallimard.
Eisenstein, E. L. (1979) *The Printing Press as an Agent of Change: Communications and Cultural Transformations in Early Modern Europe*, Cambridge: Cambridge University Press.
Elvin, M. (1973) *The Pattern of the Chinese Past*, London: Eyre Methuen.
Finley, M. I. (1985) *Democracy Ancient and Modern*, London: Hogarth.
Giddens, A. (1991) *Modernity and Self-identity: Self and Society in the Late Modern Age*, Cambridge: Polity.
Goitein, S. D. (1967) *A Mediterranean Society, the Jewish Communities of the Arab World as Portrayed in the Documents of the Cairo Geniza*, Vol. 1, Berkeley: California University Press.
Goody, J. (1986) *The Logic of Writing and the Organisation of Society*, Cambridge: Cambridge University Press.
Hobson, J. M. (2004) *The Eastern Origins of Western Civilisation*, Cambridge: Cambridge University Press.
Ong, W. (1974) *Ramus, Method and the Decay of Dialogue*, New York: Octagon Books.

Person, E. S. (1991) 'Romantic Love: At the Intersection of the Psychic and the Cultural Unconscious', *Journal of American Psychoanalytic Association*, 39: 383–411.

Rougemont, D. de (1956) *Love in the Western World*, New York: Princeton University Press.

10 Citizenship East and West

Reflections on revolutions and civil society

Bryan S. Turner

The liberal Western model of citizenship imagines society as a market place in which strangers meet to exchange goods and services. This is what we might call a 'citizenship of strangers' in which people, who have no necessary social connections with each other, interact in public. These strangers do not have or are not expected to have cultural identities that play an important role in the public domain. However, this political framework by itself was not sufficient to support civil society, which required some degree of additional social bonding through religion or nationalism. In civil society, religion was particularly important for creating social capital. We might say, for example, that in nineteenth-century England citizenship was not defined by deep cultural criteria; citizens were political actors who expressed their will through parliamentary institutions. However, these political citizens did in fact have considerable and important cultural identities, for example they were English speaking and predominantly Anglican. The key issue here is that the spread of secular citizenship constrained the relevance of cultural and kinship ties in the public domain, and replaced kinship as a principle of social organisation.

In Asia, especially in China, citizenship was slow to develop and connected with the idea of patrimony, benevolence and kinship. It was initially a citizenship of blood or what we might call a 'citizenship of kinsmen'. The state was often conceptualised in patriarchal terms as a family or clan system, in which the citizens are part of the family of the state. The obligation of the state or emperor towards citizens was understood in terms of a benefice rather than contract (Woodiwiss 1998). Like other Empires, China did not give rise to a notion of citizenship based on a market place of strangers, but there was a distinctive development of ideas of citizenship in the period 1890–1920 in which Chinese intellectuals struggled to find a language appropriate to the public domain that could express the first stirrings of political modernisation. In Japan, citizenship developed with the economic modernisation of Japan, but remained tied to the idea of a loyal subject of the emperor. With American occupation, Japan came to acquire certain institutional aspects of democracy, but Japanese society has not openly embraced cultural heterogeneity, and hence its civil society is not fundamentally a society of strangers. Indonesia – as a consequence of the national struggle against the Japanese and Dutch – has developed a notion of national citizenship in the context of an emerging nationalism. Whereas Chinese and Japanese citizenship has often been authoritarian and state dominated, Indonesia has evolved with a clear notion of national citizenship and a viable civil society.

Citizenship is typically the product of major social disruptions – invasions, revolutions, mass warfare or traumatic migrations (Turner 1986). Citizenship is often top-down (as in Germany, Russia and the Habsburg Empire) and it functions to incorporate the working class into capitalism. It can also be bottom-up (as in France, the United States and to some extent Britain). As a result, despite the historical argument that Greece and Rome were the cradles of Western democracy, Western citizenship is a relatively modern development, and specifically the product of three revolutions – the English civil war, the American War of Independence and the French Revolution. In Asia, the only comparable revolution took place in Indonesia as a war of independence, anti-colonialism and resistance.

Defining citizenship

The citizen was closely connected historically with the rise of European cities and the virtues of civility. A citizen was simply a member or denizen of a city, and as a result enjoyed certain privileges and was burdened with civil responsibilities and duties. Service in the city militia and payment of taxes were the typical duties of an urban citizen. A citizen was a burgess or freeman of a city, and citizenship has been as a result associated with burger or bourgeois culture. In the Christian West, the countryside was pagan and uncivilised. Citizens were literally urban and urbane, and were contrasted with the illiterate pagan communities of the countryside. Pagans were lacking in urbanity, whereas citizens were part of the *civitas* – the urban culture of the autonomous city and the Latin Church.

Historians have examined these cultural components of citizenship in the Greek *polis* and the early Church. However, this form of citizenship was very limited, and developed in an agrarian society in which the majority of people were domestic slaves. The public domain was reserved for men who were capable of rational conduct. Citizenship is therefore most appropriately regarded as a modern concept, emerging with the evolution of autonomous cities in medieval Europe, and coming to fruition with the revolutions that produced the modern world. Modern citizenship was produced by the destruction of the Estates and the pulverisation of feudalism by bourgeois political struggles.

In European societies, the 'citizen' was made possible by the emergence of 'civil society' (*die bürgerliche Gesellschaft*). On the one hand, the citizen emerged out of the independent associations of urban societies especially guilds, clubs and associations. On the other hand, the citizen was somebody who owed loyalty and obligation to a state that exercised sovereignty and gave the citizen security. The Western notion of citizenship (*Staatsbürger-schaf*) has this ambiguity: it is a conduit of individual rights and a reflection of the growth of state power over civil society.

The sociology of citizenship is still somewhat dominated by the analysis of Max Weber. In *The City* (1958) he emphasised the importance of Christian universalism in which faith rather than blood was recognised as the basis of social community. He contrasted the autonomous city in Europe with the city in the East as a military camp. The sharp separation of religion and politics in St Augustine's *City of God* is also thought to be important. Although we can detect the ancestry of citizenship in the urban institutions of classical Greece and Rome, there is little evidence of *social* citizenship until the modern period. Because women were excluded from participation in public life, we should hesitate in assuming that citizenship was fully developed in ancient Athens and Rome. It is more accurate to argue that classical citizenship was limited in its scope. We might suitably call the classical form *political* citizenship, and argue that the revolutionary struggles that produced modernity also produced modern or *social* citizenship. Modern citizenship has three important characteristics: it is universalistic, it does not recognise kinship ties in the public arena, and it is closely connected with the rise of effective taxation.

Causes of citizenship

Weber's account of the historical roots of democracy and citizenship has created the dominant paradigm within which citizenship has been analysed by sociologists. There are two aspects of Weber's argument that have remained influential. First, Weber in *The City* (Weber 1958) identified the medieval and renaissance city as an important location for Western democracy, because the independent guilds, the decline of slavery, the growth of independent legal institutions and the creation of an urban militia all favoured the growth of social rights. Second, military discipline meant 'the triumph of democracy, because the community wished and was compelled to secure the cooperation of the non-aristocratic masses and hence put arms, and along with the arms political power, into their hands' (Weber 1981: 324–5). Changes in the technology of warfare that encouraged the routinisation of military activity, namely taking military prowess out of 'the battle between heroes' (Weber 1981: 325), also favoured the growth of democratic institutions. The notion that the unintended consequence of the democratisation of military organisation has been to favour the general democratisation of society has been common to many accounts of citizenship, but another aspect of this argument is that the violent trauma of war on a population can destroy traditional consciousness, old forms of hierarchy and exploitation, and create new circumstances for democracy.

Modern citizenship is a product of three political revolutions – the

English Civil War, the American War of Independence and the French Revolution. These revolutions were the cradle of modern nationalism, and national citizenship means the rights and duties of a person who is a member of a national community. The creation of European nation-states from the seventeenth century necessarily involved the creation of nationalistic 'imagined communities' which assumed the existence of, and which went a long way to create, ethnically homogeneous populations. These national communities were held together, against the divisions of social class, culture and ethnicity, by nationalistic ideologies and historical narratives demonstrating the antiquity of the national community. The Treaty of Westphalia (1648) was the origin of the modern world system of nation-states, and state formation involved the creation of nationalist identities on the basis of a double colonisation, both internal and external. This political process was the cultural basis for the creation of national forms of citizenship.

National citizenship was politically important because it incorporated the working class into nascent capitalism through the creation of civil rights and in some cases welfare institutions. In practice, welfare capitalism achieved the pacification of the working class with relatively little concession to the fundamental social issue of inequalities in wealth, income and political power. Citizenship left the property structure of capitalism intact, and welfare capitalism avoided the revolutionary conflicts of the class system that were fundamental to Karl Marx's predictions of the business cycle and economic crises. However, there was considerable variation between the different capitalist regimes. While in Germany Bismarck developed social rights through welfare legislation, political rights were underdeveloped. Neither fascism nor authoritarian socialism supported civil and political rights, although they did develop welfare institutions and social rights. American liberalism combined market freedom and liberal support for individual rights, but did not favour social welfare rights.

In conclusion, in the absolutist monarchies, monarch, nobility and Church resisted universal citizenship, but they also recognised that their long-term political survival depended on some compromise with the bourgeoisie and working class, and some degree of modernisation of both society and politics. In Germany, Bismarck and Kaiser Wilhelm were founders of the modern welfare state, but social citizenship was developed with few concessions to civil and political rights. This system came into place before the First World War and according to some historians survived until the mid-1990s. Whereas in Japan, the Meiji Revolution used the monarchy as a legitimating principle in its strategy of conservative modernisation, Russia was the least successful state in developing a strategy to retain power and yet modernise the regime. It favoured repression and exclusion, followed by bouts of ineffective reform. Austria was also politically unsuccessful, and was compromised by class conflicts, nationalist struggles and a failure to develop a corporate strategy. Political success required maintaining the corporate coherence of the *ancien regime* and a partial incorporation of the bourgeoisie. These regimes, with the possible exception of Germany, did not develop social citizenship in the form of a welfare state, and civil citizenship in the shape of civil liberties was often undercut by arbitrary political interventions. Despite these limitations, Germany and Japan were relatively successful in their economic industrial-isation in a period when working class opposition was weak, given the relatively small size of the urban working class. The solidarity of the working class was also undermined by internal differentiation resulting from the growth of service sectors and the rise of the new middle class.

Revolutions and citizenship in Asia

Japan: the occupation and the imposition of citizenship

One of the most influential accounts in the historical sociology of demo-cracy was Barrington Moore's *Social Origins of Dictatorship and Demo-cracy* (1972). Broadly speaking, he argued that the paths towards either democratic or authoritarian rule were determined historically by the rela-tionship between landlord, peasant and bourgeoisie. The English case is paradigmatic. The early destruction of the peasantry through enclosures and sheep farming created a capitalist agrarian class and the early demili-tarisation of the nobility. When the bourgeoisie came to confront the rem-nants of an aristocracy, the peasant class could not act as a break on modernisation. In Germany by contrast, the continuity of the estate system in east Germany allowed a conservative *Junker* class of landlords to exer-cise considerable power over parliamentary institutions.

Perhaps the most important elaboration of Moore's argument has been developed by Theda Skocpol in *States and Social Revolutions* (1979). She has produced a distinctive theory of revolution through an examination of social revolutions in three *ancien regimes*. Revolutions occur because states are vulnerable to endogenous socio-economic processes, particularly the management of internal class conflict. Her theory rejects any role to human agency in revolutions. For example, revolutions are not produced by the revolutionary will of revolutionaries themselves; revolution is the unintended consequence of the decomposition of the state and its agrarian bureaucracy. Instead she examines the causal constraints imposed by objective historical circumstances. The three principal forms of constraint are class relations, the repressive character of the state, and the external military and other constraints on the state. Perhaps the key aspect of her argument is to reject any attempt to absorb the state into society. The repressive actions of the state have independent causal consequences for revolutions and citizenship.

What is the implication of these arguments for an analysis of the rise of citizenship and democracies in Asian societies? We need to attend to the nature of the breakdown of *ancien regimes*, their inclusion into an emerging world capitalist system, and the revolutionary opportunities for creating civil societies, civil liberties and an independent citizenry. One can argue that citizenship is the product of an emerging bourgeois class that is sufficiently powerful to protect its civil liberties, and whose social dominance over civil society eventually permits the social inclusion of subordinate classes and ethnic minorities into the social order. Alternatively, the conservative institutions of the *ancient regime* are destroyed by internal civil war and external invasion, permitting the emergence of a national consciousness and a national civil society that draws various classes into civil society.

Japanese modernisation has received considerable attention from both Western and Asian scholars. The creation of the nation-state is essential for the development of modern citizenship based on contributory rights, that is rights and duties involving taxation and social benefits, but in Japan the concept of nation did not exist historically, and was to some extent imported with Western culture after the Meiji Restoration in 1868–1873. By contrast the state as a political system had existed on the Japanese archipelago from early times. The formation of the state of Japan began to make progress from the latter half of the fourth century to the Taika Reform of 645 through integrating many independent clans by the Yamato Imperial Court. In East Asia, China and Korea had developed the highly centralised system of the ancient state much earlier than in Japan, but Japan had embraced this highly centralised system of empire from the mainland. This Chinese state was essentially the patrimonial state (Weber 1978). The old Tokugawa shogunate was transformed during the Meiji Restoration into a bureaucratic, centralised, nation-state, and this restoration was possible because of the absence of a politically efficacious upper class in Tokugawa Japan.

The modern political history of Japan starts in fact somewhat earlier. The country had been unified by three feudal barons (*daimyo*) who were able to form a coalition of powerful lords. These *daimyo* were Oda Nobunaga (1534–1582), Toyotomi Hideyoshi (1536–1598) and Tokugawa Ieyasu (1542–1616). Their main achievements were twofold – to gain greater administrative control of the land and thereby raise taxes, and to prohibit the possession of swords. The result was the emergence of a professional class of warriors, namely the *samurai*. Although Japanese and European feudalism had much in common, in Japan the Emperor system was much more highly developed, and there was no institutional religion comparable with the Catholic Church. There were no castle cities in Tokugawa Japan. These economic and social circumstances suggest that no concept of the nation-state existed under the imperial system, and consequently it also means that there was no concept of national society in the Tokugawa period (Hayes 2005).

During the Tokugawa period, political control was enhanced by Japan's seclusion and opposition to Western cultural and economic contacts. This insularity produced an almost mystical form of nationalism, in which Japan was seen as the land of the rising sun. The Chinese doctrine of the Middle Kingdom was taken over by the Japanese elite to emphasise the power and uniqueness of the Japanese state. A shared sentiment of nationalism was constituted in addressing the crisis of national defence once European and American ships began to penetrate Japanese waters. The consciousness of nation and nationalism in Japan was created with the recognition of the need for modernisation and the industrialisation of Japan. The formation of the nation-state in Japan was directly connected with an awareness of the need to create a modern industrial system. The industrial revolution in the 1890s came only three decades after national integration during the Meiji Restoration.

After Commodore Perry's visit in 1853, the eventual termination of the shogunate meant the restoration of imperial powers. The elements of participatory institutions were introduced during this period. The Charter Oath of 1868 created deliberative assemblies, the control of the state was to be influenced by both upper and lower orders, traditional customs were to be abandoned, and there were to be universal laws applying to all. The *samurai* were disbanded, and encouraged to take on new roles in society. In 1873 universal male conscription was introduced, creating not only a mass basis for the military, but also for the state. A law of 1889 recognised the emperor as sovereign, both symbolically and legally. The state's bureaucracy adopted a Prussian model. Universal suffrage for men was introduced in 1925.

Modernisation in Japan did not however involve any significant democratic institutionalisation and its rapid industrialisation resulted in an authoritarian and imperialist system. Japan's military successes in the Sino-Japanese War (1894–1895), the Russo-Japanese War (1904–1905) and the annexation of Korea in 1910 strengthened the hand of the military elite and reinforced the significance of the emperor. Modernisation was also seen to require social harmony through the leadership of the state and the emperor, and opposition was seen to be subversive. As a result, citizenship in Japan was largely passive and top-down, in the sense that it involved loyalty to the emperor and to the society; civil liberties remained underdeveloped. For example, in 1890 the Emperor had issued the Imperial Rescript on Education and employing the word *shinmin* to denote loyal officials or citizens who followed their orders obediently. Japanese nationalism and the powerful identification with the Emperor as a symbol of unity were effective in creating the illusion of ethnic and cultural homogeneity (Weiner 1997).

Perhaps the most significant event in modern Japanese political history was the American occupation which aimed to dismantle Japanese military imperialism, demobilise the six and a half million Japanese soldiers and institutionalise democracy and civil liberties. Occupation produced the paradox of an enforced system of democracy as a consequence of military defeat in line with the Potsdam Declaration of 1945. Democracy was thus imposed by decree, by a military power with overwhelming superiority of force, and by a new ruler (General McArthur) who was in some respects a *shogun* (Dower 2003). If the model of Western development in the nineteenth century had been European, after 1945 it was overwhelmingly American. Democracy in Japan as a result is seen to be an external, foreign import, not a political system that has deep roots in Japanese culture. The weakness of the political system is illustrated by the absence of vigorous opposition, a history of the corruption of politicians, the late and shallow development of women's rights, lack of tolerance of outsiders and cultural diversity, and the passivity of the judiciary. There is also a relatively weak civil society as measured by voluntary associations and NGOs.

China: from Confucianism to modern citizenship

Citizenship involves a set of duties and rights. We can explore how the rights of individuals evolve in society, or we can examine how governments come to be held accountable, and how their duty to provide citizenship with the conditions that provide both security and prosperity comes to be recognised and enforced. Confucianism in China established a tradition in which the just ruler exercised care towards his subjects. In this respect Confucian thought recognised a mutual obligation between ruler and people. Nevertheless, a distinctive notion of citizenship did not arise in China until the nineteenth century through Western influence. Intellectuals abandoned the moral discourse of Confucianism in favour of a secular, national and utilitarian notion of the participatory community in which governments were to be committed to 'wealth and power' (*fuqiang*). Although the notion of citizenship was imported, Chinese intellectuals argued that there were important national traditions that supported the emergence of citizenship. These included: a sense of national identity based on language and ethnicity; a state with a bureaucracy that was independent of the ruler; and there was a recognition of the separation between state, emperor and administration. Intellectuals also came to reject the legacy of the literati – the trained, exemplary gentleman scholar – in favour of the idea of civic virtue and public morality that applies to everybody, governor and the people.

Chinese philosophy had a notion of contract (*minyue*), but unlike the Hobbesian contract, this grew out of harmony not conflict. The notion of rights did not emerge from struggles in which individuals make claims against the state, but from the notion of shared interests. The Western idea of utilitarian individualism was generally condemned as simply selfishness. The idea of the 'sovereign individual' did not exist in China; instead individuals are always defined within relationships of mutuality. Even after the Communist Revolution the idea of paternal authority remained strong. National unity and the nation were typically conceived in kinship terms.

Citizens are like kinsmen who are bound together not by economic interest but by mutuality. Chinese intellectuals were influenced by J-J. Rousseau, especially the emphasis on popular participation. Chinese intellectuals 'did not find the cure for oppression to lie in rights but rather sought a cure for disunity and familism in peoplehood' (Zarrow 1997: 14).

Intellectuals such as Liang Qichao (1873–1929) thought of citizenship in terms of the development of the Chinese state, whereas Zhang Binglin (1869–1936) emphasised the nation, which was conceived in racial terms. Both thinkers saw the need to strengthen and rationalise the state in the context of international competition and conflict. Qichao taught that nation and citizenship were necessarily connected, and in the time of the late Qing government the extension of suffrage was connected with the idea of nation-building through popular citizenship and modernisation. With the crisis of the early 1900s when the Qing state began to collapse under domestic and foreign pressure, Qichao sought to create an active citizenry. In Liang Qichao's writing there is an important emphasis on the idea of the citizen as a new creation with a moral purpose. He used the term *xinmin* to refer to 'citizen' and 'new person'. He also referred to *guomin* to make the connection between people, the nation and citizen. At the time the discourse of citizen also included the notion of *shimin* ('urban' or 'city person'). The creation of educated, autonomous and moral citizens was an essential foundation for a free and independent nation surrounded by threats from outside. Liang Qichao saw citizens as members of a constitutional order whose development was possible only outside a despotic system. Wang Jingwei writing in 1905 referred to 'people' (*minzu*), which joins both race and nation, and *guomin*, which conflates nation and citizen to describe a constitutional framework within which 'racial citizens' could enjoy rights that were not available to subjects in a despotic system.

The development of civil society, at least in the political tradition of de Tocqueville (see for example 2003), is important in creating the conditions – such as a public space – within which citizens can participate in social life, and at the same time acquire the skills and dispositions that are necessary for active citizenship. In China, the development of scholarly study associations (*xuehui*) appears to have played an important role in creating an autonomous space between state and society within which the individual could acquire civic virtues. In organising cultural activities such as editing newspapers, publishing books and organising lectures, Chinese intellectuals in the period 1890–1910 created a platform for inculcating ordinary citizens in a civic culture. It was these study societies led by Chinese gentry in late Imperial China rather than the voluntary association of liberal philosophy that stimulated the emergence of a creative, dynamic public space (Rowe 1993).

The need to understand and implement citizenship in China arose to meet certain specific needs: to define national membership, to establish rights and duties for its members, and to encourage participation in state and society. In China there had been no real sense of the *polis* that had been important in the political philosophy of classical Greece and Rome, and the great issue in public debate had been around the respective duties of the emperor and literati. The Communist state had created popular participation at certain levels of politics and the economy. It established popular nationalism, an effective bureaucracy, and government control over local society. Although there have been important developments in civil society in China since Mao, there are chronic problems confronting citizenship: a large, subservient and poorly educated working class and rural population, absence of independent trade unions, the inability of the system to secure smooth, predictable and legitimate transitions of power, and an absence of basic civil liberties.

The limitations on citizenship in China in the twentieth century were related to the nature of the Maoist Cultural Revolution, the importance of the peasantry as a class, and the devastating impact of war and anti-colonial struggle. There were important similarities between the French, Russian and Chinese revolutions, but the Chinese communist regime was a 'politicised bureaucracy' that was not a conducive environment for civil rights. Unlike Russia, the Chinese Communist Party had direct and effective linkages to the peasantry and villages, and the revolution organised the peasantry to overthrow the traditional hierarchical control of the gentry.

Indonesia: resistance, revolution and rights

In *Imagined Communities* Anderson (1983) argued, on the basis of a historical study of the struggle for Javanese independence from Japan, that nations are created or imagined rather than naturally occurring entities waiting to be discovered. Although nationalists typically like to think of their nation as existing from the dawn of time, nations are the products of modern revolutions. He defined a nation as an 'imagined political community' that is both limited and sovereign.

It is imagined because, even in the case of small nations, the fellow-members cannot know each other, but they consider themselves or imagine themselves to be members of the nation. This community is limited in having boundaries, and it is sovereign, because the state attempts to assert its legitimate power over a territory. Finally, it is a community, because irrespective of social class divisions, members of a nation imagine themselves to be what Anderson calls a 'horizontal community'. For example, Indonesians, who occupy a complex and sprawling archipelago of islands with diverse cultures and religions, acquired a national consciousness as a result of their struggle against Japanese and Dutch occupation from 1944–1946. The Indonesian nation is an imagined community in this sense.

An argument derived from Skocpol and Anderson would suggest that Indonesia is the only Asian society that through a revolutionary conflict with Japan and The Netherlands emerged as a society with a definite sense of nationhood and nationality, that is a society in which kinship and other primordial bonds had been replaced by civil bonds. Indonesian civil society had become a society of citizens not simply a society of kinsmen. The case would prove that (bottom-up or activist) citizenship is a political effect of radical change, that is change brought about by revolutionary struggle. Of course, the actual history of the Indonesian national revolution (1945–1950) is a good deal more complicated. The collapse of the Japanese military order led to the expression of revolutionary demands, often inspired by Marxist theories of revolution, for popular sovereignty (*kedaulatan rakyat*), involvement and radical change. By contrast, conservatives feared that the termination of Japanese rule would produce social chaos. There was an unspoken assumption among the Indonesian political elite that the ethnic and religious complexity of Indonesia could only be managed by the Dutch-educated urban elite, and that a revolutionary movement of the masses would result in violence that would compromise the longer-term struggle for national independence through diplomatic means. This was a struggle between revolution and diplomacy, and between different generations. Nevertheless, what Anthony Reid (1986) has called a 'social revolution' appears to have taken place at the village level where village headmen, who had implemented Japanese rule during the occupation, were removed. The result was a social revolution 'in the manner in which authority was wielded. It had overturned the relationship between youth and maturity; between heroic spirit and legal expertise; between charisma and authority' (Reid 1986: 75). The longer-term result was that the traditional, hierarchical structures of society had been shown to be precarious, and through revolutionary action Indonesian citizenship had become a real possibility and not simply a radical theory.

Conclusion: cosmopolitanism and citizenship

In crude terms, we could conclude that Japanese democratic citizenship was imposed from outside as a result of military defeat. Chinese citizenship, although it began to emerge in intellectual debate in the 1890s, was a top-down creation of a politicised bureaucracy. In Indonesia, citizenship was produced by a social revolution against the conservative intentions of established elites that was made possible as the consequence of resistance to foreigners.

It would be all too easy to conclude from this historical sketch that citizenship is a Western invention that was imported into Asia towards the end of the nineteenth century. Against this interpretation, we need to develop a more global and critical understanding of the problem. First, European political philosophers are fond of identifying the origins of Western citizenship with classical Greece and Rome, but this connection is false. The classical world was a slave society in which the majority of the population were subjected to the *polis* and not part of it. Second, while I have argued that revolutions create citizenship, we must remember that most revolutions fail. The English revolution resulted in a restoration of monarchy after Cromwell became an autocratic political leader, and the French Revolution ended in terror. The American Revolution did not provide a solution to the underlying problem of slavery, which required a tragic civil war to transform the slave economy of the South. Third, the system of Western citizenship is under considerable strain from multiculturalism, a greying population and economic recession (Turner 2001). It is thus more accurate and more promising to argue that in the West and the East the notion of social citizenship as a form of nation-building was embraced in the late nineteenth century by intellectuals who were committed to social change and political reform, and as a result it has become a global political concept. Revolutionary struggles in both West and East have propelled the idea of participatory citizenship into a global political discourse.

Acknowledgement

I would like to thank various members of the Asia Research Institute, especially Professor Anthony Reid, for their assistance in preparing this paper. Prof. David Anthony Kelly, visiting fellow at the East Asia Institute, National University Singapore, generously helped me with the literature search on China. I am also grateful to Chen Hon Fai, Chinese University of Hong Kong, for abstracts from a doctoral thesis on *Cultivating the People. Study Association and Gentry Culture in Late Imperial China*.

References

Anderson, B. (1983) *Imagined Communities: Reflections on the Origin and Spread of Nationalism*, London: Verso.

Dower, J. W. (2003) *Embracing Defeat: Japan in the Wake of World War II*, New York: Diane.

Hayes, L. D. (2005) *Introduction to Japanese Politics*, Armonk, New York: M. E. Sharpe.

Moore, B. (1972) *Social Origins of Dictatorship and Democracy*, London: Allen Lane.

Reid, A. (1986) *Indonesian National Revolution 1945–50*, Westport, Conn.: Greenwood Press.

Rowe, W. (1993) 'The Problem of "Civil Society" in Late Imperial China', *Modern China*, 19(2): 139–57.

Skocpol, T. (1979) *States and Social Revolutions: A Comparative Analysis of France, Russia and China*, Cambridge: Cambridge University Press.

Tocqueville, A. de (2003) *Democracy in America*, London: Penguin Books.

Turner, B. S. (1986) *Citizenship and Capitalism: The Debate over Reformism*, London: Allen & Unwin.

Turner, B. S. (2001) 'The Erosion of Citizenship', *British Journal of Sociology*, 52(2): 189–209.

Weber, M. (1958) *The City*, Glencoe, Ill.: Free Press.

Weber, M. (1978) *Economy and Society*, Berkeley: University of California Press.

Weber, M. (1981) *General Economic History*, New Brunswick: Transaction Books.

Weiner, M. (ed.) (1997) *Japan's Minorities: The Illusion of Homogeneity*, London: Routledge.

Woodiwiss, A. (1998) *Globalisation, Human Rights and Labour Law in Pacific Asia*, Cambridge: Cambridge University Press.

Zarrow, P. (1997) 'Citizenship in China and the West', in J. A. Fogel and P. G. Zarrow (eds) *Imagining the People: Chinese Intellectuals and the Concept of Citizenship, 1890–1920*, Armonk, New York: M. E. Sharpe, pp. 3–38.

11 Middle Eastern modernities, Islam and cosmopolitanism

Masoud Kamali

Since the appearance of Islam in the Middle East and the Islamic revolutionary movements that swept through three continents and created new sociopolitical formations in many Muslim countries, the relation between Islam and political systems has been widely discussed and debated. Prior to the modernization movements and the entrance of European powers on the political scene of Islamic countries, Islamic formations, such as the Arabic Empire, the Ottoman Empire and the Persian Empire, created relatively long-standing socio-economic and political stability in the Middle East. This stability was to a great deal based on the existence of a relatively well-organized civil society with powerful groups, namely ulama and bazaris, and the established relationships between civil society and the state that were legally, religiously and normatively legitimized. The huge internal market, mainly controlled by the bazaris, and the web of relationships between bazaars made a suitable ground for increasing contacts, exchange of commodities and services, as well as internal migration in the Islamic empires, including Egypt. Bazaars were not only engaged in internal exchange, but also in contacts with foreign merchants, including Chinese, Indians and Italians, to mention a few. Many people were on the move and in contact with others in other parts of the Ottoman and the Persian empires and developed a cosmopolitan worldview necessary for the economic activities of the bazaars. In addition, the political doctrines and systems had to have cosmopolitan characteristics in order to manage the substantial ethnic and religious diversities of those empires.

The spreading of capitalism as a world system intensified international trade and increased the bazaars' exchange with European economic centers. However, the colonial and imperialist interests of the non-Ottoman European powers, in particular England and France, favored their own merchants and harmed the bazaris. Bazaris needed modern changes and political support in order to compete with expanding European trade and to increase their political engagements. They first used the established communication channels with the state, such as direct or indirect negotiations through the ulama. The political weakness of the state and its selective military modernization led to the growing unease with the state and gradually to nationwide social movements which demanded the establishment of a constitutional regime. These movements resulted in the establishment of constitutional governments in both the Ottoman Empire and Persia in 1908 and 1905 (Kamali 1998, 2006; Abrahamian 1983).

One of the major properties of both the Ottoman and the Persian constitutional movements was the establishment and legitimization of the compatibility of Islam and modernity. Modernization ideas and views transformed the traditional religious doctrines and created modern interpretations of Islam that appealed for modern sociopolitical changes. The necessity of approaching Christian Europe and the universalism of modernity and Islam provided new ways to interpret the place of the individual in society. New cosmopolitan ideologies and political views such as unionism, liberalism and socialism were debated and developed in the Ottoman Empire and Persia. The post-constitutional era in both empires witnessed the spread of cosmopolitan ideas in accordance with a definition that indicates a claim to universality by virtue of independence, and a detachment from the bonds, commitments and affiliations that constrain ordinary nation-bound lives (Cheah and Robbins 1998). The constitutional movements in Islamic countries generated a new Islamic/modern identity politics with strong universal views. However, there was no consensus over the political doctrines of those engaged in the movements. There were mainly two political groups with different sociopolitical interpretations and modernization programs for the countries. One group was constituted of those who advocated a completely secular modernization with the French political system as a model. The other group believed in a combination of modern ideas and transformations with Islam. This political and ideological differentiation is perhaps the most lasting controversy in Islamic countries today. Although there have been devastating conflicts between the two groups, both have strong universal ideas and creeds.

Therefore it can be said that modernity and universalism were an inseparable part of new social movements in Islamic countries. These ideas were often transformed to religiously legitimized political doctrines that were relatively free from their Eurocentric constituencies.

Particularism of Islam and universalism of modernity

According to many established and seemingly 'scientific' explanations of the modernization of Islamic countries, such as those presented by Lewis (1953) and Huntington (1993), social movements against governmental modernization initiatives and programs have been considered anti-modern. This is mainly a result of the lack of accurate historical and sociological knowledge about the social movements in many Muslim countries and an indication of the belief in the established dichotomy of modern/traditional in the social sciences.

The reactions to governmental modernization projects in Muslim countries have not been anti-modern, but anti-authoritarian against governments and leaders who tried to restructure their societies in accordance with specific understandings of modernization. Social movements, including movements led by the clergy, have been mainly reactions against authoritarian modernization and dictatorship, and have demanded participation in collective decision-making in Muslim countries. Although a few anti-modern reactions can be singled out from the mainstream body of social movements for democracy and modernization, they were marginalized and disappeared at a very early stage. The Islamic movements have had a history of modern ideas and programs for modernization that often is ignored by social scientists. However, there are some studies exploring the modern features of the new Islamic movements (for instance, Kamali 1998, 2001; Eisenstadt 1999, 2002; Abrahamian 1993).

Notwithstanding, as a result of a tradition of Orientalism and other dualistic 'scientific' constructions of 'the Muslim world' as the other side of rationality and reason, dubious pundits that provide and reinforce a simple 'us-and-them' model have been established. Even some of the contemporary scholars who believe in the particularity of 'the Muslim world', such as Gellner, Lewis, Huntington and Dahrendorf, present astonishingly simple models, typically based on a simple dichotomous world – Orientalism reinvented. The simple models and more generally, incorrect theories of Lewis, Dahrendorf and Huntington have real consequences when adopted or bought by powerful international agents. The results are: miscalculations and tragic unintended consequences, such as economic failure, political chaos, war and coup d'état. They pay selective attention to history forgetting the negative, destructive role of European powers and the USA in many instances.

As Geertz (2003: 30) stresses,

> any attempt to conceive of 'Islam' in sweeping, 'civilization' terms – Lewis's, Simon's, Akbar's, Armstrong's, or anyone else's – is in some danger of conjuring up cloudscapes mighty like a whale and concocting Joycean big words that make us all afraid. A descent into the swirl of particular incident, particular politics, particular voices, particular traditions, and particular arguments, a movement across the grain of difference and along the lines of dispute, is indeed disorienting and spoils the prospect of abiding order. But it may prove the surer path toward understanding 'Islam' – that resonant name of some things at once.

Islam is not a simple religious phenomenon, but different social and cultural constructions in different countries that cannot be forced into the simple category of the 'Muslim world'. Muslim societies and their modern histories are as diverse and multiple as anywhere else in the world. The importance of looking comparatively at modernization processes is thus to see the discontents, diversities and competitive forces and models.

Tragic developments among European and North American societies in their modernization initiatives, and also uneven and croaked developments in 'the West' and other countries in the 'non-Western' parts of the world, among Islamic countries in particular, must be studied comparatively to generate a comprehensive theory of multiple modernities as a global transformation and an inclusive cosmopolitanism behind the established dualism of modern/traditional and/or occident/orient. The traditional and established understandings and theoretical constructions of single and West-centric modernity must be challenged – as they are in the face of new sociopolitical and cultural developments of the world. Common institutional properties of modernities, such as democracy and market economy, are incorporated in a variety of ways and forms of institutional contexts in various societies. This generates different degrees of tension and conflict in different societies. Even relatively homogeneous societies with a high degree of cohesion, such as the Scandinavian countries, have had intense conflicts around questions of industrialization, commodification, capitalist development, democracy and other disruptions connected to modernization. We should not forget that Finland had a civil war during the previous century. The dichotomous sociological tradition of Western societies contra non-Western, Muslim, non-modern, non-developed, etc., have resulted in ideal-typical theories about 'the West' that deny or minimize the wayward and tragic developments in Europe: Spain, Portugal, Greece, Hungary, Romania, Russia, not to speak of Germany and Italy after the First World War.

The modern developments in Islamic countries cannot be reduced to an isolated and particular phenomenon. They shared many common features, ideological frameworks and universal claims with many other countries in the world, including many Western countries.

The Euroversalism of modernity

The modern is usually considered a historical process starting in the north-western part of Europe and spreading, with different degrees of divergence, all over the world (Wittrock 2000; Eisenstadt 2002; Therborn 1992; Giddens 1990). Although the diversities of modern development are relatively well recognized among contemporary scholars of modernity, its history and scientific research are highly Eurocentric and based on a view of an institutionally unified world. Those social scientists who try to clarify and theorize 'alternative' modernities, such as the *Sonderweg* thesis of German modernity and 'American exceptionalism' (Lipset and Marks 2000), seem to assume that there is a universal norm and everything that does not accord with it must be understood as aberrant (Delanty 2003: 4). As Arnason (2002: 64) argues, the trends of modernity that have been most extensively analyzed, such as industrialization, urbanization and the spread of education, as well as the increasing scale and scope of organization and communication, were based on views conducive to visions of a unified world. Such views were also unreceptive to the very idea of significant divergence from the common patterns. Paradoxically, this tradition of the 'uniqueness of the West' has created a theoretical challenge to the real complexity and diversity of modernity. In other words, the tradition of a single modernity has created theoretical exclusionary dichotomies, such as those between modern and traditional and between 'West and the rest'.

Such dichotomies were part and parcel of the classical sociology that influenced the theories of modernity. For example, classical theorists, such as Spencer, Hegel, Marx, Weber, Durkheim and Toennies, in their attempts to theorize the new revolutionary system, *the* modernity, all used dichotomous categories. The features by which the modern world was separated from the pre-modern ones were of great interest to classical theorists and therefore one of their major endeavors was to point out the *differences* between modern and pre-modern societies, categorized as 'traditional societies'. Theoretical constructions and dichotomies such as *traditional/modern*, *mechanical/organic* and *Gemeinschaft/Gesellschaft* came to dominate the sociological field for a very long time. This was despite the fact that the founding fathers of social theory recognized the controversies of modernity itself in terms of 'alienation', 'anomie', 'iron cage' and 'anonymity' (Lyon 1994: 28). Accordingly, an established linear evolutionist understanding of human history underpinned sociological arguments concerning the reasons for the emergence of *the* modern society in Europe. The interest for dichotomous differences between 'we' modern Europeans and the traditional 'rest' encouraged many social scientists to use even older concepts and paradigms. The established dichotomy of *Occident/Orient* was widely used, although in new terms and contexts, by many classics to explain the differences between modern European and traditional oriental societies, in particular Islamic societies. Such ideas provided a 'scientific' and ideological frame for European colonialism.

The relatively long period of internal peace between European powers, created by the Treatise of Wesphalia (1648) and victorious European colonial campaigns against weaker states, reinforced the European self-image of having a universal creed. Europeans were about to 'civilize' and 'Christianize' the world in accordance with their Eurocentric blueprints. However, to be modern came to be something impossible for 'the rest' of the world because the only way for 'the rest' to be civilized and modern was based on the authoritative formula of 'first become like us, then civilized'. The universalism was therefore nothing else than a 'Euroversalism', by which a Eurocentric understanding of an evolutionary development was extended to be a universal truth. Contrary to common understanding, the universalism of the Enlightenment was particular and nothing clear in itself. As Deleuze (1992: 162) puts it, universal claims, such as the One, the All, the True, the object and the subject, are not universals, but singular processes of unification, totalization, verification, objectification and subjectification (Deleuze 1992). The European universal creed was thus noting more than 'the imperialism of universalism', to use Bourdieu (1998: 19), that was experienced by 'the rest' of the world as colonial wars and occupation. However, the European war machinery and the industrialization of mass killing did not remain in the colonies and turned home to Europe.

The devastating First World War in Europe put an end to the optimistic belief in a peaceful and rapid development towards a better future that dominated the discourses of modernity in Europe. The appearance of new competing ideologies and blueprints for development such as Marxism, Nazism and Fascism, and the execution of such systems of governance, were partly a direct result of the failure and discretion of 'liberal universal' modernity. However, the tradition of a singular modernity was restored after the Second World War. Many scholars tried to create a coherent theoretical system that could serve to explain – in line with Weberian tradition – the *uniqueness* of Western civilization compared with other civilizations. Such researchers were not much concerned about the internal differences between Western countries. Rather, they tried to construct an ideal type of 'the West' that was theoretically and discursively separated from non-Western countries. The new wave of social theorists did not even follow the classical sort of Jekyll and Hyde theory of being modern. Instead, recognizing the advantages of 'progress', in the Cold War era they created a 'Dr Jekyll only' social theory (Taylor 1999: 14). The rather heterogeneous development of Western countries, such as developmental patterns called the French model, English model, German model, Swedish model and so forth, were not the main subject of research and/or the interest of the economic and political elites in a world where Western capitalism was challenged by its counterpart, and equally modern, 'socialist world'. The fact that there hardly existed '*a* West' but several Western patterns of socio-economic and cultural developments was overlooked in comparative research and debates in both the classics of modernization theory and their post-Second World War followers.

The paradigm of universalism considered Western experiments to be a blueprint for non-Western countries to follow. Many evolutionist social theorists and in particular sociologists tried to present it as the only way towards a lasting system in all human societies and the ultimate goal of history, in Hegelean terminology. Even research methodology has been affected by 'the universal' in modernists' comparative studies. Researchers tried to identify objects and units, such as the state and national societies, and accordingly point out universal attributes, such as political system, bureaucracy and social classes, that were assumed to have similar structures and functions in every socio-economic and cultural context, in a comparative manner. The comparison, however, was based on a linear evolutionist understanding of history. As Bach (1980: 297) puts it:

The research consisted of a search for dichotomous classifications of types of societies. Given the preoccupation of many classical theorists with the emergence of industrial society, these typologies were formed as polar ends in an evolutionary path from an immature to mature form: preindustrial to industrial, traditional to modern, folk to urban, etc. These types of societies formed the ground for comparative analysis. Whatever was common to developed societies but absent in the developed areas became a functional prerequisite for development.

Accordingly, 'empirical universals' had no capacity to explain variations between societies within 'a category'. Every society existed somewhere on the given horizontal line of development (Westernization). Both liberals and Marxists believed that modernization has a historical mission for creating a better and more developed world. Herbert Spencer (1878) already in the nineteenth century criticized patriotism as egoistic nationalism and considered it incompatible with the spirit of modern society and modern science. Although the comparative universal methodology was advocated by scholars such as Spencer, the universe for him and others was not wider than Europe. This Euroversalism, which constituted the core of classical social theory, came to dominate social sciences and create a tradition of scientific otherism.

This tradition of scientific otherism took different shapes and was organized around different constructed contents. The others, as the other side of science, reason and rationality, were defined, although in different ways, by many social scientists and philosophers of Enlightenment and modernity, from Lineaus, Kant, Montsqiue, Hegel, Marx and Weber to Giddens, Dahrandorf and Huntington. From Lineaus' categorization of 'human races' with different hierarchical biological differences, through Marx's theory of 'Asiatic mode of production', which was characterized by stagnation, the absence of dynamic class struggle and the domination of a swollen state acting as a sort of universal landlord (Hall 1996: 222), to Giddens' and Dahrandorf's claim for the defense of 'the Western values' indicate the otherism of the modern scientific history of Europe.

The dichotomous civilizational thinking, and the *'uniqueness'* of a single European modernity went so far that Marx and Engels defended colonialism as a 'progressive power of change and the progress of civilization' (Feuer 1971: 489). The legitimization of colonialism was, according to Marx and Engels, based on the assumption that the social formations of the 'Oriental world' are stagnant and that capitalism has a historical role to play in smashing the pre-capitalist modes of production (Turner 1978: 5).

Not only the critical theory of Marxism, but also other less revolutionary theories, such as those of Durkheim and Weber, have influenced our judgment about other 'less developed' or 'traditional societies', among those Muslim countries. The European social science tradition has not only influenced Western European understanding of the evolution of societies, it has also greatly influenced the ruling strata's and Westernizing intellectual elites in many Muslim countries. Both the Persian and the Ottoman intellectual elites were highly influenced by, among others, Emile Durkheim's evolutionist theory. They believed in Durkheim's formulation of 'the law of history' in his major work, *The Division of Labor in Society*: 'Thus it is a law of history that mechanical solidarity, which at first is isolated, or almost so, should progressively lose ground, and organic solidarity gradually become preponderant' (1984: 126).

Drawing on such an understanding of the evolutionary changes from 'lower' to 'higher' societies and from traditional to modern ones made the authoritative modernizers, such as Reza Shah in Iran and Ataturk in Turkey, believe that they had to lead the 'people by the hand until their feet are sure and they know the way. Then they can choose for themselves' (cited in Tomlin 1946). The influence of the Durkheimian dichotomy of modern/traditional in many Muslim countries was not only limited to the political leaders, but also affected many indigenous intellectuals and social scientists of those countries. As a result of colonial intervention, the dominant mode of sociological analysis amongst indigenous, professional sociologists has been Durkheimian. This influence of Durkheimian sociology is considerable amongst French-trained sociologists in Algeria and Tunisia, but it has also had a profound impact on sociology and historical scholarship in Turkey through the pioneering work of Ziya Göklap and Fuat Köprulu (Turner 1978: 2).

The uncritical adaptation of European social science theories by Muslim intellectuals from Morocco to Egypt, Turkey and Iran has created many problems for the sociologists of these countries. 'In the absence of an autonomous local tradition of social analysis, it is hardly surprising that many Arab intellectuals have turned toward Marxism to provide a critique of the dominant Durkheimian and functionalist sociological tradition' (Turner 1978: 2). Although, the Marxist critique of the established functionalist messianic understanding of modernity reinforced alternative interpretations of modernity – including the Islamic ones – European blueprints remained the most powerful modernization models. However, the European models were mixed with local socio economic and cultural conditions and created new paths of modernity which deviated in many ways from their European counterpart. For instance, Kemalism combined the French model (secularism), the Italian Fascist model (dictatorial, military and highly centralized state) and the Soviet model (economic planning).

Accordingly, there is neither *a* European model of modernity valid for every country and all social conditions nor an Islamic model in the imagined 'Islamic world'. Although, the European social sciences have had substantial impact on the socio-economic and political developments of many Muslim countries, these abstract theories were reformulated and used in certain social and cultural contexts. Influential agents in those countries' civil and political spheres reshaped the imported modernity models and blueprints and adjusted them to established socio-economic and cultural conditions. There is no unilinear, evolutionary path from 'traditional society' to 'modern society' and the modern history demonstrates that 'all the assumptions about the relevance and significance of European models of development ('the bourgeois revolution', 'secularization', 'modernization') fall to the ground' (Turner 1978: 81–2). Instead new models and political doctrines have been constructed for the modernization of many Muslim countries.

Selective and authoritative modernities

Almost all Muslim countries were built on the ruins of the Ottoman and, to a lesser extent, the Persian empires. They went through many modernization periods and models both as parts of those empires and as independent states. Accordingly, the term multiple modernities is appropriate to frame the modernity programs in those countries. It frames not only the variations of modernities in different countries, but also indicates various modernization programs conducted by modernization agents, in particular the state, in the same country. Modernity was not a homogeneous phenomenon or process that every agent and sociopolitical group agreed upon. It was understood and defined selectively, based on different ideological understandings of modernity. Countries, such as Egypt, Iran and Turkey, did not experience one modernization but several. Muhammad Ali's modernization in Egypt was very different from Nasser's modernization. Moreover, in Iran Qajars' (1792–1924), Pahlavis' (1924–1979), and the Islamic Republic's modernization paths showed tremendous variation. In Turkey too, the Ottoman modernization had very little in common with Kemalist modernization. The military-nationalist Ba'athi modernization of Syria (1963–) and Iraq (1952–2004) were also other models of modernization and were generated as a result of colonial occupation. The modernization of Muslim countries did not follow a predestined model and process, but can be divided into different periods with specific and various properties. For instance, the modernization of Iran can be characterized in the four following periods: (1) The Persian pre-constitutional modernization, (2) the constitutional modernization, (3) the authoritative Pahlavi modernization, and (4) the Islamic modernization. The same can be said about Turkey. The Turkish modernization can be categorized in the following periods with various and specific properties: (1) The Ottoman Imperial modernization, (2) the constitutional modernization, (3) the Kemalist modernization, and (4) the post-Kemalist modernization.

The pre-constitutional modernizations in both the Ottoman Empire and Persia were a selective modernization of the army and the administration system. The modernization of the army and the administrative system were called in both empires, *Nizam-i jadid* (New order) and *Tanzimat* (bureaucratic order). The reform policy was mainly a consequence of the inefficiency of the armies in confrontations with the new European powers and ineffective bureaucracy. The crisis of governance in both empires, and the risk of disintegration, led to social movements for constitutionalism that resulted in the change of the traditional political system and the establishment of constitutional regimes in Persia in 1905 and in the Ottoman Empire in 1908. The constitutional regimes' main attempts in both countries were to modernize the organization of government and the political system. The First World War and its devastating consequences for the Ottoman Empire and Persia, and the disintegration of the post-war period, resulted in the establishment of new visionary and authoritative regimes in both countries and in the creation of modern nation-states.

The War of Independence in Turkey, led by Kemal Ataturk (1922–1936) and Ismet Inonu, brought a revolutionary military group to power that in the early 1920s changed the traditional political system of *Kalifat* and established the Turkish Republic within the remains of the Ottoman Empire. In Persia, a military leader, Reza Khan (1924–1941), led a coup d'état in 1922 and succeeded in abolishing the reign of the corrupted Qajar dynasty (1792–1924) in 1924. He then established a new monarchy and changed the name of the country from Persia to Iran. The Pahlavi and Kemalist modernizations in Iran and Turkey had several similarities and differences. Both regimes attempted at first to create political stability, which they considered a precondition for modernizing their countries. The establishment of different political systems in Iran (monarchy) and Turkey (republic) gradually destroyed almost all organized political opposition and created dictatorial regimes which could do whatever they saw necessary for the socio-economic and cultural modernization of their countries.

The negative experiences of post-revolutionary democratic constitutionalism in Iran and Turkey that resulted in the disappearance of the two countries as nation-states created the grounds for the establishment of new authoritarian states and powerful leaders in the two countries in the early 1920s. Even the intelligentsias of the two countries were convinced of the need for centralized and powerful states to fight disintegration. Accordingly, the takeover of political power in both Iran by Reza Shah and in Turkey by Ataturk occurred without any major objections. Even the religious groups accepted the secular states of Reza Shah and Ataturk. Democracy was considered unfavorable for the modernization of the country and the creation of a powerful state.

Meanwhile, in Iran the democratic change came as a result of the occupation of the country by Allies and the abdication of Reza Shah in 1941. In Turkey, as a result of foreign pressures, the government introduced free elections and allowed opposition parties to be established after the Second World War. This resulted in the seizure of power by a moderate Islamic party, the Democratic Party, led by Adnan Menderes, in the election of 1950. For the first time in the Republic's history, the Kemalists were defeated by a moderate Islamist. Menderes also won the 1957 elections, but was overthrown by a military coup d'état in 1960 and executed. This created a democratic challenge to the Kemalist ideology and many anti-democratic military coups in order to defend 'the constitution' and the tradition of Kemalist fundamentalist secularism that formed the Turkish political sphere during the whole second half of the twentieth century. However, the premiership of Menderes in 1950 was the turning point in the political history of the Turkish Republic and a change in the Kemalist fundamental programs. Post-Kemalist modernization was more democratic and moderate Islamic parties, such as Rifah Partisi (welfare party) and Fezilet Partisi (virtue party), aimed at the democratization of the polity, reducing military power, and decreasing the gap between the haves and the have-nots.

Pahlavisian authoritarianism and rapid modernization in Iran (1924–1979) and Kemalism in Turkey succeeded in creating the most modern and powerful countries in the Middle East. Yet selective modernization also generated opposition and led to the disintegration of society. Politically, the 'fundamentalist secularism' of Pahlavis and Kemalism created religious opposition and their dictatorial regimes provoked leftist and liberal oppositions. Economically, the 'fundamentalist marketism' increased the gap between social classes and created lasting segregation. Rapid urbanization and land reform led to the mass movement of people from rural areas to the cities and coupled with ultra-liberal market economic reforms created many shanty towns in the major cities. In Iran both indigenous civil society groups, namely the ulama, the bazaris, intellectual religious groups and the secular civil society groups (such as intellectuals and political parties), were marginalized and excluded from the polity of the country (Abrahamian 1983; Kamali 1998; Arjomand 1988; Algar 1969). This resulted in the uprisings of the 1970s which led to the Islamic Revolution (1977–1979) that put an end to the thousands of year old monarchy in Iran and established a republican regime.

The establishment of the Islamic Republic in Iran created a new era of political dictatorship and simultaneously a new form of authoritarian modernization. Although the economic policy of the Shah continued more or less under the new regime, the main efforts of the new regime were directed at reinforcing its political power, which resulted in one of the most substantial attacks on both the opposition from the indigenous civil society groups, and even more on the Westernized civil society groups. The new regime considered itself to be the 'true representative' of the Iranian people with a historical zeal that gave the legitimacy to destroy all opposition and abolish any dualism between civil society and state. However, the republican nature of the regime forced it to legitimize its reign by popular elections and a modern constitution (Abrahamian 1993). In its desire to install a more authoritarian system, the Islamic regime used the war with Iraq (1981–1989) as a good pretext for realizing its blueprint by mass arrest and the execution of thousands of members of the political opposition.

However, the regime did not succeed in destroying all opposition. Using the end of the war with Iraq and the death of Ayatollah Khomeini in 1989, both civil societies of Iran, namely the indigenous and the 'Western' ones, started to organize and protest against the dictatorship. In 1997 a religious liberal group led by Muhammad Khatami succeeded in winning the election and seizing state power. This set the stage for a period of power struggle between liberal groups and religious monopolists (*enhesartalaban*) that continues today. The Khatami presidency probably put an end to a revolutionary political dictatorship which had many similarities with Fascist and communist political systems.

Modernities, histories and democracies

There is a general consensus that democracy has 'European roots'. Europe, West and democracy are often considered as synonymous concepts and developments. This is based on an assumption that 'Europe's link to unique (though restricted) democracies of classical Athens and republican Rome were never really cut off' (Therborn 1992: 65–6). This is, however, a biased conceptualization of European democratic developments. Behind these ideas, and behind modernization itself, there is a taken-for-granted geohistorical perspective which combines a Whig history with a diffusionist geography. The former is defined as a history whose story celebrates the present (Carr 1961; Taylor 1999). This takes the form of defining important features of contemporary society and tracing their lineage back in time so that the story told is one that culminates in the success of today's society (Taylor 1999: 11). Even the uneven political and non-democratic developments in the same European society, such as the differences between south and north in Italy explored by Putnam (1993), are removed from this selective diffutionist history. Accordingly, the European 'democratic nature' becomes the norm and the lack of democracy, both in the pre-modern and modern period, such as the uprising and establishment of totalitarian Fascist, Nazist and communists regimes, turns to the 'deviances of the rules'.

Such an understanding of history overlooks the fact that, for instance, in the period between the two World Wars in Europe, democratic institutions were relatively new and there existed little support for democracy at the level of the international communities. Nazism, Fascism and communism were powerful currents, and the socio-economic conditions were not sufficiently positive so as to guarantee democratic durability. Ertman's (1997) judgment is that Western Europe's first-wave democracies were highly susceptible to breakdown. Much the same can be said for the Middle East's fledgling parliamentary systems earlier this century. In one of the major European democracies, England, many citizens, such as women, were excluded from franchisement as late as the early 1920s (De Deken and Rueschmeyer 1992). However, political modernization is not to be understood as a process of democratization. 'The modern state is not necessarily democratic. A history of democratization, therefore, is not synonymous with one of state modernization' (Therborn 1992: 63). Notwithstanding, as a result of purifying 'the West' from the downside of its modernity, namely its bloody history, slavery, mass killing and genocide, modernization has been used as a parallel concept to development, progress, humanism and democracy. Even democracy itself has been purified and its very selective and 'racial' basis has been until recently ignored (see Arneil 1996 and Goldberg 1993).

This diffusionist and selective 'self-presentation', coupled with the highly theorized and widely used tradition of Orientalism in Europe, has created a dichotomous model in which 'the West' is confronted with 'the Orient'. Nowadays, the Orient is reduced to Islam across a theoretically constructed paradoxical axis. Accordingly, the established belief in the incompatibility of modernity and Islam, Islam and democracy, and civil society and Islam is a consequence of a dichotomous theoretical and discursive construction and development in the social sciences (Said 1978; Hussain *et al.* 1984; Turner 1984, 1994, 1999; Kamali 2001). Therefore, the idea of different and paradoxical civilizations clashing with each other, reformulated by Huntington (1993) among others, is nothing innovative, but a reformulation of what already existed in the social sciences in the Western part of the world. The 'clash of civilizations' is nothing more than a result of seeing and judging the world through a narrow 'Western-centric' window.

The fact is that Islamic believers and groups have been highly engaged in the democratic movements of all Muslim countries. Already in the late nineteenth and early twentieth century in Persia and the Ottoman Empire, moderate Muslim leaders and influential religious intellectuals such as Tabatabai, Bihbahani and Hairi in Persia and Namik Kemal, Zia Pasa and Nuri in the Ottoman Empire advocated constitutionalism and democratic change. Constitutionalism was religiously legitimized as a necessary transformation (see Hairi 1977 in the case of Iran, and Kuntay 1944 and Mardin 1989 in the case of Turkey). Muslim intellectuals advocated the compatibility of Islam and constitutionalism and rejected simple implementations of Western blueprints. They were influenced by European movements that they saw as more compatible with their countries' conditions. For instance, Namik Kemal, who was one of the most influential reformists among those claiming compatibility between Islam and modern reforms in the Ottoman Empire, was influenced by Garibaldi and Silvio Pellico, as well as Voltaire and Condorcet (Kuntay 1944).

A tradition of strong civil societies in both Persia and the Ottoman Empire coupled with liberal changes introduced by governmental intellectuals and reformulated and legitimized by religious agents during the course of the nineteenth century were among the conditions on which an organic democratic development could arise. The tradition of collective decision-making in both empires was improved very early (Burns and Kamali 2003). However, foreign interventions, wars and internal controversies made the governmental reforms limited and unable to change the basis of the political structures of the two empires. This led to the uprising of popular movements for constitutionalism that, as mentioned earlier, succeeded in establishing the constitutional and democratic governments in 1905 in Persia and 1908 in the Ottoman Empire. However, these changes were disrupted by wars and foreign interventions. Meanwhile, Great Britain and Russia did their best to undermine constitutionalism in Persia, and the First World War put an end to Ottoman constitutionalism. Other smaller Muslim countries were not in a better situation. The colonial powers, England and France, despite their democratic claims, hindered any attempt at democratization and development in countries such as Egypt, Syria, Algeria and Iraq. Egypt, Saudi Arabia and Iraq were put under English control, and Syria and Algeria were controlled by France.

Recent developments and a need for cosmopolitanism

The war on terror has reinforced the already existing divisions in civil societies of many Muslim countries. Meanwhile the Westernized civil societies are moving towards a more fundamentalist secularism with the French political system as a model, while the religio-modern civil societies are taking a more religious and anti-West position. This is a very dangerous development, which can jeopardize the establishment of a lasting political democracy and stability in many of those countries.

The modern history of the Middle East is a history of broken promises. The idea of a democratic and human West was paradoxically crushed by its crusaders, namely English and French colonial powers, as well as their main successor, the USA. The interventions in the Middle Eastern countries and the destruction of their democratic developments have created bitter collective memories in many countries. Simultaneously, the Western ideas of liberty and equality have been influencing many intellectuals in Muslim countries. These parallel developments have created a dilemma in those countries: an ideal-typical 'West' with a humanist and cosmopolitan creed, on the one side, and a real 'West' with colonial and imperialist intentions to subjugate non-Western, including Muslim countries, on the other.

It is important now to find a way out of the dilemma. The starting point will be to accept and respect different constellations of civil society in Muslim societies. The division and conflicts between a secular modern civil society and the religio-modern one must be accepted as one crucial condition in dealing with the socio-political developments in those countries.

Further, the existence of a 'fundamentalist secularism' of Kemalist and Pahlavi models, which paradoxically includes even leftists, must be challenged. The Iranian Islamic revolution and its aftermath, the democratic victories of Islamists in Turkey, Egypt, Lebanon, and so on, demonstrates the political power of Islam as a religio-political doctrine that will come to play, more or less, the same role as Christian Democratic parties in Europe.

Accordingly, to the extent that we accept participation of Christian Democratic parties in the polity of Western countries, we must also accept participation of Islamic parties and groups in the modern political developments of the Middle East. A successful cosmopolitanism therefore has to be free from its old Western dilemma. Western countries should reconsider their roles in the Middle East and support a democratic development that includes even Islamic parties and groups.

Turkey is making a good example so far and the military and fundamentalist secularists appear to understand the reality of the existence of Islamic political ideologies and parties that have highly influenced modern Turkish politics. The recent developments in Lebanon in the aftermath of the murder of Rafik Hariri, an oppositional leader, and the withdrawal of the Syrian troops from the country, is another field of experiment for democratic development. The role of the Western countries in supporting a democratic development that includes even the Islamic party Hezb Allah is important here. Recent Iranian elections and the victory of the religious hardliner, Ahmadi Nejad and the country's nuclear program is another field of experiment. The solution of the dilemma is at hand by respecting the democratic and socio-economic developments based on a cosmopolitan understanding of the common human destiny.

Conclusion

Social movements and political transformations in Muslim countries during the course of the twentieth century were a part of a global movement for democracy and modernization. Nationalist movements in all Muslim countries were reactions to external imperialist and colonial pressures. The devastating colonial interventions of European colonial powers and USA coups in many Muslim countries have created 'anti-West' sentiments that can easily be mobilized in political movements. Many Islamic movements are not anti-modern and anti-cosmopolitan. On the contrary, they are 'a global way of being local', and a reaction to several hundred years of socio-economic and political pressures that those countries have been subjected to.

A cosmopolitan politics should move beyond the limitations of 'us-and-them' thinking and dichotomous categories in order to generate new visions for a future in which there are no 'others'. Yet this would also require that Europe and the USA acknowledge their historical role in destroying organic forms of modernization and democratic developments in those countries.

References

Abrahamian, E. (1983) *Iran Between Two Revolutions*, Princeton: Princeton University Press.

Abrahamian, E. (1993) *Khomeinism: Essays on the Islamic Republic*, Berkeley: University of California Press.

Algar, H. (1969) *Religion and State in Iran 1785–1906*, Berkeley: University of California Press.

Arjomand, A. S. (1988) *The Turban for the Crown*, New York: Oxford University Press.

Arnason, J. P. (2002) 'Communism and Modernity', in S. Eisenstadt (ed.) *op. cit.*

Arneil, B. (1996) *John Lock and America: The Defense of English Colonialism*, Oxford: Clarendon Press.

Bach, R. L. (1980) 'On the Holism of a Word-system Perspective', in T. K. Hopkins and I. Wallerstein (eds) *Processes of the World System*, London: Sage.

Bourdieu, P. (1998) *Practical Reason: On the Theory of Action*, Stanford, Calif.: Stanford University Press.

Burns, T. and M. Kamali (2003) 'The Evolution of Parliaments: A Comparative-historical Perspective on Assemblies and Political Decision-making', in G. Delanty and E. Isin (eds) *Handbook of Historical Sociology*, London: Sage.

Carr, E. H. (1961) *What is History?* London: Penguin.

Cheah, P. and B. Robbins (1998) *Cosmopolitics: Thinking and Feeling Beyond the Nation*, Minneapolis: The University of Minnesota Press.

De Deken, J. J. and D. Rueschmeyer (1992) 'Social Policy, Democratization and State Structure: Reflections on Late Nineteenth-century Britain and Germany', in R. Torstendahl (ed.) *State Theory and State History*, London: Sage Publications.

Delanty, G. (2003) 'Rethinking Europe and Modernity in Light of Global Trans-formations: The Making of a Post-Western Europe', paper presented at Koc University, Istanbul, 2 May.

Deleuze, G. (1992) 'What is a Dispostif', in T. J. Armstrong (ed.) *Michel Foucault. Philosopher: International Conference, Paris, January 1998*, New York: Routledge.

Durkheim, E. (1984) *The Division of Labor in Society*, New York: The Free Press.

Eisenstadt, S. N. (1999) *Fundamentalism, Secularism, and Revolution: The Jacobin Dimension of Modernity*, Cambridge: Cambridge University Press.

Eisenstadt, S. N. (ed.) (2002) *Multiple Modernities*, New Brunswick, NJ: Transaction Publishers.

Ertman, T. (1997) *Birth of Leviathan: Building States and Regimes in Medieval and Early Modern Europe*, Cambridge: Cambridge University Press.

Feuer, L. S. (ed.) (1971) *Marx and Engels: Basic Writings on Politics and Philosophy*, London: Fontana Books.

Geertz, C. (2003) 'Which Way to Mecca?', *New York Review of Books*, June 12.

Giddens, A. (1990) *The Consequences of Modernity*, London: Polity Press.

Goldberg, D. T. (1993) *Racist Culture: Philosophy and the Politics of Meaning*, Oxford: Blackwell.

Hairi, A-H. (1977) *Shi'ism and Constitutionalism in Iran*, Leiden: E. J. Brill.

Hall, S. (1996) 'The West and the Rest: Discourse and Power', in S. Hall, D. Held and T. McGrew (eds) *Modernity and its Futures*, Oxford: Polity in association with Open University Press.

Huntington, S. (1993) 'The Clash of Civilizations', *Foreign Affairs*, 72(3): 22–49.

Hussain, A., R. Olson and J. Qureshi (eds) (1984) *Orientalism, Islam, and Islamists*, Vermont: Amana Books.

Kamali M. (1998) *Revolutionary Iran: Civil Society and State in the Modernization Process*, Aldershot: Ashgate.

Kamali, M. (2001) 'Civil Society and Islam: A Sociological Perspective', *European Journal of Sociology*, 42(3): 457–82.

Kamali, M. (2006) *Multiple Modernities, Civil Society and Islam*, Liverpool: Liverpool University Press.

Kuntay, M. C. (1944) *Namik Kemal: Devrinin Insanlari ve Olaylari Arasinda*, Vol. 1, Istanbul: Maarif Matbassi.

Lewis, B. (1953) 'The Impact of the French Revolution on Turkey', *Journal of World History*, 1: 114–18.

Lipset Matin, S. and G. Marks (2000) *It Didn't Happen Here: Why Socialism Failed in the United States*, New York: Norton & Co.

Lyon, D. (1994) *Postmodernity*, Buckingham: Open University Press.

Mardin, S. (1989) *Religion and Social Change in Modern Turkey: The Case of Bediuzzaman Said Nursi*, New York: State University of New York Press.

Putnam, R. D. (1993) *Making Democracy Work: Civil Traditions in Modern Italy*, Princeton: Princeton University Press.

Said, E. (1978) *Orientalism*, New York: Pantheon Books.

Spencer, H. (1878) *The Study of Sociology*, London: Kegan Paul & Co.

Spencer, H. (1898) *The Principles of Sociology*, New Brunswick, NJ: Transaction Publishers.

Taylor, P. J. (1999) *Modernities: A Geohistorical Interpretation*, Minneapolis: University of Minnesota Press.

Therborn, G. (1992) 'The Right to Vote and the Four World Routes to/through Modernity', in R. Torstendahl (ed.) *State Theory and State History*, London: Sage Publication.

Tomlin, E. W. F. (1946) *Life in Modern Turkey*, London: Thomas Nelson & Sons.

Turner, B. S. (1978) *Marx and the End of Orientalism*, London: George Allen & Unwin.

Turner, B. S. (1984) 'Orientalism and the Problem of Civil Society in Islam', in A. Hussain, R. Olson and J. Qureshi (eds) *op. cit.*

Turner, B. S. (1994) *Orientalism, Postmodernism, and Globalism*, London: Routledge.

Turner, B. S. (ed.) (1999) *Orientalism: Early Sources*, London: Routledge.

Wittrock, B. (2000) 'Modernity: One, None, or Many? European Origins and Modernity as a Global Condition', *Daedalus, Journal of the American Academy of Arts and Sciences*, 129(1): 31–59.

Part III

Between Europe and Asia

12 Borders and rebordering

Chris Rumford

Conceptually, Europe is linked to Asia through the notion of Eurasia, an unbroken (but not undivided) continental expanse, which in recent decades has been the origin or site of a number of major global struggles and conflicts. Modernity has seen Eurasia divided according to two principles which have produced a familiar pattern of bordering: an East–West divide, and a core–periphery relation. Neither of these divisions dominates Europe–Asia relations at the present time, although they both still exert an influence over political orientations and continue to inform identity politics. Contemporary bordering and rebordering processes are occurring in a post-Western Europe increasingly preoccupied with developing the means with which to govern its own social and political transformations and those taking place within the wider world. Bordering is an essential component of European Union (EU) governance, and the rebordering of Eurasia is an important dimension of EU attempts at 'global governance'.

It is no longer meaningful to divide Europe along an East–West axis. Similarly, an East–West division between Europe and Asia is no longer assumed to be enduring, fundamental or 'natural', as it was often portrayed during the Cold War era. Under conditions of postcommunism, Europeanization and globalization borders between Europe and Asia no longer take the form of an East–West division. The 'old' borders of divided Europe have been largely erased and most of the countries previously on opposite sides of the Iron Curtain now find themselves members of an enlarged European Union, whose borders now reach to Central Asia and whose political influence, economic imperatives and communication networks reach yet further afield. Likewise, in recent times the meaning of core and periphery has changed, as it has done throughout the development of the European Union. Until the 1970s and 1980s the Mediterranean would have constituted one periphery, the Celtic fringes another. More recently, Eastern Europe constituted a periphery, with important consequences for thinking about European identity, which has traditionally been dependent upon a relatively closed Eastern frontier (Delanty 2003). In its relations with the new member states of the former communist bloc the European Union conceived of itself as the core, although the composition of the core has changed as the EU has enlarged. Traditionally, Europe's core–periphery relations have been seen as an internal affair and, importantly, as an important driver of economic development, the 'blue banana' signifying the economic heartland which disseminates growth and development to the peripheries (Rumford 2002). The most recent (2004) round of EU enlargement has resulted in a major recasting of the core–periphery dimension to Europe, the existence of which has in any case come into question, from within the EU as the result of the development of the notion of the importance of polycentric development and the idea of network Europe, and from without as a result of the impact of globalization and the proliferation of borders and rebordering that this is thought to entail. Put simply, globalization has the ability to liberate localities from central authority and encourage new dynamics of growth and connectivity in such a way as to confound core–periphery expectations.

This chapter focuses on the cosmopolitan dimensions of the bordering and rebordering of Eurasia, and in particular it examines the mechanisms through which the EU constructs and reconstructs its borders with its near neighbours and how these processes are dynamic, contingent and sometimes contradictory. One problem associated with investigating bordering processes is that the very nature of borders is increasingly uncertain in a world traversed by flows, mobilities and the interconnectedness characteristic of globalization. Indeed, there exists a major tension between the notion of rebordering, which highlights the increasing securitization and impermeability of borders, and the idea of differentiated, diffuse and mobile borders consistent with a world of flows. These contradictions are embodied in the EU's attempts to develop both a 'Schengenland' model of enhanced mobility within a common space protected by 'hard' external borders, and an extended communicative and economic space – an 'undivided Europe' – embracing a Eurasian 'ring of friends' and represented by the popular notion of 'network Europe'.

The chapter also addresses the question of how cosmopolitanism can inform our perceptions of borders in the contemporary world. In this regard, there are two related arguments which are important. First, borders have not become obsolete in a world ordered by global processes (Paasi 2005). Thus, the 'borderless world' thesis, sometimes seen as a paradigmatic of globalization, does not stand up to scrutiny in a world where borders proliferate and bordering, debordering and rebordering are core components of the social transformation that is shaping Europe–Asia relations. This does not mean, however, that borders remain geopolitical and territorial. Rather, borders are also multiple, diffused and relativized. Etienne Balibar makes the point that as well as defining the political territory of the nation-state through the construction of managed perimeters, borders are increasingly dispersed throughout society (Balibar 2004: 1). It is clear that we no longer live only in a world of bounded territorial nation-states, where inside and outside, foreign and domestic are easy to distinguish.

Second, borders and mobilities are not antithetical. A globalizing world is a world of networks, flows and mobility; it is also a world of borders. It can be argued that cosmopolitanism is best understood as an orientation to the world which entails the constant negotiation and crossing of borders. A cosmopolitan is not only a citizen of the world, someone who embraces multiculturalism, or even a 'frequent flyer'. A cosmopolitan lives in and across borders. Borders connect the 'inner mobility' of our lives with both the multiplicity of communities we may elect to become members of and the cross-cutting tendencies of polities to impose their border regimes on us in ways which compromise our mobilities, freedoms, rights and even identities. The incessant mobility which is often seen as characteristic of contemporary life is only one part of the story. On the other side of the coin are the bordering, debordering and rebordering processes which point to the cosmopolitanization of society.

The chapter will explore these themes and examine the dynamics of the bordering and rebordering of Europe with respect to three tensions or conflicts: (i) the tension between the needs of territorial governance and its associated border regimes and the potential for de- and rebordering associated with flows and networks; (ii) the tension between the idea of the border as a solution and the border as problem; and (iii) the tension between the inertia of old borders and the construction of new ones.

Network Europe and 'networked borders'

The idea of network Europe and the associated notion of polycentric development have, in recent years, started to replace the more conventional idea of Europe as a 'space of places' (Castells 2000). On this view, Europe should not be thought of as an aggregation of pre-existing territorial spaces (nation-states) with fixed centres and spatial hierarchies (core and periphery, developed and underdeveloped regions, for example) but rather as a network polity linked by new forms of connectivity prompted by global flows of capital, goods and services and the concomitant mobility enjoyed by persons, enterprises and forms of governance.

While the idea of 'network Europe' has struck a chord with commentators attempting to come to terms with the rapid and fundamental transformation of Europe in the post-Cold War period, there exist other, conflicting accounts of the reconfiguration of Europe which emphasize the development of 'hard' external borders as a corollary of the increased internal mobility associated with the EU's single market and single currency (Zielonka 2002). In short, there exists a tension between the idea of 'network Europe' and the Schengen model of securitized external borders. Schengenland represents a model of unrestricted internal mobility coupled with 'hard' external borders designed to control flows of terrorists, criminals and illegal immigrants (Andreas 2003). It is common to encounter the idea that borders are becoming less significant between EU member states at the same time as the EU's external border is heavily policed, leading to a defensive shell designed to prevent seepage of the economic gains made by the EU in the face of economic globalization and the unwanted influx of migrants from the near abroad.

The unresolved tension between ideas of 'networked Europe' and Schengenland have opened up the possibility of a more nuanced account of Europe's borders, in particular an awareness that the EU's borders are becoming differentiated and can vary in scope and tightness (Hassner 2002). For example, the EU's security borders are far more rigid than the equivalent economic, telecommunication and educational borders. One problem with the 'rebordering' thesis advanced by Andreas and others, which emphasizes the need to reinforce and securitize borders, is that it relies on a rather undifferentiated notion of borders, which are intelligible only in terms of policing and security and a defence against external threats (the mobility of illegal immigrants, terrorists and traffickers in people and drugs). In fact, Schengen borders and Europe's borders more generally are not singular and unitary, and are designed to encourage various kinds of mobility, particularly for certain categories of immigrants, migrant workers and students. For example, in the UK the government scheme for recruiting agricultural students as seasonal agricultural workers (SAWS) has resulted in an estimated 20,000 (low paid) Ukrainian workers in the UK agricultural sector. This scheme previously recruited heavily from Poland and other Eastern European countries, now members of the EU. As students and workers from these countries now have new mobility rights consequent upon EU citizenship, the SAWS scheme has migrated eastward in the search for recruits.[1]

The rebordering thesis cannot easily accommodate the differentially permeable borders of 'network Europe'. At the same time, the idea of a Europe defined by flows and networks downplays the importance of territorial bordering and the ways in which political priorities can result in some borders being more important than others: what was previously the EU border with Eastern Europe (along the line of the Iron Curtain) has become relatively unimportant when compared with the enlarged border with Belarus, Ukraine, Moldova, etc. The idea of 'network Europe' and the monotopic internal space of the single market has changed the way we think about territorial spaces, but ironically has tended to work with conventional notions of borders. It is argued that 'network Europe' can only be properly understood in conjunction with a notion of 'networked borders'.

The idea of 'networked borders' draws attention to the ways in which Europe's borders are increasingly mobile and diffused throughout society. Such borders are not fixed in the way territorial borders are, rather they can be modulated within and between existing administrative entities. European borders are periodically dissolved, constructed afresh, shifted, reconstituted, etc. Examples include: common European borders replacing a collection of national borders; previously important borders – such as the Europe-defining ones between East and West Germany, and disputed ones between Germany and Poland – ceasing to be contested or troubled demarcations; the eastward movement of the 'important' borders of Europe – to the border between Slovakia and the Ukraine, or the Baltic States and Russia, for example; the 'Mediterranean' enlargement of the EU in the 1980s creating a new north–south frontier within Spain (Suarez-Navaz 2004). However, this is not the only sense in which Europe can be said to possess 'networked borders'. Europe's borders are increasingly net-worked in the sense that they attempt to manage mobility and as such are constructed in locations where mobility is most intense: at airline check-in desks and Eurostar terminals, along Europe's motorways routes and trans-European road networks (Walters 2006). Borders are no longer only to be found at the perimeter of national territory (McNeill 2004).

Borders as a problem (and an opportunity for governance)

The second tension is between the idea of the border as solution and the border as a problem to be managed. For nation-states borders are solu-tions, creating a bounded territorial entity that can be fortified, defended, administered and homogenized: recognized borders are a key element of sovereignty. What happens beyond the borders of the sovereign nation-state is not necessarily important, unless construed as a threat. The EU is not a nation-state 'writ large' nor a bounded territorial polity modelled on the nation-state, and, increasingly, the sort of borders associated with the nation-state are seen as a problem for Europe. This is particularly the case with the latest round of enlargement of the EU which is seen to contain the potential for creating economic, social and political instabilities in those countries on the other side of the new borders. Thus recent EU rhetoric has centred on 'undivided Europe' and the need to ensure that enlargement does not create new divisions in and beyond Europe. EU borders are per-ceived to be problematic in a variety of ways: in terms of potential negat-ive consequences for countries excluded by the border; in terms of the difficulty of policing them; in terms of barriers to trade; and in terms of the creation of disadvantaged regions on both sides of the border. In short, the EU is concerned that the recent round of enlargement could be responsible for creating new instabilities on the Eurasian frontier (and potential security problems) by exacerbating the difference between rich and poor regions, between neo-liberal and unreconstructed economies, and between those countries embracing EU-style democracy and human rights and those attempting to resist the external imposition of 'global' norms.

In March 2003 the European Commission published a Communication entitled 'Wider Europe – neighbourhood: a new framework for relations with eastern and southern neighbours' (European Commission 2003). The document outlined the need for the development of 'a zone of prosperity and a friendly neighbourhood – a "ring of friends" – with whom the EU enjoys close, peaceful and co-operative relations' (European Commission 2003: 4). The European Neighbourhood Policy (ENP) represents an extension of EU governance beyond EU borders (Lavenex 2004). It signals that the EU is increasingly concerned to manage non-EU space, particularly that of its neighbourhood or Eastern near abroad. Success in constructing European spaces as realms of governance which the Commission can then promote itself as being best suited to managing has led to the idea that non-Europe can also be constructed as a space of governance: countries which are not likely to become official candidates for full membership can be brought within the orbit of the Single Market and other pan-European projects.[2] The distinction between members and non-members has been replaced by a notion that integration can proceed in new ways. As such, in the wider Europe envisioned by the ENP a large number of countries of the former Soviet bloc and North Africa would be integrated (to differing degrees) within the Single Market but would not necessarily move closer to full membership of the EU. According to former Commission President Romano Prodi, the EU and its neighbours can share 'everything but institutions'; in other words, integration without enlargement.

What is notable about ENP is that it seeks to blur the distinction between candidate, member and non-member by opening up access to EU programmes to a greater extent than ever before, while at the same time ensuring that agenda-setting and policy-making remains the preserve of the EU. A suitably motivated neighbouring country could participate in EU networks, markets and common policies without the prospect of a formal accession framework. In brief, 'all the neighbouring countries should be offered the prospect of a stake in the EU's Internal Market and further integration and liberalization to promote the free movement of persons, goods, services and capital (four freedoms)' (European Commission 2003: 10). The ENP is more than another initiative to engender greater cooperation on the EU's outer limits. 'The European Neighbourhood Policy's vision embraces a ring of countries sharing the EU's fundamental values and objectives, drawn into an increasingly close relationship, going beyond cooperation to involve a significant measure of economic and political integration' (European Commission 2004).

The EU's recently evolved interest in global governance in conjunction with the 2004 round of enlargement has led to a new appreciation of the importance of the EU's lengthening borders. This interest does not simply revolve around the need to construct barriers to the outside world: on the contrary we have seen how the EU displays an awareness that rigid borders are extremely problematic and that the key to security and stability is not to create impenetrable frontiers but to increase the permeability of borders and to encourage a range of institutional and other actors to take responsibility for them. It is the EU's wish that its 'ring of friends' reinforce their border controls with other non-EU countries beyond the ENP, such as Russia. This suggests a shift away from Fortress Europe in which border lines must be policed vigilantly towards the idea of borders as buffer zones, comprising a ring of well governed and compliant states.

The recent enlargement of the EU and the accompanying discourses of 'new neighbourhood' and proximity politics have reinforced the idea that the EU is a network polity, increasingly interconnected with its near abroad. The network model is very good at accounting for the integrative capacity of the EU in its dealings with its near neighbours and broadening European space, but remains blind to ways in which the EU is increasingly blurring the inside/outside distinction in order to manage its near abroad, and misses important dimensions to the question of Europe's borders. In this context, the idea of borderlands is an important one. The EU's concern not to create rigid boundaries where the newly enlarged EU meets the former Soviet Union has prompted EU scholars to suggest that the identification of common policy spaces, coupled with the promotion of the idea of integration without enlargement, has led to the construction of the EU's eastern edges as 'new borderlands' (Batt 2003).

In the work of Saskia Sassen borderlands signify that borders should not be thought of only as dividing lines, but as circuits which cut across two or more discontinuous systems. In other words, borderlands draw out the commonalities shared by neighbouring regions. In a world of continuous border crossings represented by globalization, borderlands modify and transform spatial identity and undermine the territorial integrity of all parties. Borderlands represent a new spatiality: 'discontinuities are given a terrain rather than reduced to a dividing line' (Sassen 2001). The notion of borderlands captures an essential dimension of European space and is more useful in the study of contemporary Europe than the rather overworked ideas associated with networks. Importantly, borderlands extend to both sides of the EU border. This differentiates the notion of borderlands being developed here from the more conventional application of the term in EU studies: Batt's (2003) notion of the new borderlands of the EU, for example. The blurring of inside and outside associated with the interpenetrating flows comprising globalization means that the EU's borderlands are not simply on the 'other side' of the EU border. If borderlands are seen as spaces within which the EU attempts to accommodate global processes then Europe can be conceived of as a continuous borderland perpetually engaged in an attempt to fix its territorial and spatial arrangements into coherent patterns while global processes continually disrupt older geographical certainties.

Beyond East and West: constructing new borders

The recognition of differentiated, permeable, networked borders coupled with attempts to soften the external borders of the European Union through the development of borderlands which work to blur or shade the hard borders (or sharp edges) of the EU is, by itself, only a partial account of Europe's rebordering with Asia. In the process of shifting the EU's Eurasian border eastwards and developing modes of governance around the model of the EU as a networked polity, the EU has also been responsible for creating new borders (sometimes inadvertently) in different parts of Europe, in ways which are not easily associated with marking the new external limits of the EU; Cyprus and Russia providing very good examples. In other cases, Turkey and the Ukraine for example, rebordering has taken the form of a confounding and/or recasting of previously fixed East–West reference points. We can now give brief consideration to each of these examples.

Cyprus became a member of the EU in 2004, accession not marking an end to the island's division, however. Europe's last remaining Cold War division became, as a result of accession, a border internal to the EU, and one which separated a member state from itself. The 'Green Line' was no longer an international border between putative states, but an EU border which has created new divisions (in addition to perpetuating existing ones) between polarized communities. The rebordering of Cyprus, and the inability of the EU to overcome the Cold War division of the island, has created new internal/external, member/non-member, inclusion/exclusion instabilities within a member state.

The 2004 enlargement also led to the rebordering of Russia, but not only in the sense that the EU now possesses enlarged borders with that country. The Russian enclave of Kaliningrad, sandwiched between the Baltic Sea, Poland and Lithuania, emerged as a big issue in Russia–EU relations just prior to the 2004 enlargement due to the proposed requirement for Russians travelling to and from Kaliningrad to obtain a visa in order to travel through EU territory. The enlargement of the EU worked to reborder Russia, part of whose territory was now surrounded by the EU. In the event, the EU offered a compromise solution which required Russians travelling to and from Kaliningrad to obtain a transit document rather than a full visa. The relative isolation of Kaliningrad from Russia, coupled with the fact that it was part of Germany until the Second World War, has fuelled speculation that its future orientation is likely to be towards the EU rather than Russia.

The East–West division of Europe – represented in different ways by both of the above examples – is a powerful image, and one that has survived long beyond the period when it represented a fundamental division of the continent. Although it might be tempting to see the EU's latest round of enlargement and the subsequent development of 'neighbourhood politics' as an attempt to move Europe's borders eastward, this is at best a partial explanation. Indeed, as outlined already in this chapter the EU has acted to prevent the establishment of an 'excluded east' beyond the new member states. The EU's eastward expansion and the eclipse of Cold War demarcations means that we can start to think in terms of 'post-Western Europe' in which East and West are no longer solid reference points and markers of identity, and in which a previously marginalized East has become central to political developments (Delanty 2003).

The breakdown of the previously foundational East–West cleavage is of considerable importance in relation to the European Union's relations with Turkey, whose national identity in the Republican period has been founded on the desire to be wholly Western, an identity reinforced by Turkey's Cold War role in the architecture of Western defences against the Communist East. In the wake of the Cold War, Turkey had to reorient itself around new principles as its staunch Western vocation was no longer the same geo-strategic asset. Moreover, countries that previously identified themselves as 'Eastern' jumped the EU queue and obtained full membership while Turkey, an aspirant member since 1963, was still struggling to be recognized as an accession country.

The old notion of Turkey as a bridge between East and West lost resonance because these realms were revealed as no longer deeply divided. The West itself began to fragment without the cohesion generated by a common external enemy and it is no longer possible to identify a common 'Western' position on a range of international issues: Iraq, global warming, debt relief for Africa, agricultural subsidies. As an index of these post-Western shifts the Turkish government's refusal (despite massive financial inducements) to allow the US to launch military operations into Iraq from Turkish bases is especially significant. The post-Westernization of Turkey has been aided by domestic political changes within Turkey where the Islamicist AK Party forms the current government and has done much in a short period of time to bring Turkey closer to the EU. Importantly, the rise of liberal-conservative Islamic politics in Turkey has given voice to a contending view of modernity and progress. Whereas the traditional Kemalist political elites equate modernization with Westernization, the Islamists equate modernization with Europe and human rights. The AK Party sees Turkey as both Western and Eastern, European and Middle Eastern.

Legacies of Cold War thinking do persist, however, and it is still possible to encounter attempts to re-divide Europe along an East–West axis. In November 2004, during the Ukrainian Presidential elections, claims of ballot-rigging and election fraud precipitated a major constitutional crisis which was eventually resolved in favour of the current President Viktor Yushchenko. Mass protests against the original election results and the 'victory' of the pro-establishment Viktor Yanukovych organized by Yushchenko's oppositional Orange Bloc movement was represented in the Anglophone media as evidence of an East–West split threatening to break up the Ukraine (for example, 'East–West showdown looms as poll turmoil divides Ukraine' *The Times* 25 November 2004). Yanukovych was portrayed as the pro-Russian candidate, with a power base in the east of the country, and whose candidature was supported by Russia's President

Putin. The neo-Cold War scenario was strengthened by the portrayal of Yushchenko as a pro-Western, pro-NATO, pro-EU, democrat whose support base was in the West of the country. The future of the Ukraine was seen in either/or terms: Western or Eastern, democratic or authoritarian, progressive or backward looking. It seems that it is difficult to dispense with the analytical tools of twentieth-century modernity. What could easily have been interpreted as instability beyond the EU's borders, or even as a struggle between civil society and the state, given the recent history of popular protests against state corruption in Central and Eastern Europe, was, in the case of the Ukraine, interpreted in geopolitical terms as a tug-of-war between the EU and Russia and a struggle to establish new geopolitical spheres of influence.

Conclusion: Eurasia's cosmopolitan borders

Europe's borders with Asia are changing, both in terms of their location and their function. However, this does not mean that borders are any less significant or any less numerous. Processes of bordering, debordering and rebordering are important dimensions of the contemporary social and political transformation of Europe, and its relations with the wider world. This chapter has highlighted the rebordering of Europe that has accompanied the territorial debordering associated with the development of supranational capabilities. The shift from territorial nation-state borders to common EU borders has been marked by a tendency to view borders less as a prerequisite for sovereign governance and more in terms of problems which require novel forms of spatial management: EU governance is not primarily concerned with state or polity-building but is about the construction of European spaces within which European solutions to European problems can be deployed (Delanty and Rumford 2005). Common borders are one example of such spaces. In this context, a key argument in this chapter has been the need to go beyond the dominant models for explaining the rebordering of Europe; neither Schengenland nor 'network Europe' can adequately explain Eurasian borders. The need to go beyond territorial or networked models of spatial governance lends substance to the notion that Europe is witnessing a cosmopolitanization of its borders.

By way of a conclusion we can point to two dimensions of cosmopolitan borders which are relevant to a discussion of the rebordering of Eurasia. First, Europe and Asia can no longer be mapped according to an East–West divide. Such a simple polarity has been overtaken by contemporary realities (the recent EU enlargement to the east), overwritten by new divisions (new North–South), and erased by a post-Westernization of Europe. The interpenetration of what were previously East and West, the erosion of previous friend/enemy, inside/outside distinctions, and the concomitant development of a new sense of place in the world, have all contributed to a greater sense of continuity between Europe and Asia.

Europe and Asia no longer form the First and Second Worlds; they both inhabit one world.

Second, the tendency to see borders as problems to be governed has contributed to the proliferation of borders within (as well as between) societies. Borders are more common, more frequently shifted and more mobile. The multiplicity of communities which can emerge within and between existing polities makes for a greater number of border crossings: the negotiation of borders becomes an integral aspect of both mobilities and identities. The cosmopolitanization of Europe's borders with Asia cannot be dissociated from their multiplication: national borders have been supplemented by shifting EU borders and borders are diffused throughout society. In this sense, cosmopolitanism signals that borders are more numerous and pervasive and that borderlands are becoming the norm. The EU's New Neighbourhood Policy confuses static notions of member/non-member, candidate/non-candidate, insider/outsider by enlarging Europe's borders with Asia and projects the logic of the border into the heartland of the EU.

Notes

1 It should be noted that the SAWS scheme has been heavily criticized on the grounds that the workers are exploited (charged excessively for visas by recruitment agencies, work for low wages), bullied by 'gangmasters', and their human rights routinely infringed. One consequence of the economic hardships faced by these workers is that they tend to accumulate debts and end up overstaying their visas thereby becoming illegal immigrants. See for example, TUC 2004.
2 The European Neighbourhood Policy covers: Belarus, Ukraine, Moldova, Georgia, Armenia, and Azerbaijan, Morocco, Algeria, Tunisia, Libya, Egypt, Israel, Jordan, Lebanon, Syria, as well as the Palestinian Authority.

References

Andreas, P. (2003) 'Redrawing the Line: Borders and Security in the Twenty-first Century', *International Security*, 28(2): 78–111.

Balibar, E. (2004) *We the People of Europe: Reflections on Transnational Citizenship*, Princeton, NJ: Princeton University Press.

Batt, J. (2003) 'The EU's New Borderlands', London: CER Working Paper.

Castells, M. (2000) *The Rise of the Network Society. The Information Age: Economy, Society and Culture, Volume 1*, 2nd edn, Oxford: Blackwell.

Delanty, G. (2003) 'The Making of a Postwestern Europe: A Civilizational Analysis', *Thesis Eleven*, 72(1): 8–25.

Delanty, G. and C. Rumford (2005) *Rethinking Europe: Social Theory and the Implications of Europeanization*, London: Routledge.

European Commission (2003) Communication from the Commission to the Council and the European Parliament: 'Wider Europe – Neighbourhood: a New Framework for Relations with our Eastern and Southern Neighbours', COM(2003) 104 final, Brussels: Commission of the European Communities.

European Commission (2004) 'Beyond Enlargement: Commission Shifts European Neighbourhood Policy into Higher Gear', Press Release IP/04/308 Brussels, 12 May.

Hassner, P. (2002) 'Fixed Borders or Moving Borderlands?: A New Type of Border for a New Type of Entity', in J. Zielonka (ed.) *Europe Unbound: Enlarging and Reshaping the Boundaries of the European Union*, London: Routledge.

Lavenex, S. (2004) 'EU External Governance in "Wider Europe"', *Journal of European Public Policy*, 11(4): 680–700.

McNeill, D. (2004) *New Europe: Imagined Spaces*, London: Arnold.

Paasi, A. (2005) 'The Changing Discourse on Political Boundaries', in H. van Houtum, O. Kramsch and W. Zierhofer (eds) *B/Ordering Space*, Aldershot: Ashgate.

Rumford, C. (2002) *The European Union: A Political Sociology*, Oxford: Blackwell.

Sassen, S. (2001) 'Spatialities and Temporalities of the Global: Elements for a Theorization', in A. Appadurai (ed.) *Globalization*, Durham: Duke University Press.

Suarez-Navaz, L. (2004) *Rebordering the Mediterranean: Boundaries and Citizenship in Southern Europe*, New York: Berghahn Books.

Trades Union Congress (2004) 'Gone West – The Harsh Reality of Ukrainians at Work in the UK' at www.tuc.org.uk/em_research/tuc-7739-f0.cfm.

Walters, W. (2006) 'Border/Control', *European Journal of Social Theory*, 9(2): 187–204.

Zielonka, J. (2002) 'Introduction: Boundary Making by the European Union', in J. Zielonka (ed.) *Europe Unbound: Enlarging and Reshaping the Boundaries of the European Union*, London: Routledge.

13 Europe after the EU enlargement
'Cosmopolitanism by small steps'

William Outhwaite

Deutschland ist demokratisch
Wasser, das ist nass
Quadrate sind quadratisch
Wenn nicht das, zumindest das[1]

For some, the cosmopolitan character of Europe in general, and the EU in particular, is not in question. Is Europe not par excellence the region where humans emancipated themselves from unreflected traditions and primordial loyalties and preached, sometimes even practised, ideas of the brotherhood of man or, as we would now say, the siblinghood of humanity? And is European integration not by definition a cosmopolitan project, marked in its current version by the powerful image of the West German and French coal and steel industries fused together in the ECSC a mere half decade after the end of the War?

There is much to be said for these views, which have been powerfully argued in the recent past by Gerard Delanty, Ulrich Beck and others. Jürgen Habermas (2004), for example, has stressed the way in which Europeans have 'painfully' learned how to handle their differences and to recognise one another in their difference. Delanty (2005) has put forward the idea of Europe as a privileged site of cultural translation, while in Beck and Grande's *Cosmopolitan Europe* (2004) the adjective is built into the title. The EU's most recent enlargement in 2004 brought in an eminently cosmopolitan, or at least eclectic, mix of three former Soviet republics, one former Yugoslav republic, four members of the Visegrád group of relatively privileged postcommunist countries and one and a half Mediterranean islands.

Unfortunately, there is also a good deal to be said for the contrary, or perhaps complementary, view which sees Europe as the chief defendant in the court of world history, responsible for imperialism, 'scientific' racism, 'scientific' communism, for two world wars and for planning (and almost initiating) the third and final one.[2] Similarly, the EU can be seen as self-obsessed, protectionist and unconcerned or unable to take on a serious role in the governance of the world, thus leaving a dangerous vacuum for US hegemony. The old slogan 'Oui à l'Europe: non à Maastricht', has been echoed in some at least of the left opposition to the ill-fated 2005 constitutional treaty.

This chapter is concerned with Europe in the narrower sense, that of the EU as it has evolved over the past half-century and particularly since the end of the 'short' twentieth century in 1989. My concern is with the ways in which Europe as a whole has been reshaped by what has taken place on its own territories, as distinct from, though of course also taking account of, external or global processes, in the past 10–15 years. To put it pretentiously, and with a bow to the phenomenological tradition, I am interested not only in what is happening and is likely to happen, but in its *meaning* for Europe. And I am interested as much in what did not happen as in what did.[3]

Postcommunist transition and 2004

I am struck, in particular, in the EU Enlargement of 2004, by the mismatch between the enormous importance of what happened in May 2004 and the restricted form in which it was reflected both before and after the event. On the one hand there was the sense of a momentous transition, in which the European integration process finally embraced almost the whole of the subcontinent, including a majority of the European states excluded for forty years not just from the European Community/Union but also from the post-war democratisation process itself.[4] On the other hand, there was an essentially technical and administrative process of harmonisation and coordination. Hannah Arendt spoke (of course in an entirely different context) of the banality of evil, and we might speak here of the banality or the banalisation of accession.

The bureaucratisation of the enlargement process, though hardly unexpected, was one of its most striking features. The imposition of the Union's *acquis* was of course to be expected, though the over-neat specification of chapters and check-lists looks like an exercise in Analerotik. As my colleague Alan Mayhew (2000) pointed out, this enlargement has been more protracted (p. 7), partly because it was left in the hands of a somewhat lame-duck Commission at the end of the 1990s (p. 8), and with a much more substantial *acquis* whose adoption was made a precondition subject to verification and not just, as in the past enlargements, a condition for accession. On the other side there was some quite good public relations: a well-sustained Commission website, providing regular email reminders to check out recent developments, some imaginative activities involving schools, a fair amount of speech-making and some high-profile meetings.[5]

Alongside all this, there was a third element, the constitutional convention, contingently related to the impending enlargement in that it could (and perhaps should) have taken place well before 1989, but intrinsically linked in its mission to make a larger Union viable that the new members were fully represented in its deliberations. Although the Convention failed to produce an acceptable constitution, in other respects it was quite an impressive deliberative assembly which may be remembered when more immediately successful ventures are forgotten (Norman 2003). It was also one in which Old and New Europe met on relatively egalitarian and open terms; as Fraser Cameron (2004: 152) notes, 'it was difficult to distinguish speakers coming from existing or future member states'.[6] For all this, however, the dominant impression of the current enlargement remains that of a bureaucratic process managed in a bureaucratic manner, and tinged with arrogance on the part of the existing members. Like, some would say, the European Union itself...

We have of course been here before. I am thinking not so much of the previous accessions as of the special case of German Reunification, which produced 'Enlargement without Accession' (Spence 1991). Here, of course, even the accession was occluded by the incorporation of the territory of the GDR, without the sort of constitutional debate which Habermas and others called for. In the German case, incorporation into the Federal Republic and hence into the EU coincided with all except the first months of postcommunist transition. In the 2004 accession, by contrast, we had effectively a second transition, again widely desired in general though not necessarily welcomed in all of its details. We can only guess how this will pan out in the longer term. On the one hand, the EU's new citizens may feel that any trauma is as nothing compared with that of the 1990s. Alternatively, they may feel that, having been through all that, they are less willing to put up with such social dislocation a second time. We therefore need to reflect in rather broader terms on the transition process as a whole and what it means for Europe.

It is tempting to define postcommunist transition out of existence, suggesting that it is either essentially over, as many in East Central Europe would argue is the case in the parts of their states which interest them, or not yet seriously begun, as jaundiced observers of points further East often say. Either way, for this reductive view, the implications for the rest of Europe are seen as relatively limited and can be handled under the category of transitional arrangements, where 'transition', like 'convergence', now refers to EU accession rather than the shift from totalitarian socialism to liberal capitalism. It is certainly true that the world-historical significance of the transition, rightly stressed by analysts like Andrew Arato, hardly seems to be reflected in the observable phenomena. Everything, so to speak, was tossed up into the air, but it fell down again into relatively familiar structures and patterns. As against this view, I intend to start from the premise that 'we are all postcommunist now', not in the sense of ideological demobilisation or what Habermas, as early as 1985, called 'the exhaustion of utopian energies', but in the sense that Europe, as well as the EU, are radically transformed by what has happened. It now makes sense once again, as in the period immediately after the Second World War, to think of a political Europe which in principle includes the whole subcontinent, but where East and West have experienced radically different trajectories over half a century. Habermas's concept of the *nachholende* Revolution was prophetic of the phenomenology of the transition, especially as it appeared from a West German or West European perspective, but ultimately, I think, misleading. The apparent banality or normality of the transition, in Germany and in much of the former bloc, and reinforced in the Enlargement process, conceals, I believe, more fundamental changes.

Does more mean more cosmopolitan?

Will the new EU be more or less cosmopolitan in the sense in which theorists of cosmopolitan democracy, and most recently Ulrich Beck, have been using the term? At first sight, an enlarged EU, a real *Grosseuropa* compared with the old Western *Kleineuropa*,[7] is by definition more inclusive, embracing new languages, religions and cultures. Already the budget airlines are criss-crossing the old EU external border with more and more routes; EasyJet, Ryanair and their Eastern counterparts have taken up where Gorbachev left off and made Lviv or Vilnius realistic destinations for a cheap weekend break. On the other hand there are countervailing pressures, for objective as well as subjective reasons.

The EU will now abut some of the more problematic European states such as Russia, Belarus and Ukraine, whose citizens may have for the foreseeable future more compelling reasons to attempt to emigrate than do Poles, Czechs or Hungarians. This has the potential to ignite renewed anxieties around the EU's 'near abroad', which form part of the explanation for why 2004 came so late. It is instructive to look back at some of the surveys conducted around the turn of the century, in which existing EU citizens warmly welcomed the idea of Swiss or Norwegian (and Maltese) accession but were more lukewarm or even negative about the Eastern and Central European (ECE) countries (CEC 2000) and emphatically negative in the case of Turkey. This partly explains, in a process of reciprocal influence, the EU's remarkably slow response to 1989, which provoked considerable resentment in Poland (Blazyca 2002: 206–7, 212) and elsewhere in the region.[8] A more cosmopolitan Union, one must conclude, would have been more responsive and understanding – not least since it had just emerged from a potentially lethal cold war.[9] A more wholehearted response by the West as a whole and the EU in particular might have spared Eastern Europe a ghastly decade of negative growth and impoverishment, giving it some at least of the benefits of the capital flows accompanying German reunification, without the latter's catastrophic downside. The failure of the EU's cosmopolitan imagination when it was most urgently needed contrasts very unfavourably with earlier European initiatives such as European Nuclear Disarmament and the Helsinki process –

the latter combining official and social movement activity in an exceptionally fruitful blend.

For their part, the ECE countries tend to have a more 'traditional' and positive ('pre-postcolonial') conception of Europe than Westerners. Very many Western Europeans, for example, belong to states which have had substantial colonial empires, and although they react to this past in very different ways (compare the positive and nostalgic image of empire in the UK with the tendency to embarrassed denial in The Netherlands), it has perhaps given a more cosmopolitan and multicultural angle to their thinking about Europe. Habermas (2004: 51) emphasises the effect of the experience of colonial rule and decolonisation: 'with the growing distantiation from imperial rule and colonial history the European powers have had the chance *to take up a reflexive distance to themselves*'.[10] In the East, by contrast, 'Europe' in general and 'Central Europe' in particular have operated in part as tokens in a political strategy of distantiation from the 'asiatic' USSR.[11] To put it bluntly, Easterners, even more than Westerners, often talk about the European heritage in up-beat language which provokes hostility or embarrassment in parts of the West and the rest of the world.

The boot is perhaps on the other foot if one turns to a related issue, that of ethnocentric prejudice. The somewhat higher levels recorded in the East of Europe than in the West have generated something of a moral panic, starting with skinhead riots in the East German port of Rostock in 1991. I do not wish to belittle the unpleasant character of these manifestations, and the extremely serious levels of anti-Roma prejudice, but the pattern overall seems to be that such attitudes are driven by specific current crises rather than linked into nationalism and extreme-right ideology, as they have tended to be in the West (Hjerm 2003). Very crudely, one might say that there is an intra-European cosmopolitan multicultural tradition in Eastern and Central Europe, historically tied to local empires,[12] where the West has a more extra-European one more oriented to the Atlantic and the rest of the world via the Western European world empires. Both traditions of course are counterposed by explicit racism in the West and ethnic prejudice in the East, but the possibility of their fusion is one of the more optimistic scenarios in play here.

The ultimate destination or *finalité* of what has become the European Union remains more or less as unclear as when Andrew Shonfield examined it in 1973. Briefly, however, the EU is incipiently postnational, despite or because of its continuing symbiotic relationship with its member states. It is post-imperial, in that however much it might superficially come to resemble the Austro-Hungarian Empire it will surely retain principles of democracy more characteristic of the national state (Beck and Grande 2004). And it is perhaps (and this is part at least of its appeal), the beginning of a form of post-European cosmopolitan democracy attractive not just to Europe but to many other parts of the world.[13] Jürgen Habermas

(1991) has aptly described this as 'Europe's second chance'. A federal or semi-federal Europe which was not just a 'fortress Europe' but a Europe for others as well as for itself might be a happier transformation with which to round off the European half-millennium. As Habermas (2004: 47) puts it, why should a Europe which has at least partially solved two major problems by developing forms of postnational governance and welfare and social justice 'not also set itself the further task of defending and furthering a cosmopolitan order...?'.

Cosmopolitanism is, then, perhaps the most tempting label to attach to this vision. Ulrich Beck and Edgar Grande lay down the challenge on the back cover of their recent book (2004: 11):

> Cosmopolitan Europe is in Europe the last really effective utopia. It is about something completely new in the history of humanity, namely the projected image of a state structure which makes its foundation the recognition of cultural otherness.

This analysis of cosmopolitanism (Beck 2004) and cosmopolitan Europe builds on Beck's earlier concepts of risk society and of a second, reflexive modernity. European integration is driven, among other things, by an awareness of global risks of, in particular, environmental damage and terrorism. Neither can be meaningfully confronted just at the level of the national state. Conceptions of security must be rethought in political and social, rather than merely technical and military, terms. 'The 11th of September 2001 is the Chernobyl of the military conception of power' (Beck and Grande 2004: 376). Concretely, this means that Turkey must, if it wants, be in the EU and not just NATO; 'a continent of Europe affirming itself against Turkey would endanger itself' (p. 373). A cosmopolitan Europe is also reflexive not just in the sense of responding to humanly generated risks (the sense of reflexivity which Beck had stressed in his earlier work,[14] but also in that it relativises conceptions of inside/outside, self/other, Europe *or* the nation-state: 'Europe is another word for variable geometry, variable national interests, variable concern (Betroffenheit), variable internal and external relations, variable statehood, variable identity' (p. 16). As Beck and Grande argue at length, a reflective and cosmopolitan conception of Europe can to some extent escape the dilemmas of in/out, us/them, nation-state/federation.[15]

If this bold attempt to transcend the dilemmas which have constantly accompanied the process of European integration over the past half-century seems a little too easy, Beck and Grande stress that the cosmopolitanism of the EU is still a 'deformed cosmopolitanism', deformed economically by neoliberalism, politically by nationalism and internally by technocratic bureaucracy (chapter 5, section 3). The last of these applies also, of course, to the EU's own cosmopolitan elites: the EU embodies the paradox of a civil society *from above* aiming to establish one from below

(p. 196). The remedy however lies in more Europeanisation: the concept of European civil society offers the EU the opportunity of 'opening up the transnational space in such a way that this organises itself' (p. 197).

This is indeed a powerful image, engagingly presented. It is paralleled in the cultural sphere, as I noted at the beginning of this chapter, by Gerard Delanty's image of Europe as a site of intercultural translation (Delanty 2005; see also Delanty 2003). Against these, of course, one must set the counter-image of a Europe with a dubious past, egocentric and self-obsessed, traditionally ignorant of cultural otherness outside its borders except as something exotic.[16] An approach which takes seriously the political economy of the EU as a region of globalised capitalism is a welcome counterweight to more culturalist and voluntaristic analyses.[17] But it is at least true, I think, that to conceptualise Europe, or to pursue the project of European integration, requires a degree of cosmopolitan imagination and will which might at least anticipate a more cosmopolitan future.

The question, in a nutshell, is whether a Europe which is becoming post-Western in the trivial sense that it is no longer composed of Western and Central Europe (plus Greece) will also become post-Western in a more interesting sense of multicultural cosmopolitanism. (The Turkish case, discussed elsewhere in this volume, is of course exceptionally important in this regard.) The EU, which is on the way to becoming coextensive with almost all of the subcontinent, is of course a permanent building site. It remains to be seen whether, as a result of the 2004 Enlargement and the one which is planned to succeed it in 2007, it will be less of a fortress and more of a community, for itself and for the rest of the world.

Notes

1 'Die Rede (Deutschland ist demokratisch)', in Gebrüder Engel, *Watt 'Ne Welt*. Label: Thmv (New Music) ASIN: B00002DG7Z (1999).
2 As Étienne Balibar (2004: 24–5) has suggested, 'we should resist the illusion of believing ... that some national traditions are open, tolerant, and 'universalist' by 'nature' or on account of their 'exceptionality', whereas others, still by virtue of their nature or historical specificity, are intolerant and 'particularist'. Balibar was referring to national traditions and to their attitudes to foreigners, but the point has a more general application. See also Nederveen Pieterse (2002: 141): 'A cultural analysis of Europe points toward traveling light, in the sense of leaving behind the heavy luggage of imperialism and colonialism, racism and chauvinism, nationalism and parochialism'.
3 Of the things which did not happen, two stand out in particular. First, a rapid and much more substantial Marshall Plan-type response by the West as a whole and the EU in particular to the challenge of 1989. Second, a very different scenario in which either the EU was even less welcoming to the East, or in which part or all of the East deliberately rejected full membership of the EU in favour of a looser attachment in the European Economic Area. On the latter question, however unlikely it may look at present, the prospect of an Eastern European Norway or Switzerland should not be ruled out. More to the point, as Böröcz and Sarkar (2005: 158–9) emphasise, full membership has been and

is to be preceded by a long transitional period of dependency on EU regulations: 'For the entrants during the 2004 round of accessions (who will enjoy equal rights within the EU by 2011), this quasi-dependency status will have lasted for 18 years. For next-round members Bulgaria, Romania and Turkey – optimistically assuming only a five-year delay – it can be expected to be circa 23 years'. On further impending accessions, see also, for example, Bechev and Andreev (2005).

4 As Étienne Balibar described the situation in 1991 (Balibar 2004: 90), 'Following the disappearance of one of the two blocs, the struggle itself is vanishing, which in fact constitutes a great trial of truth: now or never is the moment for the dream to materialize, for Europe to rise up, renewed or revitalized. This is also the moment when the dream risks being smashed into pieces'.

5 Sobrina Edwards (2005) has shown the two ways in which the 2004 Enlargement was presented: first, as simply the next in a series of enlargements and, second, as a historic moment of the reunification of a Europe divided since the Second World War. See also Spohn (2000).

6 The research of Ruth Wodak and her colleagues suggests however a rather more pessimistic assessment of the Convention (Krzyzanowski 2005; Oberhuber 2005).

7 These terms are of course drawn from the nineteenth-century discussion around German unification, which in many ways can be seen as a microcosm of European integration a century later (see, for example, Garton-Ash 1993, 2004: 223; Balibar, 2004: 253 n. 23).

8 Melinda Kovács (2001) neatly describes this as 'putting down and putting off'.

9 See Baldwin *et al.* (1997: 168, quoted in Ingham and Ingham 2002: 15): 'Imagine how eager western Europe would have been in 1980 to pay ECU 18 billion a year in order to free central Europe from communism and remove Soviet troops from the region'. This figure was a current estimate of the likely cost of enlargement; the European Currency Unit (ECU) is of course the forerunner of the euro.

10 For a very different and more critical approach to this issue, see Böröcz and Sarkar (2005), who see the EU as in some ways a continuation of West European colonialism in another context.

11 Rudolf Bahro's now forgotten *Alternative* (Bahro 1977) is an interesting example among others.

12 Including the trans-European Russian empire; see Richard Sakwa's contribution to this volume.

13 On Habermas' account of cosmopolitanism, see Fine and Smith (2003). On the cosmopolitanism of European functionaries, see Shore (2000) and various studies on the Europeanisation of national administrations. On the need for, (Habermas 2004: 69–70) and the existence of elements of *deliberative* democracy in the EU, see Eriksen and Fossum (2000).

14 See the collective volume by Beck, Giddens and Lash (1994).

15 See, in particular, chapter 2, section 3, pp. 57–60. Among the divisions transcended or at least relativised is that between domestic social policy and European regional policy: 'regional policy becomes European social policy' (p. 271). More speculatively, Balibar identified in 1991 something similar in our understanding of Europe as a whole: '... in "exporting" communism to the world, after the Bible and cannons, Europe has been placed outside of itself in such a way that it is no longer able to exist as a *closed* entity. It is as much our representation of European civilization as of European political unification that is affected by the "end of communism"' (Balibar 2004: 87).

16 Beck and Grande (2004: 259) rightly point to a certain 'Western European racism'.

17 See, for example, Nederveen Pieterse (2002); Böröcz and Sarkar (2005, esp. pp.

167–8) and Srubar (2003). Nederveen Pieterse (2002: 128) puts the voluntarism issue very neatly: 'If Europeanization is part of the momentum of accelerated globalization, to what extent is the EU in the driver's seat, and to what extent is it driven?'

References

Bahro, R. (1977) *Die Alternative: zur Kritik des real existierenden Sozialismus* Köln: Europäische Verlagsanstalt, Trans. as: Bahro, R. (1978) *The Alternative in Eastern Europe*, London: New Left Books.

Balibar, É. (2004) *We, The People of Europe?: Reflections on Transnational Citizenship*, Princeton: Princeton University Press.

Bechev, D. and S. Andreev (2005) 'Top-Down vs Bottom-Up Aspects of the EU Institution-Building Strategies in the Western Balkans', *Occasional Paper 3/05*, South East European Studies Programme, European Studies Centre, St Anthony's College, Oxford.

Beck, U. (2004) *Der kosmopolitische Blick*, Frankfurt: Suhrkamp.

Beck, U., A. Giddens and S. Lash (1994) *Reflexive Modernization*, Cambridge: Polity.

Beck, U. and E. Grande (2004) *Das kosmopolitische Europa*, Frankfurt: Suhrkamp.

Blazyca, G. (2002) 'EU Accession: The Polish Case', in Ingham and Ingham (eds): 205–21.

Böröcz, J. and M. Sarkar (2005) 'What is the EU?', *International Sociology*, 20(2): 153–73.

Cameron, F. (ed.) (2004) *The Future of Europe: Integration and Enlargement*, London: Routledge.

CEC (2000) *Eurobarometer*, 53: 54.

Delanty, G. (2003) 'The Making of a Post-Western Europe: A Civilizational Analysis', *Thesis Eleven*, 72: 8–24.

Delanty, G. (2005) 'Cultural Translations and European Modernity', in E. Ben-Rafael (ed.) *Comparing Modern Civilizations: Pluralism versus Homogeneity*, Leiden: Brill.

Edwards, S. (2005) 'Explaining Enlargement: Space, Identity and Governance', unpublished paper for UACES Conference, September, University of Zagreb.

Eriksen, E. O. and J. E. Fossum (eds) (2000) *Democracy in the European Union: Integration Through Deliberation?* London: Routledge.

Fine, R. and W. Smith (2003) 'Jürgen Habermas' Theory of Cosmopolitanism', *Constellations*, 10(4): 469–87.

Garton-Ash, T. (1993) *In Europe's Name: Germany and the Divided Continent*, London: Cape.

Garton-Ash, T. (2004) *Free World*, London: Penguin.

Habermas, J. (1991) 'Europe's Second Chance', tr. in J. Habermas (1994) *The Past as Future*, Cambridge: Polity.

Habermas, J. (2004) *Der Gespaltener Westen*, Frankfurt: Suhrkamp.

Hjerm, M. (2003) 'National Sentiments in Eastern and Western Europe', *Nationalities Papers*, 31(4): 413–30.

Ingham, H. and M. Ingham (eds) (2002) *EU Expansion to the East: Prospects and Problems*, Cheltenham: Edward Edgar.

Kovács, M. (2001) 'Putting Down and Putting Off: The EU's Discursive Strategies in the 1998 and 1999 Follow-up Reports', in J. Böröcz and M. Kovács (eds) *Europe's New Clothes. Unveiling EU Enlargement*, Telford: Central European Review (www.ce-review.org/), pp. 196–234.

Krzyzanowski, M. (2005) ' "European Identity Wanted": On Discursive and Communicative Dimensions of the European Convention', in R. Wodak and P. Chilton (eds) *A New Agenda in (Critical) Discourse Analysis: Theory, Methodology, and Interdisciplinarity*, Amsterdam, Philadelphia: J. Benjamins, pp. 137–63.

Mayhew, A. (2000) 'Enlargement of the European Union: an Analysis of the Negotiations with the Central and Eastern European Countries', SEI Working Paper 39.

Nederveen Pieterse, J. (2002) 'Europe, Traveling Light: Europeanization and Globalization', in M. Kempny and A. Jawlowska (eds) *Identity in Transformation: Postmodernity, Post-Communism and Modernization*, Westport, CT: Praeger, pp. 127–44.

Norman, P. (2003) *The Accidental Constitution: The Story of the European Convention*, Brussels; Eurocomment.

Oberhuber, F. (2005) 'Deliberation or "Mainstreaming"?. Empirically Researching the European Convention', in R. Wodak and P. Chilton (eds) *A New Agenda in (Critical) Discourse Analysis: Theory, Methodology, and Interdisciplinarity*, Amsterdam, Philadelphia: J. Benjamins, pp. 165–87.

Shore, C. (2000) *Building Europe: The Cultural Politics of European Integration*, London: Routledge.

Spence, D. (1991) *Enlargement Without Accession*, London: Royal Institute of International Affairs.

Spohn, W. (2000) 'Die Osterweiterung der Europäischen Union und die Bedeutung kollektiver Identitäten. Ein Vergleich west- und osteuropäischer Staaten', *Berliner Journal fur Soziologie*, 10(2): 219–40.

Srubar, I. (2003) ' "Kampf der Kulturen" und die EU-Osterweiterung', in S. Beetz, U. Jacob and A. Sterbling (eds) *Soziologie über die Grenzen – Europäische Perspektiven. Festschrift für Herrn Professor Dr. Dr. h.c. Bálint Balla zum 75. Geburtstag*, Hamburg: Krämer Verlag, pp. 327–39.

14 Turkey between Europe and Asia

E. Fuat Keyman

In recent years, there has been an upsurge of interest in Turkey in terms of its modern history that has demonstrated that a secular, democratic constitutional democracy is possible in a social setting whose population is dominantly Muslim. The historical context in which this interest has occurred is what has come to be known as "the post-September/11 world" in which the rapid dissemination of inhuman and deadly terrorist attacks throughout the world and their link to Islam have become the central concern of international relations. Since September/11, 2001, world affairs have been increasingly framed by the discourse of "the clash of civilizations", and fundamental to this discourse has been the codification of Islam as the negation of secular modernity and liberal democracy. In this context, it has been suggested by many that the possibility of success in the ongoing global fight against terrorism depends to a large extent on the possibility of the articulation of Islam with modernity and democracy. In political and academic discourse, this suggestion has been formulated differently and in various forms, ranging in a large spectrum from the idea of "the export of democracy through war and occupation, leading to the necessary regime change in failed states" to the calls for "global democratic governance" capable of establishing an effective foundation for the co-existence of different cultures and civilizations in a manner that involves tolerance, respect and responsibility as the guiding principles of social interactions in international, regional and intra-national relations.

In the post-September/11 world, Turkey and its historical experience of modernity has constituted a significant case for the possibility of the co-existence of Islam and democracy. As a social formation with a large Muslim population, Turkey in its modern history has established itself as a modern nation with a strong secular state structure, transformed its political system into a multi-party parliamentary democracy and created a free-market economy. Moreover, as a social formation located at the intersection of the East and the West, the identity of Turkey has always been marked by its will to "reach the contemporary level of civilization", understood as Westernization and Europeanization. In other words, even though Islam has always remained a significant symbolic reference in the formation of cultural identity in Turkey, the history of modern Turkey has been characterized by Westernization as a site of secular modernity, economic progress and democracy. Moreover, despite the existence of a number of regime breakdowns and democratic-deficit problems in its multi-party system, Turkey has nevertheless persistently continued its commitment to parliamentary democracy and its norms. It is this commitment that accounts for the ability of political Islam not only to find for itself a place in the multi-party parliamentary democracy in Turkey, but also to enlarge that place to the extent of becoming the governing party of a strongly secular state, as in the case of the recent majority government of the Justice and Development Party (the AKP hereafter).

Of course, the Turkish experience of modernity and democracy has not been without serious problems and recursively occurring political, economic and cultural crises. In fact, the history of modern Turkey can be described by the simultaneous existence of "success and failure", that is, the success in establishing a necessary institutional structure of modernity, such as a nation-state, modern positive law, parliamentary democracy, market economy and citizenship, but at the same time the failure in making modernity multi-cultural, democracy consolidated, economy stable and sustainable, and citizenship operating on the basis of the language of rights and freedoms. Yet, it is due precisely to the constant and persistent commitment in this experience to secular modernity and democracy, as well as to Westernization and Europeanization, that Turkey has become one of the crucial actors of the post-September/11 world. The recent deepening in Turkey–European Union (hereafter, EU) relations, which has resulted in the European Council's historic decision in its December 2004 summit to begin full accession negotiations with Turkey on 3 October 2005 cannot be explained without taking into account the increasing importance of Turkey in today's highly insecure world. In the same vein, Turkey's ability to experience the co-existence of Islam with modernity and democracy in a generally peaceful manner has also been central to the Turkish–American relations in recent years. In its unilateral act to restructure the Middle East region through war and occupation, initiated in the name of democracy and regime change in failed states, the Bush Administration has approached Turkey and its experience of modernity as a "model" for the region. The recent interest in Turkey, especially in terms of the possibility of Turkey's full accession to the EU can also be observed in most Islamic countries, in that it was commonly suggested that the incorporation in Europe of a social formation with an Islamic religious identity has the potential and capacity to bring about the possibility of co-existence, tolerance and unity in diversity, which is needed in the post-September/11 world to resist against the increasing dominance of the essentialist discourse of the clash of civilizations.

Turkey as alternative modernity

In this chapter, I will attempt to analyze the history of modern Turkey from the perspective of "modernity". In doing so, as I have suggested elsewhere (Keyman and İçduygu 2005; Keyman 2005; Aydın and Keyman 2004), I will argue that Turkey's "alternative" route to and travel in secular modernity and democracy makes the Turkish experience interesting and important, especially in the recent restructuring of world affairs in which the question of Islam has been brought to the fore. Turkey as an alternative modernity constitutes one but effective answer to this question, and it is in this context that an account of Turkey's experience of modernity becomes necessary and timely. The perspective of modernity, in this sense, provides a useful analytical device to demonstrate in a sociological and historical way not only the peculiar nature of Turkish modernity but also its recent democratic transformation. In employing the perspective of modernity, I rely on three important theoretical interventions on the debates about modernity. First, by relying on Charles Taylor's "Two Theories of Modernity" (2001), in which he differentiates what he calls "cultural" and "acultural" theories of modernity, the chapter makes use of a cultural theory of modernity. Whereas cultural theory recognizes cultural differences and the peculiar nature of each culture, and therefore maintains that the association of modernity with the West does not result in the idea that other cultures can only modernize by following and imitating the Western modernity, acultural theory, on the other hand, sees modernity as the "development and growth" of Western reason, secularism and instrumental rationality. It is by employing a cultural theory of modernity that I will demonstrate the peculiarity of Turkish modernity as a project of political modernity (as well as its recent crisis that has given rise to the emergence of alternative claims to modernity). Second, by relying on Gerard Delanty's analysis of modernity in his important book, *Social Theory in a Changing World* (1999), the chapter locates its understanding of the emergence of alternative modernities in the conflictual nature of modernity that occurs as a result of the tension between societal modernization and cultural modernization, or between autonomy and fragmentation. Following Delanty, I approach alternative modernities as historically and discursively constructed societal claims, embedded in cultural modernization and its recent fragmentation and aiming at altering the state-centric and secular model of Turkish modernity. Third, by relying on the theory of alternative or multiple modernities (Eisenstadt 2000; Ong 1999; Berger and Huntington 2002), in which it is recognized that modernity is not one but many, and that there are different and varying articulations of economy and culture in different national sites, the chapter reads the recent criticisms of the state-centric model of Turkish modernity as having the potential to produce alternative claims to modernity with differing societal visions, cultural identity formations and citizenship demands.

On the basis of these three methodological openings, it can be suggested that Turkey with its ability to achieve the co-existence of Islam, secular modernity and democracy constitutes an alternative modernity, and it is this characteristic of Turkey that creates its recent perception in academic and political discourse as an important actor whose experience of modernity should be taken seriously by any attempt aiming at going beyond the clash of civilizations, beyond the orientalist divide between the West and the East, and more importantly beyond the culturally essentialist and fundamentalist desires to codify difference as the dangerous Other. In what follows, I will analyze Turkey's travel in modernity in three stages by focusing: first, on the arrival of Turkey at modernity in the early republican years; second, on the crisis and transformation of modernity as a result of the emergence of identity-based conflicts; and third, on the democratization of modernity and its operation as an alternative modernity in recent years.

Arrival at modernity

In his influential book, *The Making of Modern Turkey*, Feroz Ahmad correctly observes that "Turkey did not rise phoenix-like out of the ashes of the Ottoman Empire. It was 'made' in the image of the Kemalist elite which won the national struggle against foreign invaders and the old regime" (1993: 2). Moreover, in the process of "making", the primary aim was to "reach the contemporary level of civilization" by establishing its political, economic and ideological prerequisites, such as the creation of an independent nation-state, the fostering of industrialization, and the construction of a secular and modern national identity. Thus, while Turkey as an independent nation-state emerged out of an independence war against Western imperialist powers, it nevertheless accepted the universal validity of Western modernity as *the way* of building modern Turkey. For Atatürk and his followers, it was only through rapid modernization that entailed the introduction and the dissemination of Western reason and rationality into what was regarded as traditional and backward social relations that Turkey would be stronger and secure vis-à-vis its enemies.

In can be argued, in this sense, that since its inception in 1923, the process of making has involved both security and modernity, meaning that the Kemalist elite has always been concerned about the security of the new nation in a time when they accepted the universal validity of Western modernity for the possibility of Turkey to reach the contemporary level of civilization. Here the question is, how was the link between security, modernity and Westernization established in the process of making? For the Kemalist elite, the key to linking security and modernity in Westernization was the idea of "rapid modernization" through the foundation of a modern nation-state that would possess secularity and rationality, employ reason to initiate progress, and establish a modern industrial economy, thereby fostering the processes of industrialization. And, this modernization had to be "rapid", due precisely to the "time lag" between Turkey and the West in terms of their different historical arrivals at modernity (Ahıska 2003: 354). It is for this reason that for the Kemalist elite, in order for Turkey as a new independent nation to be secure and stronger, not only should it be successful in establishing the necessary political, economic and cultural institutions of what Delanty calls societal modernization, the pace of modernization should also be rapid making it possible quickly to catch up with the level of civilization in the West.

Of course, fundamental to the success in societal modernization was the idea of the state that was derived in a strategic manner from the reaction of the Kemalist elite to two fundamental problems, which they saw were the key to the decline of the Ottoman Empire. First, they saw the personal rule of the sultan in the Ottoman state as the main reason for the inability of the Empire to compete with the European nation-state system. Second, they saw the Islamic basis of the Ottoman state as the primary obstacle to progress in Ottoman society. For the Kemalist elite therefore, it was imperative to create a nation-state distinct from the person of the sultan and secular enough to reduce Islam to the realm of individual faith. Herein can be seen the association of the Kemalist elite with the Durkheimian conception of the state as the agent of rationality. The state is thus viewed as an active agent that, while taking its inspiration from the genuine feelings and desires of the nation, shapes and reshapes it to "elevate the people to the level of contemporary (Western) civilization" (Heper 1985: 50). Therefore, the Kemalist idea of the state was embedded in the question of how to activate the people towards the goal of civilization, that is, how to construct a national identity compatible with the will to civilization. Moreover, the Kemalist elite also

> took seriously the Weberian answer to the riddle of the "European miracle"; that is, that the reasons behind Western advancement could be located precisely in Western cultural practices. Kemalism understood modernization not just as a question of acquiring technology, but as something that could not be absorbed without a dense network of cultural practices which made instrumental thought possible.
>
> (Sayyid 1994: 269)

This means that the commitment to societal modernization had to be supplemented with a set of cultural practices that were to constitute the discursive and institutional foundation for a modern and secular national identity.

The state-based attempt to achieve a top-down and rapid modernization of the new republic and the construction of a modern and secular national identity was initiated through a set of reforms, namely those of republicanism, nationalism, etatism, secularism, populism and reformism (from above). These reforms defined the nation-state as the sovereign subject of modernity, operating as the dominant actor of political, economic and cultural life spheres, and aimed to construct national identity as an organic unity of the secular non-class based identity which necessarily involved the subjugation of its Other, i.e. the Kurdish identity, Islamic identity and minorities. This identity was the citizen as the symbol of secularism and civilization, virtuous enough to privilege state interest over her/his own interest, and the other was expected to accord primacy to citizenship over difference.

It should be noted at this point that in the way in which Turkish modernity reproduced itself mainly as societal modernization, that is, as a modern nation-state building process, in which the state plays a significant role as a dominant and sovereign actor/subject, its expectation to achieve a top-down construction of a modern and secular national identity through the state-based designed reforms was not very successful (Keyman 1995; Mardin 1994; Sunar 2004). As Mardin (1994) correctly suggests, even though the arrival at modernity involved success in the process of modern nation-state building, it nevertheless failed to construct a "social ethos" in societal relations. In other words, the success in societal modernization went hand in hand with the failure in cultural modernization. The remaining strong symbolic role of Islam in the identity formation of the majority of people, especially those living in rural areas, as well as in the formation of everyday life in the republican era, and also the resistance, coming especially from the Southern Anatolia and voicing the demands of the Kurdish ethnic identity, against the conceptualization of national identity as a modern and secular organic unity clearly illustrates and indicates the problem of social ethos embedded in the Kemalist elite's will to civilization through societal modernization. It is the problem of social ethos, that is, the emergence of the disjuncture between societal and cultural modernization processes in the republican era that, as will be seen in the following section, has paved the way to the identity-based conflict, mainly in the form of Islamic resurgence and the Kurdish question.

Moreover, in addition to the problem of social ethos that characterizes the nature of "arrival at modernity", the lack of reference to democracy should also be pointed out as one of the defining features of the early republican era. More than the existing one-party system, it is the need, in the minds of the Kemalist elite, to catch up with the level of civilization in the West as fast as possible, in order to make Turkey more secure and stronger, that explains the democracy deficit in this era. The main aim in the constant efforts to initiate the state-centric reforms for the top-down modernization of society as a whole, as noted, was to overcome the problem of the "time lag" between Turkey and the West, and the key to do so was "modernization without democratization". In this context, the articulation of modernity and security, framed by the discourse of Westernization, and operated mainly as a mode of the state-centric societal modernization marks the nature of the early republican era of modern Turkey.

The crisis of modernity

Even though Turkey transformed its single-party political system into a multi-party parliamentary democracy in a peaceful transition after the Second World War, it was not until the 1980s, and especially the 1990s, that the hegemony of the state-centric mode of societal modernization remained unchallenged. This statement does not underestimate the importance of the transition to democracy in modern Turkey. In fact, unlike the Latin American and South European countries, where the transition from authoritarianism to democracy was realized through a "rupture" with the old regime, Turkey's experience involved a peaceful transition with a movement of "reform" in the single-party political system (Özbudun 2000: 13–44). It is for this reason that, as has been argued by many, since its inception in 1950 parliamentary democracy has persisted and remained an accepted and dominant "political norm of governance", even if it has faced three regime breakdowns in 1960, 1971 and 1980 (Özbudun 2000; Sunar 2004). It is true that "democracy deficit" constitutes one of the main characteristics of contemporary Turkish politics, and democracy in Turkey needs to be consolidated. Yet, it is equally true that the norm of parliamentary democracy also constitutes a strong foundation for the possibility of democratic consolidation to be achieved, as well as of making Turkish modernity multi-cultural and democratic.

One of the main reasons for the simultaneous existence of "success" in transition to democracy and "failure" in consolidating democracy as a result of regime breakdown in the period between 1950 and 1980 was that this transition did not challenge the hegemony of the state-centric mode of societal modernization, its reliance on security and its approach to national identity as a modern, secular and organic unity. In other words, however important it was, the transition to democracy did not rely on societal forces and democratic struggle, nor did it activate cultural modernization. It remained ephemeral, accepted the hegemony of state-centric modernity, and has become vulnerable to regime breakdowns (Sunar 2004: 65–93). It was only after the 1980s that there occurred a set of serious challenges to state-centric modernity, which was activated within the realm of cultural modernization and initiated by the newly emerging actors of Turkish politics, namely those of economic actors acting as the strong voices of globalization, market economy and liberal state, political actors attempting to put identity politics into practice as a struggle for recognition and difference, and civil society actors and social movements trying to bring into existence a new language of politics based upon the idea of rights, freedoms and active citizenship (Keyman and İçduygu 2005; Özbudun and Keyman 2002; Kramer 2000).

During the 1990s, however, there emerged a simultaneous existence of transformation and crisis, mainly felt in the realms of politics, economics and culture. In this period, while there were societal calls for the necessary democratization of state–society relations, the development of civil society and sustainable economic development, the state and political parties have faced a serious legitimacy and representation crisis, the economic realm has experienced a serious financial and governing crisis, and the cultural realm has been confronted by religious and ethnic-based conflict. In fact, it was the identity-based conflicts, which have given rise to the process of the resurgence of Islam and the Kurdish question, that marked the crisis-ridden nature of Turkish modernity and Turkish politics during the 1990s (Keyman and İçduygu 2005). The Kurdish question, in which the ethnic identity-based demands for recognition and cultural rights and the ethnic-based violence and terror activities went hand in hand, even becoming fused, has been most politically troublesome and challenging. Not only has the Kurdish question placed ethnicity at the center of Turkish politics very effectively, it has also caused a "low-intensity war" between the state and the PKK (The Kurdish Workers Party) which has left more than 30,000 people dead. It also placed national security concerns at the center of state–society relations, and as a result, democracy was deferred in the name of security and territorial unity.

On the other hand, the process of the resurgence of Islam has created a much more complex development during the 1990s in Turkey. Similar to the Kurdish question, in which the construction of national identity in Turkish modernity as an organic, secular unity was put into interrogation, the Islamic challenge to the national identity had to do with its strictly sec-ularist and state-controlled nature (Cornell 2001). The Islamic challenge to Turkish modernity, in this sense, has been initiated on the basis of religious rights and freedoms, and directed at state-centric secularism. However, this challenge, unlike the Kurdish question, has paved the way to a multiple and multi-dimensional development of the process of resurgence. During the 1990s, the Islamic challenge has produced (i) a successful politicization process both at national and local levels, which has brought success to the Islamic-oriented parties in national and municipal elections; and (ii) successful Islamic-oriented economic actors, whose increasing presence in economic life has proved that Islam can co-exist with free market capitalism, globalization and modernity (Özbudun and Keyman 2002; Buğra 1999). The process of resurgence, then, has created Islamic-based identity claims in the political, economic and cultural realms of social life; claims whose discursive mode has varied in a large spectrum from fundamentalism to moderate conservatism, and whose success in proving that Islam can co-exist with modernity and democracy has made Turkey an example of alternative modernity. The Islamic challenge to the state-centric Turkish modernity, in fact, can be read off, in Delanty's terminology, as a challenge, emerging from within cultural modernization, and aiming at making societal modernization more open to the presence of religious identity in modernity.

Articulating modernity and democracy

During the 1990s, the state and political parties turned out to be too weak to cope effectively with these identity-based challenges, and to govern their society democratically and efficiently (Kramer 2000). The unstable coalition governments and the increasing problems of corruption, populism and clientalism, together describe the weak structure of the state and political parties in this period. However, since 2000, it has become possible to observe five crucial developments (international and national) that have generated extremely important, if not system-transforming changes in state–societal relations in Turkey. These developments have forced political and state elites to come to terms with the fact that democracy is not only a normatively good system of governance, but also constitutes a valuable strategic and political device to enable any country to be strong and stable in its homeland and in international relations. They have also created an adequate ground for the possibility of making Turkey a strong, stable and democratic country. These developments include: the February 2001 financial crisis and Turkey–IMF relations, the November 2002 national election and the AKP government, the increasing importance and role of civil society, the changing nature of Turkey–EU relations, and the war in Iraq and Turkish–American relations.

All of these developments and relations have had significant impacts in state–society relations in terms of democratization, restructuring state–economy relations, macroeconomic stability, the emergence of active and right-holder understanding of citizenship, and making Turkish modernity democratic and multicultural. The February 2001 financial crisis and Turkey–IMF relations have brought about a significant institutional restructuring of state–economy relations that aimed to fight against corruption, populism and clientalism, and also to provide a macroeconomic foundation for economic stability (Aydın 2005). The November 2002 national election demonstrated the popular feeling in Turkey that the ineffective and unstable political structure based on economic populism and democratic deficiencies had run its course and that a strong single-party government with institutional and societal support could make Turkey a democratic and economically stable country. In fact, the election result was the single majority government of the AKP. Since then, the AKP government has created political stability in Turkey and made a number of important legal and constitutional changes necessary for both further democratization of Turkey and meeting the requirements of the Copenhagen political criteria to be able to start the full accession negations with the EU. Since the AKP has emerged from the previous Islamic-oriented political parties and defined itself as a "conservative democrat" party with moderate Islamic discourse, it has played an important role in demonstrating that in Turkey Islam can co-exist with modernity and democracy. In addition to these developments, there have been strong societal calls in recent years for the further democratization of state, societal and individual relations in Turkey. Today, civil society has become an important element of Turkish politics, not only through its discourse of democratization but also its associational activities. The qualitative and quantitative importance of civil society has forced political and state actors to come to terms with democracy as well as its normative and strategic significance for making Turkey a strong and stable country in international relations (Keyman 2005).

Among these developments, it is the recent deepening of Turkey–EU relations in the post-September/11 world context that has created an upsurge of interest in Turkey both regionally (that is, mainly Europe and the Middle East) and globally. The ability and capacity of Turkey to have a secular and democratic political structure (societal modernization), and at the same time to make the possibility of co-existence of Islam with modernity and democracy an achievable reality constitutes the main reason for this interest. Since the Helsinki Summit of 1999, at which Turkey was granted the status of a candidate country for full membership, Turkish–EU relations have gained "certainty". This certainty has forced the political and state actors in Turkey to focus on democracy, since the candidate-country status requires Turkey to fulfill the Copenhagen political criteria, which means having modernity and democracy linked and upgraded in a given candidate country for full EU membership. Turkey's efforts to make a number of important legal and constitutional changes before the Copenhagen summit of 2002 was only enough to obtain a conditional date (2004 if there was no delay) for the beginning of full accession negotiations with the EU on condition that it meets the Copenhagen political criteria in terms of implementation in its state–societal relations. Turkey's efforts to consolidate its democracy in order to obtain a starting date for negotiations have been successful, as the European Council decided in its December 2004 summit that Turkey would begin the full accession negotiations on 3 October 2005. Even if there are still reactions, ambiguities and uncertainties in Europe with respect to the question of Turkey's full membership, two points are worth making. First, it is true that as Turkey–EU relations have gained certainty over time, Turkish politics have come to terms with the fact that democracy should be "the only game in town", so that these relations have the potential to generate, in fact they have begun to generate, a significant structural and institutional impact on Turkish modernity and its articulation with modernity. Second, the identity of Turkey as a secular democratic country with a large Islamic population has become an asset in Turkey–EU relations, for the incorporation of Turkey into Europe has been viewed both in Europe and globally as a way of resisting the clash of civilizations from which terrorism gains strength. This view of Turkey can be seen also in Turkish–American relations, in which Turkey has been constantly presented as a model for the failed states, as an important actor with an important role to play in the process of the creation of a stable Middle East.

These changes in Turkish–EU relations, Turkish–IMF relations, the AKP single-majority government, Turkish–American relations and the increasing importance of civil society have together brought about the possibility of making Turkish modernity more societal, liberal, plural and multicultural, as well as transforming Turkish democracy into a more consolidated and substantial democracy. Since Turkey's arrival at modernity, the history of modernity has involved ups and downs, and regime breakdowns and crises in terms of democracy and its consolidation. However, it should also be pointed out that in this history there has been a positive move towards arriving at democratic society. Today, Turkey has the chance and ability not only to continue its travel in modernity as a democratic society, but also to demonstrate that as an alternative modernity, as an example of the co-existence between Islam and democratic modernity in a secular political structure, it could make an important contribution to most needed democratic global governance for the creation of a secure, just and peaceful world.

References

Ahıska, M. (2003) "Occidentalism: The Historical Fantasy of the Modern", *South Atlantic Quarterly*, 102(2/3): 351–81.

Ahmad, F. (1993) *Making of Modern Turkey*, Routledge: London.

Aydın, Z. (2005) *The Political Economy of Turkey*, London: Pluto.

Aydın, S. and E. F. Keyman (2004) *Democratization and European Integration in Turkey*, CEPS Working Papers.

Berger, P. L. and S. P. Huntington (eds) *Many Globalizations*, Oxford: Oxford University Press, pp. 296–321.

Buğra, A. (1999) *Islam in Economic Organizations*, İstanbul: TESEV.

Cornell, E. (2001) *Turkey in the 21st Century*, Richmond: Curzon.

Delanty, G. (1999) *Social Theory in a Changing World*, Cambridge: Polity.

Eisenstadt, S. N. (2000) "Multiple Modernities", *Daedalus*, 129(1): 1–31.

Heper, M. (1985) *The State Tradition in Turkey*, North Humberside: The Eothen Press.

Keyman, E. F. (1995) "On Relation Between Global Modernity and Nationalism: The Crisis of Hegemony and the Rise of Islamic Identity in Turkey", *New Perspectives in Turkey*, 13, pp. 93–121.

Keyman, E. F. and A. İçduygu (eds) (2005) *Citizenship in a Global World: European Questions, Turkish Experiences*, London: Routledge.

Keyman, E. F. (2005) "Modernity, Democracy and Civil Society", in F. Adaman and M. Arsel (eds) *Environmentalism in Turkey*, Aldershot: Ashgate, pp. 35–53.

Kramer, H. (2000) *A Changing Turkey*, Washington: Brookings Institution Press.

Mardin, S. (1994) *Religion and Politics* (Devlet ve Din), İstanbul: İletisim.

Ong, A. (1999) *Flexible Citizenship*, Durham: Duke University Press.

Özbudun, E. (2000) *Contemporary Turkish Politics*, Boulder: Lynne Riener.

Özbudun, E. and E. F. Keyman (2002) "Cultural Globalization in Turkey", in P. L. Berger and S. P. Huntington (eds) *Many Globalizations*, Oxford: Oxford University Press, pp. 296–321.

Sayyid, B. (1994) *The Fundamentalist Fear*, London: Zed.

Sunar, I. (2004) *State, Society and Democracy in Turkey*, Istanbul: Bahcesehir University Publications.

Taylor, C. (2001) "Two Theories of Modernity", in D. P. Gaonkar (ed.) *Alternative Modernities*, London: Duke University Press, pp. 172–97.

15 Russia as Eurasia

An innate cosmopolitanism

Richard Sakwa

Russia is not a country; it is a world.

(Russian saying)

In the great struggle of Europe against the rest, Russia stands to one side. Its identity as a European nation is questioned internally and externally, while its status as a European power is perceived as one of the fundamental challenges facing the continent. In tsarist guise the Russian empire expanded to fill the Eurasian landmass and ultimately challenged the Nordic powers to carve out space for its new 'window on the West', the city of St. Petersburg, and in the south Russia imposed relentless pressure on the decaying Ottoman empire to seize the southern steppes and Crimea, and entertained dreams of occupying Constantinople. In Soviet guise Russia became the kernel of an alternative modernity in which capitalism would be superseded and collectivist forms of life practised. Today a democratising post-imperial Russia looms over to the East, too big to join the European Union but too important to be left out. Multiple layers of identity clash and complement each other: imperial, Byzantine, European and Eurasian, while the very concept to describe the country remains contested – a nation-state or a civilisational alternative to the modernity characteristic of the West. In geographical and cultural terms Russia appears to have an innate cosmopolitanism in that its very existence refutes narrow definitions of East and West, Europe and Asia, nation-state and empire, modernity and backwardness. Russia's multiple identities transcend dominant narratives of what it means to be 'Western', while not always sure of the nature of the alternative that it seeks to embody. In this chapter we will survey some of the positions and examine whether indeed this very diversity endows Russia with elements of an innate cosmopolitanism. Never having been a nation-state in the accepted definition of the term, perhaps Russia really has been able to skip stages of development and move on to become a cosmopolitan social order internally and a post-national entity in external relations.

Facets of identity

While contemporaries in late nineteenth-century Western Europe expounded on the theme of the distinctiveness of national destinies or imperial missions, the Russian intelligentsia endlessly agonised over the deeper spiritual mission of the country and its own role in bringing enlightenment to the nation and the world. Among the best examples of this trend of intellectual evolution are the works of Nikolai Berdyaev and Vladimir Soloviev, joined by a host of other writers. The emergence of revolutionary socialism as an ersatz national utopianism was contested by this religious-cultural trend, most notably in the *Landmarks* collection of 1909 (*Vekhi* 1994 [1909]). Authors such as Semyon Frank in his article 'The Ethics of Nihilism' in that volume stressed moral development and personal responsibility against the revolutionary romanticism that afflicted the Russian liberals of that time as much as it did the socialists and radical agrarians. The challenge of reconstituting this philosophical-spiritual strand remains to this day as Russia attempts to democratise and find a new place in the world. As James Billington puts it (2004: xv), 'an enduring positive identity will be possible only if Russians are able harmoniously to synthesise Western political and economic institutions with an indigenous recovery of the religious and moral dimensions of Russian culture'.

The debate continues over whether Russia is no more than the Eastern flank of a common European civilisation, or whether it constitutes a separate and distinct civilisation of its own (Bova 2003). The distinctive pattern of Russian national development, where a land-based empire expanded by absorbing its neighbours, together with the delayed development of a modern civic political community, means that sub-national identities remain strong on the Eurasian landmass. The Chechen wars are in part a reflection of this phenomenon. It also means that the very notion of a 'nation-state' is alien to the Russian tradition. The homogenising 'nation-building' processes that were characteristic of the major West European states in the late nineteenth century largely passed Russia by, although the policy of Russification from the 1880s was a response to the perceived problem of disloyalty among some of the incorporated peoples. The Russian people as an ethnic group was seen as just one, even if the leading one, in a broader pan-Eurasian national culture that encompassed not only Belarus and Ukraine, but also a host of other peoples, religions and cultures. For every strain of dominating discourse, there were a myriad sub-cultures and alternative identities. This cultural heterogeneity and civilisational irresolution was one reason for the delayed development of a hegemonic nation-building project, and instead the emphasis was on a state power that became increasingly brittle. The Russian empire had a supranational character that allowed significant diversity of social forms and political identity for its constituent parts. Indeed, the failure to achieve modern forms of political integration was in part the reason for the collapse in 1917.

The Soviet system, while destroying formal expressions of traditional identities, failed to create a fully inclusive national model of the Soviet citizen. While the territory under its control became more socially homogeneous, it was not fully 'nationalised' in the sense of Brubaker's (1996) notion of 'nationalising states'. While the regime, in particular under Leonid Brezhnev, declared the creation of a 'new historical community, the Soviet people', its own policies impeded the creation of such a 'Soviet people'. The notorious point 5 in Soviet passports required an individual to choose whether they were Russian, Jewish or whatever at the age of 16, based on either the maternal or paternal lines, but once entered it was very difficult to change. This perpetuated, and in some cases effectively created, sub-national ethnically-based identities. Indeed, one author (Martin 2001) characterised the Soviet system as an 'affirmative action empire'. Although in the post-Stalin period leaders spoke of the creation of a 'new Soviet people', Soviet policy in regards to what it called 'the nationalities question' remained within the confines of the policy of *sblizhenie* (the coming together as in convergence of peoples) rather than their *sliyanie* (merging).

For post-communist Russia the problem of forging a new national identity remains as sharp as ever. Several competing designs are in tension with each other. Vera Tolz (2001) describes them as imperial, based on a supranational state; the Eastern Slav idea based on a common origin and culture; the nation based on the Russian language, irrespective of ethnic origin or domicile; an ethnic identity based on narrow racial blood ties; and the idea of a civic Russian nation that would transcend religious, ethnic and other traditions. All these ideas exist at the same time and for what is probably the majority of the people, a number of them are not mutually exclusive: each in turn represents a layer of identity. This is one reason why post-communist Russian leaderships have focused so much on finding a new 'national idea', something that could provide some sort of common purpose and orientation. President Boris Yeltsin's competition to find a new national idea in 1996 collapsed in a welter of ridicule, while president Vladimir Putin, in office from 2000, in part derived his popular support from the ability to encompass several facets, even contradictory ones, simultaneously. For example, in his state of the nation speech of 25 April 2005 he argued that 'the collapse of the Soviet Union was the greatest geopolitical catastrophe of the century. And for the Russian people, it was a real drama. Tens of millions of our citizens and fellow-countrymen found themselves outside the Russian Federation'. Nevertheless, he did not advocate the recreation of some sort of neo-imperial bloc, and indeed he spoke dismissively of the Commonwealth of Independent States (CIS), the rather weak body that was intended to act as some sort of surrogate for the disintegrating USSR when established in December 1991. Even unification between Russia and Belarus was put on the back burner. For Putin the priority was the development of the sinews of the Russian state, confined within its 1991 borders, and integrated into the world economy and society. However, the very multiplicity of identities challenged his government to find a convincing hegemonic project under which the endlessly divided people could rally.

Eurasianism

Concepts of Russia's place in its region and the world are equally multifaceted. Various alternative discourses were vigorously debated in the postcommunist period. Most are effectively oriented towards the idea of 'civilisation' as the most convincing operative unit of analysis. The nation-state is too small, and in the Russian case anachronistic even before it has developed, while the CIS or its equivalents were clearly not viable. Instead certain metaphorical concepts were advanced, rooted in beliefs and aspirations but at the same time reflecting genuine elements of Russian history and its anomalous place in the community of nations. Notable among these is the idea of Eurasianism. This is based on the nineteenth-century idea that Russia is a separate and distinct civilisation and not part of a broader European or even Western civilisation. In the émigré movement of the 1920s this took on a stronger form by disassociating Russia entirely from the West and insisting that its destiny lay in Asia. The organising category is 'civilisation', rather than nation-state or even empire, and thus the supra-nationalism that is characteristic of much of Russian thinking on issues of identity takes a particularly strong form in the Eurasianist model. The 1920s-style Eurasianism reinforced Lenin's view of the Soviet system as anti-Western. In effect Leninism can be considered a civilisational alternative to the West, and thus the civilisational aspect of Eurasianist thinking was a natural complement to Leninism.

In its contemporary manifestations the leader of the Communist Party of the Russian Federation, Gennady Zyuganov, continued this two-pronged rejection of the West as barbaric and decadent. He seized on Samuel Huntington's 'clash of civilisations' as confirmation of traditional Russian ideas that civilisation rather than nation-state is the measure of all things, and that Russia constituted a separate and distinct civilisation of its own. Authors such as A. S. Panarin (1999) called for a 'United States of Eurasia', established in the framework of dialogue between Orthodox Christianity and Islam and based on their common hostility to Western secularism and individualism. There is a powerful tradition in Russia, only some of it in the Eurasian tradition, that condemns the West, and in particular the United States, for its artificial, mechanical, individualised and materialistic nature. The philosopher Igor Shafarevich, for example, is consistent in his condemnation of Western values and the exposition of Russian exceptionalism.

Anti-Westernism remains an important component in Russian national identity, with its roots in nineteenth-century debates between developmental paths, notably between so-called Slavophiles and Westerners, but with a powerful resonance to this day. We can characterise much of this as a form of Russian occidentalism, in which the West is homogenised, its divisions and inner tensions blurred, and then portrayed as the antithesis of Russian values and the obstacle to the achievement of Russian aspirations and the fulfilment of its national destiny (see Buruma and Margalit 2004: 79–99). The Eurasianist strand of Russian occidentalism has a philosophical-cultural 'civilisational' face, but it also has a geopolitical dimension. The various facets are well-described by Andrei Tsygankov (1999), identifying expansionists, civilisationists, stabilisers and geoeconomists. He notes that while some versions take a relatively benign view of the West, others are 'openly isolationist and expansionist'. Despite its heterogeneity, reflecting the broader fragmented character of Russian occidentalism, Eurasianism focuses attention on the almost universal belief in Russia, and in particular among its elites, that the source of many of Russia's woes are geopolitical in character (Tsygankov 1999: 102).

In part this is a reflection of notions that Russia is the heartland of Eurasia, and on the basis of this geographical centrality visions of its civilisational destiny are projected. The influential thinker Alexander Dugin is on the civilisational part of the Eurasianist spectrum. He views globalism as a major threat to Russia, and insists that the multinational (imperial) nature of the Russian state incorporates the four traditional religions (Orthodoxy, Judaism, Islam and Buddhism) as well as the Mongol legacy: 'The mission of Holy Russ is expressed in defending a distinctive Eurasian culture, an original social order, which in its key features differs from the Catholic and Protestant West'. Eurasianists for him are the vanguard of the East, wider than the Third World, against the West, 'as the forward line of traditional society against the society that is secular, atheistic and subservient to mammon'(Dugin 2002: 8). For Eurasianists such as Dugin, in keeping with their view of Russia as a land-based geopolitical empire, Siberia is the heart of Russian identity. As Egor Ligachev (2004) put it, 'Without Siberia there is no Russia. Russia can only develop with Siberia'. By comparison with neighbouring Chinese provinces, Siberia is relatively depopulated, although in terms of absolute economic rationality, Siberia still has an excessive population. Siberia for Eurasianists, of course, is not so much an actual territory but a country of the mind on to which they can project their dreams. Alexander Solzhenitsyn in an earlier generation had done much the same as he urged Russia to cast off the burden of empire and focus on spiritual renewal and development of the Siberian heartland.

Employing a constructivist approach, Tsygankov argues that the response of the Russian intelligentsia to the West following the communist collapse has been overwhelmingly negative. Russians in his view have an alternative vision of world order to that generated in the West, above all through the works of two authors that he takes as archetypal in the post-Cold War world, Francis Fukuyama (the triumph of liberalism) and

Samuel Huntington (the clash of civilisations). In Tsygankov's (2004) view, these two authors are, respectively, excessively cosmopolitan and ethnocentrically realist. Cosmopolitanism from this perspective lacks cultural sensitivity in projecting the circumstances of a particular time and place as a universal norm; the West really is the best from this perceived Huntingtonian perspective. Cosmopolitanism is a highly contested concept in Russia, and is heavily overlain with connotations of the past and anti-national sentiments in the present. In his attack in 1948 on Sergei Prokofiev and others, Andrei Zhdanov sought to reconcile Soviet nationalism with a broader vision, contrasting 'healthy' and 'formalist' approaches to music. '[I]nternationalism in art', Zhdanov (1950: 62–3) argued, 'does not spring from the depletion and impoverishment of national art; on the contrary, internationalism grows where national culture flourishes. To forget this is to lose one's individuality and become a cosmopolitan without a country'. By this time 'cosmopolitan' had become a barely disguised euphemism for anti-semitism, and reminds us that the concept of cosmopolitanism in the Russian context has a highly ambivalent history.

Today Russian thinking stretches from national democrats to the outer reaches of Eurasianism and imperialism. For example, Igor Chubais seeks to reconcile the Russian and Western traditions to establish a viable synthesis between the West's market and democratic values and Russia's moral culture. A visible example of the achievement of this lofty ambition is Dmitry Likhachev, who was able to combine the three positive forces in Russian culture identified by Billington (2004: 106): traditional religious beliefs, receptivity to borrowings from the West, and a distinctive affinity for the land and nature. There is, however, by and large a consensus that Russia is a separate and distinct civilisation, while at the same time an integral and important part of the international community. Russia has a project for world order that in some ways complements that of the United States but in other respects comes into contradiction with it, above all in Russia's insistence of retaining its independence from the West (Tsygankov 2004: Chapter 6). As always, Russia was unable to find an adequate political form for its cosmopolitan realities and great power ambitions.

Time and place: Russia and Europe

Russia has had a distinctive path of development that distinguishes it from other European countries, however diverse and conflictual their own relations may have been. From early on Russia defined itself as both Europe and not-Europe, seeking a non-European path to modernity while incorporating some aspects of European development. Russia was able to develop its sui generis model because, as Marshall Poe (2003) has argued, it was hard to reach by sea and because of the coherence of the centralised political system. The European challenge was beaten back, and in the Soviet form Russia's independent path became attractive to non-European societies, and indeed to segments in European states themselves who looked for an alternative pattern of development. It was this 'Russian Moment in World History' that ended in 1991 when Russia's leaders abandoned attempts at sustaining an alternative. The best that they could hope for thereafter was a degree of autonomy.

After the Cold War the West was not so much an alternative as a triumphant model. It became for Russia the spatial substitute for the temporal utopia of communism that it had lost, and became the model to which the country aspired. At the same time, there were numerous points of resistance to 'Westification', rooted above all in a strong sense of the value of its own autochthonous path of development. The patriotic philosopher Sergei Kara-Murza (2001: 494–500; 2002), for example argues that Eurocentrism reflects the Russian intelligentsia's oedipal complex towards an over-bearing other. For him Eurocentrism is a set of ideological myths predicated on the assumption that European civilisation is the one and only correct path that all other cultures and civilisations should follow. The internalisation of this myth during perestroika in his view led to the collapse of the USSR.

In broad terms Russia remains Europe's 'other'. Many studies have demonstrated how the emergence of the idea of Europe was accompanied by an uneasy relationship with internal difference and external threats. R. W. Southern (1961) describes the nightmares haunting medieval Christendom, beset by the Mongol threat abroad, Islam and domestic heretics. As Le Goff (2005) notes, the history of Europe is torn between the concepts of 'territory' and 'time': the tension between consolidation and fragmentation remains a permanent feature, accompanied by the struggle between the affirmation of what would become national units and more supranational cosmopolitan definitions of identity; while the obsession with notions of progress associated with the ability to measure time accurately dates back 700 years. A 'Russian question' has been evident for nearly as long. Ivan III may have brought together the territory of a consolidated Muscovite state, but although he ruled over a Christian country, Russia has always remained outside of the idea of Europe while being part of Europe in all significant ways. The destruction of the power of Byzantium in 1453 deprived Russia of a cultural ally, but allowed the exaltation of its own distinctive civilisational mission as the 'third Rome'.

The Eastern borders of Europe have always been blurred. While in conceptual terms some layers of European identity reach out across the Siberian tundra to the Pacific, others firmly stop at the borders of what is currently the European Union. The 'European question' for Russia is decisive. As Sergei Karaganov, the chair of the Council for Foreign and Defence Policy, put it, 'Relations with Europe have and will determine Russia's self-identification and development'. For him this is not just a matter of geography, with the formal border of Europe running along Russia's Urals mountains, or of growing trade flows between Russia and

Europe, since equally high levels of economic interaction are enjoyed by several North African countries. Russia and Europe share many aspects of history and culture, but the Europe of the EU now expresses some fundamentally new normative features. In terms of politics and security Europe seeks to overcome the legacy of endless wars, desists from the use of force in conflict resolution, repudiates the old balance of power politics, and places human rights, religious tolerance and ethnic and social inclusiveness above the interests of nations. In his view, 'A new post-European civilisation, and the first relatively successful prototype of world government, are taking shape today'. Over the last three centuries Russia borrowed eclectically from the European developmental model, including 'the utopian communist path (also borrowed from Europe), which distanced the country further from Europe'. With the fall of communism Russia was able to catch up with the rest of Europe incredibly fast, 'covering three years in one'. However, as Europe and Russia drew closer, they realised just how different they were. 'Russia was moving towards the Europe of De Gaulle, Churchill and Adenauer, and when it got closer, it saw the Europe of the Brussels bureaucracy and new political correctness' (RIA Novosti, 26 May 2005).

The tension between necessary adaptation to the West and loyalty to a nativist path of development was at the heart of debates in the post-communist era. By contrast with the communist era, the contradictory nature of the Western experience was well understood. Some in Putin's government were sensitive to the multiple meanings of the West (for example, German Gref, *Itogi*, 8 February 2000: 24). The West is susceptible to a number of geographical and ideological interpretations. Geographically, there is a tension between the American and the European versions, while Japan represents a world of its own. The ideological ambiguity of the West is reflected above all in the tension between perceptions of the West as a security community (primarily NATO), as a zone of capitalist prosperity (in particular the EU), or as the core of a set of universal values based on human rights and a set of international ethical norms (represented, for example, by the Council of Europe). Thus some Russian thinking has deconstructed the West, no longer a monolithic unitary actor, into a more dynamic conception as the site of conflicts, divergent interests and economic dynamism. It was this more subtle understanding of the West that allowed the transcendence of traditional 'Russia versus the West' discourses.

The transcendence of the Cold War meant more than simply putting an end to the dynamic of conflict but also dealing with its material and institutional legacies. The new era had a dual meaning: liberation from communism but also loss of status and territory. Russia lost its superpower status and an empire that had taken four hundred years to assemble. A vast military-security establishment remained barely changed, despite endless reforms. The predictability and certainties of the Cold War had gone, but the rules and modalities of the new world order were far from clear. Cosmopolitanism in the guise of Western universalism, and its accompanying ideology of 'humanitarian intervention', particularly in the Balkans, was perceived as a threat by Russia, but its alternative model of internationalism, based on multipolarity and the coexistence of civilisations, lacked a sufficiently convincing platform as the Russian economy and society languished in crisis. Russia was both a defeated power (losing the superpower status that had been achieved by the USSR) and an undefeated power (since Russia could justifiably disassociate itself from the fate of the Soviet system).

This ambiguity pervaded not only Russia's relations with the world, but perhaps even more importantly, the world's relations with Russia, in particular when it came to dealing with the other post-Soviet republics. Russia's erstwhile Cold War adversaries, and its neighbours in the so-called 'near abroad', could not bring themselves to believe that the new Russia had really changed its spots, and all in one form or another feared the revival of 'Russian imperialism'. Russia's pursuit of constrained regional hegemony reflected trans-national ambitions that could variously be interpreted as cosmopolitanism or neo-imperialism. Russian supranationalism in whatever guise was perceived as a threat, and reinforced the nation-state building efforts of its neighbours. The former Soviet republics are seen as an area of threat rather than fulfilment, and for many the Western path is the only one that would allow Russia to overcome its 'Asiatism', where power and property fuse and an authoritarian regime claims to fulfil some transcendent mission and thus justifies its domination over society (Shelov-Kovedyaev 2004).

At an Asia-Pacific Economic Co-operation (APEC) meeting in May 2001 Putin acknowledged the Eurasian factor by calling Russia 'Euro-Asia' ('Soblazn evraziistva', *Moskovskie novosti*, 8 May 2001) although in general he has consistently repudiated the ideological elements of Eurasianism. While Putin insists that it would be foolhardy for Russia to claim to be an alternative to the West, he vigorously defends Russia's autonomy. This sometimes leads to the adoption of contradictory positions. Following the political debacle during the Ukrainian presidential elections of late 2004, Gleb Pavlovsky, the Russian strategist most responsible for Russia's failures in Ukraine, argued 'If we believe that the institutions of Western democracy cannot be accepted in the Euro-East, why can't we discuss this openly?' (*Moskovskii komsomolets*, 21 December 2004). This was not a position that Putin would share, since he is well aware that if any specific content were to be put on 'Euro-Eastern values', they would most likely be reactionary, isolationist and regressive, all things against which he has fought. This does not mean that Putin has renounced a special role for Russia in Eurasia, but for him historical traditions and human ties are pre-eminent. Vitaly Tretyakov, the former editor of *Nezavisimaya gazeta*, argued that in addition to these two, CIS states are united by 'anti-Americanism' (*Ekspert*, 6 December 2004), precisely the sort of sentiment that Putin seeks to avoid. Putin is well aware, as Tretyakov put it, 'We have nothing that would be equal in ideological might to Soviet communism or Western liberalism'. Russia was not able to generate an alternative social model that could in any way be attractive to its neighbours. The post-Soviet states are engaged in the modernist nation-building project, whereas post-modern cosmopolitanism in Eurasia encounters a powerful dynamic of resistance.

Polity and cosmopolitanism

For Ulrich Beck (2005), globalisation transforms traditional notions of a world of nation-states with fixed borders, measured sovereignty and exclusive identities into new forms of cosmopolitan political community that transcend traditional categories and are open to difference and otherness. In his view, there is a traditional European version of cosmopolitanism whose recovery is made possible by the second modernity ushered in by the age of globalisation. The development of a cosmopolitan social order internally also comes up against resistance. A poll by Gallup International in early 2005 found that 61 per cent of Russians were hostile in one way or another to globalisation, slightly higher than the world average of 56 per cent ('Global'nyi antiglobalizm' 2005: 11). In part this could be because of a lack of understanding of what globalisation entailed, but at the same time it reflected fears that globalisation was a covert way of universalising American global hegemony. For many Russians a cosmopolitan world would be a Westernised one, and these fears are not baseless. President George W. Bush used the word 'freedom' 25 times in his second-term inauguration speech in January 2005. As Martin Jacques (2005: 17) comments, 'The neoconservative strategy is quite explicit: to bend the world to America's will; to reshape it according to the interests of a born-again superpower', and despite the problems in Iraq, 'the United States does not recognise the constraints on its own power and ambition'. He argues that for historical reasons American modernity differs from that of Europe, and even more so both differ from that in China and India, stressing that 'modernity is not simply a snapshot of the present, but a product of history, not only a function of markets and technology, but the creation of a culture'.

The question asked by Ernest Renan takes on redoubled force when applied to Russia. The problem for us is not so much 'What is a nation?', but 'What is the Russian nation?'. The failure of the USSR to define the features of a Soviet nation was one of the major contributory factors to the Soviet collapse. There were attempts to create a single 'Soviet people', but this remained an abstraction and was undermined, as we have seen, by the perpetuation of distinct ethnic identities. The introduction of the Russian passport in the mid-1990s raised the question once again in the sharpest form. While the independent Russian state was constitutionally committed to its development as a civic multi-ethnic community, the dropping of ethnic affiliation in the passport led to vigorous protests by some of the more self-confident ethnic groups, notable the Tatars and Bashkirs. They argued that without an ethnic signifier, they would be liable to be absorbed into an amorphous 'Russian' nation and lose their cultural specificity and would be unable to assert autonomous political aspects of their identity. The introduction of new passports in some Volga regions was delayed for a number of years until a compromise was found under Putin's leadership whereby an insert in the language of the titular population was allowed in passports, and with an entry on ethnicity in birth certificates. These were to be voluntary (Simonsen 2005). There is thus a strong domestic resistance to the development of an internal Russian cosmopolitanism, however civic in form. As far as Russia's ethno-federal republics were concerned, a multiplicity of polities was preferable to the development of a single Russian cosmopolity. They feared that the establishment of a single bounded polity would be accompanied by the homogenisation of political and cultural space. In theory, however, cosmopolitanism could transcend this zero-sum logic and provide a way of reconciling diversity with coherent governance.

Debates over nationality policy continue. Much of the focus was on the distinction between the supranational concept of 'Rossiiskii' citizenship, favoured by Yeltsin and which gave rise to the notion of a 'Rossiyanin', a citizen of Russia with no indication of ethnic identity, and the more traditional notion of 'Russkii', an ethnic Russian person. The 2002 census had identified 160 distinct peoples in Russia, 80 of whom had a population of over 10,000. In an attempt to move away from the traditional ethno-territorial way of giving expression to ethnic aspirations, Russia in the mid-1990s had gone a long way towards providing a framework to allow the development of national-cultural autonomy (Bowring 2002). Discussions over the adoption of a new nationalities policy from late 2004 focused on defining various permissible forms of national self-determination and included ideas for the establishment of a social council to manage nationality affairs. However, minority groups feared that these proposals suggested a return to Brezhnev-era ideas of the creation of a 'new historical community'. Old debates re-emerged between two visions of the nation: the civic approach in which ethnicity remained a personal matter and had no role in state organisation; and others for whom the multinational character of the federation was decisive. One thing is clear: the history of Russian state development demonstrates that the classic distinction between a Western nationalism that is civic and inclusive and an oriental nationalism based on ethnicity and intolerance is false, a finding confirmed by much recent scholarship (Marx 2005).

Conclusion

Russia's developmental tragedy has been described in terms of Achilles and the tortoise: no matter how fast he hurries, he cannot catch up with the tortoise. As one commentator puts it, 'Our revolutions and military victories have only led to us falling further behind Europe, which has always moved forward, if only at the pace of a tortoise. We really don't want to be seen as Asians. Yet history has turned out in such a way that Europe is constantly ahead of Russia' (Leskov 2005). While Europe may be undergoing a process of cultural self-transformation in which universal normative aspirations combine with national traditions to forge a new cosmopolitan identity, in Russia the narrative of development remains linear, and thus the current model of modernisation repudiates elements in its own history. Russia is already a microcosm of a cosmopolitan state, and the nation-state may not be the natural political community in Eurasia, although today all the post-Soviet states are struggling to develop within its constraints. Finding an adequate political form for this innate cosmopolitanism, both in Russia and Eurasia, however, remains elusive. The innate features of cosmopolitanism mediate between traditional state building and the transformation of international relations in Eurasia and beyond. Countries are torn between their desire to complete nation-state development, of which they have been deprived for so long, and engagement with processes of international integration. In Russia the completion of the national project competes with post-national exigencies. Russian citizens are equally torn between national and cosmopolitan identities, although these are not necessarily opposed but provide the basis for a 'rooted cosmopolitanism' (Beck and Grande 2004). Rather than embracing the cosmopolitan elements of their past, most states today are seeking to suppress them just at the time when cosmopolitanism is emerging on the global stage as a new stage of post-Western development. As always, Russia is seeking to achieve a model of development that is already becoming anachronistic.

References

Beck, U. (2005) *The Cosmopolitan Vision*, Cambridge: Polity.

Beck, U and E. Grande (2004) *Das kosmopolitische Europe*, Frankfurt: Suhrkamp.

Billington, J. H. (2004) *Russia in Search of Itself*, Washington and Baltimore: Woodrow Wilson Center Press and Johns Hopkins University Press.

Bova, R. (ed.) (2003) *Russia and Western Civilization: Cultural and Historical Encounters*, Armonk, New York: M. E. Sharpe.

Bowring, B. (2002) 'Austro-Marxism's Last Laugh?: the Struggle for Recognition of National-Cultural Autonomy for Rossians and Russians', *Europe-Asia Studies*, 54(2): 229–50.

Brubaker, R. (1996) *Nationalism Reframed: Nationhood and the National Question in the New Europe*, Cambridge: Cambridge University Press.

Buruma, I. and A. Margalit (2004) *Occidentalism: The West in the Eyes of its Enemies*, London: Penguin.

Dugin, A. G. (2002) 'Evraziya prevyshe vsego: Manifest sovremennogo evraziiskogo dvizheniya', in *Osnovy Evraziistva*, Moscow: Arktogeya tsentr.

German Gref (2000) 'Sostavitel's kontrakta' (Interview with Sergei Parkhomenko), *Itogi*, 8 February.

'Global'nyi antiglobalizm', *Newsweek* (Russian version), 31.01–06.02.2005.

Goff, J. Le (2005) *The Birth of Europe*, Oxford: Blackwell.

Jacques, M. (2005) 'No Monopoly on Modernity', *Guardian*, 5 February.

Kara-Murza, S. (2001) *Sovetskaya tsivilizatsiya ot velikikh pobedy do nashikh dnei*, Moscow: Algoritm.

Kara-Murza, S. (2002) *Evrotsentrizm – edipov kompleks intelliigentsii*, Moscow: Algoritm.

Leskov, S. (2005) 'An Adult Russia, With No Utopias', *Izvestiya*, 20 May.

Ligachev, E. K. (2004) 'Oblik Rodinu: Russ s Sibiriyu', *Sovetskaya Rossiya*, 29 May.

Martin, T. (2001) *The Affirmative Action Empire: Nations and Nationalism in the Soviet Union, 1923–1939*, Ithaca: Cornell University Press.

Marx, A. W. (2005) *Faith in Nation: Exclusionary Origins of Nationalism*, Oxford: Oxford University Press.

Panarin, A. S. (1999) *Rossiya v tsiklakh mirovoi istorii*, Moscow: Moscow University.

Poe, M. T. (2003) *The Russian Moment in World History*, Princeton NJ: Princeton University Press.

Shelov-Kovedyaev, F. V. (2004), 'Fantomy Evraziistva', *Politiya*, 2(33): 234–43.

Simonsen, S. G. (2005) 'Between Minority Rights and Civil Liberties: Russia's Discourse Over "Nationality" Registration and the Internal Passports', *Nationalities Papers*, 33(2): 211–29.

Southern, R. W. (1961) *The Making of the Middle Ages*, New Haven, CT: Yale University Press.

Tolz, V. (2001) *Russia: Inventing the Nation*, London: Arnold.

Tsygankov, A. P. (1999) 'Mastering Space in Eurasia: Russia's Geopolitical Thinking After the Soviet Break-up', *Communist and Post-Communist Studies*, 36: 481–500.

Tsygankov, A. P. (2004) *Whose World Order? Russia's Perception of American Ideas after the Cold War*, Lanham, MD: Rowman & Littlefield.

Vekhi: Landmarks (1994) translated and edited by M. S. Shatz and J. E. Zimmerman. Armonk, New York: M. E. Sharpe.

Zhdanov, A. A. (1950) 'Concluding Speech at a Conference of Soviet Music Workers, 1948', in E. Fox, S. Jackson and H. C. Feldt (trans and eds), *On Literature, Music and Philosophy*, London: Lawrence & Wishart.

16 Out of Europe but not in Europe

Israel between ethnic nation-state and Jewish cosmopolitanism

Natan Sznaider

Imagine for a moment what would happen if Israel applied for membership in the European Union. What would be the response? Its application would either be deferred like Turkey's, or flatly rejected. Why? Is Israel not European enough? Does it even belong to Europe even though geographically it is located in Asia? Even though founded in Europe, Israel is out of Europe but not in Europe. It lies in Asia and like Turkey connects Asia to Europe. Turkey is of course the looming question that has brought this long-buried discourse of origins out of hiding. People who want to keep Turkey out have suddenly discovered that the roots of Europe lie in its Christian heritage. Those who share the European continent, but do not share this Christian heritage, are seen as Europe's Other. Thus the same should apply for Israel and for Europe's Jews. Israel is certainly not a Christian country. One can almost claim that it is the opposite with its particularistic and ethnic self-definition as a Jewish state. And Israel – like Turkey – is not a Western Liberal state. Israel (like Turkey) rose out of the Ottoman Empire and constantly has to balance processes of Europeanization, Americanization, the expectations of international institutions and the pressure of local groups and tradition. On the one side the European Union, the European Council and the United Nations, on the other side Kurds and Palestinians, who are in ethnic and national conflicts with both states. Both states struggle to find their own special path to modernity, which looks different from most Western states with their post-Enlightenment separation between state and religion – a Christian-based notion of just that Western Enlightenment. Turkey attempts its own way as a Muslim democratic modernity, while Israel goes its own way as a Jewish democratic modernity. Both countries show Europeans a not-yet-existing diversity beyond their participation in European song and sporting events.

The Jewish nation and Israeli polity

Israel defines itself ethnically and its criteria of citizenship are exclusive. Wouldn't the term "European" imply, at least politically, the demands to change the basis of the Israeli national definition and found it on the conventional territorial principle – equality before the law of all citizens living within Israeli territory, irrespective of ethnic origins, race, community, religion or sex? Shouldn't Israel first of all "Europeanize" and stop opposing those who think that nations are either "imagined" or "invented" and, as a consequence, live with the illusion that nationalism will disappear when shown and "proven" that the nation is a creation of the mind? However, the continuation of the Israeli–Arab conflict and the resistance of anti-Semitism will resist these kinds of tendencies. Israel attempts to be universal democratic and particular Jewish at the same time and with that reaches its limits of universality. However, in a global network society universalism and particularism do not have to exclude each other. Thus, Turkey and Israel address through their existence the praxis of a new European–Asian cosmopolitanism that cannot be limited by Christian European notions. It is cosmopolitanism beyond universalism. Israel suggests a different reading of European history undermining the project of reconciliation between former enemies enabled by the breakdown of the socialist regimes. Israel's alternative reading of European history keeps the memory of destruction alive for which Nazi Germany and its allies were responsible. Its existence presents a challenge to European reconciliation.

Israel is rooted in the particular historical experience of Eastern and Central Europe. Herein lies the source of the well known tension between two fundamental definitions of nationhood: the first, territorial and political with its political and historical roots in Western Europe, and the second ethnic, and which is typical of the historical experience of Eastern and Central Europe. In order to become "European", Israel is supposed to shift its national identity to Western European categories without dismissing nationalism altogether. The terms of these debates are "civic nationalism" versus "ethnic nationalism", both at the same time empirical as well as normative criteria of belonging. Both are conceptualized through the boundaries of the state. The Western type also forcefully reinvigorated by many so-called "post-Zionists", is associated with the "rational" principles of citizenship and democratic virtues. The second type is organic and associated with "irrational" beliefs that supersede the voluntaristic character of the Western type. On this view, a developmental approach is involved as well. "Enlightened" political nationalism was gradually replaced by organic forms of nationalism that were embraced in Central and Eastern Europe and went on to become the origins of the Jewish Nation in Israel. But are these the only alternatives? Can there be a "rooted cosmopolitanism" which goes beyond classical notions of the nation-state while not forgetting why the Jews wanted a state of their own altogether?

Zionism and Diaspora

Usually, debates regarding citizenship are framed around the state. It is very difficult to think about citizens without a state. Just the opposite, a state of statelessness is a state of limbo, a state of misfortune, a state without rights. Not only a Jewish problem, but very much informed by Jewish fate, statelessness became the central problem for Jews in the twentieth century (see Arendt 1951). The strongest manifestation of this statelessness was, of course, caused by the destruction of European Jewry in the Holocaust. Only Zionism could allegedly make whole what the German Nazis broke: to give the Jews a state and to make a stateless people a people with a state and a home. It is bringing to end the experience of Diaspora, which often enough has been identified with a form of Jewish cosmopolitanism. Is Israel therefore the antithesis to Jewish cosmopolitanism? I would suggest that Israel is an ethnic state based on social pluralism preserving the roots of Jewish cosmopolitanism of the Diaspora. I suggest not to confuse Diaspora with cosmopolitanism per se.

The experience of the Diaspora is the counterpoint to living in a group defined by territory and nationality. Thus Zionist ideology was first of all based on the "negation of Diaspora". Diaspora produces a sense of belonging and connectedness to groups and places that are outside the national borders of where one has settled. The de-territorialization of social identities poses a challenge to the nation-state, with its demand for absolute loyalty. Multiple identities and sometimes even multiple citizenships are becoming increasingly widespread in the context of globalization. In these cases, opponents of diasporic formations talk of conflicting loyalties; supporters regard these types of affiliations as prototypes for defining the global citizens of the future. Whichever way one looks at it, clearly defined diasporic communities strengthen the tendency whereby identities are not necessarily formed through exclusive allegiance to a single political or geographic entity. Instead, there emerge multiple loyalties to various entities (e.g. other countries, religious communities, etc.). In light of multiculturalism, the pressure to assimilate has subsided and the preservation of cultural identity has become more legitimate in many cases. Consequently, minority identity is no longer necessarily defined by one's connection to a homeland.

One should note that the concept of the Diaspora that has taken hold in the social sciences refers back directly to the concrete Jewish experience. In Jewish history, the notion of a life outside of the nation-state is nothing new (Boyarin and Boyarin 1993). Prior to the Holocaust and to the founding of the state of Israel, there was a mixture of longing for territorial independence (Zionism) with a fascination and direct contact with and in other cultures (assimilation, new religious trends). This state of affairs came about not only because of Judaism, but was a result of the tension between civil rights issues, citizenship and cultural identities. These struggles are also present within the Israeli homeland and are particularly relevant for the European context of Jewish society in Israel. A large part of the Jewish population does not originate in Europe but comes from Arab countries. Have they come home? Zionism started in Europe. Before 1939,

90 per cent of the world's Jews either lived in Europe or were descendants of European Jews and only 10 per cent were "Jews from Arab lands". It was in Europe that the emergence of modern nationalism made the position of Jews precarious (when nationalism reached the Arab world in the mid-twentieth century, the same processes developed in countries like Iraq, Egypt or Morocco). Clearly, after 1948 the Israeli establishment, mirrored in European conceptions of assimilation attempted to assimilate Jews from Arab lands into a so-called melting-pot based on Western customs and norms. Only later did a multicultural and more tolerant approach develop, which then in turn allows the intellectual elite of the Jews from Arab lands to romanticize the old Arab world as cosmopolitan and the state of Israel as a narrow ethno-centric state based on European Orientalism (e.g. Nimni 2003 for a good collection of essays presenting that view).

From early on, Jews in the Diaspora saw themselves as both citizens of a country and as cosmopolitans – they experienced directly the above-mentioned tension between universalism and particularism. At the time, this state of affairs was not common but, as we have noted, it has increasingly become the norm in Western democracies. The Diaspora was never, nor is it now, a closed culture; hence, Jewish culture has always mixed with others. If one understands culture as something open to the outside (and not homogeneous), one can see how the newly emerging cosmopolitan culture is becoming "Jewish". At the beginning of the twentieth century, the Jewish Diaspora experience and its cosmopolitan exponents stood in crude opposition to the national-territorial forms of memory constitutive of the European nations. Today, identification with a group (be it ethnic, national or religious) whose historical roots are outside of the spatial and temporal coordinates of the adopted homeland is often a matter of preference and, not infrequently, of pride. In addition to its social impact, this stance also has political repercussions. In the face of oppression or real disadvantage, maintaining a status that is not based upon fixed geographic boundaries fuels political strivings and protests (Clifford 1994).

The Jewish Diaspora can serve as the paradigm for de-territorialization as such. A particular awareness of place and the relationship to being Other are played out on an immediate experiential level here. However, the Diaspora was never a closed-off sphere. Lived Jewish culture was not only mixed with other cultures, it was itself a mixture of cultures. In a certain sense, its cosmopolitanism lay in judaizing the mixture of cultures it absorbed – it gave them a unifying cast without negating them. The experience of Diaspora, of life in exile, is the clearest example modernity offers of a sustained community life that did not need a territorial container to preserve its history. In Jewish experience, life outside the nation-state is nothing new. Prior to the Holocaust and to the founding of the state of Israel, the Jewish experience was determined by a mixture of yearning to be territorially independent as well as to be universal ambassadors of Diaspora. Nowadays, however, these can no longer be considered specifically Jewish concerns, but instead constitute the broader arena in which issues of citizenship, civil society and cultural identity are played out. Jews were simultaneously cosmopolitan and citizens of a particular country. Although the Jews were more aware of needing to straddle the poles of universalism and particularism, this state of tension has increasingly become the norm in today's world. Jewish existence before the Holocaust and before the founding of the state of Israel mixed longing for territorial independence with attraction and enmeshment in other cultures. This condition of Diaspora did not grow out of Judaism per se, but out of tensions among citizenship, civil society and cultural identity. But one should not over-extend the concept. Not all ex-territorial experiences are diasporic (for criticism of the over-extension of the concept in the cultural sciences, see Brubaker 2005). Does Diaspora indeed offer an alternative to life in territoriality and nationally marked groups? For Jews, these alternatives were never mutually exclusive.

Jewish cosmopolitanism and nationalism

Jews were both a nation *and* cosmopolitan. Jews lived therefore in a tension between universalism and particularism that is increasingly becoming the norm for all nations. Franz Rosenzweig once said that Jews lived in two dimensions, the Now and the Eternal. But this tension between territorial identity (the Now) and de-territorialized existence (the Eternal) is increasingly the destiny – or in modern terms, the danger and opportunity – of all people (Hertzberg 1998). Historically, this was played out by Jews at exactly the same European sites where Zionism was born: Central Europe. Central Europe was already the venue for a struggle between cosmopolitanism and nationalism, in which Jews played a big role (Hacohen 1999). This was the site of ethno-national tensions, the Holocaust and the expulsions after the Second World War. But cosmopolitanism was only the refuge of a small circle of intellectuals, of people who thought they had nothing to gain from an emerging ethno-politics. Cosmopolitanism is often confused with "universal enlightenment", which undermines individual national culture. One need only think of Karl Popper's *The Open Society and Its Enemies*, a seminal Cold War text that defended the openly cosmopolitan imperialism of the West. As Hacohen's analysis of Popper shows, because of anti-Semitism, this type of universalism was not able to mediate between nationalism and cosmopolitanism. Their antidote to nationalism was an "Enlightened Imperialism", be it the Habsburg Empire or later for Popper and others the British one. It was also that milieu which created one of Zionism's seminal texts: *The Jewish State* by Theodor Herzl. Popper's hostility to Zionism (as to any other form of ethno-nationalism) was typical for a dichotomous world view which confused cosmopolitanism with universalism and could not see how cosmopolitanism could be squared with nationalism. Popper's imagined

"Open Society" became the "assimilated Jewish philosopher's cosmopolitan homeland" (Hacohen 1999: 136). It was an imperial homeland, a kind of Westernized modernity in its global (and today American) form, it is the late Hellenic culture of bygone ages, dominant, progressive, wave of the future, assimilationist, admirable, seductive and beautiful as it always was and is for Jewish particularism. It was a vision of a democratic cosmopolitan empire which attracted many Jews like Popper to Great Britain and attracts them today to the USA, whereas Zionists recognized the need of Jews to secure a common history that is strongly connected with cultural properties and national history. If we take the long historical view, the fundamental meaning of Jewish cosmopolitanism for both its proponents and its antagonists was a sign of Jewish civilization (Eisenstadt 1992). Diaspora for the Jews meant that they were an ethnic–religious–national community, at the same time trying to mediate all of those components.

In my opinion, this view has never been expressed more clearly than in Leon Feuchtwanger's novel *The Jewess of Toledo* (1956). The story is set in Spain in the twelfth century. It is a country on the frontiers between Christianity and Islam, and thus on the frontlines of the original Crusades and Jihads, when those words were more than metaphors. There, in the interpenetration of those frontiers lives Feuchtwanger's main protagonist, Jehuda Ibn Esra. He accepts the post of finance minister under King Alfonso – essentially the post of an economic czar, who takes a cut of the overall profit in return for personally putting up capital and bearing huge risks – because he sees this Christian country as full of productive potential that he can bring to fruition, if, and only if, he can keep the country out of war. The King, a knight of the old stamp, wants to go to war as soon as possible, of course, for that is the only sure road to glory. He only grudgingly accepts that he must build up the economic strength of his exhausted country first, and with the same grudgingness, he accepts that Ibn Esra has a genius for peacetime management that he himself lacks. And so the two struggle with and against each other for many years, in a partnership and a rivalry with very high stakes. It is not an accident that Feuchtwanger wrote this book just after the Nazis and the Second World War destroyed his German-Jewish world of educated and wealthy "burghers". For Feuchtwanger, the knightly ideals that would destroy everything that other people have built up for the sake of glory were all too close to home. He opposes to them the strivings for wealth and commerce that are carried on by the citizens of towns, by Jews and by women, who counteract the destructive force of knights and barons with the quiet pleasures of enjoying material things. In his "Josephus" trilogy, Feuchtwanger, through the role of Jewish historian Josephus Flavius, outlines the dilemmas of a man torn between Jewish patriotism and Hellenist/Roman imperial cosmopolitanism. Feuchtwanger's was a desperate attempt to defend a cosmopolitan European identity composed of Jewish, Greek, Christian and Muslim identities against the rise of National-Socialism. Therefore, his Ibn Esra and Josephus were not only fictional and were not only restricted to Europe.

The anthropologist and writer Amitav Gosh (1992) tells the story of the Jewish Arab Ben-Yiju of the twelfth century, when being an Arab Jew was no contradiction in terms as it is in today's Israel. Ben-Yiju was a merchant travelling the Orient, being in communication with peoples of all cultures and worlds. And if we look at Weimar Germany for instance, we can find several Ibn Esras and Ben-Yijus each trying to work out economic and political arrangements which would connect Germany to England and avoid war. Like Ibn Esra and Ben-Yiju, they were between cultures and regarded with suspicion. And they saw themselves playing the same dangerous game for the same high stakes: for the preservation of civilization and all that they had built. But it was the virtue of these men that they were between cultures and cosmopolitan. It is what gave them their sophistication, their breadth of vision and their tolerance. Their culture came from many places and existed mixed with them. All of it felt familiar, as if it belonged together. They embodied the ideal of integration. It was inextricably part of their ideal of individual cultivation. Among men like this, rootedness – being fixed in one place and submerging one culture – was regarded as a limitation. And limited people could extend their boundaries only by war. That is why their cosmopolitanism was always threatened by the warriors they tried to civilize. It expresses also a vision of multi-ethnic European civilizations. It connects to Delanty's (2003) vision of a Europe based on multiple modernities and composed of three civilizational constellations: (i) the Occidental Christian; (ii) the Byzantine-Slavic Eurasian; and (iii) the Ottoman, Islamic one. But it was exactly that kind of Jewish cosmopolitanism which was destroyed during the Second World War.

Memories of the Holocaust: cosmopolitan and national

This chapter is also one of reconstruction. It aims to add an additional civilization to the three existing ones, namely Jewish Civilization. However, this civilization does not exist any more and will only exist as a vision. Jewish civilization was destroyed by the Nazis and Europe has turned into a big graveyard for most Jews. Jewish life does still exist in Europe, but Jewish civilization has moved outside of Europe: it exists in the USA and it exists in Israel and both constellations are from Europe but not in Europe. To add the dimension of Jewish civilization to Europe today is, therefore, an exercise in memory. On the other hand, Israel's legitimacy to exist as an ethnic nation-state for the Jews rests partly on the Holocaust and, therefore, on the cosmopolitan memory of that tragedy. Understood in this sense, the memory of the Holocaust is not just a monument to Europe's sense of the tragic. It is a memorial specifically to the

European barbarism that was made possible by the marriage of modernity and the nation-state. It is a mass grave upon which the new Europe made an oath and chose a different path. Europe's collective memory of the Holocaust recalls the basis of the EU. It is a warning sign that when modernity develops exclusively in the grooves of the nation-state, it builds the potential for a moral, political, economic and technological catastrophe without limit, without mercy, and without even any consideration for its own survival. That is how the memory of the Holocaust was understood in Europe's own self-image. But it also laid the foundations for Israel's existence as a particular ethnic nation-state where the Jews can feel protected after the Holocaust. A European project all together. I also argue that a self-critical European remembering of the Holocaust, rather than destroying the European tradition, has been and will continue to be a vital resource for reconstituting the identity of Europe. It is what enables Europe to find its continuity at the very point at which it breaks from the past. It allows it to establish future-oriented forms of memory, against national founding myths and myths of warfare and for a cosmopolitan self-critique of Europe. However, this is not how the memory of the Holocaust is perceived in Israel. Just the opposite. For the Jews, the memory of the Holocaust meant first of all that it should never happen again to Jews. Therefore, to protect the Jews at all cost became one of the pillars of Israel's identity. Thus, Israel was founded at the very same moment that the new Europe rose out of the ruins of the Second World War. Both entities were formed on the same background, but former perpetrators and former victims drew very different conclusions from the memory of the Holocaust, but drawn together. To legitimize the Jewish existence in the Middle East through the negation of former Jewish life in Europe has to turn Israel into a European project. It recognizes the Holocaust as a universal event which happened to the Jews. Thus, for many critics of Israel, modern Zionism turned against this cosmopolitan ideal (see e.g. Judt 2003), even though it reacted to modern European nationalism and its unwillingness to incorporate the Jews, unlike in the USA where Jews became part of the religious pluralist framework. But critics of Israel reject the very idea of a "Jewish state" – the idea of an ethnic state in which Jews enjoy privileges as rooted in a Europe prior to the Second World War and leading to Europe's catastrophe. Israel, in their eyes, is an anachronism. It was in some ways an ironic turn back to the ideals of warrior virtue. The Jewish cosmopolitan ideal was destroyed in the Holocaust and Jewish Israelis turned into warriors as an attempt to avoid the next one; they rejected the cosmopolitan and partly diasporic notions of multinationality in their own lands, as if these were exclusive notions. Opponents criticize Israel's willingness and constant preparedness for war.

However, if one thinks dichotomously, the only alternative to the softening, peace-seeking and compromising cosmopolitanism is nationalism constantly stoked to be ready to fight, or even to ethnically cleanse. This kind of nationalism is about war, and war is about wearing one's poverty and hardship as a sign of virtue – rather than as a sign of shame, as it appears in peace. And the reverse is also true: market cosmopolitanism is about wearing one's luxury as a sign of virtue, rather than being ashamed of it as a sign of sinful indulgence. They look like opposed moral schemes. Within such an alleged opposition, in the last decade or so, the cultural and business elite in Israel have tried to cultivate an image of Western secularism and cosmopolitanism. Their objective has been to create a permissive, consumerist, high-tech, non-traditional Israel in a "new Middle East". For these new "Yuppies" the prospect of increased consumption was a major incentive to support the Israeli–Arab peace process (see also Peled and Shafir 1996). Many Israelis of the middle classes favoured a new civil discourse. However, this civil discourse is not only about a discourse of "rights", but also about a discourse of "fun". Liberalism, in Israel as well, was increasingly viewed as the pursuit of individual pleasure and the privatization of social life. In short, the peace process increased consumption for people with money, and their desire for more consumption reinforced their support for the peace process. Thus, the cosmopolitanization and consumption patterns that came along with it also meant that ethnic identities became plural and commercialized. In today's Israel, being an Israeli can mean that one reads Russian papers, goes to a Russian theatre and listens to Russian rock music, maintaining a different identity through the medium of a separate language. But being an Israeli can mean equally that one takes one's Jewish Oriental identity seriously and, paradoxically thanks to the influence of Western multiculturalism, rejects everything Western and with it the memories of the Holocaust. Thus, Israel's self-definition of being out of Europe but not (yet) in Europe is being challenged and, even though the origins of Israel lie in Europe, the presence of Jews from Arab countries pushed Israel further away from Europe.

Being an Israeli also means that non-Jewish Israelis, Palestinians with an Israeli passport, can claim cultural autonomy for themselves. Thus, Israel is a pluralist and multicultural society while at the same time an ethnic state. Ethnic and national discourses are clearly separated here. And the increased pluralism within Israeli society allows Jewish communities outside of Israel to free themselves from the burden of being exclusively potential citizens of Israel, even though the globalizing Middle East conflict and signs of increasing anti-Semitism are drawing Jews within and outside Israel closer together. A parallel process is also developing in the Islamic countries of the Middle East. Not universal, but rooted, where people from the safety of the particular identity can negotiate these identities with others (for rooted cosmopolitanism see Appiah 1998; Cohen 1992; Beck 2002).

Conclusion

Walking the streets of Tel-Aviv, and especially the more affluent neigh-
bourhoods, might create the illusion that one was in a "normal" Western
country displaying the hedonism and optimism of its corresponding cosmopolitanism. There is a sense of "normalcy" in the air, a joyful, even
eroticized secularism. The Tel-Aviv flâneur passes by McDonald's, Burger
King, Tower Records, Blockbuster Videos, The Gap, Banana Republic,
Haagen Dasz, Ben & Jerry's and many other symbols of the global homogenizing consumer culture. However, the post-modern winds of Tel-Aviv
are located in a specific cultural, religious and historical context. People in
Israel may have the same cell phones as anywhere else, but the gulf
between classes and cultural groups is growing increasingly more visible.
When a country enters world markets, and increases its consumption, it
increases the gulf at the same time as it begins to share tastes with other
countries. Furthermore, these class and cultural divisions reinforce existing
divisions present in every such society between Westernizers and tradition-
alists. Huntington (1996) states that the essence of Western culture is the
"Magna Carta" not the "Magna Mac". He argues that Westernization is
basically a cultural process that is completely distinct from economic modernization. In his view, Westernization is the spread of the world view of
Christianity and the liberalism that grew out of it (see also Siedentop
1989). He believes the fundamental dichotomies that mark the "Western"
worldview – the distinctions between state and civil society and between
public and private spheres – derive ultimately from Christian assumptions.
He even sees the birth of the "individual" as a Christian achievement.

We are back where we started: Israel of course is not a Christian
country. Unlike Christianity, Judaism is an ethnicity as much as a belief
system and this understanding is written into the very foundation of the
state, and its citizenship laws. Israel can thus never be a neutral state on
the French or American model. Every attempt to make it one threatens the
essential Jewishness of the country. This in turn leads to strong and violent
conflicts – not commodifiable conflicts, but fundamental conflicts that do
not accept compromise. How can modernity be defined such that it is compatible with Jewishness? Taking the pure Western model as the only definitive standard in the Middle East may also be a mistaken calculation. It is
difficult to imagine that an American model incorporating pluralism or tolerance or a French model of an aggressively secular state with highest
honours going to anti-religious intellect could be relevant to Israel. These
are only partial models for the struggle in an essentially and essentialist
Jewish state. What is clear is that it may even be disastrous to take these
models formulated somewhere else as comprehensive and complete. Israel
since its inception has always been conceived of as a Jewish state, even by
people who consider themselves secular. But it could also be conceived of
as a modern democratic state, even by people who consider themselves

religious. Clearly, Zionism is not the same as Judaism. Zionism is Judaism plus liberalism, Liberalism with a capital L, Liberalism as the founding creed of a modern nation-state. Thus Europe would have to accept reluctantly that the Jewishness that lurked in the subconscious of the "secular" founding fathers was Judaism as a modern nationality, Judaism that was no longer a "spaceless" religion, but as a people with a land and with a history. Perhaps in the final analysis, there is no reason, according to such a view, to take the details of the land's history more seriously than the details of the land's present. What is important here is that there is a land, and the paramount goal is to make it a normal land, a land at peace, a land that is no longer disputed, and a land that is accepted by the world – the only recognition that will finally make religion into peoplehood. Not only Israeli liberals believe that modernity is unalterably secular. America, however, is the most religious country in the industrialized world. What actually happens during the process of modernization is that religion is individualized and commodified. America and Europe may look secular when compared with their medieval and puritan pasts. When compared with Israel, theirs is a Christian secularism, and not only because their weekend runs through Sunday. The fundamental divisions that Huntington quite rightly points out as the salient and constant features of Euro-American culture – the division between public and private, between civil society and the state – are the deep cultural markers of its secularized Christianity. It is possible to have modernity without them. And when European and Israeli liberals accept that Jewishness is part of the identity of the Israeli state – and that such Jewishness is not opposed to the essence of modernity, but simply to its secularized Christian form – then compromise between Europeans, Palestinians and Israelis will be possible. It does not violate the essence of modernity, because that essence is not secularism per se, but a moral order based on individuation. It is a patriotic and rooted cosmopolitanism.

References

Appiah, K. A. (1998) "Cosmopolitan Patriots", in P. Cheah and B. Robbins (eds) *Cosmopolitics: Thinking and Feeling Beyond the Nation*, Minneapolis: University of Minnesota Press, pp. 91–114.
Arendt, H. (1951) *The Origins of Totalitarianism*, New York: Meridan.
Beck, U. (2002) "The Cosmopolitan Society and its Enemies", *Theory, Culture and Society*, 19(1–2): 17–44.
Boyarin, D. and J. Boyarin (1993) "Diaspora: Generation and the Ground of Jewish identity", *Critical Inquiry* 19(3): 693–726.
Brubaker, R. (2005) "The 'Diaspora' Diaspora", *Ethnic and Racial Studies*, 28(1): 1–19.
Clifford, J. (1994) "Diasporas", *Cultural Anthropology*, 9(3): 302–38.
Cohen, M. (1992) "Rooted Cosmopolitanism", *Dissent*, 39: 478–83.
Delanty, G. (2003) "The Making of a Post-Western Europe: A Civilizational Analysis", *Thesis Eleven*, 72: 9–25.

Eisenstadt, S. N. (1992) *Jewish Civilization*, New York: Oxford University Press.

Feuchtwanger, L. (1956) *Die Jüdin von Toledo*, Frankfurt: Fischer.

Gosh, A. (1992) *In an Antique Land*, New York: Vintage Press.

Hacohen, M. (1999) "Dilemmas of Cosmopolitanism: Karl Popper, Jewish Identity and Central European Culture", *Journal of Modern History*, 71: 105–49.

Hertzberg, A. (1998) *Jews: The Essence and the Character of a People*, San Francisco: Harper.

Huntington, S. (1996) "The West Unique, Not Universal", *Foreign Affairs*, 75(6): 28–46.

Judt, T. (2003) "Israel: The Alternative", *New York Review of Books*, 50(16).

Nimni, E. (ed.) (2003) *The Challenge of Post-Zionism*, London: Zed Books.

Peled, Y. and G. Shafir (1996) "The Roots of Peacemaking: The Dynamics of Citizenship in Israel, 1948–93", *International Journal of Middle East Studies*, 28: 391–413.

Siedentop, L. (1989) "Liberalism: The Christian Connection", *Times Literary Supplement*, March 24: 308.

Part IV

Otherness in Europe and Asia

17 Europe's otherness

Cosmopolitanism and the construction of cultural unities

Heidrun Friese

Herrlich ist der Orient
Übers Mittelmeer gedrungen;
Nur wer Hafis liebt und kennt,
Weiß was Calderon gesungen.

Wer sich selbst und andere kennt
Wird auch hier erkennen
Orient und Okzident
Sind nicht mehr zu trennen

Johann Wolfgang von Goethe
West-östlicher Diwan, Hafis-Goethe Monument, Weimar[1]

It seems we no longer comfortably take a seat on this *West-östlicher Diwan*, a semantic space which had been united by a hyphen and was held together by an undividable, shared space and the common logos of poetry, it looks as if the common seat has been separated into two distinct, if not opposed entities, namely East and West. However, what is meant by 'East *and* West' and how is the 'Beyond' in the title of this book to be understood? In a literal sense, the terms indicate first of all marks of orientation that operate from a privileged, stable and secure point of view, namely 'Europe'. If Hegel – Goethe's Zeitgenosse – remarks that Asia 'is a West to America, but just like Europe is the centre and the end of the old world and the absolute West, Asia is the absolute East' (Hegel 1992: 130), what is indicated are not neutral geographical or cartographical positions, rather, the spatial metaphors open up to a broader semantic field, its historically widely branched legacy and its inherent work of spacing and timing. Thus, the term 'West' designates not just quite specific cultural, socio-historical and political configurations, but points to specific concepts of time and space. The following remarks will take up some of the discursive components of the ambivalent legacy which are to ground the (historically) exceptional occidental configuration, or to be more specific: the European particularity that attained universal significance, validity and force, elements at the same time that show how questions of what might be the distinctive features of Europe, its specific modernity and its – alleged – identity have been negotiated (Friese 2004a).

In early modern time, Europe learned to comprehend – as Peter Sloter-dijk remarks – not just the 'unity of the human species within the variety of cultures' (Sloterdijk 2002: 10), a notion which established specific relations and tensions between the universal and the particular and subsequently was expressed in the Declaration of Human Rights, concepts of a cosmopolitan order and visions of global justice. At the same time, colonial expansions and domination produced powerful spatio-political narrations and images of a familiar 'one's own' and the uncanny 'stranger' as well. An all too easy criticism of Eurocentrism, however, does not just flatten the recognition of differences but fails to realize that the imaginaries in which Europe recognizes and negotiates itself are always already inhabited by internal caesuras, rifts and an otherness at work within these narratives (Friese 2004a).

In this context, what will be recalled in the following is the mechanism of constructing a cultural identity that was considered to constitute, to enact Europe's – alleged – unity. The by now well-established culturalist paradigm assumes stable and unequivocal identities and allocates those in space and in time, one world-history, a single time with universal validity that only allows for the unity to be established. Against assumptions of unrejectable stages of development and a despotic universal time, what is advocated is the questioning of a homogeneous world-time and well-integrated societies and cultures, be it the West or the East, a critique allowing for a perspective to evolve that interprets the particularities of social worlds, cultural cosmologies and imaginaries as multiply authored inventions, shifting paradoxes, non-consensual negotiation and ongoing translations.

These highly problematic notions thus point toward a variety of tensions: the tension between the (civic) universal and the (ethnic) particular, between cosmopolitism and (cultural) singularity, the dilemma between universalism and (ethical) particularity, universally applicable norms, particular values and cultural differences, between egalitarians and multi-culturalists which are challenging and limiting the basic concerns of liberalism. An attempt to engage with these tensions will be pursued in three steps. In the first step, the ambivalent discursive heritage narratives of Europe's unity will be recalled. I will not, however, draw on the familiar narratives of the political constitution of Europe and on concepts such as liberty, statehood and democracy (Friese and Wagner 2002). Rather, and in the second step, the focus will be on the modes of creating spatial and temporal demarcations that are to constitute cultural unities. Against the exercised dualisms and powerful politics of identities in a 'globalizing' world – currently discussed under the label 'Orientalism' and 'Occidental-ism', in the third step, I aim to recall perspectives which brought attention to the occurrence of being-othered (*Veranderung*) that trouble assumptions of cultural coherence and point towards Europe's cosmopolitism.

Europe's unity – Europe's otherness

'The sun, the light arises in the East ... World history moves from East to West since Europe is by all means the end of world history whereas Asia is its beginning' as Hegel (1992: 133, 134) remarks, relating a geographical synopsis to the idea of freedom and to the teleological course of history. Whereas the New World, 'land of the future' is still out of reach for history, whereas Africa is not a 'historical region' and excluded from the 'transition of human Spirit from East to West' and thus does neither know 'movement nor development' (Hegel 1992: 129), whereas Asia is the origin of history, Europe is the scene, the theatre of world history, centre and end of the Old world and the stage on which Spirit reaches itself as Spirit: 'there are entire regions of the world which didn't have this idea or do not have it yet' (Hegel 1986: 301, §482). The positivity of Spirit and freedom thus are tied to its negation and the spatial and temporal exclusion, it progresses in a temporal dimension of a not yet and a never ever. Substituting natural consciousness, philosophy, aesthetics and freedom inaugurate in the West, it is only 'in the Occident that the light becomes sudden inspiration which, struck by this lightning, creates its world' (Hegel 1993: 121).

An easy gesture to denounce this attitude, the rejection of this teleological philosophy of history or Europe's fascination with the Orient, however, fails to take into account the historical circumstances – the staggering socio-political and cultural upheavals – and thus loses out of sight the will for emancipation but the tensions and aporias of these notions. Nevertheless, this thought and the tropes of inversion represent 'one's own' by means of spacing and setting boundaries. In this negative definition and via including differences in an – alleged – homogeneous identity, otherness cannot but show itself as non-intelligible. The *mise-en-scène* of a mythical-solar course of history – which was not really interrupted by Columbus' inauguration of the Western option that constituted the Western hemisphere as the West (Sloterdijk 1999: 832) – allows for the dualism Orient and Occident to persist (Chattopadhyaya 1997). Even the grand *récits* of the 'decline of the Occident' (Oswald Spengler), the 'dis-enchantment of the world' (Max Weber), the 'crisis of European sciences' (Edmund Husserl), and the mechanization of life in Western modernity (Martin Heidegger) do echo this topos.

A quite familiar narration states that the consolidation of the modern European nation-state led to more or less homogeneous cultural and ethnical entities. Within this broad legacy, however, there are to be found – at least within the eighteenth century – not just narrations that are to ground Europe's alterity. Within this legacy there are as well discursive elements pointing to Europe's blurring the 'original character of peoples' which increasingly 'do mix and melt into another' (Rousseau [1762]: 498). The progress of technology, increasing traffic and long distance voyage that establish common or agonistic political interests and dense commercial relations became driving forces, wiping out the self-containment of nations: 'Today, traffic between Europe and Asia is a hundred times more frequent than the one between France and Spain in former times. The parts of Europe were more disconnected than the entire globe in our times' (Rousseau [1762]: 499). Not just Jean Paul shares this diagnosis and remarks in 1804 that technological inventions had led to an unprecedented mobility and the way of life has incredibly been accelerated: 'Our book of life resembles the more and more a thin and restless leaflet that flies around and vanishes – from airships to steamers and express post: it is evident that Europe is on the move and one migration of peoples meets the other' (Jean Paul 1959–1963: 494). Twenty years earlier – in 1784 – Johann Gottfried Herder notes that Europe is distinguished 'by its diversity of Nations, by the diversity of customs and arts'. Europe's impact is the result of its heterogeneity, it is based on the fact that it assembles particularities and hosts its otherness. 'In no part of the world the peoples have mixed in such a large proportion..., a melting without which the Europe's general spirit [*Allgemeingeist*] would not have been aroused' (Herder 1965: 289). This humanism is far from considering Europe as a shining universal example for leading a good life, but recognizes the worth of the varieties of languages and cultures in which humankind expresses itself.

Europe's characteristic features are to be found not just in an inaugural heterogeneity or the confident faith in inevitable progress in the name of reason. The assertion of freedom and the various concepts of cosmopolitism are considered to be European attributes. The idea of freedom has been related to Christianity because the individual is being embraced by God's love that destines man to freedom (Hegel 1986: 301–2, §482). From a different standpoint, Novalis' fragmentary pamphlet 'Christendom or Europe' (*Die Christenheit oder Europa* 1799) addressed the unifying, individualizing principle of Christendom as an ideal, peaceful and brotherly cosmopolis, advocated the Renaissance of Europe and its holy unity and justice. Johann Gottlieb Fichte related the Europe to come to a renewed Christendom as well which unites the formerly divided peoples to one nation. This renewed Europe will determine the relations of single nations that compete to permit individual freedom, equality before the law, freedom of religion and of (political) judgement 'wherever one part lacks' as he confidently notes, 'they long for being away; where they are granted, they long to gather' (Fichte 1845/1846a: 204–5). The unifying moment of single nations – even in their mutual competition to allow for freedom – is to be found in the undeniable course of history striving for the realization of reason and with it, the citizen once tied to its soil becomes the cosmopolitan European: 'In this cosmopolitan sense we can be perfectly calm with regard to the actions and the destiny of the States, for our generation, for those who are to come until the end of days' (Fichte 1845/1846b: 211–12). From quite different viewpoints, enlightened visions assume that humankind would unite in a global association grounded in particularity that illustrates universal humanity. It advocated a peaceful cosmopolis allowing for freedom, the rule of law, freedom of religion and a rational, secular and humanist morality – be it contractual or utilitarian, based on rights or on duty – that convey universal principles of judgement.

These notions relate Europe not just to a cosmopolitism but to its shared historical responsibility as well. The critique of religion, 'superstition' and the 'political tricks' of papacy (Lessing 1970: 263–4) which brought unspeakable suffering to humankind becomes a unifying moment. Europe thus is united in the indignation about the deeds done in its name and in the name of Christianity. Europe is not founded in heroic deeds; it is founded in an act of unnameable atrocity, frenzy, the otherness of reason which remain 'an eternal accuser of the therein insulted humankind' (Herder 1965: 404). If Europe is united by this shared history of misdeeds, only consideration, compensation and enlightened reason can guide Europe. Europe's future comes into being in remembering extermination and despotism, it incurs and bears responsibility.

Against blind nationalism Friedrich Nietzsche still refers to the European cosmopolitan heritage. Neither God nor nation but modern homelessness and permanent exile shape the 'good European', who, because he has grown within Christendom has grown out of it. Europe, therefore, is founded in a 'We' of those who are 'homeless' and who resist a 'We'. 'We, the homeless ... are by race and descent all too mixed and therefore not inclined to participate in ... self-adoration of race and its prostitution [*Unzucht*]...' (Nietzsche 1988: 630–1, no. 277). Such modernity, understood both as legacy of and as obligation and indebtedness to the European spirit, can hardly tolerate apologetic and regressive national atavisms (Nietzsche 1988, 180–1, no. 241).

Max Weber takes up this heritage and the topos of Europe's singularity that has to be explained. Situating the text in a specific genealogy ('the son of the modern European world'), the inaugural gesture in the Preface to the *Sociology of Religion* however restricts assumptions of a strict law of development and opens to the – tragic insight – of the enchainment of historical circumstances and contingencies that gained universal importance and threaten to overwhelm everything else. At the same time his protocol of what lacks elsewhere enacts a negative method. For Hegel, the particularity of the European spirit is made of its inclinations to freedom and self-consciousness, negation and the detachment from unquestioned traditions. Weber, in turn, relates the uniqueness of the Occident to specific institutions, such as systematic science, a rational doctrine of law, the State, a rational statutory constitution and administration. It is only here that the 'fateful force' of capitalism, the bourgeoisie and the proletariat developed: by means of a negative comparison Europe becomes the other that has to be explained. At the same time, the comparative method – the determination of positive and distinguishing marks of a way of life via exclusion and figures of absence has consequences not just for an understanding of other peoples. The *reductio ad unum* conceptualizes Europe as a monolithic structure opposed to other monolithic structures or ways of life as well. In one breath, the structural identity of Europe is determined and its inner unity is proclaimed. Accordingly, different variations of modernity which are not based on adaptation to external impulses but on creations of different histories are excluded.

Europe's singularity, its distinctive features set out by these accounts are based on the idea of freedom, the autonomy of the individual against unquestioned tradition and the need to legitimize political action. Europe's singularity is based on religion as well as on its critique and secular orientations, on remembrance and the quest for responsibility. Its singularity is made up by specific social institutions of organized curiosity, science and technology, a bureaucracy, the state, a rational system of law and the specific mode of capitalistic economy. Briefly, it is based on specific institutionalized forms of reason and rationality. Additionally, concepts such as cosmopolitism, civil society, citizenship, public sphere and justice are indebted to this heritage which now became globalized. A feature of this – quite heterogeneous – European heritage, however, is dissent as well; the unifying moment is scarcely continuity but rupture and therefore cannot easily be accommodated in a unifying narrative. Europe's legacy is made up by remembering its unredeemed promises, the remembrance of 'what lacks' or has historically been missed. Europe is inaugurated in 'a rift, a caesura, an incision' (Marramao 2003: 60). Therefore, it is constituted not via an external segregation and the spacing of clear borders but by 'inner polarities', an original 'eccentricity' (Jaspers 1963: 93; Brague 1999).[2] Europe thus locates its non-founded foundation in an otherness as well as in its otherness.

Demarcations: spatial and temporal

The terms East and West are based on a double denial that sets spatial and temporal demarcations. Space and time are fundamental categories of the various practices and symbolizations of social life which mark boundaries as well as commonalties and therefore are far from being merely neutral definitions. For a long time social sciences relied on concepts that were to demarcate otherness not just by setting spatial borders in order to identify commonalties, but by situating the Other on a homogeneous axis of time which was to guarantee cultural unity and ontological stability of social life. The spatial and temporal continuum, the congruence of space and time respectively – the 'here' and 'now' of modernity vs. the 'there' and 'then', 'not yet' of tradition (Fabian 1983; Chakrabarty 2000) – which rely on the assumption of a linear world-time, were to mark the socio-cultural identity of Western modernity.

The procedure of analysis and cross-cultural comparison, therefore, was the construction of segregated, homogeneous and well-integrated entities; it was based on the presupposition of an epistemological break between 'subject' and 'object' and of a congruence between spatial-historical distance and cultural difference. In the course of the establishment of academic disciplines, geographical spaces have been assigned socio-cultural commonalities, not least with a view to constitute autonomous fields of research and to gain legitimacy within the academic canon. The focus of attention therefore, was not the particularities, the whole range of varieties of cultural forms and imaginaries, languages and symbolical worlds. On the contrary, the search was for correspondences of heterogeneous elements within one space and one frame of time; the search was for cultural identity and the uniformity of its traits. Given the distance between the researching subject and the researched object – a distance that is precisely meant to safeguard difference – what came into view were hardly the reciprocal and power-laden processes of translation and interpretation, but the analysable identity of the 'objects', an identity without which, indeed, the whole procedure would appear as rather dubious.

Both procedures inscribe the varieties of cultural practices into a generalized time and history dominating the entirety of humanity. Particularity is turned into a generality, indeed it only permits the very assumption of a self-identical generality that in turn guarantees the possibility of uniformity and thus the constancy of its objects of cognition. Time and history are not only spatialized, i.e. one time and one history are located in a common space, both are also represented as an empty continuum in which action is only represented, without being enabled to become effective. Neither, however, is identical action thinkable, since one would need to think it as timeless eternity, nor – and this would be Kant's epistemological and Hegel's thesis on the philosophy of history – do action or history move *in* time. Kant anchored time in the form of an apriori intuition which as a (transcendental) form is situated before history and Hegel gave a consistent teleological direction to history which appeared in the concept of progress. Theoretical arrangements declaring that history moves in a homogeneous time still determine scientific procedures. Similarly, this procedure has inscribed into itself the construct of a general history in which particularity enters as nothing but a moment of that generality, to dissolve into the generality. It is not history, not historical action or historical practices, that found time (or better: times), but it is the general that is said to determine action.

Predominant macro-sociological perspectives, which located socio-cultural configurations on a unilinear axis of development to characterize them as 'people without history', 'tribal', 'feudal', 'early-capitalist', 'traditional' or more recently 'pre-modern', have lost legitimation. However, the 'externalist' paradigm focusing on the impact of Western colonial history or on the penetration of capitalist world markets – recently analysed under the term 'globalization' – is still quite common. Thus, it is not the historical practices of the respective society under consideration, but external factors that lead to the dynamics of socio-cultural change.

Current concepts are influenced by these assumptions as well and have passed on the legacy of the philosophies of history. In the first instance, such reasoning assumes a drastic rupture with former conceptions which relied on tradition and postulate an omnipresent orientation towards the future in modern times (without, however, explaining which specific social configurations are characterized by such modernity and by the infinite possibilities allegedly opened by it). Western modernity thus is characterized by the break with the conceptions of time in 'traditional' societies and is substituted by the emergent 'open horizon of future possibilities' (Habermas 1985). It is marked by the scission of 'the time of life' and the 'time of the world' (Blumenberg 1986) and a precarious relation between finitude and of infinite possibilities and contingencies is opened up (Koselleck 1979). As a result, different ontologies of time and versions of modernities are measured against the yardstick of a specific, yet dominant variation and the conquest of space through time.

Attempts of theorizing 'multiple modernities' thematize again the interdependencies of social configurations and – like similar explorations of the mutual interrelationships between micro- and macro-structure, between family, local community and capitalist world-market – provide a conceptual space for varieties of modernity. The integration of those various forms of modernity into a 'global history', however, again locks such particular constellations into a unity and into the general developmental process of 'globalization'. The 'externalist' perspective and a procedure which already constituted the demarcations of Orient and Occident are repeated, a procedure which neglects the diversities of cultural practices, the variety of local landscapes 'within' such constellations. The creation of clear borders indicating breaks and continuities between forms of life is, as Geertz (2000: 247) remarks, 'a good deal easier in theory than it is in practice' and concepts of cultural homogeneity, identity and consensus as well as simplistic slogans of a 'global village' or a homogenizing 'global capitalism' fail to take into account the 'reworking and multiplication' of cultural traits (Geertz 2000: 247).

Migration and the increasing mobility of people troubled the familiar correspondence of time and space and led to a reasoning emphasizing uncertain identities, blurred borders, intersections and 'contact zones' (James Clifford). Concepts such as 'transnationalism', 'travelling cultures', 'diasporas' and 'dislocation', seem to indicate the weakening of the congruence of time, space and culture. Notions like 'acculturation', 'syncretism' or even 'assimilation' which once described linear processes from one culture to another, the overlapping of two different systems or the dissolution of a distinct and confineable culture, its practices, symbols into another distinguishable and confinable culture (Clifford 1999: 7), have been replaced by concepts that focus on the interrelation of socio-cultural configurations. Furthermore, these shifting formations are seen as always having been constituted reciprocally, as part of ambivalent, dynamic transnational and power-loaded processes which escape the establishment of clearly identifiable borders and identities (Friese 2002b).

Following Edward Said's classical discourse-analysis of 'Orientalism' that effectively gained force from the eighteenth-century onwards, patterns have been scrutinized that assert the unity and identity of Europe or the West in tropes of 'Occidentialism' (Said 1978; Carrier 1995). (Romantic) self-representations – not just those of the elites – have developed a counter-discourse against Western narratives and images about the Orient that in turn develop essentialist images of the identity of the West. These narratives take up the topoi already addressed above and become an integral part of the social imagination. Accordingly to such assertions, the West is to be considered as the reign of unlimited freedom, unrestrained individualism, materialistic orientation, nihilistic and destructive negation and corrosion of belief, custom and tradition. Such persuasive representations enter into an alliance with the modern critique of modernity and the legitimization of traditions which seem to vanish due to modernity and the processes of globalization. Revealing an astonishing analogy, what is proclaimed it not just the unity of 'Asian values' etc. but – paradoxically – the unity of one's 'own' alterity based on a variety of glaring contrasts and antinomies repeating the tensions that constitute 'modernity' (Kaiwar and Mazumdar 2003). Western political liberalism is contrasted with a substantial political order, secular life bluntly set against a way of life rooted in religious prescriptions and the promises of salvation, materialism against the legacies delivered by tradition.

Such constructions are immediately interwoven with a powerful politics of identity – such as new nationalisms or the fusion of ethnicity and territory – that mystifies one's own and distinct 'authenticity' and seeks to safeguard 'difference' (Friese 2004b). In redress of a closed – alleged – homogeneous and monolithic identity of 'logocentric and Eurocentric thought' or a flattening and uniforming cosmopolitism, 'counter-concepts' of identity are constructed which assume opposing primordial cultural dispositions. Ironically, such obsessions are consolidated at a point in time in which ontological essences, primordial, collective identities and reifications are questioned, a critique which in the meantime has been adjoined to various 'postmodern ethics' of difference and alterity that take account of the irreducible singularity of an Other and focus on responsibility, friendship, hospitality and a renewed openness (Derrida 1992; Bauman 1993; Irigaray 1999).

Europe's cosmopolitism

Europe again is asked to allow for an open space, a space of an active otherness which is not only marked by the presence of an Other within it but points towards an otherness already at work that halts any notion of cultural identity. Such an opening towards an Other has been demanded not just by Edgar Morin (1987). From another point of view Jacques Derrida insists on 'an opening and a non-exclusion for which Europe would in someway be responsible', an opening that includes unconditional hospitality (Derrida 1992: 28–9).[3]

This proposal is of course already related to a specific, if heterogeneous and branched tradition, it is bound to a cosmopolitanism and concepts of universal rights even if it distances itself clearly from them. In contrast to Kant's cosmopolitanism which puts forward the law of universal citizenship (*Weltbürgerrecht*), limited and conditioned by general hospitality and a general law of hospitality which are bound to the authority of the state, the control of residence and its duration,[4] Derrida proposes a notion of cosmopolitan justice beyond both the nation-state and this cosmopolitanism. 'Absolute hospitality' requires the commitment to unconditional accommodation of the 'absolute, unknown, anonymous' Other, it requires to accept an Other 'at home' (chez moi, chez nous), to donate, to 'give him a place', without enquiring as to origin or identity (Derrida and Dufourmantelle 1997: 29). Unconditional, absolute hospitality – which suspends reciprocity, does not require identification and is beyond the order of law, its application and a judgement – breaks with the law and its regulations which bestow hospitality with conditions and limits. This unconditionality is equitable with a regulative idea that dynamizes action and political decision, without applying a normative continuum which guarantees its realization because it remains as alien from law as justice from law. The relationship between absolute hospitality and the laws and rules which should serve its unconditionality thus becomes part of political negotiation and (cosmo)political deliberation. Although it is not clear, who – beyond membership and citizenship – is to be considered to be the subject(s) of political negotiation and deliberation (Friese 2004b), an active otherness is introduced which cannot be removed beyond political or cultural borders.

Any fetishization of cultural unity does not only fail to see the contingencies that inhabit cultural practices, but falls short of perceiving the caesuras which indicate (one's 'own') otherness. Assumptions of stable unities or ascertainable cultural identities do not account for the constitutive *Veranderung* (being-othered) enacted in socio-cultural practices. In accordance with, but as well against theories of intersubjectivity, dialogue and a hermeuneutics of empathy and understanding and drawing on Edmund Husserl, Michael Theunissen (1984) brought a perspective into play which focuses on the event of *Veranderung*.[5] With the occurrence of reciprocal *Veranderung* already at work, the singular human being becomes estranged by an Other and at the same time becomes an Other among others. The subject thus is deprived of its world-constituting power, s/he is decentralized and experiences him/herself as constituting as well as being constituted by the Other, to whom s/he gives himself as well as s/he is given. This perspective cannot advocate for demarcated personal and/or cultural identities but evidences an otherness which is already at work. Such a perspective undermines the certainties of clear demarcations and fixed identities. It neither subscribes to an emphasis of identity and alterity nor inscribes a singular Other into a cultural collectivity.

A further elaboration of such a perspective would work in two directions. It would address the epistemological problems, i.e. the constitution of the 'object' and at the same time the powerful politics of identity: neither could socio-cultural essentials be identified that are to form a stable identity, nor could an unbridgeable distance between the subject and the 'object' of research be assumed. Far from being dominated by common underlying internal structures which are to guarantee their identity, what could be shown is the heterogeneity of spaces, the various regional ontologies of time and the varieties of historical landscapes which are constituted by different practices, narratives and ways of writing. At the same time, identity could not be tied to a common, universal time, but could be seen as already postponed, displaced and exceeded.

Once the constitutive *Veranderung* is taken into account, boundaries of an – alleged – inner and outer dimension and unfruitful dualisms can be avoided, without inscribing different (historical) times into one despotic world-time. A perspective that evidences the constitutive *Veranderung* already at work thus does not just recognize the Other in the supposed own self and that which is one's own in the Other, but is aware of and insists on the principled impossibility of a clearly defined 'own' and/or 'other', a clearly defined Occident, a 'European Modernity' as opposed to an Orient and other forms of modernities.

Goethe related self-cognition to the recognition of the Other within oneself that prohibits strict demarcations. Beyond that, what could be indicated is a Beyond already at work.

Notes

1 Literally: 'Across the Mediterranean, magnificently, the Orient made its way/only the one who loves and knows Hafis/does know what Calderon has sung.// The one who knows himself and others/ here will recognize as well/Orient and Occident can no longer be divided' (Goethe, 1998: 57). In the following, all translations are mine and page numbers follow the original edition.

I am indebted to Naomi Salmon for friendship and hospitality, her inquiries with the '*Stiftung Weimarer Klassik*', late night faxes and Volkart Knigge for a wonderful walk through Weimar.

2 Rémi Brague has argued that being secondary culturally towards ancient Greece and religiously towards Judaism is Europe's specificity. For a critique of Brague's focus on Roman Catholicism, see Friese (2004a).

3 Derrida uses both the terms 'responsibility' and 'obligation, duty'. The astonishing shift in concepts from 'brotherhood' to 'duty', from 'solidarity' to 'responsibility' would merit a detailed critique. For a critique of the current emphasis on

'responsibility', a concept which is deeply rooted in the Judaeo-Christian tradition, see Friese (2004b).
4 The concept of a peaceful community is not an 'ethic-philanthropic' venture but, as Kant stresses, a 'legal principle'. Nations are not legal communities of propriety (*communio*) but of interrelation (*commercium*). The law that guarantees this, is cosmopolitan law (ius cosmopoliticum) which entails the right to visit but not to stay. For the latter, Kant insisted on the need of a 'special treaty' (Kant, 1997: 475–7, §62). For an interpretation of Kant, see Benhabib (2004); Bohmann and Lutz-Bachmann (1997).
5 According to Theunissen, three interconnected perspectives can be identified. Transcendental approaches, drawing on Edmund Husserl, first, focus on the constitution of the Other in and through world-projecting subjectivity. Dialogical approaches, as in Martin Buber, second, emphasize the encounter of the Other and the birth of self in and through the encounter. Approaches as elaborated by Wilhelm Dilthey, Max Weber or Alfred Schütz, finally, have proposed a hermeneutics of understanding and empathy. Whereas transcendental approaches seek the original being of the Other in the 'strange-I' and its existential modifications, dialogical thinking encounters the Other in the Thou. Hermeneutic approaches, in turn hope to 'overcome' the 'gap' between self and Other by interpretative means.

References

Bauman, Z. (1993) *Postmodern Ethics*, Oxford: Blackwell.
Benhabib, S. (2004) *The Rights of Others: Aliens, Residents and Citizens*, Cambridge: Cambridge University Press.
Blumenberg, H. (1986) *Weltzeit und Lebenszeit*, Frankfurt am Main: Suhrkamp.
Bohmann, J. and M. Lutz-Bachmann (eds) (1997) *Perpetual Peace: Essays on Kant's Cosmopolitan Ideal*, Cambridge, MA: MIT Press.
Brague, R. (1999) *Europe, la voie romaine*, Paris: Gallimard.
Carrier, J. G. (ed.) (1995) *Occidentalism: Images of the West*, Oxford: Clarendon Press.
Chakrabarty, D. (2000) *Provincializing Europe: Postcolonial Thought and Historical Difference*, Princeton: Princeton University Press.
Chattopadhyaya, D. P. (1997) *Sociology, Ideology and Utopia: Socio-political Philosophy of East and West*, Leiden: Brill.
Clifford, J. (1999) *Routes: Travel and Translation in the Late Twentieth Century*, Cambridge, MA: Harvard University Press.
Derrida, J. (1992) *The Other Heading: Reflections on Today's Europe*, trans. P.-A. Brault and M. B. Naas, Bloomington: Indiana University Press.
Derrida, J. and A. Dufourmantelle (1997) *De l'hospitalité*, Paris: Calmann-Lévy.
Fabian, J. (1983) *Time and the Other: How Anthropology makes its Object*, New York: Columbia University Press.
Fichte, J. G. ([1800] 1845/1846a) 'Der geschlossene Handelsstaat', in *Fichtes sämmtliche Werke*, ed. by I. H. Fichte, Vol. 3, Berlin: Veit & Comp.
Fichte, J. G. (1845/1846b) 'Die Grundzüge des gegenwärtigen Zeitalters', in *Fichtes sämmtliche Werke*, ed. by I. H. Fichte, Vol. 7, Berlin: Veit & Comp.
Friese, H. (2002a) 'L'Europa a venire', in H. Friese, T. Negri and P. Wagner (eds) *Europa politica: Ragioni di una necessità*, Rome: manifestolibri, pp. 59–77.
Friese, H. (ed.) (2002b) *Identities: Time, Boundary and Difference*, Oxford: Berghahn.

Friese, H. (2004a) 'La otredad de Europa', *Política y sociedad*, 41(3): 99–112.

Friese, H. (2004b) 'Spaces of Hospitality', *Angelaki: Journal of the Theoretical Humanities*, 9(2): 67–79.

Friese, H. and P. Wagner (2002) 'The Nascent Political Philosophy of the European Polity', *Journal of Political Philosophy*, 10(3): 342–64.

Geertz, C. (2000) *Available Light: Anthropological Reflections on Philosophical Topics*, Princeton: Princeton University Press.

Goethe, J. W. v. (1998 [1819]) 'Hikmet Nameh, Buch der Sprüche', *West-östlicher Divan. Hamburger Ausgabe*, Vol. 2, Hamburg: DTV.

Habermas, J. (1985) *Der philosophische Diskurs der Moderne*, Frankfurt am Main: Suhrkamp.

Hegel, G. W. F. ([1837/1838] 1993) 'Vorlesungen über die Geschichte der Philosophie', in *Werke*, Vol. 18–20, ed. by E. Moldenhauer and K. M. Michel, Frankfurt am Main: Suhrkamp.

Hegel, G. W. F. (1986 [1830]) 'Enzyklopädie der philosophischen Wissenschaften im Grundrisse, Dritter Teil. Die Philosophie des Geistes', in *Werke*, Vol. 10, ed. by E, Moldenhauer and K. M. Michel, Frankfurt am Main: Suhrkamp.

Hegel, Georg Wilhelm Friedrich (1992 [1837]) 'Vorlesungen über die Philosophie der Geschichte', in *Werke*, Vol. 12, ed. by E. Moldenhauer and K. M. Michel, Frankfurt am Main: Suhrkamp.

Herder, J. G. (1965 [1784]) *Ideen zur Philosophie der Geschichte der Menschheit*, Vol. 1 and 2., ed. by H. Stolpe, Berlin: Aufbau Verlag.

Irigaray, L. (1999) *Entre Orient et Occident: De la singularité à la communauté*, Paris: Grasset.

Jaspers, K. (1963 [1949]) 'Orient und Okzident (Morgenland und Abendland)', in *Vom Ursprung und Ziel der Geschichte*, Munich: Piper, pp. 93–7.

Kaiwar, V. and S. Mazumdar (eds) (2003) *Antinomies of Modernity: Essays on Race, Orient, Nation*, Durham: Duke University Press.

Kant, I. (1997 [1797A/1798B]) 'Die Metaphysik der Sitten', in *Werkausgabe*, Vol. 8, ed. by W. Weischedel, Frankfurt am Main: Suhrkamp.

Koselleck, R. (1979) *Vergangene Zukunft: Zur Semantik geschichtlicher Zeiten*, Frankfurt am Main: Suhrkamp.

Lessing, G. E. (1970 [1767/1969]) 'Hamburgische Dramaturgie', in *Werke*, Vol. 4, ed. by H. G. Göpfert in collaboration with K. Eibl, H. Göbel, K. S. Guthke *et al.*, Munich: Carl Hanser.

Marramao, G. (2003) *Passaggio a Occidente: Filosofia e globalizzazione*, Torino: Bollati Boringhieri.

Morin, E. (1987) *Penser l'Europe*, Paris: Gallimard.

Nietzsche, F. (1988, 2nd edn) 'Jenseits von Gut und Böse', in *Kritische Studienausgabe*, Vol. 5, ed. by G. Colli and M. Montinari, Munich: DTV/de Gruyter, pp. 9–243.

Nietzsche, F. (1988, 2nd edn [1882/1887]) 'Die fröhliche Wissenschaft', in *Kritische Studienausgabe*, Vol. 3, ed. by G. Colli and M. Montinari, Munich: DTV and de Gruyter, pp. 343–651.

Novalis (1981/1999) 'Die Christenheit oder Europa', in *Werke*, ed. by H.-J. Mähl and R. Samuel, Munich: Hanser.

Paul, J. (1959–1963 [1804/1812]) 'Vorschule der Ästhetik, Über Tagblätter und Taschenbücher', in *Werke, 1. Abteilung*, Vol. 5, ed. by N. Miller and G. Lohmann, Munich: Carl Hanser.

Rousseau, J.-J. (1998, 13th edn [1762]) 'Emil oder Über die Erziehung' (trans. L. Schmidts), Paderborn, Munich: UTB, Ferdinand Schöningh.

Said, E. W. (1978) *Orientalism*, London: Penguin Books.

Sloterdijk, P. (1999) *Sphären*, Vol. 2, Frankfurt am Main: Suhrkamp.

Sloterdijk, P. (2002) *Falls Europa erwacht: Gedanken zum Programm einer Weltmacht am Ende des Zeitalters ihrer politischen Absence*, Frankfurt am Main: Suhrkamp.

Theunissen, M. (1984) *The Other, Studies in the Social Ontology of Husserl, Heidegger, Sartre, and Buber*, Cambridge, MA: MIT Press.

Weber, M. (1988, 9th edn [1920]) *Gesammelte Aufsätze zur Religionssoziologie*, Vol. I, Tübingen: Mohr Siebeck.

18 Is there such a thing as Eurocentrism?

Rémi Brague

In a book on European cultural identity, to be precise in the American translation of a book written originally in French, I wrote some lines, which I will now quote. "No culture was ever so little centred on itself and so interested in the others as Europe. China called itself 'the Middle Kingdom' Europe never did. Eurocentrism is a misnomer. It is even the contrary of truth" (Brague 2002a: 133ff.). In a review of recent books on Europe, Gerard Delanty quoted some of those words and saw in them a "seductive argument" in which, however, "there is a philosophical sleight of hand". As a consequence, "this problem is not adequately addressed" (Delanty 2003: 471–88, especially 486). I cannot see where the legerdemain resides, but I can agree on the sketchy character of this somewhat provocative thesis. The aim of what follows is to flesh it out.

Eurocentrism

I am sorry to have to confess that I have been unable to discover exactly who coined the word Eurocentrism, and when this took place and for what purposes. The earliest occurrence of the term that I could locate, albeit after rather superficial inquiry, is in the title of a book written in 1988 by Samir Amin. Mr. Amin is an economist, apparently of Marxist persuasian, and an opponent of "globalization". He was born in 1931 to an Egyptian father and a French mother (which explains why his book was written in French).

Obviously, "Eurocentrism" combines two substantives: "Europe", shortened into a prefix of sorts, "centre", and the suffix "-ism". The latter adds a derogatory shade. It implies that it is wrong to consider Europe as the centre of the world. In the same way, "geocentricism" is the name that was given to Ptolemy's geocentric cosmology, when it was proved wrong.

I understand the word "centrism" as standing for an intellectual phenomenon. For, in order to describe the concrete stance of European peoples towards the rest of the world, a great deal of other words are available. They are more to the point than Eurocentrism. Some are merely descriptive, such as colonization. Some capture the inner stance that is supposed to have triggered the former, such as imperialism. For the most part, they imply a judgement of value, and a negative one. I understand Eurocentrism as meaning the way in which Europeans are supposed to look at other cultures from their own point of view, to measure them according to their own standards.

"Centrism" as a universal phenomenon

What I should like to call "centrism" is a common phenomenon among cultures. If we are allowed to draw a parallel between cultural and biological phenomena, and I know full well that this cannot be done without due care, a "centrist" view of things is a common feature of living beings. They do not take in their environment as it is. Their perceptive apparel selects what is "interesting" for them in the constant struggle for life, i.e. what can be a danger, like predators, or what can be useful for the individual or the species: food supply, sexual partners, etc.

The same holds true, *mutatis mutandis*, for human societies. Many among them consider themselves as being identical with mankind. People in them often call themselves "men" *tout court*, whereas the other peoples are animals. Each culture looks at the other ones from its own vantage point. Claude Levi-Strauss tells us the story of an Indian from the Brazilian heartland who is brought to Rio de Janeiro. Asked about the differences he sees between Indians and "Europeans", he says that the main one is that, unlike Europeans, Indians never pluck flowers.

Europe makes no exception. What distinguishes European "centrism" from other instances of the same attitude is merely quantitative in nature. The fact that Europe has conquered the whole world had to swell the European view of the world to gigantic proportions. Of course, one could invoke the famous "law" of dialectical materialism according to which quantity allegedly becomes quality. One could plead that such a switch must occur when a definite world-view becomes so broadly accepted that its possible rivals are automatically out of court. Hence, if I had to answer my question with a blunt yes or no, I should acknowledge that Eurocentrism existed, and still exists. Drawing a list of what bears witness of a Eurocentric stance, unmasking it and exposing it is quite an easy task. There are some people for whom it is interesting. In my opinion, the results of this kind of enquiry have the unbearable tediousness that belabouring the obvious produces when it is presented as a feat of scholarship and insight.

Europe as eccentric

Let us now have a look at the other component of the word I am trying to scrutinize, i.e. the prefix "Euro". If Europe is Eurocentric, is Eurocentrism typically European? My answer is emphatically "no". In the book I have just alluded to, I endeavoured to show that Europe fed upon previous cultures from which it felt estranged. This is what I called Europe's secondarity. What I called "eccentric identity" is a feature of European culture, nay its backbone. I need not repeat what I explained there.

To the best of my knowledge, cultural secondarity and eccentricity do not exist except in Europe. We are not that prone to acknowledge this, because of a difficulty that was pointed out in its whole breath by a famous legal historian: "In spite of overwhelming evidence, it is most difficult for a citizen of Western Europe to bring thoroughly home to himself the truth that the civilization which surrounds him is a rare exception in the history of the world" (Maine 1970 [1861]: 13f.).

In order to show once more European cultural eccentricity, I will proceed indirectly. Being eccentric necessarily leads to an eccentric view of oneself. Russian literary theorists of the pre-First World War period, the so-called "formalists", coined the concept of singularization (остранение) to capture the very essence of literature: "whereas everyday experience is inevitably worn out by habit, the writer enables the reader to look at it with fresh eyes by making it look strange through various devices" (Chklovski 1965 [1917]: 83). Later on, the idea was taken up by Brecht with his *Verfremdung*, distantiation. Now, I will try to show that European culture as such shows phenomena that can be grouped under the heading of distantiation.

In order to do so, I will focus on the Middle Ages. Since this period is anterior to Europe's overseas expansion, it will be easier to grasp its cultural features in some sort of state of chemical purity, unalloyed by any feedback phenomenon from the countries that it later conquered. Let me highlight three aspects. I will deal with them with a decreasing brevity.

Far away

First, the very place that people knew they were occupying on the map was far from being central. If we look at medieval maps (see, for example, Maurolico's map in Bertola 1996: 130), we observe that a basic agreement obtains between European, Byzantine Greek and Islamic cartographers. The shape of the world, such as it was known, differs only in details. In each case, the centre of the world was located somewhere in the Near East, for instance, Iran and the Arabic Peninsula (see, for example, Al-Amiri 1988: 66ff.). Furthermore, a centre is more than geometry. It means a point of reference. The mathematical centre does not always coincide with what I should call the axiological centre. I showed this elsewhere for pre-Copernican cosmology (see Brague 1997: 187–210). Now, such a centre for the medieval man is definitely not Europe, but again the Middle East: for the Jews and Christians, it is Jerusalem; for the Muslims it is Mecca.

This is shown in a famous poem by a medieval Jew and apologist of his religion, Jehuda Halevi, who lived in Andalusia and died in 1140 in

Alexandria, on his way to the Holy Land. He writes: "my heart is in Orient, but I am dwelling in the farthest West". Now, the heart is more than a metaphor for affectivity. Halevi does not mean only that his longing is towards the holy city of Jerusalem. The Hebrew *lev* actually had this meaning, among other ones, in the ancient language. But it had taken a new shade that it did not yet possess in Biblical time, but had borrowed from the Arabic *lubb*. This word means the kernel of a fruit. In medieval parlance, it is a common metaphor for the innermost core of a being. This is the case in Halevi's own writings, especially his masterpiece the *Kuzari*, where the idea plays a decisive part: Israel is claimed to be the kernel of mankind.[1] What Halevi means in the poem is that his centre of gravity, his point of reference, the hard core of his religious identity is in the East, i.e. Jerusalem, whereas his concrete abode, the place of his body, is Spain.

Interest

Second, I contend that Europe is the only culture that ever became interested in the other cultures. Let me qualify this somewhat provocative thesis. I spoke of a culture as a subject and said that European culture did this and failed to do that, and so forth. This is obviously shorthand for more careful formulas that competent people could formulate more aptly. Individuals can qualify as subjects of actions and, to some extent, social groups, too. What I mean with "European culture did this", etc. is something like: a definite practice was commonly received for a long time and in social groups large in number and powerful in influence.

Now, we can find in pre-European or extra-European cultures examples of individuals who became interested in other cultures and tried to study them in a fair way. Herodotus did precisely that in ancient Greece with his accounts of Egypt, Persia, etc. Al-Biruni (d. 1053) did that in medieval Persian Islam with his reports on India. He even reflected on parochialism, an intellectual flaw that he ascribed to the Indians of his time. For them, the earth is their country, mankind is their people, the kings are their leaders, religion is their sect, knowledge is what they know (Al-Biruni 1983: 20). But people like Herodotus and Al-Biruni remained shooting stars and left no intellectual posterity. A swallow does not make a spring.

A notable fact is that Arab travellers explored each and every nook and corner of the Islamic world. But we find no examples among them of people who went to European countries (see Fletcher 2003: 163). And few examples of people who listened with interest to what foreign travellers told them about their country of origin (see the cases in Malvezzi 1956: 116ff. and 125, cited in von Grunebaum 1973: 232). On the other hand, we find many instances of foreign peoples who cannot understand why Europeans came and visited them just for the fun of it. In the late seventeenth century, the French traveller Jean Chardin recorded the surprise of the Persians – the real ones, not Montesquieu's – when they understood that he had undertaken a long and dangerous trip just for the sake of curiosity.[2]

In Europe, interest for foreign mores became common and fostered a whole literary genre. There exists a long tradition of travel literature. In the thirteenth century, monks were sent to the Mongols, like John of Piano-Carpini, OFM (d. 1252). William Rubruk, OFM went to Karakorum to the court of the Grand Khan. The latter was sent by the Pope and the King of France in order to try and win the alliance of the Mongols against Islam. In 1258, he took part in a religious disputation in the presence of the Khan. One could mention other people like William of Boldensele, OP, John of Montecorbino (d. 1328) or Odoric of Pordenone, OFM (d. 1331) who went as far as China.

What is revealing for us are not the travellers, let alone their diplomatic aims, but the fact that they wrote their travel diary and published it. Marco Polo perhaps never went to China and simply listened to sailors' yarns somewhere in Bassorah or such places (see Wood's provocative 1995 book: 208pp.). But his book was immensely successful. In the same way, Sir John Mandeville, the imaginary author of an imaginary travel book that appeared in 1356–1357 in Anglo-Norman French met a huge success and was translated into many languages. The forger took the existence of an interested readership for granted.

The other as vantage point

I should like to make my third point on the basis of the second one. Getting interested in something is more than a sheer token of curiosity; or, rather, there are several levels of interest. The deepest one consists of understanding that the other one is interesting also because of the light it throws back on the observer (Brague 2002b: 183–201, especially 184). This is what European culture did.

A well-known literary device among European writers consists of pretending that a traveller from a remote country looks at Europe and describes it naively. This enables a veiled critique of one's own basic assumptions. Montesquieu's *Lettres Persanes* (1721), a classical work that every French person has read at high school, is the most famous example of this literary genre. But Montesquieu was in the wake of an older tradition of European self-criticism and endeavouring to look at oneself through foreign eyes.

In modern times, the first to make use of this literary device probably was an Italian who lived mainly in France, Giovanni Paolo Marana (1642–1693) in his *L'esploratore turco* (1682), in Marana's own French *L'Espion du Grand Seigneur* (1684). The book presents itself as a collection of reports allegedly translated from the Arabic of a Turkish spy by the name of Mahmut.[3] In the last decade of the seventeenth century, the French polygraph Charles Dufresny in his *Amusements sérieux et comiques* (1699) already reflects on this practice.

Let me quote my English translation:

> For us to be more vividly struck by a variety that the *prejudices of*
> *habit* make appear almost uniform, let us imagine that a Siamese
> enters Paris. What fun could it be for him to examine *with the eyes of*
> *a traveller* all the pecularities of this large city [...] we will see in
> which manner he will be struck by some things that the prejudices of
> habit make look reasonable and natural to us.
>
> (Dufresny 1992: 994–1050 – my emphasis)

This passage is interesting because, amongst other reasons, of the stress
it lays on the idea of prejudice. This idea originated in Descartes and Male-
branche. It was already a lively topic of discussion during the *Querelle des*
Anciens et des Modernes (see Longepierre 2001 [1687]: 286–9), and it was
to become a catchword of the Enlightenment.

As for Montesquieu's *Lettres Persanes*, nobody challenges their place as
the masterpiece of this literary genre. Little wonder that they were largely
imitated, so that the trick became simply hackneyed in the eighteenth
century. Let me mention some instances following the chronological order.

Jean-Baptiste de Boyer, marquis d'Argens (1704–1771), a French polygraph, siding with the "Philosophes", published two series of Letters, first
Jewish, then Chinese, that contain a scathing critique of "superstition" –
code-word for Christianity (Boyer d'Argens 1736–1737 and 1751).

In England Oliver Goldsmith, more famous for his novel *The Vicar of*
Wakefield (1766), published between January 1760 and August 1761 a
series of 119 "Chinese Letters" that were published in the next year with
the new title of *The Citizen of the World* (Friedman (ed.) 1966 [1762]:
XIX, 476pp.). An imaginary Chinaman, Lien Chi Altangi, mocks London
life and manners. The works draws heavily on d'Argens previous work,
which Goldsmith from time to time simply cribbed, and on various reports
on things Chinese.

In L'Ingénu (1767), Voltaire dropped the genre of letters and wrote of a
red Indian, a Huron, in Paris. The contrast is between the refinement and
corruption of Parisian high life and the innocence of the noble savage.

In Spain José Cadalso (d. 1782), an officer, in his *Cartas Marruecas*
(posthumous, 1789), has a traveller from Morocco, helped by a Spaniard,
write a satire on Spanish mores (Cadalso 1956: XLVI, 232pp.).

After the French Revolution, the procedure seems to have lost its
charm, although some examples are still to be found nowadays, as in the
case of the German writer Herbert Rosendorfer who took up the rather
obsolete form of the letters to have a Chinese mandarin of the tenth
century describe with amazement the mores of contemporary Munich
(1994 [1983]: 275pp.).

To be sure, this conjunction of works bears witness to the spirit of the
Enlightenment. Interestingly, it lasted for slightly more than one century,

and this century is precisely the one which we commonly call by the name of Enlightenment. The oldest work, Marana's, was published at a mighty intellectual watershed: the 1670s and 1680s, a period that the French historian of ideas Paul Hazard called, in a book by this title that he published in 1935, *The Crisis of the European Conscience*. The last one, Cadalso's, was printed in the very first year of the French Revolution and had been written a few years earlier. All those works actually contribute to the strategy of the Enlightenment.

The Middle Ages

We then must ask: is this ability to look at oneself from afar a feature of European culture as such? Or does it belong to the modern period only? Seeing from afar is a common trait of modernity, after the discovery of America, the circumnavigation of the world, and so on. This does not hold true for geographic distance only. More generally, the astronomic revolution brought about by Copernicus may have opened up a new perspective, although the idea of an ascension towards the highest spheres that enables us to literally look down on our own everyday world is very ancient (see Brague 2003: 73, 88, 90).

In the same way, attempts at looking at oneself through foreign eyes are far earlier than Modern times. Examples are to be found several centuries earlier, i.e. in the Middle Ages, too. In the twelfth century, the French philosopher Pierre Abélard (d. 1142) wrote a dialogue between a Christian, a Jew and a Philosopher, who happens to be a Muslim in origin. He has a cue in which the Jew complains about the situation of humiliation in which his people have been living under Christian domination.[4] What is remarkable is not the content of such an outburst, but the fact that it was written by a Christian. Abélard had to suffer from some of his fellow Christians and had first-hand experience of persecution. In his autobiography, he even confesses that he has toyed with the idea of settling in Pagan (i.e. Islamic) countries, in order to live there as a Christian, paying the special poll-tax for non-Muslims, but enjoying a greater freedom than in Christendom.[5] We have another example of a comparison between one's own habits and foreign practice to the benefit of the foreign: Ibn Jubayr, a Muslim traveller who visited Palestine at the time of the Crusades, compares the situation of Muslims under Islamic rule and under Frankish rule, to the advantage of the latter (Ibn Jubayr 1953 [1907], cited in Lewis 1990: 93). Nevertheless, what is remarkable in Abelard is the ability to put into the mouth of the other one arguments against oneself.

Another example of this stance is to be found in the travelogue of a Franciscan monk whom I have already mentioned: William of Rubruk. The Great Khan taunts William's brothers in the faith with inconsistency: they allegedly were given a Holy Scripture, but they hardly abide by its regulations (Rubrouck 1993: 182–6). There may be a grain of truth in this.

Yet, what is really interesting is that such accusations levelled against Christianity by a foreign prince became a topos in medieval travel literature (see Kastner 1997: 280–95).

Honoré Bouvet as a key example

Let me spend some time on another medieval work. Its author, by the name of Honoré Bouvet, was a Benedictine monk, trained in Canon Law, who lived in the abbey of Selonnet (in the French département of the Alpes de Haute-Provence, near the dam of Serre-Ponçon). He was born around 1340 and died in the first decade of the fifteenth century. Bouvet was not exactly a dove. On the contrary, he had a lively interest in military things and wrote a compendium of military rules, some sort of mirror of the noble soldier, by the title of *L'Arbre des Batailles* (*The Tree of Battles*) (1387), which remained his most successful production and was translated into several languages.

I will deal here with another work, *L'apparicion maistre Jean de Meung*, written in 1398 (Arnold 1926: 1–68).[6] The author dreams that the famous author of the second part of the *Roman de la Rose* appears to him. The great writer engages in a dialogue with a physician, a Jew, a Saracen and a Jacobin monk, four people who, for different reasons, were in disrepute.[7] Through them, Bouvet expresses his strictures against the mores of his contemporaries. Some of them are put into the mouths of foreigners, the Jew and mainly the Saracen. We will see that he hardly pulls his punches.

The Jew had to come in hiding,[8] because of the ban published by the King in 1394, expelling the Jews because of their sins, especially usury.[9] He asks that the ban be lifted, for the Christians do far worse. They practice usury under the veil, by pretending to engage in lawful commercial transactions. Why should the Jews, who are not a match against Christian cupidity, remain in exile? If they were granted permission to come back, they would ask for lower interest than Christians do: "Et nous serions plus gracioux / De prendre plus petite usure".[10]

Bouvet puts into the mouth of his Saracen a far longer speech. His character is a black man, "aussy noir comme charbon"; he is an interpreter, of noble breed, and steeped in the Muslim religion: "...je suy plus franc trossimant / Qui soit en Sarrasisme grant, / Car je sçay parler tout langage; / Et sy suy home de paraige / Et suy bon clerc en nostre loy".[11] He was sent to study French people in order to report upon their habits, their creed, their political system: "...nos seigneurs de la / Sy m'ont envoyé par deça / Pour vëoir l'estat des crestians. [...] Pour ce suy venuz en partie / Pour vëoir des Françoys leur vie, / Leur fait, leur noble contenance, / Quel foy ilz ont, quel ordonnance."[12] The critique he levels against French Christians is harsher still than the Jew's. The first one betrays Bouvet's interest in things military: Christians live in luxury and effeminacy. Hence, they are weak soldiers.[13]

But there are far worse things. Among Saracens, the Christian law, i.e. the Christian religion, is said to rest on charity. But Saracens are more charitable to each other than the Christians vis-à-vis their neighbours. Among Christians, there is neither charity nor mercy: "On dit entre nous une fable / Que vostre loy est charitable, / Mais je vous dy pour verité / Que nous avons plus de charité / Entre nous autres Sarrazins / Que vous n'avez a vos voisins".[14] In particular, Christians do not care about the sad condition of their prisoners in Muslim countries. Therefore, they know neither charity nor even pity: "Pour ce dy je que charité / N'est entre crestiens ne pitié".[15] Christian tradesmen swear upon their faith and commit perjury all the same. Christian people commit adultery and theft. Christian soldiers prey upon their own folks, and on and on.[16]

The content of this critique is interesting. But it is not original. We read very much the same things at the same period, for instance in Eustache Dechamps.[17] What is more interesting still, is the literary device. The Saracen is put into scene by a Christian to put his fellow Christians to shame. The device is even doubled, for the Saracen begins with reminding the Latin Christians of the hatred of their brothers, the Greek Christians of Byzantium against them: "j'ay ouÿ par plusieurs foys / Parler aux Rommains des Françoys, / Mais c'estoit bien vilainemant: / Ilz les prisent moins que neant, / Car ilz les ont pour scismatiques."[18] The wheel comes full circle: a Latin Christian writer has a Muslim character report about the critique of Byzantine Christians against Latin Christians.

Conclusion

We find hardly any match to this attitude outside Europe. André Miquel contends that some Muslim geographers praised foreign, far-eastern mores as a mirror held to their own world for it to improve itself. Yet, the passages of his large work on the geographers which he refers to are not convincing (Miquel 2000: 108–14).

Now, as a matter or course, all this is mere fiction. The alleged foreigners are described on the basis of reports of European travellers. They are hardly more than mouthpieces for the author's own assumptions. One could say that such a device is the heyday of Eurocentrism. Moreover, the writers who make use of this device are not free of prejudices against other European countries. For instance, Montesquieu has his Persian traveller lampoon France, but he has him criticize Russia, too, so harshly that this elicited an answer from a German who wrote in French, Strube de Piermont, who chose the same literary form of a correspondence to launch a counter-attack on *L'Esprit des Lois* (Strube de Piermont 1978: 219pp.).

Nevertheless, we are not allowed to reduce these texts to sheer Eurocentrism, since it would not have been possible without what I alluded to a while ago, i.e. the tradition of travel literature and the interest for the other that made it possible. Even if the "other" is a construction, his place remains as a possibility of self-distantiation for European consciousness. To be sure, the other is an imaginary focus. But it is enough to change the circle of which Europe would be the centre into an ellipse that displaces it from itself.

In a nutshell, Eurocentrism as a concept is either too broad or too narrow. As a subspecies of "centrism", it is too broad to capture Europe and does not tell us anything specific about it. In so far as it is supposed to describe Europe as such and to the exclusion of whatsoever else, it simply misses the mark.

I could even go farther and claim: speaking of Eurocentrism, i.e. applying this broad concept to Europe only, is a typically Eurocentric move. Nothing is more Eurocentric than the critique levelled against Eurocentrism. Perhaps the very idea that there is such a thing as Eurocentrism is the only genuine Eurocentric stance.

Notes

1 Jehuda Halevi, *Kuzari*, I, 95; II, 12; IV, 15, etc.
2 *Voyages du Chevalier Chardin en Perse, et autres lieux de l'Orient* [...], Amsterdam 1735, Vol. 3 [...] *Description générale de la Perse*, ch. 11, 53.
3 Unfortunately, I could not access the text and had to rely on secondary literature (see Roscioni 1992: 518pp.; also see Berger 2002: 57–91 for an English translation of another work by Roscioni that draws on the same device).
4 Abélard, *Dialogus inter Judaeum, Philosophum et Christianum*, PL, 178, 1617d–1618d.
5 Abélard, *Historia calamitatum*, ch. 12; PL, 164b.
6 I owe my acquaintance with the work of Bouvet to I. Fletcher, op. cit., 153ff.
7 Bouvet, *Apparicion*, I. Arnold's Introduction, XVII.
8 Bouvet, *Apparicion*, V. 289–92, p. 17.
9 Bouvet, *Apparicion*, V. 234, p. 15.
10 Bouvet, *Apparicion*, V. 246–92, p. 16ff.
11 Bouvet, *Apparicion*, Prose 116ff., p. 9; V. 303–6, p. 17ff.
12 Bouvet, *Apparicion*, V. 311–13, 319–22, p. 18.
13 Bouvet, *Apparicion*, V. 420ff., p. 21ff.
14 Bouvet, *Apparicion*, V. 631–6, p. 30. Interestingly, the characterization of Christianity as a religion of love alone is not an invention of Bouvet. It is to be found, with a critical slant, in Muslim authors, e.g. in al-Biruni, op. cit., 433.
15 Bouvet, *Apparicion*, V. 665ff., p. 31.
16 Bouvet, *Apparicion*, V. 767–80, p. 36f.
17 Bouvet, *Apparicion*, I. Arnold's Introduction, XXV–XXVII.
18 Bouvet, *Apparicion*, V. 357–61, p. 19.

References

Al-Amiri (1988) *Kitab al-amad 'ala' l-abad*, II, 18, in E. Rowson *A Muslim Philosopher on the Soul and its Fate* [...], New Haven: American Oriental Society.
Al-Biruni (1983) *India*, edited by A. Safâ, Beirut: 'Alam al-kutub.
Amin, S. (1988) *L'Eurocentrisme: Critique d'une ideologie*, Paris: Anthropos: 162pp.

Arnold, I. (1926) *L'apparicion maistre Jehan de Meun et le Somnium super materia scismatis d'Honoré Bonet* [wrongly for Bouvet], Paris: Belles Lettres and Oxford: Oxford University Press: 1–68 [here: Bouvet, *Apparicion*].

Berger, R. W. (ed. and trans.) (2002) *An Anthology of Source Descriptions, 1323–1790*, New York: Italica Press.

Bertola, F. (1996) *Imago mundi: La représentation de l'univers à travers les siècles*, French translation by A. Hayli, Bruxelles: La Renaissance du Livre.

Boyer d'Argens, J.-B. (1736–1737) *Lettres juives, ou correspondance philosophique, historique et critique, entre un juif voyageur à Paris et ses correspondants en divers endroits*, 4 volumes, Amsterdam.

Boyer d'Argens, J.-B. (1751) *Lettres chinoises, ou [. . .] entre un chinois [. . .] à la Chine, en Muscovie, en Perse et au Japon*, 5 volumes, La Haye.

Brague, R. (1997) "Geocentrism as a Humiliation for Man", *Medieval Encounters*, 3: 187–210.

Brague, R. (2002a) *Eccentric Culture: A Theory of Western Civilization*, translated by S. Lester, South Bend, Indiana: Saint Augustine's Press.

Brague, R. (2002b) "Is Physics Interesting?", *Graduate Faculty Philosophy Journal*, 23(2): 183–201.

Brague, R. (2003) *The Wisdom of the World: The Human Experience of the Universe in Western Thought*, English translation, T. Fagan, Chicago: The University of Chicago Press.

Cadalso, J. (1956) *Cartas Marruecas*, edited by J. Tamayo y Rubio, Madrid: Espasa-Calpe: XLVI, 232pp.

Chklovski, V. (1965 [1917]) "L'art comme procédé", French translation in T. Todorov (ed.) *Théorie de la littérature: Textes des formalistes russes réunis, présentés et traduits par T. Todorov*, Paris: Seuil.

Delanty, G. (2003) "Conceptions of Europe: A Review of Recent Trends", *European Journal of Social Theory*, 6(4): 471–88.

Dufresny, C. R. (1992) "Amusements sérieux et comiques", in J. Lafond (ed.) *Moralistes du XVIIe siècle*, Paris: Laffont.

Fletcher, R. (2003) *La Croix et le Croissant. Le Christianisme et l'Islam, de Mahomet à la Réforme*, translated by C. Loiseau, Paris: Audibert.

Friedman, A. (ed.) (1966) *Collected Works of Oliver Goldsmith, Volume II: The Citizen of the World*, Oxford: Clarendon Press.

Grunebaum, G. E. von (1973) *L'Identité culturelle de l'islam*, translated from French by R. Stuvéras, Paris: Gallimard: 232, n. 2.

Kastner, H. (1997) "Das Gesprach des Orientreisenden mit dem hiednischen Herrscher: Zur Typik und zur Funktion einer interkulturellen Dialogsszene in der Reiseliteratur des Spatmittelalters und der fruhen Neuzeit", in H. Wenzel (ed.) *Gesprache-Boten-Briefe: Korpergedachtnis und Schriftgedachtnis im Mittelalter*, Berlin: Erich Schmidt Verlag.

Lewis, B. (1990) *Comment l'islam a découvert l'Europe*, translated by A. Pélissier, Paris: Gallimard.

Longepierre, H. B. de (2001 [1687]) "Discours sur les Anciens", in M. Fumaroli (ed.) *La Querelle des Anciens et des Modernes*, Paris: Gallimard, pp. 286–9.

Maine, H. S. (1970 [1861]) *Ancient Law*, edited by J. H. Morgan, London: Dent.

Miquel, A. (2000) *L'Orient d'une vie*, Paris, Payot, and *Géographie humaine du monde musulman*, Paris: Colin, Volume 2, pp. 108–14.

Roscioni, G. C. (1992) *Sulle tracee dell: "Esploratore turco"*, Milan: Rizzoli.

Rosendorfer, H. (1994 [1983]) *Briefe in die chinesische Vergangenheit*, Munich: Deutscher Taschenbuch Verlag.

Rubrouck, G. de (1993) *Voyage dans l'empire mongol, 1253–1255*, translated by C-C. and R. Kappler, Paris: Payot.

Strube de Piermont, F.-H. (1978) *Lettres russiennes*, edited by C. Rosso, Pisa: La Goliardica.

Wood, F. (1995) *Did Marco Polo Go to China?*, Boulder, CO: Westview Press.

19 Rethinking Asia

Multiplying modernity

Alastair Bonnett

Asia is a persistent idea. Despite its shifting political and geographical contours, it has gained a seemingly secure place in the modern geopolitical vocabulary. Yet 'Asia' is also persistently represented as something supplementary: as an idea dependent on and derivative of the ur-continent of Europe. Ravi Palat (2002: 687) assures us that, '[s]imply put, Asia's unity derives from, and derives only from, its historical and contemporary role as Europe's civilisational other'. Grounding the argument in etymology, Sakai adopts a similarly commonsensical tone: 'It is well known that the word *Asia* was coined by the Europeans in order to distinguish Europe from its eastern others' (2000: 791). Leo Ching theoretically elaborates the point as follows:

> The principle of [Asian] identity lies outside itself, in relation to (an)Other. If one can ascribe to Asia any vague sense of unity, it is that which is excluded and objectified by the West in the service of its historical progress. Asia is, and can be one, only under the imperial eye of the West.
>
> (1998: 70)

The theoretical heritage behind Ching's depiction is certainly weighty. Deconstruction, psychoanalysis, existentialism and a dialectical theory of the formation of self are all put to work on what is, essentially, a political argument. In this way philosophical abstractions are given historical resonance and spatial content. Fanon and Sartre showed us how rhetorically powerful this combination could be. Yet it is a formula that, in relying on Europe (and 'the West') as the original site of definition, overlooks the ambiguous, transcultural origins of notions of orient and occident, Asia and Europe, both in pre-modern (see Toynbee 1954; Korhonen 2002) and modern Asia.

This chapter addresses 'Asia' as an idea that responds to particular Asian intellectual projects, lineages that relied on and called forth images of Europe and the West. This kind of 'turning of the tables' between Asia and Europe is already a familiar device. It is often allied to a positioning of

'Asia' as an historical agent which 'invented' both itself and the West: examples include Clarke's (1997) *Oriental Enlightenment* and Hobson's (2004) The *Eastern Origins of Western Civilisation* (we might also wish to add Keene 1969 and Hay 1970). However, I intend to offer a more limited argument, one which relies on the identification of the geopolitical imagination of specific Asian intellectuals and resists extrapolation to the anthropomorphic impulse that demands consideration of the 'ambitions' or 'achievements' of nations or regions (see also Sun 2000a, 2000b). I will also exemplify two other, closely related, arguments: (i) that ideas of Asia were developed in relationship with constructions of the West and Europe; and (ii), that these geographical visions were employed and deployed within and through different visions of Asian modernity.

These arguments are sketched through brief assessments of the starkly different images of 'Asia' and 'Europe' offered by two of the most influential interpreters of both of these categories – the Japanese 'Westerniser' and nationalist Fukuzawa Yukichi (1834–1901) and the Indian poet and advocate of spiritual Asia, Rabindranath Tagore (1861–1941). Tagore's pathway led to a rhetoric of 'soulless' and 'industrial' West and an attempt to imagine a non-materialist Asian modernity. Fukuzawa's route demanded a distinction between an advanced and aggressive Europe and a backward, passive Asia; a contrast from which a Japanese project of national modernity (through 'leaving Asia') emerged. The comparison of the geographical imaginations of these two men has far more than purely historical interest. For its legacies and strains can be found at work within many of the contemporary dilemmas that surround Asian identity. The example that I use to show this is the late twentieth-century debate surrounding 'Asia values'. At once a novel moment of Asian self-invention, the idea of 'Asian values' both employed and inverted Fukuzawa's binary, offering a lazy West and a hard-working, productive Asia. Yet it also remained haunted by Tagore's aspiration that Asia could be an utterly different and better place than the West, a community that is more than merely a site of material progress.

Tagore's spiritual Asia

It is difficult for us to sense the excitement and political provocation contained in the opening words of Kakuzo Okakura's *The Ideals of the East* (which first appeared in 1904), that 'Asia is one'. Yet, what a stupendous and improbable idea it is. The notion that there is some shared essence between all the different cultures of this vast space – or, at a more particular level, between, for example, 'Indian culture' and 'Japanese culture' – is an imaginative leap of considerable proportions.

Tagore and Okakura claimed to detect such an essence in spiritual traditions that stretch across a greater portion of the continent, most notably in Buddhism. Yet to even begin naming commonalties immediately opens up the implausible nature of any vision of Asia as a single entity. Buddhism, after all, is a minority religious current in Asia. Moreover, its absorption into regional cultures, from India to Japan, has taken different paths. Thus any claim of contemporary solidarity based upon Buddhism becomes a reclamation and reinvention of a distant past. Okakura, like Tagore, acknowledged that his was a project of historical retrieval, a necessary fabrication of identity: 'For the shadows of the past are the promise of the future' (Okakura 2000: 240).

Paying homage after Okakura's death in 1913, Tagore said, 'from him we first came to know that there was such a thing as an Asiatic mind' (cited in Hay 1970: 38). For Tagore, the West and Europe (terms he used interchangeably) were mechanical, officious civilisations, the antithesis of the organic culture found within Asia. This distinction mapped onto another: the West was essentially urban, and spread itself around the world by way of urbanisation. '[D]ead monotony is the sign of the Nation. The modern towns', Tagore wrote in *Creative Unity* (1922: 144), 'are everywhere the same, from San Francisco to London, from London to Tokyo. They show no faces, but merely masks'.

Tagore cast Asia as a community of tradition that could and should modernise on its own terms. This also implied a vision of Asia as united by its status as a victim of European (per)versions of modernity. The issue of what is meant by freedom was central to Tagore's concerns. He came to associate the term with the possibility of individual and social creativity, a process that he identified in the Asian relationship to the spiritual. Thus, although critical of many areas where freedom and individual development are stymied in the East, he cited Buddhism and the epic poem of Hinduism, the Mahabharata, as an illustration of the possibilities of free expression: 'full of freedom of enquiry and experiment' (1922: 137). Tagore, who travelled extensively and for long periods in both Europe and the USA, was cynical about the claims he heard there about the value Westerners' placed on freedom. In a open letter from New York, published in 1922, he writes that 'In my recent travels in the West I have felt that out there freedom as an idea has become feeble and ineffectual' (Tagore 1922: 133). What Tagore saw in the West was not freedom but a 'spirit of repression and coercion', driven by the industrialisation of social relations and the 'immense power of money' (1922: 136). Tagore was also clear that, as freedom had diminished, the personality and individuality of Westerners had become what he called 'professionalised'; that is, made superficial and vulnerable to political manipulation:

Man as a person has his individuality, which is the field where his spirit has its freedom to express itself and grow. The professional man carries a rigid crust around him which has little variation and hardly any elasticity. This professionalism is the region where men specialise their knowledge and organise their power, mercilessly elbowing each other in their struggle to come to the front.

(1922: 145)

Tagore wanted to break the association, not just between freedom and Westernisation, but also between modernisation and Westernisation. 'Modernism is not in the dress of the Europeans; or in the hideous structures, where their children are interned to take lessons' he argued, 'These are not modern but merely European' (cited in Hay 1970: 70). 'True modernism', he continued, 'is freedom of mind, not slavery of taste. It is independence of thought and action, not tutelage under European schoolmasters. It is science, but not its wrong application in life'.

Tagore was scornful of the way Japan had dramatically 'proved itself' as a modern nation by virtue of its military victory in the Russo-Japanese war (1904–1905). In one of the angriest passages in *Nationalism* (1991; first published 1917), he argues that, Westerners 'admit Japan's equality with themselves, only when they know that Japan also possesses the key to open the floodgate of hell-fire upon the fair earth whenever she chooses' (1991: 39–40).

Tagore's books swarm with fond images of the English romantic poets and he was keenly alert to the utility of science and technology in the alleviation of poverty and oppression. Indeed, his reformist, conciliatory approach made him vulnerable throughout his life to accusations of being a Westerniser. Yet, however much Tagore protested his faith in a 'creative unity' of East and West, his dialectical logic was constantly interrupted by the stereotypes of both Europe and the West he had worked so hard to develop. What I mean by this is that, because Tagore's West was a place of instrumentalism and soulless anomie, it was also a place quite unsuitable for 'creative unity'. It was a civilisation that did not want real contact with others and that was, at root, inherently destructive: 'The dominant collective idea of the Western countries is not creative ... It is wholly wanting in spiritual power to balance and harmonise; it lacks the sense of the great personality of man' (1991: 99).

Tagore's modernity contrasts sharply both with the nationalism fostered by Fukuzawa as well as with the ubiquitous portrayal of modernity as interwoven with industrialisation. However, the inventive capacity of Tagore, his willingness to re-align old identities into new patterns of belonging, suggest he was embarked on a project that is formally similar to these other modernist enterprises. Another parallel can also be drawn, one that concerns the way that the logic of modernity is aligned to a self-questioning and critical sensibility. Themes of uncertainty and reflexivity, along with the challenge of living in 'post-traditional' communities, have become staple topics within Western social theory. They are usually employed to describe the state of consciousness that accompanies post-Fordist capitalism (Beck 1994; see also Lash 1999). Since Tagore wished to defend certain traditional values it is understandable that he does not appear in the kind of historical overview offered by Beck. Yet, Tagore considered himself a defender of the modern. What he was concerned with is the identification of progress and modernity with the West, the conflation that continues to render provincial so much Western social theory. Tagore's notion of a spiritual modernity idea developed mystical and meditative Buddhist and non-doctrinal Hindu traditions, where emphasis is placed on inner reflection and the removal of dogmatic conceit. It is an individualistic exploration that has the restless quality of a perpetual and dissatisfied seeking for 'unity' and 'reconciliation'. 'In dogmatic religion', Tagore tells us, 'all doubts are laid to rest'. Tagore's own understanding of religion is, he says, 'indefinite and elastic': it offers 'no doctrine or injunction' and 'never undertakes to lead anybody anywhere to any solid conclusion; yet it reveals endless spheres of light, because it has no walls round itself' (1922: 16). This language of spiritual self-discovery found a following in the West, partly because it appears to offer transcendental experience without succumbing to the rigid anachronisms of conventional Christianity. However, there is little that is 'alternative' about Tagore's approach to the spiritual. It represents, rather, a reflexive, self-questioning approach to the problem of modernity, an approach that hopes to embrace modernity without being over-impressed by the instrumental logic that, Tagore claimed, characterises its Western incarnation.

Fukuzawa: nationalist modernity in and against Asia

Fukuzawa Yukichi is the most well known and influential of the nineteenth-century Japanese Westernisers. Born in 1834, as a child Fukuzawa studied *rangaku* ('Dutch learning') at school in Nagasaki, at a time when the Dutch were the only Westerners allowed even limited entry into the country. In 1862 he was part of the Takenouchi mission to the West, the first of a series of official Japanese investigations of Western society, industry and economic development. His glowing account of what he saw was published in 1866 ('Conditions in the West', 1958) and became an immediate best seller. Fukuzawa later wrote the primary school textbook, *World Geography* (1959; first published 1869), which drew on similar material and explicitly placed Europe at the centre of world civilisation.

In terms of the structure of Fukuzawa's argument, China has as important a role in *An Outline of a Theory of Civilization* (1973) as the West. It is China that is represented as static and passive, China that is cast as hopelessly archaic and vulnerable to national humiliation. Where these attributes are located in Japan they are cast as stemming from the age-old domination of Japanese culture by China. The following passage exemplifies this 'othering' of China, as well as hinting at the aggressive and nationalistic foreign policies that Fukuzawa's work was later taken to condone. Such phrases as 'be gentle, modest, and deferring to others', or 'rule by inaction', or 'the holy man does not have ambition' ... all refer to inner states which in the West would be described as merely 'passive' (Fukuzawa 1973: 79).

For Sakamoto (2001: 149), Fukuzawa may be identified as holding 'Western racialist-Orientalist images' of China. However, the notion that Fukuzawa's vision of Asia was a mere repetition of a master discourse of East and West disseminated from the West is inadequate. 'Asia', 'the East' and 'the West' were ideas already in circulation in Japan before their elaboration in the West. Iida (1997: 412) notes that, as early as 1715, Arai Hakuseki had offered a 'proto-type of the notion of Asia' when he contrasted the East as 'spiritual civilisation' to the 'material civilisation' of the West. In *Japan's Orient*, Stefan Tanaka (1993) details the long history of orientalist and occidentalist commentary. Tanaka also argues that the 'shift' from China to the West as the dominant influence on Japanese culture,

> did not entail the simple replacement of China by the West ... The difference between the use of China and the use of the West was that the previous world was one in which all life was construed as being part of a fixed realm ... The West brought a different perspective, the probable future; knowledge was infinite.
>
> (1993: 32–3)

The most well known slogan associated with Fukuzawa concerns the relation between Japan, the West and Asia. The title of his essay *Datsu-a nyu-o* (1997), first published in 1885, has been translated as 'On leaving Asia', 'Disassociating Asia' and, more simply, 'Good-bye Asia'. It suggests that Japan must now consider itself part of Western civilisation and thus 'dissociate' itself from its barbaric and doomed neighbours:

> We do not have time to wait for the enlightenment of our neighbors so that we can work together toward the development of Asia. It is better for us to leave the ranks of Asian nations and cast our lot with civilized nations of the West. As for the way of dealing with China and Korea, no special treatment is necessary just because they happen to be our neighbors. We simply follow the manner of the Westerners in knowing how to treat them.
>
> (Fukuzawa 1997: 353).

This stance did not suggest that Japan should cut itself off from Asia but, rather, that Japan was a nation of a different order, a higher type. Saying good-bye to Asia meant being more involved with it; not as an equal but in a similar fashion to other Western powers. This position was also developed by Fukuzawa to suggest that Japan was the natural leader and defender of weak and anarchic Asian nations against Western military might. As Sakamoto (1996) has shown, this attitude to Asia, whilst more explicit and clearly colonialist towards the end of Fukuzawa's life, was present throughout his work. He goes on to argue that Fukuzawa's work 'annuls the West/Japan dichotomy', leaving the 'civilisation/non-civilisation dichotomy' intact, and ' "Asia" [to function] as the negative Other of civilised Westernised/hybridised Japan' (1996: 125). Sakamoto's real target here is the political naiveté of contemporary theories of hybridisation. He concludes that 'the construction of a hybrid discourse, at least in Japan's case, led to the exclusion of another Other, which Bhabha's theory ignores. To "go beyond" one dichotomy without creating yet another may not be an easy project' (1996: 126).

Clearly, Fukuzawa's work does not sustain a vision of hybridity as a kind of 'open' and reflexive third moment. Indeed, to extend Sakamoto's argument, I would cast doubt on the utility of conceptualising his work as an example of hybridity at all. Fukuzawa actively fashioned a certain representation of the West to suit his own (and, in large measure, his social class's) particular political ambitions. This process is best understood as a creative and original intervention in the history of the idea of the West that can be positioned alongside the contributions of Kidd, Spengler and Toynbee in Europe (Gogwilt 1995; Bonnett 2004), as well as other intellectuals in the 'non-Western' world (such as Tagore): intellectuals engaged with the challenge of working out the meaning of modern national and international identities.

It is through Fukuzawa's desire to invent and shape identity that his modernity emerges most clearly. This attitude, one of the few he shares with Tagore, ensures that collective identities become denaturalised and emerge as 'foci of contestation and struggle' (Eisenstadt 2000: 7). The central identities for Fukuzawa are Europe, the West, Asia, China and, above all, Japan. For Fukuzawa modernity is a discourse of national independence. It is a form of resistance to Western hegemony that co-opts Western civilisation in order to both preserve national autonomy and ensure its continued existence. Despite Fukuzawa's reputation as a reformer, his primary motivation is to conserve the nation. 'Japan's uniqueness', Fukuzawa notes 'lies only in the fact that she has preserved national polity intact from earliest antiquity and has never been deprived of her sovereignty by a foreign power' (2000: 27). At the end of *An Outline of a Theory of Civilisation* he reminds readers that his 'ultimate goal' is 'national independence and all aspects of life [should be] made to converge on this single goal ... Whether institutions, learning, business, or industry, they are all means to this end' (1973: 196).

The ideas of 'the West' and of 'Asia' are employed and deployed by Fukuzawa in order to fashion not just a new Japan but a Japan that is capable of surviving in an increasingly aggressive and predatory world. Fukuzawa's West is a place of meritocracy and rational learning, a place where the middle class thrives and where a sense of national community and solidarity ensures an active, participatory population. Yet despite Fukuzawa's desire for a profound cultural shift towards the West, he also continued to conceptualise the West as a set of traits that could be bolted on to an existing primordial national unit: 'Western civilization is the best possible means of making our country strong and our Imperial line flourish, so why should we hesitate to adopt it' (cited in Blacker 1969: 33). Thus he made fun of unthinking Westernisers who had forgotten the national *raison d'être* of the modernising impulse. Such folk, says Fukuzawa, believed 'in the new with the same belief that they had believed in the old' (cited in Blacker 1969: 39).

Asian values and the idle West

In 1931 Budhhadev Bose had already announced that 'the age of Tagore was gone' (cited in Chakrabarty 2000: 160). The transition from predominantly colonial to post-colonial regimes across Asia that occurred from the late 1940s onwards ushered in new generations of leaders keen to assert modern, forward-looking, national agendas. The rise of Asian independence corresponded with a shift in the way Europe and the West were imagined. Most obviously, the association of power, of political and economic decision making, with Europe and the West, could be challenged, not just by Japan and China, but by countries across the continent.

It was predictable that, as the levers of power became decolonised, and the institutions and ideologies of nation-building took an ever more dominant position, the post-national, anti-political, aspirations articulated by Tagore would appear increasingly utopian. Indeed, the themes of creativity and individual freedom, which Tagore saw as being crushed in the West, were given a negative spin and associated by those who, in the 1980s and 1990s, came to espouse 'Asian values' with chaos, decline and decadence. By the end of the century the 'Asian image of the West' was transformed: not so much soulless as work-shy; not a ghastly, efficient machine stamping conformity and alienation across the planet but an individualistic, welfare-dependent yet anti-social creature that could no longer 'keep up' with Asia. It is a curious transition: for it turned Asia into the scold of the West for not possessing the very qualities that Tagore most despised. Fukuzawa's caricature of a passive Asia which must be rejected in order to embrace national modernity was also turned on its head. Within 'Asian values' narratives, it is the passive, idle West that must be rejected, in order to embrace a regional modernity centred on the cliché of 'hard working Asians'.

One constant within this transition is the centrality of representations of Europe and the West to claims on modernity and Asia. 'The West' is employed and deployed in ways that suggest, not simply or merely its fictive character, but that Asia has continued to be a site for its imaginative construction. Today, the arguments of both Tagore and Fukuzawa may appear to have been rejected. Yet each man is associated with images of Asia that continue to haunt the present. Fukuzawa's quest for national modernity remains a potent model, not only in Japan. The nationalisms formed through independence struggles have combined with the continuing difficulty of instituting Asian regional governance to ensure the prominence of the 'modernising nation-state' amongst Asian visions of the future. Indeed, after the East Asian economic crisis of 1997 the Malaysian social scientist Khoo Boo Teik described how quickly the regional aspirations implied by 'Asian values' could evaporate,

> Now the miracle has turned to meltdown in the short period of one and half years, Asians have been scrambling to distinguish themselves from other Asians – not least in the eyes of a Western-dominated international money market. Under the conditions which began in July 1997, the consensus of the Asian state elites over critical issues – so to speak, a surrogate measure of the workability of the principle of 'Asian consensus' – has been almost nowhere in sight.
>
> (1999: 188)

Neither has Fukuzawa's stereotype of Asian passivity entirely disappeared. The nagging, anxious fears it plays on have a clear presence in the attempts by proponents of 'Asian values' to create a region-wide *disciplinary* and *transformatory* culture based on an 'Asian work ethic'.

An irony within narratives of 'Asian values' is the lack of interest they exhibit in the diverse heritages of Asia outside of those deemed to sustain economic progress. At the same time, it is revealing that 'Asian values' are routinely rooted in 'Asian traditions', even in 'Asian religious traditions'. This reminds us that Tagore's distinction between Asian spirituality and Western soullessness is not quite dead. Despite being cast into a strange, sentimental, limbo, it retains a certain symbolic power. What it symbolises is *cultural depth*. Asian spirituality remains attached to – or, perhaps, we should say clings to – the idea of Asia. I shall return to this attachment later, after addressing the reciprocal relationship between 'Asian values' and 'Western values'.

Asian values bring together economic goals with supposedly *traditional* family values and *traditional* networks. Such a combination of old and new is said to promise a different, less disruptive and less inhumane, route to modernisation (as compared, inevitably, with Western industrialisation). A related notion, once surprisingly prevalent even in Europe and the USA, had it that business practices in the Far East are less brutal and instrumental than those in the West. In the words of business journalist Shui-shen Liu, the Chinese 'pay more attention to human relations than to "things" ... In the West "things" are more important than human relations' (cited in Tai 1989: 19). However, it is significant that, although strong family ties and collectivism can both be found across Asia, it is the supposed *absence of the work-ethic* that differentiated Asians outside the fold of the Asian values debate (especially South Asians) in the 1980s and 1990s, from those at its centre (East Asians). East Asians, the Malaysian intellectual, Noordin Sopiee has argued, are characterised by their ability to 'work very hard' and a disposition to 'saving and thriftiness' (cited in Milner and Johnson 2002). Indeed, Asian religious and mystical traditions have been emptied of transcendental content and put to work to suggest that the work-ethic has a specific, East Asian, heritage. Thus, for example, Japanese Buddhism, and Confucianism in a number of East Asian countries, have been used to explain and illustrate a disposition towards asceticism, self-discipline and self-sacrifice. By contrast India, as Francis Fukuyama puts it, has the wrong kind of Asian religion: it suffers from the 'toper and inertia' encouraged by Hindu mysticism. Hinduism, Fukuyama tells us, 'is in many respects the opposite of the spirit of capitalism' (1992: 228).

Asian values perspectives emphasise social cohesion and community. However, societal progress is measured, overwhelmingly, in economic terms. In *Can Asians Think?*, the Singaporean ambassador to the United Nations, Kishore Mahbubani, was unapologetic about the primacy of wealth creation as the focus and destiny of Asian culture. Answering 'yes' to the bizarre question he poses in his title, Mahbubani finds the conclusive evidence from a single source, 'the incredible economic performance of East Asian societies in the past few decades' (1998: 23). As with nearly all proponents of Asian values, Kishore Mahbubani's idea of Asia relies on an interpretation of what is wrong with the West. Tagore's concern with soulless and mechanical Westernisation is replaced by a West of decadence and indulgence. The debauched, idle and self-destructive West is not a new image, either in the West or Asia. However, its ubiquity and unrivalled deployment in the 1980s and 1990s to shape what Asia is, more specifically to shape the Asian ideal, was unprecedented. The West's 'undoing' is not merely a favourite theme amongst advocates of Asian values but a *defining* theme: without 'Western decadence' the notion that real or good Asians are devoted to wealth creation would be incomprehensible and easily rendered as a shallow and materialistic subversion of Asian identity. Mahbubani provides a fairly typical account of Western decline:

> Only hubris can explain why so many Western societies are trying to defy the economic laws of gravity. Budgetary discipline is disappearing. Expensive social programs and pork-barrel projects multiply with little heed to costs. The West's low savings and investment rates lead to declining competitiveness vis-à-vis East Asia. The work ethic is eroding while politicians delude workers into believing that they can retain high wages despite becoming internationally uncompetitive.
>
> (1998: 97)

The twin themes of the work-shy West and the violent, 'out of control' West can be found throughout Asian values narratives. It is an assessment that carries a historical judgement. For it shows, as Singapore Prime Minister, Goh Chok Tong, put it during his National Day speech on 21 August 1994 that 'societies can go wrong quickly':

> US and British societies have changed profoundly in the last 30 years. Up to the early 60s they were disciplined, conservative, with the family very much the pillar of their societies. Since then both the US and Britain have seen a sharp rise in broken families, teenage mothers, illegitimate children, juvenile delinquency, vandalism and violent crime.
>
> (cited in Sheridan 1999: 72)

The Singaporean sociologist Soek-Fang Sim has highlighted the suspiciously over-zealous way that anti-social behaviour is presented as Western. This kind of geographical despatching of the sins of modernity never rings true. 'With the increasing realisation that the 'West' is within and inevitable, that Singaporeans are indelibly Westernised', Sim (2001: 51) argues, this kind of rhetoric is required, 'not only to protect the Singapore nation from the dangerous West but also to protect Singapore from Singaporeans'. In other words, Goh's and Mahbubani's attitude towards the West represents a displacement of internal problems. It is a process of purification of the nation that sanctions and demands strict protection and self-discipline as well as the perpetuation of an image of the West as an external, ever looming, 'folk-devil'.

The shift, in the late twentieth century, to notions of an Asian regional identity that are eagerly submissive to neo-liberal globalisation has subverted the appeal of Asian spirituality. Some will be tempted to describe this shift in terms of a decline in the ability of South Asia to determine the meaning of Asia and the rise of pragmatic, secular East Asia.[1] However, since such an explanation would have the effect of cementing stereotypes whose creation is part of our enquiry, it is better to approach these regional attributes as changeable and temporary. Moreover, the ideal of Asian spirituality is not entirely dead in Asia today. It is, rather, petrified: frozen into cultural capital, into a symbol of Asian ethnic specialness. It is sustained as a marketable cultural distinction, one that implies that, no matter how ferocious and flexible the labour market may be in East Asia, certain values, especially those associated with the family, will remain unchanged. In this way, a non-instrumental essence of Asianess continues to be invoked, in large measure, because it consolidates the legitimacy of the dominant paradigm of economic growth. Perhaps, though, it is retained for another reason too. Asian spirituality clings to our imagination because it is an idea made necessary by the revolutions of modernity; it offers a necessary hope. For whilst Asian values and Western values now chorus that, in the words of Deng Xiaoping, 'to get rich is glorious', many continue to sense that materialistic, industrialised lives are not full lives; that there may be some other type of value in Asia.

The vision of Asia as containing the potential to transcend both the West and industrialised modernity, a vision associated with 'Asian spirituality', continues to be hard to dispatch entirely. It casts its shadow over the debate, especially whenever Asian 'family values' are relied on as the uncommercialised, bedrock of humane conduct that will help Asia get through its latest economic crisis. It also has a certain sickly presence in the conduct of Asian statism: the state that directs all, knows all, looks after the righteous and punishes the wrong-doers, takes on the role of an omnipresent and all-knowing deity. More concretely, it was political nous rather than woolly liberalism that seems to have spurred the Malaysian deputy Prime Minister, Anwar Ibrahim to flesh out a conception of a more democratic and less soulless Asia – to be achieved by what he called an 'Asian Renaissance' – in the early 1990s (Ibrahim 1996). Ibrahim's project explicitly cited Tagore as an inspiration. It also directly challenged Mahathir's 'Asian values', an act of insubordination that many consider to have provoked Ibrahim's persecution (and lengthy jail sentence). Ibrahim's contention that 'Asian man at heart is *persona religiosis*' (cited in Milner and Johnson 2002), reflected not simply a renewed interest in Muslim identity in Malaysia but also the continuing ability of the idea of Asia to imply another kind of modernity.

Conclusions

Tagore worried that Western colonialism had become the paradigm for all intercultural contact:

> The modern age has brought the geography of the earth near to us, but made it difficult for us to come into touch with man. We go to strange lands and observe; we do not live there. We hardly meet men: but only specimens of knowledge. We are in haste to seek for general types and overlook individuals.
>
> (Tagore 1922: 95)

For Tagore, the development of alienated, instrumental relations between people encourages a hollow cosmopolitanism, in which people are able to travel extensively, encountering many different cultures, yet never experience any vulnerability or desire for genuine exchange. '[O]ur knowledge of foreign people grows insensitive', wrote Tagore (1922: 95), coming to resemble the way that 'Western people' know about other people yet 'do not recognise any obligation of kinship'.

Europeans and Asians know each other and themselves through a range of stereotypes, which, as we have seen, have been central to the construction of particular visions of Asia (including Tagore's own). I have crudely sketched two very particular visions – Tagore's 'Asian spirituality' and Fukazawa's 'passive Asia', and shown some of the connections each has with a more general and contemporary expression of Asian identity, namely 'Asian values'. All three of these imaginative geographies are structured around representations of Europe and the West, representations which were used to develop different 'Asian visions' of modernity. The multiplicity of modernity is now an established theme in historical and international research (Gaonkar 1999; Sachsenmaier *et al.* 2002; Bonnett 2005). The phrase 'Western modernity' is becoming less and less available as a tautology. This chapter has sought to evoke the intimate association that exists between the articulation of modernities and the creation of images of Europe and Asia. To trace these patterns may, perhaps, help us challenge the kind of arrogance that is the target of Tagore's observations; thus unshackling cosmopolitanism from the presumption that either modernity, or the great geographical ideas of our era, are rooted permanently in the West.

Note

1 In the country once seen as the home of Asian spirituality – India – Asian identity has been increasingly ignored. National considerations and the rise of more immediate and pressing regional, South Asian and East Asian identities led towards Indians' disassociation from a wider sense of 'their continent'. By the end of the century Ravi Palat, writing in *The Hindu* in December 2000, felt able to be unequivocal about 'India's excision from dominant conceptions of Asia'. This process, he noted, has occurred 'both in the West and in much of Southeast and East Asia, as indicated by [East Asian focused] debates on "Asian values"'. Another reflection of this process is that Tagore's Asianist imagination is barely mentioned by recent 'post-colonial' writers. Rather, Spivak (2001) and Chakrabarty (2000: 178) stress his contribution in terms of an 'irreducible ... aesthetic moment' in the politics of colonialism.

References

Beck, U. (1994) 'The Reinvention of Politics: Towards a Theory of Reflexive Modernisation', in U. Beck, A. Giddens and S. Lash (eds) *Reflexive Modernization: Politics, Tradition and Aesthetics in the Modern Social Order*, Oxford: Polity.

Blacker, C. (1969) *The Japanese Enlightenment: A Study of the Writings of Fukuzawa Yukichi*, Cambridge: Cambridge University Press.

Bonnett, A. (2004) *The Idea of the West: History, Culture and Politics*, Houndsmills: Palgrave

Bonnett, A. (2005) 'Occidentalism and Plural Modernities: Or, how Fukazawa and Tagore Invented the West', *Environment and Planning D: Society and Space*, 23: 505–25.

Chakrabarty, D. (2000) *Provincialising Europe: Postcolonial Thought and Historical Difference*, Princeton: Princeton University Press.

Ching, L. (1998) 'Yellow Skins, White Masks: Race, Class, and Identification in

Japanese Colonial Discourse', in K. Chen (ed.) *Trajectories: Inter-Asian Cultural Studies*, Routledge: London, pp. 65–8.

Clarke, J. (1997) *Oriental Enlightenment: The Encounter Between Asian and Western Thought*, London: Routledge.

Eisenstadt, S. (2000) 'Multiple Modernities', *Daedalus*, 129(1): 1–29.

Fukuyama, F. (1992) *The End of History and The Last Man*, London: Hamish Hamilton.

Fukuzawa, Y. (1958) 'Seiyo Jijo' [Conditions in the West], in *Fukuzawa Yukichi Zenshu*: Vol. 1, Tokyo, Iwanami Shoten, p. 511.

Fukuzawa, Y. (1959) 'Sekai Kunizukushi' [World Geography], in *Fukuzawa Yukichi Zenshu*: Vol. 2, Tokyo, Iwanami Shoten, pp. 591–668.

Fukuzawa, Y. (1973) *An Outline of a Theory of Civilization*, Tokyo: Sophia University Press.

Fukuzawa, Y. (1997) 'Good-bye Asia (Datsu-a), 1885', in D. Lu (ed.) *Japan: A Documentary History: The Late Tokugawa Period to the Present*, Armonk: M. E. Sharpe.

Gaonkar, D. (1999) 'On Alternative Modernities', *Public Culture*, 11(1): 245–68.

Gogwilt, C. (1995) *The Invention of the West: Joseph Conrad and the Double-mapping of Europe and Empire*, Stanford: Stanford University Press.

Hay, S. (1970) *Asian Ideas of East and West: Tagore and his Critics in Japan, China, and India*, Cambridge: Harvard University Press.

Hobson, J. (2004) *The Eastern Origins of Western Civilisation*, Cambridge: Cambridge University Press.

Ibrahim, A. (1996) *The Asian Renaissance*, Singapore: Times Books International.

Iida, Y. (1997) 'Fleeing the West, Making Asia Home: Transpositions of Otherness in Japanese Pan-Asianism, 1905–1930', *Alternatives*, 22: 409–32.

Keene, D. (1969) *The Japanese Discovery of Europe, 1720–1830*: Revised edition, Stanford: Stanford University Press.

Korhonen, P. (2002) 'Asia's Chinese Name', *Inter-Asia Cultural Studies*, 3(2): 253–70.

Lash, S. (1999) *Another Modernity, A Different Rationality*, Oxford: Blackwell.

Mahbubani, K. (1998) *Can Asians Think? Understanding the Divide between East and West*, South Royalton, Vermont: Steerforth Press.

Milner, A. and D. Johnson (2002) 'The Idea of Asia', at www.anu.edu.au/asianstudies/ideas.html, accessed 28/08/02.

Okakura, K. (2000) *The Ideals of the East, with Special Reference to the Art of Japan*, ICG Muse, New York and Tokyo.

Palat, R. (2000) 'India and Asia', *The Hindu*, Monday 4 December at www.hinduonnet.com/thehindu/2000/12/04/stories/05042524.htm, accessed 28/08/02.

Palat, R. (2002) 'Is India part of Asia?', *Environment and Planning D: Society and Space*, 20: 669–91.

Sachsenmaier, D., S. Eisenstadt and J. Riedel (eds) (2002) *Reflections on Multiple Modernities: European, Chinese and Other Interpretations*, Leiden: Brill.

Sakai, N. (2000) ' "You Asians:" On the Historical Role of the West and Asia Binary', *The South Atlantic Quarterly*, 99(4): 789–817.

Sakamoto, R. (1996) 'Japan, Hybridity and the Creation of Colonialist Discourse', *Theory, Culture and Society*, 13(3): 113–28.

Sakamoto, R. (2001) 'Dream of a Modern Subject: Maruyama Masao, Fukuzawa Yukichi, and 'Asia' as the Limits of Ideology Critique', *Japanese Studies*, 21(2): 137–53.

Sheridan, G. (1999) *Asian Values, Western Dreams: Understanding the New Asia*, St Leonards, New South Wales: Allen & Unwin.

Sim, S. (2001) 'Asian Values, Authoritarianism and Capitalism in Singapore', *Javnost: The Public*, 8(2): 45–66.

Spivak (2001) 'The Burden of English', in G. Castle (ed.) *Postcolonial Discourses: An Anthology*, Oxford: Blackwell.

Sun, G. (2000a) 'How Does Asia Mean? (Part II)', *Inter-Asia Cultural Studies*, 1(2): 319–41.

Sun, G. (2000b) 'How Does Asia Mean? (Part I)', *Inter-Asia Cultural Studies*, 1(1): 13–47.

Tagore, R. (1922) *Creative Unity*, London: Macmillan.

Tagore, R. (1991) *Nationalism*, London: Macmillan.

Tai, H. (1989) 'The Oriental Alternative: An Hypothesis on Culture and Economy', in H. Tai (ed.) *Confucianism and Economic Development*, Washington: Washington Institute Press.

Tanaka, S. (1993) *Japan's Orient: Rendering Pasts into History*, Berkeley: University of California Press.

Teik, Khoo Boo (1999) 'The Value(s) of a Miracle: Malaysian and Singaporean Elite Constructions of Asia', *Asian Studies Review*, 23(2): 181–92.

Toynbee, A. (1954) *A Study of History: Volume VIII*, London: Oxford University Press.

20 Critical intellectuals in a global age

Asian and European encounters

Fred Dallmayr

So long as it remains true to itself, philosophy partakes in the lived experience of its time, including its traumas and agonies. Among the most prominent features of our age is the process of globalization, that is, the perceived shrinkage of the globe into a commonly shared space. Although acutely felt in the domains of economics and information technology, the significance of this process is not always sufficiently acknowledged by philosophers and social theorists. Sometimes geographical labels are attached to perspectives or schools of thought, like "Continental philosophy", "Frankfurt School" and so on – labels whose meaning is often belied by what is happening on the ground. Thus, travelers in distant lands may find there more vibrant resonances of "Continental" thought than can be found in Europe today, just as seminal ideas of the early "Frankfurt School" are sometimes more intensely discussed in Asia or Latin America than in their native city. This does not mean that European perspectives are simply disseminated across the world without reciprocity or reciprocal learning. Nor does it mean that local origins are simply erased in favor of a bland universalism (since local origins are often inscribed with concrete and singular sufferings). What it does mean is that landscapes and localities undergo symbolic metamorphoses, and that experiences once localized at a given place increasingly find echoes or resonance chambers among distant societies and peoples.

Symbolic migration today is characteristic of several intellectual or theoretical perspectives – including, perhaps most prominently, the perspective of "analytical" or "Anglo-American" philosophy (whose teachings sometimes exert hegemonic claims around the world). However, a similar outreach also marks Continental-European thought and social theory. No doubt, the latter perspective exhibits a great variety of distinct orientations and emphases. Yet, for purposes of the present discussion, I want to highlight what I consider the chief common traits of Continental-European thought as it developed (roughly) during the past century. As it seems to me, the central common trait of this thought – especially when compared with the "analytical" perspective – is its close attention to the theory–praxis connection, that is, the connection of thinking and doing.

This entails an opposition to "pure" theory or a purely spectatorial theorizing which, aiming at objective knowledge, distances the spectator or analyst rigidly from the targets of his/her analysis. The basic underpinnings of this spectatorial approach can be found in the modern Cartesian worldview which, in separating subject and object (*cogito* and extended matter), provided the engine for the rise of modern science and technology (and generally the replacement of quality by quantity). The difference of outlooks has social implications: while spectatorial theory is congenial to, and favored by, people satisfied on the whole with "the way things are" and "the powers that be", practical theorizing appeals mainly to people alienated from the way of the world and bent on some kind of transformation. Seen in this light, Continental-European thought (in its different versions) has tended to be mostly critical and self-critical – by mounting a sustained critique of the modern cult of science, technology and the market and, more broadly, of the "underside of modernity". In the following I shall first highlight the "critical" dimension pervading Continental-European thought in recent times. Next, I shall discuss parallel critical arguments advanced in the content of non-Western societies, with special attention to Indian social thought. In doing so, I follow in a way the lead of Ulrich Beck who, not long ago, called for "a new critical theory with a cosmopolitan intent" (Beck 2003: 453–68). By way of conclusion, I offer some comments on the prospects of a global critical theory.

European critical thought

As indicated, Continental-European thought (as the term is used here) comprises a number of distinct strands. For present purposes I shall refer to three main perspectives: critical theory (Frankfurt School); phenomenology and hermeneutics (Freiburg School); and deconstruction (French School). Early critical theory provides us with a document which, in instructive fashion, highlights both the practical (or praxis-related) and critical dimensions of European thought of the period: Max Horkheimer's programmatic essay on "Traditional and Critical Theory" (of 1937). In this essay, Horkheimer sharply opposes to each other two kinds of theory: namely, "traditional" theory (corresponding to what I have called a purely spectatorial mode of theorizing) and a critical outlook steeped in practical social engagement. Following the French philosopher of science, Henri Poincaré, Horkheimer defines the gist of traditional theory as "the sumtotal of propositions about a subject, the propositions being so linked with each other that a few are basic and the rest derive from these". The definition contains two components: the propositional and the factual. While the validity of such a theory depends on the correspondence of propositions with actual facts or states of affairs, the propositions themselves aim at the greatest possible parsimony and logical transparency. Following again Poincaré, Horkheimer adds that traditional (or scientifically verifiable) theory constitutes a matrix of "stored-up knowledge, put in a form that makes it useful for the closest possible description of facts". In line with the "unified science" movement popular at the time (and supported by Poincaré), the ultimate perfection of pure theory consists in a limited set of highly abstract propositions whose validity extends to the largest possible number of data, and in the end to all phenomena in the world: "The general goal of all theory is a universal systematic science, not limited to any particular subject matter but embracing all possible objects" (although we are still "rather far from such an ideal situation") (Horkheimer 1972 [1937]: 188–9; see also Poincaré 1905: 105).

As Horkheimer points out, the origins of this mode of theorizing are not of recent date but can be traced to "the beginnings of modern philosophy", and particularly to the Cartesian worldview with its division of subject and object, *cogito* and extended matter, where the former is placed in the analytical judgment seat. In accord with Descartes' conception of method, knowledge properly speaking resides in a set of "clear and distinct" ideas, linked together through chains of deductive reasoning, and ultimately translatable into mathematical formulas. Insofar as this conception of theory shows a tendency, the essay states, it is "toward a purely mathematical system of symbols" – a tendency which by logical necessity progresses from the natural sciences to the human and social sciences as well. In more recent times, the Cartesian worldview has been continued especially by positivists and logical positivists whose overall emphasis has been on transforming philosophy (or theorizing) into a "handmaiden" of science. Although more attentive to practical and social concerns, even the so-called "pragmatists" followed the positivist lead by construing praxis in a purely "instrumental" sense, thereby subjecting it to the efficiency criteria of existing society. What persists from Descartes to positivism and pragmatism is the predominance of the Cartesian paradigm (with its "dualism of thought and being") which assigns to the theorizing scholar an extra-mundane or purely spectatorial position – although this position on closer inspection turns out to be illusory. For, no matter how "independent" and "detached" the expert's knowledge may claim to be, the scholar and his/her theorizing remain "incorporated into the [existing] apparatus of society". To this extent, the scholar's achievements and "original" contributions are "a factor in the conservation and continuous renewal of the existing state of affairs, no matter what fine names s/he gives to what s/he does" (Horkheimer 1972 [1937]: 189–90, 196–7).[1]

By contrast to this spectatorial outlook, "critical" theorizing presupposes the participatory engagement of the theorist in his world. In Horkheimer's account, the task of critical intellectuals is not to be pliantly supportive of an existing state of affairs, but to problematize and call into question this state from an existential and normative angle; hence, the relation between such intellectuals and their society is necessarily "marked by tension" and this tension characterizes "all the concepts of the critical mode of thinking". Given its accent on participatory engagement, critical theorizing clearly departs from the Cartesian worldview with its separation of *cogito* and nature, observer and target of analysis. In the words of the essay: "The inability to grasp in thought the unity of theory and praxis, and the limitation of the concept of necessity to inevitable [causal] events are both due, from the epistemological viewpoint, to the Cartesian dualism of thought and being" – a dualism which is "congenial both to nature and to bourgeois society insofar as the latter resembles a natural mechanism". In the traditional mode of theorizing – this is for Horkheimer the "decisive" point – the targets of analysis are not at all affected by the theorist's endeavors, nor are these endeavors in turn affected by, or responsive to, dilemmas in the "external world". Being a part of the prevailing "mode of production", the traditional mainstream scholar simply registers and acknowledges existing social conditions (which seem to be ineluctable like forces of nature) without taking a stand. Critical intellectuals are unable to operate in this fashion. In their case, theorizing responds to and inserts itself in the ongoing dilemmas and agonies of social life, from a practical and normative perspective. Simply put: "Critical theory of society is, in its totality, the unfolding of a single existential judgment" (Horkheimer 1972 [1937]: 208, 227–9, 231).

The notion of an "existential judgment" brings into view the conception of a social ethics which is not purely cognitive but rooted in historical experience – without being merely subjective or arbitrary. Proceeding from a broadly Marxian vantage, Horkheimer sees modern Western history as exhibiting a dialectic of progress and regress, of growing emancipation and domination. As he writes, the kind of commodity economy on which modern history rests "contains in itself all the internal and external tensions of the modern era; it generates these tensions in an increasingly heightened form, and after a period of progress ... [may drive] humanity into a new barbarism". Deviating from even a non-orthodox Marxian ideology, Horkheimer does not find any historical assurance that the decline into barbarism can be averted – except for the efforts of resistance on the part of critical intellectuals who at all times are in short supply. "The idea of a transformed society", he writes soberly, "does not have the advantage of widespread acceptance". In the general course of events, "truth [meaning: existential-ethical truth] may reside with numerically small groups of people". Yet, he adds, "history teaches us that such groups, hardly noticed even by those opposed to the status quo, outlawed but imperturbable, may at the decisive moment become the leaders because of their deeper insight". Returning to the notion of existential judgment, Horkheimer concludes his essay by stressing the crucial importance of such judgment whose place cannot be usurped by pure theory, formal logic or mathematical algorithms, for all its insight into social life and social change:

critical theory has no specific influence on its side, except the abolition
of social injustice. This negative formulation, if we wish to express it
abstractly, is the materialist content of the idealist concept of reason.

(Horkheimer 1972 [1937]: 227, 241–2)

Despite a diversity of philosophical and political premises, many of the
basic points of Horkheimer's essay find a parallel in both Continental
phenomenology and deconstruction. A major affinity resides in the effort
to overcome traditional "metaphysics" (or pure theory), and especially the
predominance of the Cartesian egocentric worldview. In the latter respect,
Edmund Husserl's life-work constitutes a crucial waystation in the formation of contemporary Continental thought. From the time of his early writings, Husserl's central aim was to breach the Cartesian subject–object split
through the accent on the "intentional" directedness of human consciousness, captured in the motto "to the things themselves" (*zu den Sachen*).
Far from celebrating the pure self-confinement of reason in a kind of metaphysical narcissism, his practice of "phenomenology" urged reason to
venture into the world of phenomena and to allow itself to be nurtured
and enriched by this experience. To be sure, despite his principled remon-
strations, Husserl's approach in many ways remained heir to the Cartesian
(and neo-Kantian) paradigm – a fact evident in his attachment to "transcendental idealism" and his fondness for mathematical logic. Nevertheless, his later writings amply testify to his dissatisfaction with this legacy.
A major text of that period is entitled *Cartesian Meditations* – a magister-
ial work showing the phenomenologist wrestling with the spirit (or ghost)
of the Cartesian method. Still later, his disenchantment with positivism
and logical empiricism led Husserl to launch a sustained assault on the
rootlessness of the modern scientific enterprise, that is, its growing divorce
from practical engagement and the concrete experiences of the social "life-
world".[2]

Husserl's life-work was carried forward in novel directions by Martin
Heidegger's "hermeneutical phenomenology" with its accent on "worldli-
ness" – human existence being defined as "being-in-the-world" – and a
further move away from metaphysical theorizing. In his *Being and Time*
(of 1927), Heidegger offered a sustained critique of modern metaphysics,
insisting on the implausibility or untenability of both the Cartesian *cogito*
and Kant's transcendental consciousness. In turning to the linkage of
"being" and "time", the text underscored the importance of the experience
of finitude or mortality – stylized in the expression of "being-toward-
death". At the same time, the central trademark of being human was
shifted in the text from "reason" (or animal with reason, *animal rationale*)
to the dimension of "care" (*Sorge*) – a shift which marks a decisive move
from cognition to praxis. In fact, it is possible to argue that all of Heidegger's central terms – from "being" to language to "*Ereignis*" – should be
seen not as nouns (amenable to pure theorizing) but as verbs calling for a

transformative praxis. As in the case of Husserl, it is true that Heidegger himself did not always draw the required conclusions from his thought (and at least in one instance drew precisely the wrong conclusion). Nevertheless, the practical as well as critical-social implications of his work can hardly be denied. In terms of praxis-orientation, many observers have pointed to certain affinities with Aristotelian ethics as well as a certain non-instrumental form of pragmatism. As Lawrence Hatab observes correctly, for Heidegger human existence "*is* what it *does*", disclosing itself in "its living dealings and movements"; to this extent, Heideggerian ethics is released from the subject–object and fact–value binaries of the Cartesian paradigm while approximating the Aristotelian notion of the self as "essentially an activity, not a static essence". In terms of social-historical critique, Heidegger's work is well known for its sharp denunciation of the modern cult of science and technology, especially the cult of giant control mechanisms (*Gestell*) from whose vantage human beings appear as mere cogs in a machine (see Heidegger 1974 and Hatab 2000: 63, 72, 102).[3]

The practical orientation of (Freiburg-style) Continental thought is even more pronounced in the case of Hans-Georg Gadamer whose "philosophical hermeneutics" is basically centered on engaged praxis – where the latter means an engagement with texts, with fellow-beings, and with social-historical constellations. As Gadamer notes in an essay specifically titled "Hermeneutics as Practical Philosophy", hermeneutics or the endeavor to make sense of texts and experiences is indeed "philosophical", but in the sense of what traditionally has been called "practical philosophy". This means that, seen as an ongoing effort to understand, hermeneutical interpretation cannot be stabilized in an abstract metaphysical system, nor can it be reduced to a mere technical skill or a mechanically applied recipe. Rather, given the variety of concrete contexts, understanding has to remain constantly open and responsive to situational challenges, precisely in the way of an engaged social praxis. In Gadamer's words, there is a "mutual implication" between understanding and practical action – and it was Aristotle who first thought through this implication "with complete lucidity" in his ethics with its central category of *phronesis*. This outlook stands again in complete contrast with the modern Cartesian worldview with its emphasis on spectatorship and the instrumental mastery of nature through technical fabrication or construction. This "ideal of technical production" implicit in the concept of mechanics, Gadamer states at another point, has had a triumphant ascendancy in modern times and has in fact "become an arm prolonged to monstrous proportions" – a development which has made possible "the nature of our machines, our transformation of nature, and our outreach into space" for purposes of planetary control. What is eclipsed and threatened with erasure in this development is the domain of practical engagement in collaborative understanding, that is, "the realm of all that transcends utility, usefulness, and instrumental calculation" (Gadamer 1981: 70–1, 77, 111; compare with Taylor 1985: 91–115).

The practical and social-critical components were further intensified in French existential phenomenology, particularly the writings of Jean-Paul Sartre and Maurice Merleau-Ponty. Specially memorable in the case of Sartre was his denunciation of orthodox Marxism – and of any comprehensive ideology – for celebrating an abstract "scholasticism of the totality", while neglecting the inevitably "heuristic" character of every inquiry and the praxis-orientation of social theorizing (Sartre 1963: 22, 26–8).[4] In the case of Merleau-Ponty, critique of dominant ideologies was from the beginning part and parcel of his "genetic" phenomenology (concerned with the "becoming" of phenomena) and extended from Communist to liberal political doctrines. His book *Humanism and Terror* (1947) contains this startling passage (whose relevance has only increased with time): "An aggressive liberalism exists which is a dogma and already an ideology of war. It can be recognized by its love for the empyrean of principles, its failure ever to mention the geographical and historical circumstances to which it owes its birth, and its abstract judgment of political systems without regard for the specific conditions under which they develop". Turning to the praxis-dimension of political life, the book added: "It is not just a question of knowing what the liberals have in *mind* but what in reality is *done* by the liberal state [or the state professing to defend freedom] within and beyond its borders" (italics added). For Merleau-Ponty, the relation to praxis was endemic not only to political thought, but to philosophy in general – despite an acknowledged need to avoid narrow partisanship. Far from allowing the philosopher to abscond into an ivory tower, his *Eulogy of Philosophy* ascribed to theoretical reflection a practical task: "One must be able to withdraw and gain distance in order to become truly engaged, which is also, always, an engagement in the truth". Yet, "the very detachment of the philosopher assigns to him a certain kind of action among fellow-men". Here is a passage from the same text which eloquently captures the gist of critical Continental thought:

> At the conclusion of a reflection which at first isolates him, the philosopher, in order to experience more fully the ties of truth which bind him to the world and history, finds neither the depth of himself nor absolute knowledge, but a renewed image of the world and of himself placed within it among others.
>
> (Merleau-Ponty 1969, 1963)

Despite a certain intellectual sea-change – which happened around 1968 – many of the discussed accents of hermeneutics and phenomenology continue to reverberate in late twentieth-century European thought, including French post-structuralism and deconstruction. To some extent, this persistence can even be detected in the writings of Jacques Derrida – a thinker whose work is often associated with radical rupture and a complete dismissal of social agency. What is correct about this reputation is Derrida's undeniable radicalization of the critique of the Cartesian *cogito* and his dismantling of human self-identity in favor of a resolute openness to the "Other's" initiative. Yet, precisely in light of this dismantling, a transformed kind of agency comes into view bent, no longer on predatory mastery but on a generous hospitality toward others (akin to Heidegger's "letting be"). In his famous "Reflections on Today's Europe", Derrida urged Europeans (and people in the West more generally) to open themselves up to the rest of the world more hospitably than was the case in the past (when colonialism and "white man's burden" were the preferred policies). In the same text, he also encouraged liberal democrats, comfortably ensconced in "lands of the free", to ponder the possibility of a more generous mode of democratic life – what Derrida called a "democracy to come" or a "democracy that must have the structure of a promise" (thus cannot now be cognitively mapped or managed). For Derrida, the same openness or generosity is also the hallmark of philosophical thinking as such – a thinking which is not the privilege of mandarins nor the monopoly of self-appointed experts but a general human birthright in need of practical cultivation. As he stated at one point (echoing Merleau-Ponty): "The right to philosophize becomes increasingly urgent", as does the call for philosophers to evaluate and critique perspectives that "in the name of a technical-economic-military positivism" tend to reduce the field and the chances of an "open and unrestricted philosophizing" both in colleges and in international life (Derrida 1992: 77–9; 2002: 15).

Non-Western critical thought

Derrida's call for a critical kind of theorizing or philosophizing – one opposed to the hegemonic "positivism" (in technological, military and economic domains) – obviously is not restricted to the confines of Europe, but has a "cosmopolitan intent". The French philosopher's cosmopolitan or cosmopolitical leanings are well known – having been voiced on numerous occasions, including his text *On Cosmopolitanism* (of 2001).[5] As it happens, his summons today finds echoes or resonances in many parts of the world, from Asia to Africa and Latin America. Actually, given the intrusive and oppressive effects of the reigning "positivism" in most non-Westerns societies, critical theorizing tends to be widespread and at a premium precisely in those parts of the world. In the following, I shall be able to give only a very limited sample of non-Western critical intellectuals voicing their opposition to mainstream positivism as well as to a purely spectatorial (and ethically irresponsible) mode of theorizing. In view of my own frequent and extended visits to India, I shall concentrate my discussion first on theoretical initiatives on the subcontinent, before extending my review to other parts of the world.

In post-independence India, the closest parallel to the outlook of the early Frankfurt School – as articulated in Horkheimer's programmatic essay – can be found in the Centre for the Study of Developing Societies (CSDS) operating in Delhi since 1963. In its structure and design, the Delhi Centre from the beginning resembled its German counterpart: particularly in its emphasis on interdisciplinary cooperation (comprising scholars from the humanities, the social sciences and psychology) and its concerted effort to bridge the theory–praxis divide. As a result of its interdisciplinary character, studies sponsored or published by the Centre have dealt with a broad spectrum of topics: ranging from the ethnic and social-psychological components of social change to problems of rural development and ethnoagriculture to the role of science and technology in the modern world. In terms of theoretical orientation, a primary role has always been played by Rajni Kothari, the initial founder and longtime director of the Centre.[6] Trained both in India and the West, Kothari has distinguished himself (like Horkheimer) as a scholar and institution builder; in addition he has been an activist on all levels (local, national and international) of politics. About ten years after founding the Centre, he was instrumental in launching the quarterly *Alternatives*, a journal that soon emerged as a leading forum in India for the discussion of issues relating to social change and global transformation. Both his scholarly and his practical-political talents coalesced in 1980 when, together with other Centre colleagues, he inaugurated the movement "*Lokayan*" (meaning "dialogue among people"), designed as an arena for the meeting of academics, policy-makers and activists concerned with grassroots initiatives. His moment of greatest public visibility came in 1989 when, following the defeat of Rajiv Gandhi, he joined the National Front government as a member of the national Planning Commission.

Among Kothari's prolific writings, I want to single out for present purposes these four: *State Against Democracy* (1988), *Transformation and Survival* (1988), *Rethinking Development* (1989) and *Growing Amnesia* (1993). Subtitled "In search of humane governance", the first volume was written mainly in protest against the policies of Indira and Rajiv Gandhi whose regimes were denounced for their attempt to marshall state power – what Derrida might have called state positivism – against the democratic aspirations of the people. In large measure, the book was meant as a challenge to the relentless process of centralization that, during the post-independence period, was steadily molding India into a uniform "nation-state" along Western lines. Buttressed by the resources of modern technology and corporate business, this nation-state – in Kothari's view – was re-erecting or deepening the structure of social inequality which the struggle against colonialism had aimed to erase. The situation was further aggravated by the progressive militarization of the state promoted in the name of "national security". These and related factors conspired to produce a socio-political crisis which, according to Kothari, was changing or perverting the character of the state: namely, from "being an instrument of liberation of the masses to being a source of so much oppression for them" (see Kothari 1988a: 60).[7] The critique of state-centered accumulation of power was extended into the global arena in the second book, *Transformation and Survival*. Paralleling the growing stratification of domestic society, the operation of the international state system – in Kothari's account – promoted and reinforced a global structure of asymmetry between North and South, "developed" and "developing" societies, and center and periphery. As on the national level, this global asymmetry was compounded by the concentration of technological, economic and military resources in the hands of hegemonic (developed) states or superpowers. In combination, these forces posed a threat to the natural environment, international peace and ultimately the survival of humankind itself.

As an antidote to these dangers, the two cited volumes formulated an alternative vision of human existence and socio-political life that was not beholden to any of the reigning ideologies of the time. In fact, as Kothari insisted, it was necessary to move beyond both the liberal-capitalist and the orthodox Marxist paradigms, since both derived from the same Cartesian worldview: they were both "offshoots of the same philosophic pedigree of the Enlightenment and nineteenth-century (mechanistic) humanism" with their unlimited faith in progress fueled by technological mastery over nature. In lieu of this "modernist" and positivist pedigree, the books invoked the legacy of Mahatma Gandhi whose life-work had challenged Western imperialism while at the same time enlisting popular grassroots beliefs and traditions for democratic purposes. In both his writings and his actions, Gandhi had thus honored "the moral imperative of treating [ordinary] people as a source in the recovery of a humane order". In addition to Gandhian teachings, the texts also drew inspiration from various left-leaning modes of political radicalism wedded to the promotion of human freedom and social justice. As used by Kothari, "freedom" was not a synonym for the pursuit of libertarian self-interest nor for a retreat into public abstinence, but rather denoted the capacity (or capability) for public participation and the promotion of social well-being. To this extent, the notion of "human rights" signaled not only private entitlements or privileges as rather basic constituents of a good and "humane" social order (see Kothari 1988a: 2–3, 151; also 1988b: 6, 170–1).

Kothari's *Rethinking Development* sought to expose both the pitfalls and the muddle-headedness of much of the dominant literature and planning in this field. Both in mainstream writings and mainline policy-making, he noted, "development" has tended to be equated with unfettered economic and industrial expansion propelled by advances in modern science and technology. As was to be expected, this approach has engendered not only a deadly arms race and a wasteful, consumption-driven economy, but also a pernicious class structure on both the national and the global levels. As a consequence, democracy was under siege both at home and in the world at large. For Kothari, the trouble with the dominant approach was that it was not only difficult to implement but inherently flawed and misguided. Echoing again Horkheimer, his text located the root problem of the "developmental" ideology in its attachment to a dominant worldview or philosophical doctrine which, although originating in Europe, was now encircling the globe: the "doctrine of modernity" according to which "the end of life is narrowly defined as to be within the grasp of all – progress based on economic prosperity". Fueled by Enlightenment teachings, this doctrine presented social advancement entirely as a matter of social engineering, backed up by "science-based technology"; all that human beings and societies had to do according to this model was to "discard tradition and superstition and become rational and 'modern' ". In language reminiscent (but also sharpening the edge) of the "dialectic of Enlightenment" articulated by Horkheimer and Theodor Adorno, *Rethinking Development* asked these questions:

> Isn't the theory of progress, as developed in the West, based on an anthropocentric view of nature and a positivist conception of knowledge and science, which are responsible for a model of development spelling domination and exploitation? And if these be the essence of Occidental culture and its contribution to human thought and values shouldn't we discard large parts of it, and look for alternative modes of thought and values embedded in some other cultures?
>
> (Kothari 1989: 3–5, 48–9, 51)[8]

Growing Amnesia was published four years later, in the wake of the dismantling of the Soviet Union and the vanishing of the so-called "nonalignment" policy (sponsored by India and other "developing" countries). Although widely hailed in the West as the dawn of a new "world order", the emerging global situation raised serious worries and apprehensions for Kothari. In his view, the turn of events signaled basically the triumph of corporate capitalism, a triumph that augured ill for the cause of social justice and participatory or grassroots democracy. Given the concentration of power and wealth in developed countries and multinational conglomerates, the existing gulf between North and South, centre and periphery was prone to be further deepened, while the fate of underprivileged masses around the world was bound to be abandoned to apathy or else consigned to "growing amnesia". Above all, the priority granted to policies of "deregulation" and "liberalization" of the market was bought at a steep price: its overall effect was to "destabilize the democratic polity, put the masses under severe strain, turn against labor and further marginalize the poor". To be sure, the remedy for deregulation could not reside in a centralized state bureaucracy controlling and planning every facet of social life in a top-down fashion. In opposition to the dystopias of both the Leviathan state and unchecked market forces, *Growing Amnesia* sponsored a social-democratic alternative where the apparatus of the modern state was retained but sharply refocused in the direction of democratic participation and self-rule. Embracing again aspects of the Gandhian legacy, the alternative placed a strong accent on political and economic decentralization as an antidote to technocratic or corporate elitism. Such a shift of accent, Kothari argued, was guided and inspired by a commitment to "take people seriously", by "respecting their thinking and wisdom" and by fostering institutions that would "respond to their needs". Only by following these guideposts was it possible to avoid both plutocracy and rampant consumerism and to establish an economic system that, in Gandhi's words, "not only produces for the mass of the people but in which the mass of the people are also the producers" (Kothari 1993: 8–9, 123, 134, 149–51).

Next to Kothari, the most prominent member of the Delhi Centre is Ashis Nandy, a senior fellow and sometime director of the institute. In its basic thrust, Nandy shares Kothari's political orientation: the commitment to democratic transformative change – but a change popularly or locally legitimated rather than imposed by hegemonic (colonial or neocolonial) forces. A main difference between the two thinkers has to do with disciplinary focus: whereas Kothari has tended to center-stage issues of political economy and sociology, Nandy – a trained psychologist and psychoanalyst – has been more concerned with psychic or psychocultural sources of popular resistance as well as the inner traumas of colonial oppression. One of his early publications, *At the Edge of Psychology* (1980), traced the intersections linking politics, culture and psychology, especially as experienced in non-Western societies. His next book, *The Intimate Enemy* (1983), probed these linkages more concretely by focusing on the introjection or internalization of the colonizer's worldview, which, among the colonized, can lead to self-hatred and "loss of self". Nandy's own alternative vision was outlined in *Traditions, Tyranny, and Utopia* (1987), especially in the chapter "Toward a Third World Utopia". The chapter deliberately took its stand at the grassroots level by viewing the world "from the bottom up". As Nandy emphasized, the notion "Third World" was not a timeless, metaphysical idea but rather a political and economic category "born of poverty, exploitation, indignity and self-contempt". Given this stark historical background, the formulation of an alternative future for non-Western societies had to start from the experience of "man-made suffering" – not for the sake of inducing self-pity, but in order to permit a therapeutic "working through" of the traumas of oppression. As helpmates in this process of coping and working through, the text invoked the healing powers latent in indigenous traditions, especially powers like those tapped in the Gandhian struggle for independence. An additional helpmate was the relative distance of non-Western cultures from the modern Cartesian paradigm with its dualisms and dichotomies – between subject and object, humans and nature, and colonizers and colonized (Nandy 1987a: 21, 31–5; see also 1980 and 1983).

In still more forceful terms, Nandy's alternative vision for the future was spelled out in his essay "Cultural Frames for Social Transformation: A credo", published in the Centre's journal *Alternatives* (in 1987). The essay took its point of departure from the anti-colonial struggle in Africa, especially from Amilcar Cabral's stress on popular or indigenous culture as a counterpoint to hegemonic oppression. In Nandy's view, this outlook could be extended to other colonial or postcolonial societies. Basically, the stress on indigenous legacies signaled a defiance of the modern (Western) idea of intellectual and scientific "expertise" uncontaminated by popular customs or beliefs; it gave voice to societies and peoples "which have been the victims of history and are now trying to rediscover their own visions of a desirable society". In our time of relentless globalization and Western-style standardization, this kind of self-assertion and defiance gained global significance. To this extent, the stress on "cultural frames of social transformation" constitutes in our time "a plea for a minimum cultural plurality in an increasingly uniformized world". One of the prominent features of global standardization was for Nandy the imposition of the model of the "nation-state" and Western-style nationalism in all parts of the world, including the Indian subcontinent. This topic was pursued further in his subsequent study, *The Illegitimacy of Nationalism* (1994), which launched a blistering attack on the rise of centralization and nationalist standardization which have become dominant traits of post-independence India. In Nandy's portrayal, nationalism and nation-state structures are basically Western imports foisted indiscriminately on non-Western societies and cultures. Indigenous cultural resources are again marshaled as antidotes to this imposition. Following the lead of Gandhi and Rabindranath Tagore, Nandy stressed the highly ambivalent role of nation-states as agents of both liberation and oppression; as an alternative he postulated a global perspective rooted in "the tolerance encoded in various traditional ways of life in a highly diverse, plural society" (Nandy 1994: x–xi; see also 1987b: 113–16).

In his critique of nationalism and the nation-state, Nandy comes close to the position of another major intellectual school in post-independence India: the so-called "Subaltern Studies" project launched by the historian Ranajit Guha around 1982. By comparison with the Delhi Centre, the Subaltern Studies movement (in its early phase) was more directly inspired by the teaching of Antonio Gramsci and humanist Marxism. For members of the movement, the gaining of independence and the erection of the Indian nation-state were only very superficial and ambivalent accomplishments, involving basically the transfer of power from Britain to post-colonial bourgeois and capitalist elites. A major articulation of this outlook was provided by Partha Chatterjee, a prominent social scientist working and teaching in Calcutta. In his *Nationalist Thought and the Colonial World* (1986), Chatterjee denounced nationalist independence as a borrowed ideology and purely "derivative discourse": concealing and legitimating a mere shift in the agents of domination. His subsequent book, *The Nation and Its Fragments* (1993), offered a more nuanced and differentiated assessment, attentive to recent post-Marxist and post-structuralist tendencies. In this respect, Chatterjee's work is representative of a broader intellectual realignment characterizing the Subaltern Studies movement as a whole. In writing a preface to a volume seeking to provide an overview of the movement, Edward Said perceptively registered a certain shift away from the school's earlier Marxist and Gramscian moorings. As he observed: "None of the Subaltern Scholars is anything less than a critical student of Karl Marx"; moreover, today "the influence of structuralist and post-structuralist thinkers like Derrida, Foucault, Roland Barthes and Louis Althusser is evident, along with the influence of British and American thinkers, like E. P. Thompson, Eric Hobsbawm, and others" (Said 1988: x; also compare Chatterjee 1986 and 1993).

Apart from multi-member institutes and research agendas India is, of course, replete with talented and innovative individual thinkers. For present purposes (given limitations of space), I want to single out three prominent recent philosophers: Daya Krishna, Sundara Rajan and J. L. Mehta. Trained both in India and the West, Daya Krishna has been keenly attentive to, and critical of, dominant paradigms promulgated by Western social scientists during the Cold War era. Foremost among these were the formulas of "development" and "modernization" postulating the progressive assimilation of non-Western societies to Western yardsticks. For Krishna, these formulas were both theoretically confused and socio-politically obnoxious. As he queried in his book *Political Development* (1979), how could one speak of linear development in the case of cultural frameworks, more specifically when comparing artworks of modernity with those of Greek antiquity or else with the masterpieces of India and China? Socio-politically, he added, the relevant distinction should not be between "developed" and "undeveloped", but between "good" and "bad" or legitimate and illegitimate political regimes. His compatriot Sundara Rajan has been similarly critical of linear or one-dimensional schemes of social advancement, relying for his purposes on a combination of social phenomenology and Frankfurt School critical theory. As he wrote in his book *Innovative Competence and Social Change* (1986): "If the alignment of [Frankfurt-style] communicative competence and [phenomenological] social theory could be defended, then I suggest we have a possibility of carrying over a 'transcendental' point of view into the domain of social theory". In Rajan's later writings, the influence of Continental hermeneutics – especially Paul Riceour's version – became steadily more decisive, leading him to differentiate between contextual "signification" and a more de-contextualized critical-emancipatory "symbolization". In J. L. Mehta's case, finally, the most striking features of his work are the resonances he developed between Indian classical thought and aspects of Heideggerian ontology and Gadamerian hermeneutics.[9]

Turning to East Asia, one finds again a plethora of innovative and critical perspectives, developed by both Buddhist and Confucian intellectuals and scholars. In the Buddhist camp, one must mention first of all the renowned Kyoto School of philosophy in Japan, inaugurated by Kitaro Nishida and further developed by such thinkers as Keiji Nishitani, Hajime Tanabe, Hisamatsu Shin'ihi and Masao Abe. In the case of all these thinkers the resonances with Continental thought are pronounced: while Nishida's work makes frequent appeal to Kierkegaard, Bergson and Husserl, the writings of Nishitani and others reveal a more distinct Heideggerian slant. Given the heavy emphasis of the entire school on such key Zen notions of "nothingness" and "emptiness" (*sunyata*), one may wonder about the practical implications of their perspective. However, as soon as the affinity of "*sunyata*" with Heidegger's "nihilating nothingness" is taken into account, the practical and critical impulses spring instantly into view. For clearly, from the angle of nihilation, Buddhist thought can have no truck with totalizing modes of domination (with Derrida's "technical-economic-military positivism"). The only proper and legitimate form of action or agency, under Zen Buddhist auspices, is a non-possessive and non-domineering kind of action – traditionally called "*wu-wei*" (again akin to Heidegger's "letting be").[10] Outside the confines of Kyoto, more resolutely praxis-oriented forms of Buddhist thought have emerged in recent decades in many parts of Asia and South Asia. Sometimes labeled "Buddhist liberation movement" or movement of "engaged Buddhism", this outlook – often aiming at radical social transformation – is represented by such figures as Thich Nhat Hanh (from Vietnam), the Dalai Lama (from Tibet), Sulak Sivaraksa (Thailand), A. T. Ariyaratne (Sri Lanka) and the late Dr Ambedkar (India). (Compare, for example, Hanh 1967, Sivaraksa 1994 and Ambedkar 1984. See also Queen and King 1996.) Despite limitations imposed by the regime in mainland China, Confucianism has also experienced a remarkable revival in East and Southeast Asia, often with a critical edge against centralizing or totalizing types of government. (Compare, for example, Tu 1985, Bell and Hahm 2003 and Dallmayr 1998b: 123–44.)

Contrary to simplistic assumptions much in vogue in the West, Islamic societies today are not uniformly dominated by dogmatic-clerical or "fundamentalist" doctrines, but display a rich welter of intellectual orientations – some of them with clearly practical-critical overtones. In Southeast Asia, the prototype of a critical Muslim intellectual is Chandra Muzaffer, head of an NGO called "Just World Trust", whose publications and public statements have been exemplary in denouncing both Western aggressive or imperialist policies and unjust or corrupt practices in the Islamic world (see, for example, Muzaffer 2002 and 1993). Some of the liveliest intellectual debates in that part of the world are carried on today in Iran, with "reformers" and "conservatives" engaging each other in sustained exchanges on philosophical and political issues – often with a high degree

of erudition and sophistication. As in India and East Asia, European resonances can readily be detected in these exchanges, particularly in the arguments of reformers whose writings frequently appeal to Continental
perspectives, ranging from the Vienna School to Husserlian phenomenology,
Heideggerian ontology, Gadamerian hermeneutics and French-style postmodernism.[11] The influence of phenomenology and hermeneutics can also be
found in the works of other Muslims thinkers, such as the Egyptian philosopher Hassan Hanafi (2000), while aspects of Frankfurt School critical
theory surface in the publications of the Moroccan Mohammed al-Jabiri
(see, for example, Hanafi 1965 and Abed al-Jabiri 1999). Limitations of
space prevent here a discussion of intellectual debates in Africa and Latin
America – except to say that, in the one case, the legacies of Frantz Fanon
and Aime Césaire continue to provide powerful support to critical praxis
while, in the other case, the writings of Paolo Freire, Enrique Dussel and
others testify to their unflagging commitment to a "pedagogy of the
oppressed" (see, for example, Freire 1982; Dussel 1995; Schutte 1993;
Fanon 1968; Césaire 1968; Hountondji 1996; and Masolo 1994).

Toward a global public sphere

The preceding discussion was meant to provide a glimpse into arenas of critical theorizing in many parts of the world, and thus to counteract parochial
assumptions of a European (or Western) monopoly in the domain of critical
philosophy and social thought. As has been shown, networks of critical
intellectual life are present around the globe, stretching from East and South
Asia to the Middle East, Africa and South America; as has also been indicated, many of these networks stand in close and reciprocal interactions
with schools or perspectives originating on the Continent. In our age of
globalization, these interactions are bound to multiply and to deepen,
leading to the emergence of a global community of critically engaged intellectuals – an updated and cosmopolitan version of the traditional "republic
of letters". This development is crucially important in our time of immense
superpower predominance, a domination which – following the model of
earlier imperial systems – is hostile to the cultivation of critical scrutiny and
contestation. To speak with Jacques Derrida, it is imperative in our time to
defend the "right to philosophy", that is, the right to critical theorizing
among ordinary people around the world, as an antidote and response to
the dictates of a coercive "technical-economic-military positivism". In
Derrida's sense, this defense is necessary in order to preserve the open spaces
needed for unregimented and "unrestricted" inquiry and questioning – open
spaces which, in turn, serve as heralds or anticipations of a "democracy to
come". To express the point in somewhat different language: the emerging
global networks of critical thinking can be seen as waystations to the formation of a global public sphere – a sphere indispensable for anything like a
democratically constituted cosmopolis.

In his plea for a "critical theory with a cosmopolitan intent", Ulrich Beck mentions a number of challenges or tasks which must be tackled by the emerging networks of critical global theorizing. Foremost among these tasks is the need to break through and dismantle the ideological tactics and obfuscations employed by dominant hegemonic or nationalist powers, above all "the forms and strategies used to render cosmopolitan realities [or possibilities] invisible". These strategies are particularly evident whenever existing global institutions or norms are bypassed or erased in the name of the protection of "national security" interests. Prominent examples that come to mind are the evisceration of provisions of the United Nations Charter, the shuttling of the Geneva Conventions, and the erosion of codes of military conduct. Next to the need to contest such strategies, Beck stresses the role of innovative social and political imagination, that is, the endeavor to make theoretical room for open spaces going beyond the confines of national sovereignties (but without merely surrendering to a global superpower). In his words, what is called for is a "re-imagination of the political" which would explore and experiment with "the difference between the national viewpoint of political actors and the cosmopolitan perspective" becoming available today. Specifically reserved for critical intellectuals everywhere is the additional task of rethinking and reformulating prevailing conceptual categories – especially categories used in social and political analysis – in favor of new and more "hospitable" theoretical frames of reference. As Beck summarizes his argument, the main focus in contemporary debates revolves around "gaining a new cosmopolitan perspective on the global power field, pushing new actors and actor networks, power potentials, strategies, and forms of organization of 'debounded' politics into the field of vision" (Beck 2003: 467).

To return to some points made at the beginning of this chapter: critical theory situates itself in the prevailing agonies and dilemmas of the age and is willing to take a practical and normative stand in opposition to injustice, cruelty and oppression. This does not mean that critical theory does not think or theorize – which would render it blind or myopic; but it does allow its thinking to be informed and nurtured by practical experience. In doing so, critical theorizing stands opposed to what Max Horkheimer called "traditional theory" and what I have termed a purely spectatorial stance – the assumption that human beings can be mere spectators or onlookers in a world torn apart by so much turmoil, misery and suffering (and today the possibility of a nuclear holocaust). As indicated before, this spectatorial stance was in large measure promoted by the modern Cartesian worldview and its offshoots (as well as by certain modes of traditional metaphysics). What is required in our time is perhaps not a complete dismantling of this worldview but its resolute recasting and reformulation – in such a manner that spectators can return as participants in their experienced life-world. The old dispute between theory and praxis is thus not resolved in favor of a blind activism, but in favor of a more thoughtful and responsible praxis. Given the retreat of Cartesian egocentrism, this praxis is destined to be non-domineering, enabling and liberating – without insisting at any point on its own meritorious agency or achievements. To recall a passage penned by Horkheimer toward the conclusion of his essay: "Critical theory has no specific influence on its side, except concern for the abolition of social injustice. This negative formulation . . . is the materialist content of the idealist concept of reason".

Notes

1 The essay includes in the category of traditional or spectatorial theorizing also the "neo-Kantianism of the Marburg School" with its emphasis on universal categories and the pure "*logos*" of the world-mind (1972 [1937]: 198). As Horkheimer acknowledges (1972 [1937]: 204), Hegelian philosophy tried to overcome the Kantian antinomies (of noumena/phenomena, of activity/passivity) by "sublating" them on the level of objective and absolute spirit. However, this solution remained "a purely private assertion, a personal peace treaty between the philosopher and an inhuman world".

2 Compare in this context Husserl (1973) and (1970).

3 As Hatab adds (2000: 109): "In a way we can understand Heidegger's ontology as a radicalization of Aristotelian teleology that inscribes creative openness into temporal development". Compare with Zimmerman (1990).

4 The *Search* served as prefatory essay to Sartre's ambitious *Critique of Dialectical Reason* (1960).

5 The text *On Cosmopolitanism* is based on an address by Derrida to the International Parliament of Writers in Strasbourg in 1996, titled "*Cosmopolites de tous les pays, encore un effort!*"

6 A brief introduction to the perspective and work of the Centre is provided by Kothari (1989: 23–43). For a more detailed discussion of Kothari and the Centre see Dallmayr (1998a: 219–40).

7 As one should note, Kothari did not entirely condemn the modern state. In a progressive democratic vein, he endorsed the state provided it served as an agency of democratization and a guardian of the common people.

8 Among the alternative modes of thought, Kothari included cultural and religious traditions of non-Western societies. In his words (1989: 50): "The religions and civilizations of India, of the Islamic world, of the complex of humanist thought that has informed China, and of Buddhism provide major streams of thought that could substantially contribute to the present search for alternatives". As one should note, however, the text in no way supported a simple anti-Western or anti-modern stance, but rather conceded (1989: 52) that modernity is "part of us all" just as "the West is part of us all".

9 Compare with the above Krishna 1979: 187, 190, 201, and 1965; Rajan 1986: 87–9, 1987 and 1991; and Mehta 1976, 1985 and 1990. For a fuller development of these thinkers' views, see the chapters "Heidegger, Bhakti, and Vedanta" and "Modernization and Postmodernization" in Dallmayr 1996: 89–114, 149–74. Apart from these philosophers there are several social and political theorists who, in their own ways, have articulated a critical Indian perspective. Among them I should mention Thomas Pantham (University of Baroda); Vrajendra Raj Mehta (former Vice-Chancelor of Delhi University); Rajeev Bhargava (Delhi University); Ananta K. Giri (Center for Developing Societies, Chennai), and the prominent expatriate political theorist Bhikhu Parekh (now Lord Parekh), a leading student of Gandhi's thought.

10 For some writings of Kyoto School thinkers, see Nishida (1958), Nishitani (1982), Tanabe (1987) and Shin'ichi (1971). An important recent development the Kyoto Forum for Public Philosophizing in Common: see Kim 2006.
11 On intellectual debates in Iran, see, for example, Boroujerdi 1996, Jahanbaksh 2001, Mirsepassi 2000 and Jahanbegloo 2004. Compare also the section "Toward an Islamic Modernity?" and the chapter "Islam and Democracy: Reflections on Abdolkarim Soroush" in Dallmayr 2002: 100–4, 167–84.

References

Abe, M. (1985) *Zen and Western Thought*, Honolulu: University of Hawaii Press.
Abed al-Jabiri, M. (1999) *Arab-Islamic Philosophy: A Contemporary Critique*, trans. A. Abassi, Austin: University of Texas.
Ambedkar, B. R. (1984) *The Buddha and His Dharma*, 3rd edn, Bombay: Siddarth Publications.
Beck, U. (2003) "Toward a New Critical Theory with a Cosmopolitan Intent", *Constellations*, 10(3): 453–68.
Bell, D. and C. Hahm (eds) (2003) *Confucianism for the Modern World*, Cambridge: Cambridge University Press.
Boroujerdi, M. (1996) *Iranian Intellectuals and the West*, Syracuse, NY: Syracuse University Press.
Césaire, A. (1968) *Return to My Native Land*, trans. E. Snyders, Paris: Présence Africaine.
Chatterjee, P. (1986) *Nationalist Thought and the Colonial World: A Derivative Discourse*, Tokyo: Zed Books.
Chatterjee, P. (1993) *The Nation and Its Fragments: Colonial and Postcolonial Histories*, Princeton: Princeton University Press.
Dallmayr, F. (1998a) *Beyond Orientalism: Essays on Cross-cultural Encounter*, Albany, NY: State University of New York Press.
Dallmayr, F. (1998b) "Global Development? Alternative Voices from Delhi", in *Alternative Visions: Paths in the Global Village*, Lanham, MD: Rowman & Littlefield.
Dallmayr, F. (2002) *Dialogue Among Civilizations: Some Exemplary Voices*, New York: Palgrave MacMillan.
Dallmayr, F. (2003) "Humanity and Humanization: Comments on Confucianism", in *Alternatives Visions*, pp. 123–44.
Derrida, J. (1992) *The Other Heading: Reflections on Today's Europe*, Bloomington, IN: Indiana University Press.
Derrida, J. (2001) *On Cosmopolitanism and Forgiveness*, London: Routledge.
Derrida, J. (2002) "The Right to Philosophy from the Cosmopolitan Point of View", in P. P. Trifonas (ed.) *Ethics, Institutions, and the Right to Philosophy*, Lanham, MD: Rowman & Littlefield.
Dussel, E. (1995) *The Invention of the Americas: Eclipse of the "Other" and the Myth of Modernity*, trans. M. D. Barber, New York: Continuum.
Fanon, F. (1968) *The Wretched of the Earth*, New York: Grove Press.
Freire, P. (1982) *Pedagogy of the Oppressed*, New York: Continuum.
Gadamer, H-G. (1981) "Hermeneutics as Practical Philosophy", in Gadamer, *Reason in the Age of Science*, trans. F. G. Lawrence, Cambridge, MA: MIT Press.

Hanafi, H. (1965) *Les méthodes d'exégèse*, Cairo: Conseil des Arts.

Hanafi, H. (2000) *Islam in the Modern World*, 2 vols, Cairo: Dar Kebaa.

Hanh, T. N. (1967) *Vietnam: Lotus in a Sea of Fire*, with a foreword by T. Merton, New York: Hill & Wang.

Hatab, L. J. (2000) *Ethics and Finitude: Heideggerian Contributions to Moral Philosophy*, Lanham, MD: Rowman & Littlefield.

Heidegger, M. (1974) *The Question Concerning Technology and Other Essays*, trans. W. Lovitt, New York: Harper & Row.

Heidegger, M. (1996 [1927]) *Being and Time*, Albany, NY: State University of New York Press.

Horkheimer, M. (1972 [1937]) "Traditional and Critical Theory", in M. Horkheimer *Critical Theory: Selected Essays*, trans. M. J. O'Connell *et al.*, New York: Herder & Herder.

Hountondji, P. J. (1996) *African Philosophy: Myth and Reality*, 2nd edn, Bloomington, IN: Indiana University Press.

Husserl, E. (1970 [1954]) *The Crisis of European Sciences and Transcendental Phenomenology*, Evanston, IL: Northwestern University Press.

Husserl, E. (1973) *Cartesian Meditations: An Introduction to Phenomenology*, trans. Dorion Cairns, The Hague: Martinus Nijhoff.

Jahanbaksh, F. (2001) *Islam, Democracy, and Religious Modernism in Iran, 1953–2000*, Boston: Brill.

Jahanbegloo, R. (2004) *Iran: Between Tradition and Modernity*, Lanham, MD: Lexington Books.

Kim, T. and N. Yamawaki (eds) (2006) *Kyoto Forum and Public Philosophy*, Osaka: Kyoto Forum.

Kothari, R. (1988a) *State against Democracy: In Search of Humane Governance*, Delhi: Ajanta.

Kothari, R. (1988b) *Transformation and Survival: In Search of a Humane World Order*, Delhi: Ajanta.

Kothari, R. (1989) *Rethinking Development: In Search for Humane Alternatives*, New York: New Horizons Press.

Kothari, R. (1993) *Growing Amnesia: An Essay on Poverty and the Human Condition*, New Delhi: Viking.

Krishna, D. (1965) *Considerations Toward a Theory of Social Change*, Bombay: Manaktalas.

Krishna, D. (1979) *Political Development: A Critical Perspective*, Delhi: Oxford University Press.

Masolo, D. A. (1994) *African Philosophy in Search of Identity*, Bloomington, IN: Indiana University Press.

Mehta, J. L. (1976) *Martin Heidegger: The Way and the Vision*, Honolulu: University of Hawaii Press.

Mehta, J. L. (1985) *India and the West: The Problem of Understanding*, Chico, CA: Scholars Press.

Mehta, J. L. (1990) *Philosophy and Religion: Essays in Interpretation*, New Delhi: Manoharlal.

Merleau-Ponty, M. (1963) *In Praise of Philosophy*, Evanston, IL: Northwestern University Press.

Merleau-Ponty, M. (1969) *Humanism and Terror: An Essay on the Communist Problem*, trans. John O'Neill, Boston: Beacon Press.

Mirsepassi, A. (2000) *Intellectual Discourse and the Politics of Modernization: Negotiating Modernity in Iran*, Cambridge: Cambridge University Press.

Muzaffer, C. (1993) *Human Rights and the New World Order*, Penang, Malaysia: Just World Trust.

Muzaffer, C. (2002) *Rights, Religion and Reform*, London: Routledge Curzon.

Nandy, A. (1980) *At the Edge of Psychology: Essays on Politics and Culture*, Delhi: Oxford University Press.

Nandy, A. (1983) *The Intimate Enemy: Loss and Recovery of Self Under Colonialism*, Delhi: Oxford University Press.

Nandy, A. (1987a) *Traditions, Tyranny and Utopias*, Delhi: Oxford University Press.

Nandy, A. (1987b) "Cultural Frames for Social Transformation: A Credo", *Alternatives*, 12(2): 113–16.

Nandy, A. (1994) *The Illegitimacy of Nationalism*, Delhi: Oxford University Press.

Nishida, K. (1958) *Intelligibility and the Philosophy of Nothingness*, Honolulu: East–West Center Press.

Nishitani, K. (1982) *Religion and Nothingness*, Berkeley: University of California Press.

Poincaré, H. (1905) *Science and Hypothesis*, trans. W. J. Greenstrect, London: Walter Scott.

Queen, C. S. and S. B. King (eds) (1996) *Engaged Buddhism: Buddhist Liberation Movements in Asia*, Albany, NY: State University of New York Press.

Rajan, R. S. (1986) *Innovative Competence and Social Change*, Ganeshkind: Poona University Press.

Rajan, R. S. (1987) *Toward a Critique of Cultural Reason*, Delhi: Oxford University Press.

Rajan, R. S. (1991) *The Primacy of the Political*, Delhi: Oxford University Press.

Said, E. W. (1988) "Foreword", in R. Guha and G. C. Spivak (eds) *Selected Subaltern Studies*, New York: Oxford University Press.

Sartre, Jean-Paul (1963) *Search for a Method*, trans. H. E. Barnes, New York: Alfred Knopf.

Schutte, O. (1993) *Cultural Identity and Social Liberation in Latin American Thought*, Albany, NY: State University of New York Press.

Shin'ichi, Hisamatsu (1971) *Zen and the Fine Arts*, Tokyo: Kodansha International.

Sivaraksa, S. (1994) *A Buddhist Vision for Renewing Society*, Bangkok: Thai Interreligious Commission for Development.

Tanabe, H. (1987) *Philosophy as Metanoetics*, Berkeley: University of California Press.

Taylor, C. (1985) "Social Theory as Practice", in *Philosophy and the Human Sciences: Philosophical Papers 2*, Cambridge: Cambridge University Press.

Tu, W.-M. (1985) *Confucian Thought: Selfhood as Creative Transformation*, Albany, NY: State University of New York Press.

Zimmerman, M. E. (1990) *Heidegger's Confrontation with Modernity: Technology, Politics, Art*, Bloomington, IN: Indiana University Press.

21 Chinese thought and dialogical universalism

Tong Shijun

Many arguments have been made by European and Chinese thinkers against the current American foreign policy and its underlying political philosophy. This article explores the possibility of combining the argument based on the traditional Chinese idea of *"tian xia"* or "All under Heaven" with the argument for a dialogical universalism versus the subject-centered or monological universalism advanced by German philosopher Jürgen Habermas.

The Chinese idea of *"tian xia"* vs. the Western idea of the "world"

Habermas's criticism of the "imperialist claim" of the American neo-Conservative strategists (see Habermas 2002, 2003) may seem to some people to be a good case for making a distinction within "Western values" between "European values" and "American values", and this distinction more or less amounts to that between a dialogical and de-centerized version of universalism and a monological and self-centered version of universalism. In the view of the contemporary Chinese scholar, Zhao Tingyang, however, it is still limited by the same political tradition shared by Westerners across the Atlantic: Habermas's "inter-subjectivity" is still an "inter-ness" between the subjects (or the nation-states in this context), but not a "transcendence" over the subjects. The real alternative to either the nation-states or the empire with one nation as its core is what the ancient Chinese imagined as *"tian xia"* or "All under Heaven".

"Tian xia" is one of the most frequently used words in ancient Chinese classics. Literally meaning "All under Heaven" or "All the land under Heaven", it was used by ancient Chinese to refer to the whole world as they knew or imagined. It is different both from Heaven, which is above us, and from the smaller parts within it. As something different from Heaven, *tian xia* is actually the intersecting point of the *"tian dao"* or Heavenly Dao and *"ren dao"* or Human Dao. In other words, the principle regulating *tian xia* is the Heavenly *Dao* in the form of Human *Dao*. As something different from smaller parts within it, *tian xia* is the ideal

towards which ordinary people approach and by which their everyday activities are judged. In a famous passage in the Confucian classics *Great Learning*, *tian xia* is at the top of a hierarchy of ideas: *tian xia* (the world), *guo* (states), *jia* (families), shen (individual persons), which is followed by a series of ideas with regards to the individual persons: *xin* (minds), *yi* (will), *zhi* (knowledge).

Although the word "*guo*" or state is mentioned here, the ancient Chinese minds typically care more about *tian xia* or the world, which is supposed to be shared by everybody under *tian* or Heaven, than about *guo*, which is ruled by a *jia* (family) – the common Chinese equivalent of the English word "state", *guo jia*, actually is composed of the two words respectively meaning state and family. The most famous contrast between "*tian xia*" and "*guo*" was made by Gu Yanwu (1613–1682), who said:

> There is the perishing (*wang*) of *guo*, there's also the perishing of *tian xia*. The changing of names and titles (of dynasties) is the former, while blocking of *ren* [humanity] and *yi* [righteousness] even to the degree of eating each other like beasts is the latter.... Therefore one knows to protect *tian xia* before he knows to protect his *guo*. Protecting guo is the obligations of *guo*'s emperors, ministers and officials, while protecting *tian xia* is the duty of everybody, including those in the lowest rank.

Here Gu seems to be making a distinction between "institutional obligations" and "natural duties" in John Rawls's sense: what one owes to *tian xia* is a natural duty, which needs no justification, while what one owes to a *guo* or state is an institutional obligation, which needs justification on the basis of one's natural duties.

This contrast between *tian xia* and *guo/jia* was noticed by many modern Chinese thinkers when they tried to understand the meaning of nation-states when people's obligation to their *guo/jia* justified by their duty to the supposedly everybody's *tian xia* was severely challenged by some nation-states who neither belonged to the Chinese *guo/jia*, nor accepted the claim that the Chinese guo/jia was the embodiment of the principle of *tian xia*. To many Chinese thinkers, the trouble is not only the fact that this claim was not recognized by Western "barbarous" powers, but also the fact that a nation that traditionally care more about *tian xia* than about *guo/jia* is extremely vulnerable to foreign invaders in the age dominated by a system of nation-states developed first in the West. Though few of them wanted to give up their claim for the moral superiority of this idea of *tian xia*, many of these Chinese thinkers warned that if we are going to survive as Chinese at all, we should have our own sense of national identity and national dignity defined according to the game rules of this world of nation-states, rather than defined according to our traditional understanding of *tian xia*.

While Modern Chinese thinkers like Liang Qichao (1873–1929) and Liang Shuming (1893–1988) referred to the traditional idea of *tian xia* in order to remind the Chinese people of the importance of developing something between *tian xia* and *jia* (family) while respecting their values, that is, the importance of cultivating the "group life" in Liang Shuming's words, contemporary Chinese thinkers like Shen Hong and Zhao Tingyang referred to the idea of *tian xia* in order to claim that the traditional Chinese political culture contains important insights that might be helpful in solving the problems facing us at the global level.

The most important problem in our times of globalization, according to Zhao Tingyang, is the fact that the system of nation-states has become outdated: it is irrelevant when it comes to many problems at the global level. As a reaction to this situation, some alternative projects have been proposed, or even pursued, but none of them, in Zhao's view, is satisfactory, because all of them are afflicted by the problem of failure really to go beyond the horizon of the model of nation-state. The United Nations is basically still a "world organization" rather than a "world institution"; the difference between the two is that while a "world institution" needs an idea of "the world" that transcends nations as its basis, a "world organization" is still an *inter*national arrangement. In theory, the UN has the problem of trying to integrate the two incompatible things, that is, pluralism and universalism, into a coherent unity; in practice, the UN has the problem of failure to do anything that any of the powers in the world does not agree upon. It is true that the United States is now the only superpower in the world, but then the UN seems to be even weaker compared with the USA in implementing its wills. Here comes the idea that the world is turned to be a new empire, an empire of the age of globalization. This "global empire", as Michael Hardt and Antonio Negri described in their *Empire*, is to Zhao's idea actually a model of American imperialism, in which America is not only the overwhelmingly powerful game player, but also the sole game rule maker. Thus "the United States managed to become the sole outlaw state in the world game" (Zhao 2005: 105). The fact that America is now behaving lawlessly, in Zhao's view, is not only a result of the imperialist ambition of the USA, but also a result of the fact that the world does not yet have a "world idea", neither does it have a world institution and the power to support it. "It is this", Zhao said, "that is the severe problem posed in our times" (Zhao 2005: 105).

The traditional Chinese idea of *tian xia*, thought Zhao, is a good candidate for this kind of world idea. Basically the idea *tian xia* has the following three levels of meaning:

- First it is its geographical sense, referring to "all the lands under heaven" in the geographical sense. It amounts to the "*di*" (earth) in the traditional Chinese triad of "*tian* (heaven), *di* (earth), *ren* (people)", or the whole world that can be inhabited by human beings.

- Second it is its psychological sense, referring to the mentality of all those who live upon the earth, or what Chinese calls "*min xin*" or "popular sentiments". In traditional Chinese political culture having supreme power over *tian xia* in the geographical sense is not "*de tian xia*" or "acquiring the world" in the real sense. "Acquiring *tian xia*" in the real sense is to have support by all the people on the earth and under the heaven.
- Third it is its ethical-political sense, referring to the ideal or Utopia of everybody under heaven treating each other like members of one family. What is special with this part of the idea of *tian xia* is that in it there is an imagination of and aspiration for a certain "world institution", and a certain "world government" supported by it.

Compared with the Western idea of "the world", the Chinese idea of *tian xia* is, according to Zhao, a philosophical rather than scientific idea, a conceptually completed world that contains all the possible meanings of the world and excludes none of them. Compared with Husserl's idea of "the life world", which is also filled with human meanings, the idea of *tian xia* contains the institutional dimension that the idea of lifeworld lacks. Compared with the Christian worldview, the Chinese idea of *tian xia* is not afflicted with all kinds of divisions, conflicts and struggles, and does not deprive us of the ability to imagine a perfect future in this world, the human world.

It is interesting to note when he was arguing for the importance of the idea of *tian xia* to our times, Zhao Tingyang was criticizing Habermas and Rawls as well. Zhao's criticism of Rawls is very harsh. Rawls's thinking follows the line of Kant, which is regarded by Zhao as the best one can do before one goes beyond the paradigm of the non-world. But, according to Zhao, Rawls's idea of "law of peoples" implies two gravely dangerous ideas: the refusal to extend the principle of difference, which is in favor of the disadvantaged, from the domestic societies to the global society, and the suggestion that the so-called "liberal and decent peoples" are justified not to tolerate the outlaw states. "Rawls's theory amounts to advocating a new imperialism, which is exactly what is carried on by the USA, a country that is willing to invest more in wars than in the orderly international community" (Zhao 2005: 98).

Compared with Rawls, Habermas received less harsh criticism from Zhao Tingyang. Habermas, in Zhao's view, neglected two critical questions. On the one hand, Habermas does not see that some matters can never be agreed upon by different parties, however rational a dialogue that has been undergone might be, and even though the parties concerned have understood each other perfectly. On the other hand, some issues involve immediate interests, which would be lost if no action is taken immediately. In addition to these two problems, Habermas's approach is wrong mainly because it has still not gone beyond the typically Western habit of taking entities like "individuals" and "nations-states" as the decisive units of consideration. By contrast, in Chinese philosophy the basic unit of consideration is a relational structure, such as family and *tian xia*. A philosophy based on "relationships" instead of "individuals" thus provides "the view from everywhere" rather than "the view from somewhere" (Zhao 2005: 108).

"View from everywhere" vs. "view from somewhere"

Although the idea of *tian xia* is considered by Zhao Tingyang to be able to provide a view from everywhere rather than a view from somewhere, Zhao himself was making this claim from a very clearly expressed "somewhere": China. The introduction to his book *The System of Tian Xia: An introduction to a philosophy of the world institution*" is titled "Why should we discuss the Chinese worldview?" Zhao's answer to this question is put forward against the background of the so-called "China's rise" or even "China threat".

The reason why we should clearly state the Chinese conception of the world, according to Zhao, is that China's importance in thinking should match its importance in economy. And this is also required by China's now growing responsibility to the world. "China threat" or "China's rise", two phrases reflecting the growing importance of China in the world from different positions, are both misconceptions of China. The former is a negative misconception of an "Other" by the non-Chinese, while the latter is a positive (self-)misconception of the Chinese themselves. In some sense, all developed countries or large countries are threats to others, because they consume large amounts of energy, and create pressure upon others. But the key issue is to identify China's possible contributions and responsibility for the world, or to redefine the positive meaning of the idea of "China". Zhao said:

> To the world, the positive meaning that China can contribute is to become a new type of power, a power that is responsible to the world, a power that is different from various empires in the world history. To be responsible to the world, rather than merely to one's own country, is, theoretically speaking, a perspective of the Chinese philosophy, and practically speaking, a brand new possibility, that is, to take "*tian xia*" as a preferred unit of analysis of political/economic interests, to understand the world from the perspective of *tian xia*, that is, to analyze problems with "the world" as the unit of thinking, going beyond the Western mode of thinking in terms of nation/state, to take responsibility to the world as one's own responsibility, and to create a new world idea and a new world institution. World idea and world institution are values and orders that this world has ever lacked. Both the Great Britain, the power over the world in the past, and the USA, the power over the world now, have no other ideas than the idea of

nation/state, and no other considerations than their own national interests, and with regards to the administration of the world they have had no legitimacy either in political or in philosophical senses. The reason is that their "world thinking" is nothing but advocating their particular values, and universalizing their own values.... The problem is not that the Western nations do not think about the world; actually they always do. But "to think about the world" and "to think from the perspective of the world" are two totally different spheres of thinking. With regards to world politics, the Chinese world-view, or its theory of *tian xia*, is the only theory that takes into consideration the legitimacy of the world order and the world institution, because only the Chinese world-view possesses the idea of "*tian xia*" as a perspective of analysis that is higher and larger than "nation". Therefore our real problem is what kind of obligation that China is prepared to take for the world, and what kind of ideas China is prepared to create for the world.

(2005: 3–4)

That is to say, the real importance of China to the world is that only in Chinese tradition there is a way of thinking that is against not only other powers' egocentric thinking, but also its own egocentric thinking. Here Zhao seems to imply that according to this tradition, a "threat from China" would thus become a "threat against China" as well, and the only correct understanding of "China's rise" is the rise of China's responsibility to the world – not a responsibility in the sense of a "mission" to universalize its values and distribute them all over the world, but in the sense of a duty to "think of *tian xia* from the perspective of *tian xia*", and to regard nobody as others or outsiders, because in relation to *tian xia* there are, by definition, no outsiders.

The core of Zhao's idea is a vision of a cosmopolitan order that calls for a higher sense of responsibility rather than a stronger sense of power and hegemony, and a perspective that is neither other-worldly transcendental, nor this-worldly utilitarian, but in a sense this-worldly transcendental. Zhao regards this "immanent transcendental" perspective as "ontological" and "a priori", but I would rather interpret it as a perspective concerning "who we are" or "who we want to be" instead of "what we have" or "how much we have", nor "what we should do" as one would think on a deontological position. A cosmopolitan order or an order of *tian xia* is justified not from any particular interest positions, nor from any supposedly universalized or universalizable interest positions, which is the core of Habermas's version of Kantianism, but from the perspective of *tian xia* itself, which is the "ontological condition" for our happiness, or our "well-being", which is our real being. In other words, a cosmopolitan order, or the peaceful coexistence and cooperation among all the peoples under heaven, is justified neither on the basis of the instrumental value of coexistence and cooperation, nor on the basis of some other-worldly meanings, but on the basis of the this-worldly immanent values of coexistence and cooperation.

A utilitarian justification for coexistence and cooperation is limited because interest-relations between different persons or different groups of people could easily change with time, situation and particular considerations of the people concerned at particular moments. If one's interest is the major reason for his or her engagement in the coexistence and cooperation, he or she may well break this relationship easily for the very same reason of self-interest.

One may then say that coexistence and cooperation should be justified by long-term rather than short-term interests: in the long run cooperation between different peoples is beneficial to each of them. Even if the current cooperation is not very beneficial to us, we may say, we can rely on our long-term interest-calculation, which would tell us that we would be guaranteed of a share of benefit of the cooperation in the future sooner or later. At first sight this way of thinking seems much better than the above one, the one based on short-term interest relations. On closer look, however, it is also somehow problematic. Actually, those who argue for competition rather than for cooperation are making the same type of consideration: although competition on the basis of self-interests is harmful in many cases, it will bring about beneficial results in the long run according to certain laws or meanings governing human society or human history as a whole. Behind both arguments we can perhaps see the following same way of thinking: to base our hope or activity on our conviction of some deep-seated laws or meanings of human society and history, no matter what these laws and meanings say about the result of our hope or action. What is problematic about this way of thinking is that in the human world, what our future will be like depends, to a large degree, on what we choose to do now and here, rather than some hidden or deep-seated laws and meanings. To justify something on the ground that it will bring us beneficial results in the future according to certain transcendental goals or objective laws could lead, in my view, to easing our sense of urgency with regard to what we should do now and here, while it is much more dangerous in our times than in previous periods for us to sit and wait until what Kant called "providence" or "the secret plan of Nature", what Hegel called the "cunning of Reason", or what Marx called the "law of history", show us what our real destiny will be in the remote future. In our times, modern science has already peeped into human genes, weapons of mass destruction can be easily used for different reasons, and large-scale harmful ecological changes have begun to influence our everyday life. This means that what we choose to do now can easily delete any chance of our further choices in the future, and we are no longer in the situation where we can be sure that any mistake now can be corrected and its consequence be compensated in the long run. This concerns the very "being" of us, rather than the mere "having" of us. Against this background it is really very important to emphasize our (Chinese) responsibility that is growing together with our economic and technological power, and to consider the problem of the world from the perspective of the world itself, rather than the perspective of any particular interests. This is the implication in Zhao Tingyang's idea of *tian xia*, which is very important indeed.

"View from everywhere" as "ideal role-taking"

To see *tian xia* from the perspective of *tian xia* itself is to justify coexistence and cooperation on the basis of the immanent non-utilitarian value of coexistence and cooperation themselves, and to say that coexistence and cooperation have an immanent non-utilitarian value in them is to say that to live together with each other in a friendly and cooperative way is to live in a genuinely human way: when we are asked to define the meaning of a genuinely human life, we have to mention friendship and cooperation and include them in that definition. For this kind of thinking I want to give a formulation that is less metaphysical than Zhao's and which is developed on the basis of my understanding of Confucianism.

The focus of Confucianism is to teach how to be a human being in the full sense. To be a human in the full sense, according to Confucius, is to cultivate "*ren*" in ourselves. "*Ren*" is the kernel concept of Confucianism, and it is composed of " 人 " "(man) and " 二 "(two). One becomes a human individual in the full sense only through interaction with other people; "intersubjectivity" comes before "subjectivity" in this sense. Interaction with other people is first of all a process of getting mature as a human being, or a process of learning to be a human being in the full sense, instead of a mere process of benefiting each other. The first passage of the *Analectics* records the Master's saying that "Is it not pleasant to learn with a constant perseverance and application? Is it not delightful to have friends coming from distant quarters? Is he not a man of complete virtue, who feels no discomposure though men may take no note of him?" (*Analectics* 1992: Ch. 1). What is most relevant to the topic of this chapter is the second sentence: "Is it not delightful to have friends coming from distant quarters". Having friends coming from distant quarters is something delightful, and it is delightful by itself, not because of any other things. Of the same nature is "learning with constant perseverance and application". It is also something that is pleasant by itself and not because of anything else. Put these two sentences together and we may say that Confucius teaches us both to love others and to educate or cultivate ourselves, and these two things are actually closely connected with each other: according to Confucius, loving others is a great way of cultivating ourselves, or a great way for us to learn to be human beings in the full sense. That is why the concept "*ren*" is so important in the doctrine of Confucius and later Confucians. It is, of course, not an easy thing to love others;

otherwise it would not be so important to our personal development. "Others" are others because they are different from us, and it is a great challenge for us to learn to deal with differences between people. To have a harmonious relation with others is not to reduce all the differences between them and us. That is what Confucius means when he says that "the gentleman aims at harmony, not uniformity; the small man prefers uniformity, not harmony" (*Analectics* 1992: Ch. 12). Harmony, according to Confucianism, is a relation between different elements, like what we have in a "thick soup". Given the differences and diversities between different people, it is only natural that misunderstandings can arise from time to time. In order to deal with this kind of situation, Confucius asks us to be patient, to be optimistic, and not to give up easily in striving for mutual understanding and trust. That is why the third sentence of the first paragraph of the *Analectics* goes like this: "Is he not a man of complete virtue, who feels no discomposure though men may take no note of him?" (*Analectics* 1992: Ch. 1).

If we expand our understanding of coexistence and cooperation as the "ontological condition" for our (well-)being, then we can see that when we are engaged in friendly coexistence and cooperation, we should not only avoid trying to benefit us alone, but also avoid trying to benefit others according to our own understanding of "benefits" or "interests". The first principle in Confucianism in dealing with others is "Not to do to others as you would not wish done to yourself" (*Analectics* 1992: Ch. 12). This, as we all know, is the Confucian version of the "Golden Rule". In addition to this basically negative rule there is another Confucian rule, a positive one: "Now the man of perfect virtue, wishing to be established himself, seeks also to establish others; wishing to be enlarged himself, he seeks also to enlarge others" (*Analectics* 1992: Ch. 6). Here the expressions "to establish others" and "to enlarge others" should not be understood as simply "making others live the same kind of life as we do". It is well known that to impose what we think to be good upon other people very often inflicts great harm upon them instead. To have the view of *tian xia* in our times means that we should not only do good things for others, but also respect others' understanding of the meaning of "a good life". In order to show our respect for other people's right to interpret the meaning of "good", and, in order to seek mutual understanding between different people (and different peoples) over the problem "what is a good life", we should take an active part in cooperation not only in trade, finance and economy in general, but also in culture, in cultural exchange and intellectual dialogue.

What is said above is, contrary to Zhao Tingyang's view, not very different from Habermas's position. Or in other words, the traditional Chinese idea of "*tian xia*" can be translated into the language of Habermas's theory of communicative action. Both Habermas and Zhao Tingyang want to find some *a priori* condition for our being as human beings, but it is Habermas, instead of Zhao, who seems to be closer to

Confucius: Habermas, like a good Confucian typically would do, starts from what is nearby, that is, everyday communication, while Zhao argues that *tian xia*, the least probable Utopia, has the "logical precedence" over all other orders. Zhao does not see that with Habermas, as with Confucius, subjectivity and intersubjectivity presuppose each other, rather than the latter unilaterally depends on the former. Like many other people, Zhao does not see clearly that Habermas's idea of "ideal speech situation" is not a purely regulative idea, but also something constitutive, or something we have already presupposed if interpersonal communication is to be possible at all. And Habermas needs his theory of dialogue or argumentation not only because of the importance of dialogue and argumentation to decision-making on domestic, international and global issues, but also because of the importance of study of dialogue and argumentation to answering some key questions in theory of knowledge, morality and law, such as whether it is still possible to keep and defend the ideas of truth, justice and goodness, and why we should bother to be moral at all. These questions were answered by appealing to traditional worldviews in the past, and thus were not real questions at all. In our times, however, they become questions just because they no longer have ready-made answers. Now both Confucius and Habermas can be said as accepting Herbert Mead's thesis of "individualization through socialization" (see Habermas 1992: 149–204). With the help of this thesis, we can see that to a person who has become a mature individual through a process of social interaction in which rationalized social norms are internalized in him, "why moral" is a problem that has already been solved in everyday life before it is raised in expert discourse. At a higher level, in our times, one is developed into a mature individual not only through a process of socialization in one particular cultural community, but also through a process of being engaged in the process of communication between different cultural communities in the global society as well as in domestic societies. A mature individual is one who has learnt to take everybody's perspective, which is called by Mead (and Habermas) "the ideal role taking": "In moral discourse, the ethnocentric perspective of an unlimited communication community, all of whose members put themselves in each individual's situation, worldview, and self-understanding, and together practice an ideal role taking (as understood by G. H. Mead)" (Habermas 1996: 162). This, I think, is just what Zhao Tingyang means by "the view from everywhere".

Confucianism, of course, can be and has been interpreted in many ways. What I have proposed above is more or less a mutual translation between the Confucian idea of "*tian xia*" or Zhao Tingyang's "the view from everywhere" on the one hand, and the idea of "ideal role-taking" in Mead and Habermas, on the other. Preserving the traditional Chinese idea of "*tian xia*" and interpreting the idea of "*tian xia*" with the help of the idea of "ideal role-taking", we can, on the one hand, connect the traditional idea with the contemporary discussions on various relevant issues, including the issue of institutional framework for implementing the idea of "*tian xia*", and, on the other hand, bring the achievements of these contemporary discussions, of which Habermas's dialogical universalism is a very important one, into touch with the traditional Chinese culture, especially its idea of "*tian xia*" as a this-worldly transcendental Utopia.

References

"Analectics" (1992) *The Chinese/English Four Books*, translated by James Legge, Changsha: Hunan Press.

Habermas, J. (1992) *Postmetaphysical Thinking: Philosophical Essays*, translated by William Mark Hohengarten, Cambridge: Polity Press.

Habermas, J. (1996) *Between Facts and Norms: Contributions to a Discourse Theory of Law and Democracy*, translated by William Rehg, Cambridge, Mass.: MIT Press.

Habermas, J. (2002) "Letter to America", *Nation*, 275(21), 12/16/2002.

Habermas, J. (2003) "Was bedeutet der Denkmalsturz?", *Frankfurter Allgemeinen Zeitung vom 17*, April.

Zhao, T. (2005) *The System of Tian Xia: An Introduction to a Philosophy of the World Institution (tian xia ti xi: shi jie zhi du zhe xue dao lun)*, Jiangsu Education Press.

Index